TAKING SIDES

Clashing Views in

Special Education

THIRD EDITION

Mc Graw Hill **Contemporary Learning Series**

A Division of The McGraw-Hill Companies

TAKING SIDES

Clashing Views in
Special Education

THIRD EDITION

Selected, Edited, and with Introductions by

MaryAnn Byrnes
University of Massachusetts–Boston

Contemporary Learning Series

A Division of The McGraw-Hill Companies

Photo Acknowledgment
Cover image: Digital Vision/PunchStock

Cover Acknowledgment
Maggie Lytle

Manufactured in the United States of America

Third Edition

123456789DOCDOC9876

Library of Congress Cataloging-in-Publication Data
Main entry under title:
Taking sides: clashing views on controversial issues in special education/selected, edited, and
with introductions by MaryAnn Byrnes.—3rd ed.
Includes bibliographical references and index.
1. Special education. I. Byrnes, MaryAnn, ed. II. Series.
371.9

0-07-351500-0
978-0-07-351500-7
ISSN: 1537-0739

Printed on Recycled Paper

Preface

Special education is full of questions, emotions, and opinions. Public responsibility for the education of children with disabilities is a relatively new endeavor that is still forging its identity and boundaries. Sometimes it seems that just as one set of issues is resolved (such as the creation of a range of services in public schools), a host of new challenges (such as leaving no child behind) arises. Other issues, including appropriate funding and inclusion, seem to defy resolution. Through *Taking Sides: Clashing Views in Special Education*, I invite you to consider several current issues in this volatile and rewarding field.

Some basic principles guided the choice of selections for this book. Each reading needed to represent a point of view on the question at hand. Other opinions surely exist, but the ones presented needed to be broadly held. Each had to employ solid reasoning; its position could not be easily refuted because of faulty logic. Finally, each selection needed to be interesting to read. If an article did not captivate my attention, I did not want it included.

Taking Sides: Clashing Views in Special Education has two major goals: first, to introduce key questions in special education, so that readers can learn about the field from authors who have thought extensively about educational policy and practice, and second, to encourage thinking and discussion, so that readers can explore possibilities and debate the consequences of positions and actions. I hope you will find yourselves engaged and enlivened by the conversations these topics begin. Most of all, I trust your deliberations will contribute to constructive solutions to puzzles that demand careful thinking and dedication to all our children.

This book includes 19 issues, addressing active debates in the field. There are three parts. Part 1, "Special Education and Society," introduces questions of social policy and practice. Part 2, "Access and Accountability," highlights perspectives on educational expectations and outcomes. Part 3, "Issues about Disabilities," presents critical considerations about specific disabilities and treatments.

Each issue is framed as a question and begins with an *Introduction*, designed to set the stage. Two readings, presenting contrasting points of view, come next. Each issue closes with a *Postscript*, summarizing the expressed points of view, suggesting other points of view, and presenting additional readings on the topic. The Introductions and Postscripts also feature questions to stimulate your thinking as you weigh the topic at hand and its relationship to schools. Each question represents challenges to be resolved in the policy and practice of educating children with disabilities.

Due to page constraints, most selections have been edited. Use the citation to locate the entire article, along with its bibliography.

To further expand your thinking, you may want to reference the *Internet References* pages that precede each section. These contain a sampling of Internet site addresses (URLs) that present varied points of view as well as links to related sites and bibliographies.

The YES and NO positions on every issue express strongly held opinions. You may agree or disagree with the authors, or you may find that your own view lies somewhere in between. Perhaps you will identify additional perspectives as you study the issues more thoroughly. You will certainly find connections between issues. Class discussions may lead you to formulate a fresh response to the issue question. Doubtless, as you continue in your professional and personal life, your ideas will change and develop. What is critical as you read this book is that you reflect on positions, possibilities, and emotions so you can form opinions you can use to guide your actions and decisions.

A word to the instructor   An *Instructor's Manual with Test Questions* (multiple choice and essay) is available through The McGraw Hill Contemporary Learning Series for the instructor using *Taking Sides* in the classroom. Also available is *Using Taking Sides in the Classroom,* a general guidebook that presents strategies and examples of using the pro-con method in classroom settings. Faculty members using this text also have access to an online version of *Using Taking Sides in the Classroom* and a correspondence service, located at http://www.mhcls. com/usingts/.

Taking Sides: Clashing Views in Special Education is only one title in the Taking Sides series. The table of contents for any of the other titles can be found at the Taking Sides Web site at http://www.mhcls.com/takingsides/.

Changes to this edition   This third edition includes five completely new issues: "Has the ADA Accomplished Its Goals?" (Issue 1); "Does IDEA 2004 Contain Substantial Changes?" (Issue 2); "Does NCLB Leave Some Students Behind?" (Issue 8); "Will NCLB Requirements Produce Highly Qualified Special Education Teachers?" (Issue 9); and "Can Scientifically Based Research Guide Instructional Practice?" (Issue 10). Four issues have been reframed and have new articles: "Do Funding Systems Create a Perverse Incentive to Place Students in Special Education?" (Issue 4); "Can One Model of Special Education Serve All Students?" (Issue 11); "Is Full Inclusion the Least Restrictive Environment?" (Issue 12); and "Should Students with Cognitive Disabilities Be Expected to Demonstrate Academic Proficiency?" (Issue 15). In all, there are 18 new selections. The Introduction, as well as issue Introductions and Postscripts, have been revised to reflect IDEA 2004. Finally, this edition begins with a unique section entitled "Individuals with Disabilities Education Improvement Act (IDEA 2004): Emerging Issues." This section introduces readers to the newly released final regulations and alerts them to controversial issues that will be developing.

Acknowledgements   Spirited debate about "the right thing to do" has been part of my life since I became a teacher. So long as we keep children in mind, debating possibilities is exhilarating. First, and most importantly, I thank the children, educators, and parents who frame the questions and continually teach me almost anything is possible—not always easy, but possible. I have appreciated the helpfulness of Susan Brusch, stepping into the *Taking Sides* family, and all the efforts of supporting staff at McGraw-Hill. And, of course, Joe.

MaryAnn Byrnes
University of Massachusetts–Boston

Contents In Brief

Contents

John Hockenberry, an award-winning television commentator, radio host, and foreign correspondent, who happens to use a wheelchair, celebrates the increased accessibility brought about by the past 15 years' implementation of the Americans with Disabilities Act. Patricia Jordan Rea, assistant professor in educational leadership at The George Washington University, and Judy Davis-Dorsey, director of human resources with the York County (VA) Schools, believe the promise of this act cannot be realized until its many unintended confusions are resolved.

H. Rutherford Turnbull III, co-founder and co-director of the Beach Center on Disability at the University of Kansas, sees major changes in IDEA 2004. In line with the Bush administration's priorities, Turnbull identifies a shift toward requiring parents and students to take more responsibility for their own behavior and for relationships with schools. Tom E. C. Smith, professor at the University of Arkansas, focuses his research on disability law and inclusion. Reflecting on IDEA 2004, Smith believes that, although some changes seem significant, they will make little difference in the daily practice of special education.

M. Suzanne Donovan and Christopher Cross, researchers representing the findings of a National Research Council (NRC) study on minority students in special and gifted education, believe overrepresentation issues are complex and not easily resolvable. While teachers can make a difference, environmental factors, and poverty have a large impact and require interventions beyond schools. Daniel J. Losen and Gary Orfield, both policy experts, present the results of research commissioned by the Civil Rights Project of Harvard University. While agreeing with some of the NRC recommendations, these findings suggest that patterns will change with stricter enforcement of federal and state regulations.

Jay P. Greene, senior fellow, and Greg Forster, senior research associate, both with The Manhattan Institute for Policy Research, assert that the number of students identified as disabled is increasing at an excessive rate, especially in states where funding systems provide a "perverse incentive" in favor of placement. Kanya Mahitivanichcha, research analyst, and Tom Parrish, managing director for the Education and Human Development Program, both at the American Institutes for Research, maintain that funding formulas are only one reason behind increases in special education placement.

Lewis M. Andrews, executive director for the Yankee Institute for Public Policy, reviews the experiences of a number of countries with considerable school choice experience. He maintains that children with disabilities will find unexpected opportunities in choice-sponsored schools. Barbara Miner, a freelance writer and former managing editor of *Rethinking Schools*, explores experiences with the pioneering Milwaukee voucher systems, and discusses exclusionary policies and practices that limit access for students with disabilities.

Kay S. Hymowitz, a regular contributing editor to *The City Journal* (published by The Manhattan Institute), cites inclusive educational programming for students with disabilities and the legal limitations of IDEA as primary contributors to the destruction of effective discipline in today's schools. James A. Taylor and Richard A. Baker, Jr., president and vice president of Edleaders.com, respectively, believe that school administrators who design and implement an effective disciplinary code that applies to all students, including those with disabilities, can create a more orderly environment for everyone.

The National Council on Disability (NCD) is an independent federal agency composed of 15 members appointed by the president and confirmed by the U.S. Senate, dedicated to promoting policies, programs, practices and procedures that guarantee equal opportunity and empowerment for all individuals with disabilities. NCD found all 50 states to be out of compliance with special education law, a condition that must be remedied by increased federal attention. Frederick M. Hess, assistant professor of education and government at the University of Virginia, and Frederick J. Brigham, assistant professor of education at the same school, share Virginia's experience that increased federal monitoring will only deepen the separation between general and special education, drawing resources away from true educational excellence for all.

Jennifer Booher-Jennings, a doctoral candidate at Columbia University, finds the accountability pressures of No Child Left Behind are leading some administrators to advise teachers to focus only on those children who will improve their school's scores; other students don't count much. The U.S. Department of Education FAQ Sheet on IDEA and NCLB advises readers that the link between these two statutes is sound, emphasizing how they work together to ensure that every student's performance and needs receive appropriate attention.

Rod Paige, then-Secretary of the U.S. Department of Education, and former Houston, Texas, superintendent, believes the promise of No Child Left Behind can be realized by mandating that every teacher be highly qualified by increasing their focus in the content areas they teach and decreasing time spent on pedagogical skills. James McLeskey and Dorene D. Ross, teacher education faculty at the University of Florida, present competing views of what constitutes "highly qualified" special education teachers, one based on deregulation and one based on professionalization; they encourage ongoing consideration to determine the value and impact of each.

Samuel L. Odom, Ellen Brantlinger, Russell Gersten, Robert H. Horner, Bruce Thompson, and Karen R. Harris, all college faculty members and educational researchers, begin their article with definitive support for research-based methodology. They herald proposals for quality indicators, to establish rigor in an array of research methods that can identify effective educational practices. Frederick J. Brigham, associate professor at the University of Virginia, Charlottesville; William E. Gustashaw III and Andrew L. Wiley, both doctoral candidates at the University of Virginia, Charlottesville; and Michele St. Peter Brigham, a special education practitioner, believe that disagreement, mistrust, and the shifting general education environment preclude the usefulness of scientifically based research to guide daily instruction.

Wayne Sailor, professor of education and associate director of the Beach Center on Disability at the University of Kansas-Lawrence, and Blair Roger, an educational consultant based in Oakland, California, believe that a school-based model of support services for all students would successfully increase inclusionary practices. Naomi Zigmond, professor of education at the University of Pittsburgh, maintains that promoting one model of services over another is the wrong approach and advocates that educators and researchers need to focus attentions on individual students.

Rosalind and Joe Vargo, parents of Ro, use their voices to tell a powerful story of their daughter's success in fully inclusive educational programs, from kindergarten through college. Amy Dockser Marcus, staff reporter at *The Wall Street Journal,* records the voices of Eli's parents and teachers as they react to his message to leave a fully inclusive program in favor of a separate special education class.

Rex Knowles, a retired college professor, and his daughter Trudy Knowles, an education faculty member at Westfield (MA) State College, feel that federal mandates for all students to master the same curriculum fail to consider students' individual differences and needs. Jerry Jesness, a special education teacher, stresses that students who complete school without learning the basics will be ill-equipped to succeed as adults and that any program that avoids teaching these essentials fails to address the long-term needs of students.

James M. Kauffman, a faculty member at the University of Virginia, along with Kathleen McGee and Michele Brigham, both special education teachers, maintain that special education has pursued its goal of normalization to an extreme. The emphasis has shifted from increasing competence to perpetuating disabilities through the unwise use of accommodations. MaryAnn Byrnes, a University of Massachusetts–Boston faculty member, former special education administrator, and editor of this *Taking Sides,* argues that relevant accommodations are necessary to ensure that people with disabilities have a fair chance to demonstrate what they know and can do.

Kevin S. McGrew, educational researcher and the director of the Institute for Applied Psychometrics (IAP), and Jeffrey Evans, consultant and educational researcher for IAP, are wary that stereotypes of individuals with cognitive disabilities are used to form limited (and limiting) expectations and self-fulfilling prophecies. James M. Kauffman, professor emeritus of education at the University of Virginia, Charlottesville, and special education philosopher-researcher, believes that educators and parents must acknowledge that some students with cognitive disabilities cannot reach high academic standards and are best served by programs that develop other skills.

PART 3   ISSUES ABOUT DISABILITIES   315

Sally and Bennett Shaywitz, codirectors of the National Institute of Child Health and Human Development—Yale Center for the Study of Learning and Attention, and Yale University professors, summarize their recent research findings suggesting that advances in medicine, together with reading research, can virtually eliminate reading disabilities. Gerald Coles, an educational psychologist and former member of the Robert

U.S. Supreme Court Justice John Paul Stevens, writing for the majority of the Court, affirms the "bright line test," establishing that school districts are required by IDEA to provide one-on-one nursing services and any other health-related services that can be delivered by individuals other than a licensed physician. U.S. Supreme Court Justice Clarence Thomas, representing the dissenting minority opinion, asserts that continuous one-on-one nursing services for disabled children are indeed medical and, as such, beyond the scope of congressional intent in IDEA. He concludes that such services are not the responsibility of special education programs within school districts.

Introduction

I introduce . . . a bill . . . to insure equal opportunities for the handicapped by prohibiting needless discrimination in programs receiving federal financial assistance. . . . The time has come when we can no longer tolerate the invisibility of the handicapped in America. . . . These people have the right to live, to work to the best of their ability—to know the dignity to which every human being is entitled. But too often we keep children whom we regard as "different" or a "disturbing influence" out of our schools and community altogether. . . . Where is the cost-effectiveness in consigning them to . . . "terminal" care in an institution?

—Senator Hubert H. Humphrey (D-Minnesota), January 20, 1972, on introducing to Congress a bill mandating education for children with disabilities (as quoted in "Back to School on Civil Rights," National Council on Disability, 2000)

Unfortunately, this bill promises more than the federal government can deliver, and its good intentions could be thwarted by the many unwise provisions it contains. . . . Even the strongest supporters of this measure know as well as I that they are falsely raising the expectations of the groups affected by claiming authorization levels which are excessive and unrealistic . . . [This bill also contains a] vast array of detailed complex and costly administrative requirements which would unnecessarily assert federal control over traditional state and local government functions.

—President Gerald Ford, November 29, 1975, upon signing federal legislation to mandate education for children with disabilities (as quoted in *Congress and the Nation, IV*)

Special education was born of controversy about who belongs in schools and how far schools need to stretch to meet student needs. The debate continues.

When was the first time you saw someone with a disability? Think hard about your school experience. What do you remember? Compare your recollections with those of someone one generation older—and one younger. The differences will be startling.

Some of you might remember The Room at your elementary school. Usually it was in the basement of the school. Hardly anyone went into The Room. Hardly anyone came out. The kids in The Room never seemed to be part of recess or plays or lunch or gym. The teachers were invisible, too. Sometimes the windows of The Room were covered with paper. Usually the shades were drawn. Kids in your class whispered about The Room, but no one really knew what happened "in there."

Likely, the students who went to school in The Room seemed older, bigger, and not as smart as most of the other kids in the school. They had few books to learn from and rarely studied anything but the most basic academic tasks. No one really knew what happened to the kids in The Room once they left elementary school. There never seemed to be a Room at high school. Hard as it is to believe, those who made it inside The Room may have been the lucky ones.

Thirty years ago, if you were the parent of a child with a disability, your local school had the option to tell you that your child was not welcome—that there was no place in the school for your child. Choices were limited—you could teach your child at home (or just have him spend his days there), you could try to find a space in a kind school run by dedicated religious people; or you could have your child "put away" in a faceless institution for life. Try looking at Burton Blatt's *Christmas in Purgatory: A Photographic Essay on Mental Retardation* (Human Policy Press, 1974) for a view of some of the worst options.

I remember The Room in the elementary schools I attended, but I never knew much about its students. I also remember the Catholic school for girls with Down syndrome, where I volunteered as a Girl Scout. The residents learned cooking and sewing while I was getting ready for high school and college. I never saw the girls outside the school and didn't know what they did when they became adults.

I also remember the boys who sat in the back row of my classes and tried to avoid the teachers' attention. The teachers hoped these boys would just be quiet and behave. The boys dropped out of school as soon as they could.

Years later, in the early 1970s, I moved from being a fourth grade teacher to a special education teacher because I was intrigued with unlocking the puzzles that made learning so hard for some of my students. One of my early jobs was as a teacher in an updated version of The Room. It was my first experience in a small district. The day before school began, all the teachers and their students were listed in the local newspaper, along with their bus routes. I eagerly looked for my name, but instead of Mrs. Byrnes, I read "Emotionally Disturbed Classroom." For the entire time I worked at that school, I was the "emotionally disturbed teacher."

Times had changed a little since I attended school. My classroom was on the main floor, next door to the third grade; we had academic books, and we had lunch and recess with everyone else. But we were still different. Each day, my students and I needed to leave our room from 11:30 to 1:30 so that it could be used by the gym teacher while the gym was used as a cafeteria. Since there were only 10 of us, it seemed to be an easy solution to take our classroom space. No one seemed to care where we went or what we did during that time. Plenty of people were surprised to see us camp out in the library, tackling "real" school work.

In contrast, I think about the schools of today. Children with learning problems significant enough to be disabilities are the focus of concentrated attention. Trained professionals and researchers strive to understand disabilities and address them with specific teaching methods and approaches. Parents and teachers actively consider ways to adapt instruction. Program options seem limitless. Many children with disabilities grow into adults who hold jobs and contribute to society instead of spending their lives in isolation at home, in institutions, or on the streets.

Despite this progress, I still know schools in which students with disabilities are separated into sections of the school where no one else ever goes. There are still districts where people must be reminded to include students with disabilities when counting the number of new math books that need to be ordered. And once formal schooling ends, there are still many young adults who sit at home without jobs because there is no guaranteed support.

Has the promise of special education been met, fallen short, or been exceeded? Has society done too much or not enough? Despite what feels like progress, arguments about special education continue. Many of them are included in this book.

As you consider the issues ahead, think about the people with disabilities *you* first remember. How would their lives have been changed by today's special education? What could be done to help them be more productive citizens? How have the dreams of Hubert Humphrey and the cautions of Gerald Ford been realized?

Recent History and Legal Foundations

The history of special education in American public schools is short and defined by legislation. Private or religious schools have long offered specialized options for students who were blind, were deaf, or had mental retardation. Until the last quarter of the twentieth century, public options were largely limited to residential institutions and a few "Opportunity Classes" in public schools.

Following the civil rights struggles of the 1960s came the realization that another significant segment of our children—those with disabilities—were not offered a quality education. While a few states instituted their own policies and regulations regarding education of children with disabilities, districts could still refuse to admit these students.

Successful state court cases established that children with disabilities had rights to an education. They led to the 1975 passage of federal Public Law 94-142, which offered federal funds to every public school district delivering a free and appropriate public education to all children with disabilities. Renamed the Individuals with Disabilities Education Act (IDEA) in subsequent reauthorizations, the regulations connected to these statutes form the foundation of special education for every state. In addition, individual states constructed local legislation to clarify federal language or to extend commitments beyond the federal standard.

Even if districts chose not to seek federal funds, sidestepping IDEA regulations, the education of students with disabilities would be covered by other legislation. Section 504 of the Rehabilitation Act of 1973 is a civil rights statute prohibiting organizations that receive federal funds from discriminating against any individual based on a disability that substantially limits a major life activity. Reasonable accommodations must be implemented so that individuals with disabilities have equal access to the activities of such organizations. Curb cuts, lowered water fountains, and signs in Braille all came to be in response to Section 504. Since all school districts receive federal funds, Section 504 forbids the exclusion of students with disabilities, although it does not address education with the detail of IDEA.

The Americans with Disabilities Act (ADA), which was passed in 1990, expands the protections of Section 504 to the private sector. The ADA forbids businesses, governmental agencies, or public accommodations (other than churches or private clubs) from discriminating against any individual who has a disability that substantially limits a major life activity. The ADA carries the same responsibility for accommodations as Section 504, impacting the practices of almost every employer. One widely discussed ADA case established the right of a golfer to use a cart as an accommodation so that his physical condition did not prevent him from playing golf.

Most recently, elements of the No Child Left Behind Act of 2001 (NCLB) have been mirrored in the newest IDEA reauthorization. This merger holds schools accountable for student performance, sets exacting standards for teacher qualifications, and requires that educators implement research-based instructional practices.

Many say that the elements of these laws are vague and undefined. Terms are interpreted differently across the states, and businesses struggle with the range of accommodations, the meaning of "reasonable," and conflicting research results. Clarity is often achieved through the resolution of legal challenges, some of which have reached the Supreme Court. Because of the continually changing natures of disabilities and society, a single court decision can radically alter the obligations of an employer.

The ground shifts for schools as well. For example, as you proceed through the readings, you will encounter the debate between "least restrictive environment" and "free and appropriate public education." Each term is critical to the development of a school's special education program, but each is also fluid in meaning. Federal law does not provide solid definitions that can be used with precision. Schools do their best to apply these terms to individual children with widely varying needs. As with businesses and the ADA, court cases about individual children continue to define what is "restrictive" and what is "appropriate."

Essential Terms and Concepts

Special education has its own unique vocabulary and terms, just as any other field. Being familiar with the concepts discussed below will increase your understanding of the issues ahead.

Disabilities.   All federal laws refer to the following list of disabilities: autism, deaf-blindness, deafness, developmental delay, emotional disturbance, hearing impairment, mental retardation, orthopedic impairment, other health impairment, specific learning disability, speech or language impairment, traumatic brain injury, and visual impairment. Autism and traumatic brain injury are relatively recent additions to the list, because their occurrence has increased. State laws frequently amplify the federal definitions of each disability with particular diagnostic criteria, satisfied through the administration of appropriate assessment tools in the "language and form most likely to yield accurate information about what the child knows and can do academically and functionally" (IDEA 04). It is important to note that this list of disabilities does not include children who need instructional assistance solely because of language differences, cultural differences, or lack of instruction. In order for a child to be eligible for special education, the school's educational team must determine whether a disability exists.

Federal definition of a child eligible for special education.   According to IDEA, this is a child with a disability who is not making effective progress in school because of that disability and who requires specially designed instruction and/or related services in order to make progress in school. Federal legislation applies to individuals from birth to the receipt of a high school diploma or age 22. In most states, public schools are charged with educational responsibility beginning on a child's third birthday.

Individualized Education Program (IEP).   IDEA requires each child's educational team, including parents, to meet at least annually to formulate this agreement, which describes the education of a child with a disability. The IEP outlines the impact of the student's disability, current educational status, necessary accommodations, the nature and amount of services to be provided to the child, and target goals for each year. Services cannot be delivered—or ended—without a parent-approved IEP. Parents who disagree with evaluations or services have the right to seek redress through administrative hearing and/or legal suit. All educators are bound to abide by the terms of an approved IEP.

Related services.   These supportive, noneducational services permit a child with a disability to access the general curriculum. Related services can include, but are not limited to the following: transportation, various therapies, mobility instruction, social work, and medical services for diagnostic or evaluation purposes.

Free and appropriate public education (FAPE).   This cornerstone of IDEA guarantees that special education and related services are provided at no cost to parents. The word "appropriate," never clearly defined, has been the source of much controversy and litigation.

Continuum of services.   Special education services take many forms and are delivered in varied settings. Inside the classroom, these can range from consulting with a teacher on the format of a test to the team teaching of a special educator and an English teacher. Outside the general education class, specialized instruction might be delivered to small groups of children with disabilities. A few children are taught in separate classes or schools (day, residential, or hospital) that enroll only children with disabilities. The entire spectrum of options, known as the continuum of services, must be considered when designing individualized special education programs.

Least Restrictive Environment (LRE). Another key element of IDEA, this phrase refers to each school's responsibility to ensure that "to the maximum extent appropriate, children with disabilities . . . are educated with children who are nondisabled; and that . . . removal from the regular educational environment occurs only if the nature or severity of the disability is such that education in regular classes with the use of supplementary aids and services cannot be achieved satisfactorily" (IDEA, Section 300.550). Here, too, differing interpretations of many undefined terms can lead to disagreement and litigation.

Inclusion. This term may be one of the first that comes to mind when special education is mentioned. Surprisingly, the word "inclusion" does not appear in any federal legislation. Its meaning differs across states, across districts, and even within schools, and can change from year to year. Defining and applying this term has resulted in inspiration as well as confusion, frustration as well as opportunity, creativity as well as litigation. The common element in all definitions involves increasing the participation of children with disabilities in general education classes.

Differing Orientations

Underlying the controversies in this *Taking Sides: Clashing Views in Special Education* are three separate perspectives, each of which affects the way in which people envision a solid special education program. Although disagreements cannot always be reduced to one of these, it is likely that people who support differing sides of an issue question will also be on opposite sides of the following dynamics.

Medical or Educational Model?

The medical model of special education views disabilities as conditions that can be improved, remedied, remediated, or perhaps prevented. Medical model adherents seek a specific treatment or therapy to address the physical, psychological, or cognitive issues that result in school problems. Those who follow an educational model aim to address directly the impact of a disability on school performance. Proponents focus on improving educational success through teaching skills or particular strategies that sidestep the areas of difficulty. Is it wiser to deliver occupational therapy to improve the penmanship of a child with cerebral palsy or to teach the child how to use voice-activated software to enable his or her words to become print?

Special Need or Disability?

The federal list of disabilities does not mention children who need instructional assistance solely due to language differences, cultural differences, poverty, or lack of instruction. Neither does it include students who are gifted and talented. Yet children in each of these groups may not have their needs met in a standard classroom without extra attention. In addition, almost everyone can remember struggling with learning at one point in life. Special education does not help children covered by any of these descriptions unless those children also have disabilities.

Special education is about the education of children who have a disability rather than those who struggle. This delineation causes controversy. If we know children whose lives make them at risk for failure, should we wait until that failure occurs before we give them help or should we expand special education to include them? If we expand special education by including these children, are we helping them or burdening them with a stigmatizing label?

General or Special Responsibilities?

In the early 1970s, millions of children with disabilities were excluded from school. Federal laws mandated their education, which initially occurred mostly in secluded locations by specialized teachers. Seeing these students grow, teachers and parents began to seek out special education services. In many districts, special education ceased being a stigma and became a desired and protected resource, particularly when budget stress increased class sizes and reduced overall supports.

As the number of children receiving services increased, resistance rose to the expansion and costs of special education and to its separation from the overall school curriculum. This backlash resulted in tighter definitions, restricting services to those who are truly disabled and increasing expectations that classroom teachers assume responsibility for a wider range of children.

No Child Left Behind takes these deliberations one step further, introducing the idea that students should not be considered for special education if it can be determined that they have not experienced research-based classroom instruction.

The accountability provisions of No Child Left Behind are redefining the connection between general and special education personnel. Since schools must be answerable for the progress of students in special education, everyone must focus less on "where" the students learn, and more on what knowledge they acquire.

Will schools initiate and sustain general education supports for all children, lessening the pressure for special education? Will heightened standards result in better outcomes for students with disabilities?

Understanding Controversy

Precisely because the issues surrounding special education are so powerful, and the stakes for children so high, it is vital that we actively engage in their resolution. To achieve this end, it is essential to recognize differences and collaborate to find common ground.

Disagreements about Applying the Law

Parents and teachers must come to agreement about the best way to meet the needs of a child with a disability. Honorable people may be equally committed to the goal of a free and appropriate public education in the least restrictive environment, but differ on the definition and application of these terms. Although few would argue about the meaning of "free," some parents and teachers prefer focused instruction in small groups of children with similar learning needs, while other parents and educators feel the letter and spirit of the law can be met only when all children (regardless of individual need) are taught within the general education classroom all day. Two children may be very similar but have dramatically different special education programs because the preferences and reasoning of their educational teams differ. Since each child is unique, and can experience only one option at a time, it is impossible to know which choice will lead to the best outcome. In fact, the "best" option may change as the child grows and develops.

Sometimes the differing interpretations of parents and teachers can result in heated arguments. The keys to coming to consensus involve listening, learning, and being open to new information and different perspectives. Equally important is evaluating each source of information, and each course of action, in a measured, careful way, even if it differs substantially from what you feel to be right. Often, putting yourself in the other person's place helps. What would I do if this were my child? What would I do if I were the teacher?

As with most issues regarding children, the best solution is achieved when the adults involved put their attitudes, emotions, and pride aside to understand what the other persons want and why they want it.

Disagreements about Interpreting Facts and Figures

While some of the questions in this *Taking Sides* address decision making about individual children, others require the interpretation of objective facts. Analyzing these controversies requires a different approach.

For example, educators and legislators often argue about the significant increase in special education numbers and costs. While this is a debate that deserves examination, it is also one that highlights the importance of evaluating information carefully. The meaning of seemingly objective facts often depends on the context used for interpretation.

Consider the following statement, "Student enrollment in special education programs increased from 3.6 million in 1976–77 to 6 million in 1996–97. During that same time, the total student population increased by only 4.4%" (Center for Special Education Finance (CSEF) *Resource,* Winter, 1999–2000). A truly alarming increase.

What a terrible situation! This is a system run amok. The number of children in special education has doubled at a time when the number of children in schools has barely increased at all. There must be a way to slow this trend. At this rate there won't be any money to buy books. Perhaps the law is poorly written. Perhaps districts are not evaluated closely enough. Perhaps parents are too unreasonable or administrators too ready to provide any service requested. Or is it?

Additional information might change the interpretation. The cited enrollment statistics begin with 1976, the first year after federal law called for a free and appropriate public education for all children with disabilities. In 1973, the Senate Labor and Public Welfare Committee documented "more than seven million deaf, blind, retarded, speech-impaired, emotionally dis-turbed or otherwise handicapped children in the United States . . . only 40 per cent were receiving an adequate education, and many were not in school at all" (*Congress and the Nation, IV,* 1973).

Millions of children with disabilities were not *in* school in 1976, so their addition to the rolls made a big impact. Many children were in institutions, which declined in size and scope as school doors opened. Many children became identified as having a disability and entered the special education count—do the statistics subtract them from the "total student population"?

Background information about statistics or seemingly objective facts can affect your understanding of their meaning and, with it, your position on the issue. Bringing to light the assumptions made by others may do the same.

Some believe that special education enrollments have risen due to the creation of "invisible disabilities" invented by those looking for a cause or an excuse for poor performance or any way to get extra help for their children. Others contend that science is becoming more adept at understanding learn-ing and behavior. In doing so, research identifies real reasons to explain why some students struggle and provides productive strategies to facilitate learning.

Some maintain that society has become looser and more permissive. Drugs and alcohol are more available. Children are not supervised the way they used to be and are influenced heavily by exposure to media representa-tions of violent behavior. Others point to statistics on poverty, one-parent homes, three-job parents, and the disintegration of family and community supports to explain increasing numbers of students who push the limits of courtesy, tolerance, and the law.

Some are proud that medicine is making remarkable strides, sustaining one-pound babies and victims of tragic accidents or chronic illnesses, who live to come to school ready to learn. Others are concerned that these miracles of life require extensive support and extraordinary methods beyond the scope of schools.

Each point of view puts a different spin on the analysis of enrollment figures in special education. The interpretation you choose to accept depends on the argument you find most compelling. Careful deliberation of all infor-mation helps you formulate your own opinion.

Being Ware of Bias

Each of us brings to every discussion our own background and inclinations. We cannot help but apply these to the issues in this book. In fact, those indi-vidual experiences may very well lead to creative options that change the course of a debate. As you begin to tackle your first issue, I offer the following reflections, gathered from students, parents, and colleagues.

Acknowledge and be mindful of your own experiences. If you, or a family mem-ber, encountered special education (or the lack of it), you will have formed strong opinions about its worth. If you have not had direct experience, your community's media coverage of special education may have shaped your thoughts. Recognize the impact of your experience and consider its influence as you debate the issues.

Be cautious of solutions that claim to apply equally to every situation.   Two children with Down syndrome can be as different from each other as two "typical" seventh grade children. Urban and suburban elementary schools pose very different sets of possibilities and limitations. Appropriate strategies in kindergarten transfer poorly to tenth grade. Ideas can usually be adapted, but rarely duplicated.

Think of possibilities rather than limitations.   It is easy to say, "That can't be done," and be constrained by what you have already observed. Creative solutions emerge from asking, "How can it be done?"

Consider the impact of roles, motivations, and perspectives.   Teachers come to their work because they want to help children grow and learn. Special education professionals believe in the ability to help children conquer the limitations of their disabilities to become productive learners and adults. Parents seek educators who are dedicated to helping children reach their potential. District administrators serve two masters. First, they believe in the power of education and want to clear financial and legal hurdles so teachers can do their job as well as possible. Second, they understand that they are entrusted with the finite resources of a community and need to be answerable for their decisions in a way that will sustain the confidence of the citizens. Finally, legislators are committed to ensuring equal treatment and benefit to constituents whose lives span a wide range of circumstances.

Each of these roles demands responsibility and accountability. The tasks of each role shape opinions and decisions. The outlook of people holding each role can lead to widely different perspectives, powerful arguments, and creative solutions. Consider the background of each of the authors you read in this *Taking Sides* as you evaluate their point of view. What in their backgrounds led them to their respective conclusions?

Final Words

As you read the selections in this book and discuss them with your colleagues, your challenge is to sort through competing arguments and information to form your own opinions about the education of children with disabilities. Perhaps you will have the opportunity to apply your point of view to an issue within your community or school. Perhaps you will discover practices in those schools that will change your opinion on an issue.

Controversies in special education will likely endure. The topics will change, but there will always be arguments about the right thing to do for children who seem to need so much. You might be tempted to search for global answers. You might find yourself frustrated by limited options. You might come to a unique solution that works perfectly for your district and your school.

As a special education administrator, especially in the spring, I often woke up in the middle of the night with a seemingly irresolvable problem running and running and running through my brain. Usually it involved balancing competing views of how to help a child. None of the options seemed totally satisfactory. A wise friend suggested I let go of the feeling that I needed to solve the problem alone and, instead, ask others to discuss together the pros and cons of each avenue. This suggestion has always served me well as I struggle over issues of doing the right thing for children. I hope the issues in this *Taking Sides* keep you thinking at night and that my friend's suggestion helps you come to your own conclusions about educating children with disabilities.

Individuals with Disabilities Education Improvement Act (IDEA 2004): Emerging Issues

Taking Sides is based on current issues. Nothing could be more current than the new reauthorization of IDEA, the federal law upon which special education is built. Throughout the development of this edition, I kept the reauthorization of IDEA 2004 in mind. I am pleased to include an early evaluation of the regulations that became final in October 2006.

Despite promises, predictions, and good intentions, it took almost two full years for the final IDEA 2004 regulations to be published—and even now they are not totally complete. Perhaps the delay had something to do with the receipt of over 5500 comments on the draft regulations.

The final regulations (except for the areas of early intervention, multi-year IEPs, and paperwork reduction pilots) appeared in *The Federal Register* in mid-August 2006, and became official in mid-October 2006. Although some changes became operative in July, 2005, states will now take some time to formulate policy directives that districts can implement. Teachers will then learn exactly how they must change their practice.

The final regulations are over 1700 pages long. Should you want to consult them as a primary source, they can be found at http://www.ed.gov/policy/speced/guid/idea/idea2004.html. The newest federally sponsored Web site on IDEA 2004 can be found at http://idea.ed.gov. Professional and advocacy associations dove into these regulations and will be issuing analyses and commentaries in the coming months. Check the Web site for your state's department of education for updates on how IDEA 2004 final regulations will apply to your schools.

Highlighted Changes—And Questions to Consider

Keep your eyes and ears open for information on the following selection of changes, bearing in mind that your own state's laws may affect implementation. Be on the alert for controversial issues that may develop as educators and parents strive for understanding.

Alignment with No Child Left Behind

U.S. Secretary of Education Margaret Spellings used the following words to herald the final regulations of IDEA 2004: "No Child Left Behind and the Individuals with Disabilities Education Act have put the needs of students with disabilities front and center. We now have a laser-like focus on helping these kids."

Indeed, IDEA 2004 has embraced many of the elements of No Child Left Behind. There are differences, to be sure, but the two now hold common ground on several issues, including teacher qualifications, student expectations, and teaching practices.

Highly Qualified Teachers

IDEA 04 adopts the NCLB requirements for highly qualified special education teachers. This element received a large number of comments. See Issue 6, "Will NCLB Requirements Produce Highly Qualified Special Education Teachers?". Expect more controversy about how these new content requirements will affect the teacher shortage. Also, expect unhappiness that these regulations do not extend to private schools, which may be paid by public schools to educate students who need a more restrictive environment. Are all the special education teachers you know highly qualified?

Identifying Students with Specific Learning Disabilities

Responding to criticisms about the large number of students labeled as having a specific learning disability, schools are encouraged to forsake reliance on an aptitude/achievement gap in favor of determining first if a student demonstrates response to intervention (RTI). Students must not be found eligible for special education if they have not experienced sound instruction in the basic elements of reading. Will this reduce the number of students in special education? How will general education teachers react to this new responsibility?

Flexibility in Team Practices

School staff and parents may agree to hold meetings through videoconferences, conference calls, or virtual meetings. School staff and parents may agree (in writing) to excuse a member if their area is "not being modified or discussed," especially if a written report is provided. Will this save time or create paperwork? Will participation agreements be reached easily?

Elimination of Short-Term Objectives

In an attempt to respond to complaints about paperwork, short-term objectives are only required for students with significant cognitive disabilities who are taking alternate assessments. Does this apply to your state? Will this save time? How will parents react?

Transition

IEPs must address transition more formally, including both functional and academic goals, to address the student's plans after leaving school. How will teams balance these goals with those required to meet standards-based curriculum requirements? See Issue 13, "Should Students with Disabilities Be Exempt from Standards-Based Curriculum?".

Research-Based Instruction

Closely tied to No Child Left Behind elements, all instruction must be based on peer-reviewed and validated practices. See Issue 10, "Can Scientifically Based Research Guide Instructional Practice?". Do you know if your teaching practices are research based? Do you know how to tell if they are? What will teachers do if asked by parents to try a promising approach that does not have research support? Or worse, one that has been proven ineffective? What if parents and teachers discover practices that address the unique needs of a specific child, but have never been studied?

Discipline

Schools have been given more latitude to remove students for disciplinary reasons, even if they do have a disability. Standards of proof for manifestation determinations have become more stringent. See Issue 6, "Do Students with Disabilities Threaten Effective School Discipline?". Will these changes make a noticeable difference in school climate? In the way students with disabilities are disciplined?

Updates in This Edition

In addition to the targeted issues noted above, you will gain much information from Issue 2, "Does IDEA 2004 Contain Substantial Changes?". Many of the changes contained in IDEA 2004 are also discussed in the Introductions and Postscripts to other issues.

In Closing

As you absorb the new regulations, consider the following points. Which elements of the reauthorization are most likely to affect students? How should/will teaching practice change? As a future special education teacher, who can help you understand and be informed? How can you divide the task of learning the new elements and share the information you learn? How can educators and parents collaborate in understanding the changes?

Internet References . . .

National Institute of Mental Health

A branch of the National Institutes of Health, the National Institute of Mental Health (NIMH) is focused on generating and disseminating information regarding mental health conditions. This site contains information regarding the full range of behavioral disorders and conditions as well as up-to-date research information related to their existence, causes, and treatment.

http://www.nimh.nih.gov

Center for Special Education Finance

Established in 1992, the Center for Special Education Finance (CSEF) addresses fiscal and policy questions related to the delivery and support of special education services in the United States. This Web site provides access to CSEF publications, studies, and research activities.

http://www.csef-air.org

OSEP Technical Assistance Center on Positive Behavioral Interventions and Supports

This federally funded technical assistance center maintains an extensive Web site dedicated to informing educators and school systems about an array of school-wide behavioral interventions. Examples of positive practice are available for use with families, entire schools, classrooms and individuals. The Web site includes links to practicing schools, a newsletter and online information and supports.

http://www.pbis.org

Thomas B. Fordham Foundation

Affiliated with the Manhattan Institute for Policy Research, the Thomas B. Fordham Foundation supports research, publications, and action projects, with a special interest in education reform. This site contains a link to Rethinking Education for a New Century, a compilation of thought-provoking essays about the status of special education in today's schools.

http://www.eexcellence.net/foundation/global/index.cfm

Job Accommodations Network

The Job Accommodations Network, operated through the Office of Disability Employment Policy of the U.S. Department of Labor, has as its mission to facilitate the employment and retention of workers with disabilities by providing employers, people with disabilities, their family members, and other interested parties with information on job accommodations, self-employment and small business opportunities, and related subjects.

http://www.jan.wvu.edu

Individuals with Disabilities Education Improvement Act (IDEA) of 2004

The final IDEA regulations are over 1700 pages long. Should you want to consult them as a primary source, they can be found at this site:

http://www.ed.gov/policy/speced/guid/idea/idea2004.html

PART 1

Special Education and Society

It seems simple enough. *Individuals with disabilities should have access to our environment. All students have a right to education. Unfortunately, society needed to be compelled by force of law to provide access and education. The boundaries of required services are interpreted as frequently by the words of litigation as by the decisions of educators. Opportunities for some are interpreted as limitations for others. As budgets strain, the costs of the commitment to include everyone become increasingly contentious. As society changes, the definition of acceptability evolves. The spirit and the letter of the law are not always clear, but remain the source of heated discussion.*

- Has the ADA Accomplished Its Goals?

- Does IDEA 2004 Contain Substantial Changes?

- Is Eliminating Minority Overrepresentation Beyond the Scope of Public Schools?

- Do Funding Systems Create a Perverse Incentive to Place Students in Special Education?

- Does School Choice Open Doors for Students with Disabilities?

- Do Students with Disabilities Threaten Effective School Discipline?

- Will More Federal Monitoring Result in Better Special Education?

ISSUE 1

Has the ADA Accomplished Its Goals?

YES: John Hockenberry, from "Yes, You Can," *Parade Magazine* (July 24, 2005)

NO: Patricia Jordan Rea and Judy Davis-Dorsey, from "ADA in the Public School Setting: Practitioners' Reflections," *Journal of Disability Policy Studies* (vol. 15, no. 2, 2004)

ISSUE SUMMARY

YES: John Hockenberry, an award-winning television commentator, radio host, and foreign correspondent, who happens to use a wheelchair, celebrates the increased accessibility brought about by the past 15 years' implementation of the Americans with Disabilities Act.

NO: Patricia Jordan Rea, assistant professor in educational leadership at The George Washington University, and Judy Davis-Dorsey, director of human resources with the York County (VA) Schools, believe the promise of this act cannot be realized until its many unintended confusions are resolved.

As discussed in the Introduction, three basic federal laws govern the lives of individuals with disabilities: Section 504 of the Rehabilitation Act of 1973, the Individuals with Disabilities Education Act (IDEA), and the Americans with Disabilities Act.

Section 504 is a civil rights statute prohibiting organizations that receive federal funds from discriminating against any individual based on a disability that substantially limits a major life activity. Reasonable accommodations must be implemented so individuals with disabilities have equal access to the activities of the organization. Since all school districts receive federal funds, Section 504 applies to two groups: students and employees.

The regulations of IDEA form the foundation of special education, upon which individual states base local legislation to clarify federal language, establish practices, or extend commitments beyond the federal standard. Students served under IDEA are automatically covered by Section 504. Other children with disabilities, who do not require the specially designed instruction of IDEA, are eligible to receive 504 plans, which outline any necessary accommodations to ensure equal access to the educational experience.

Finally, the Americans with Disabilities Act (ADA), passed in 1990 by the first President Bush, extends the protections of Section 504, prohibiting businesses, governmental agencies, or public accommodations (other than churches or private clubs) from discriminating against any individual who has a disability that substantially limits a major life activity. The ADA carries the same responsibility for reasonable accommodations as Section 504, impacting the practices of almost every employer.

While ADA court cases frequently attract notice, attention to the ADA rose in 2005, its fifteenth anniversary. Several groups reflected on the gains that it had brought about. Others questioned its accomplishments.

John Hockenberry is a prominent journalist and foreign correspondent. At the age of 19, he became a paraplegic in a car accident. He now uses a wheelchair in his daily travel and in his overseas assignments. Reflecting on his experiences under ADA, Hockenberry reminds readers of the increased access that we now take as commonplace. Citing several examples, he observes that ADA-based accommodations have made life more accessible for those who do not have disabilities.

Patricia Jordan Rea and Judy Davis-Dorsey identify themselves as practitioners who endeavor to implement the ADA in public school settings. While acknowledging that the ADA creates opportunity for some, they find that the three legal mandates (Section 504, IDEA, and the ADA) often conflict with each other. Referencing a range of competing claims to access, Rea and Davis-Dorsey are concerned that the uncertainty and ambiguity of implementing the ADA might actually limit opportunities.

As you read these articles, consider the strides that IDEA has made for children with disabilities. Access and expectations have greatly increased. Federally, eligible students are covered until they reach the age of 22 or receive their high school diploma. What happens when individuals covered by IDEA leave the schoolhouse and enter the workplace and adult society—the ultimate inclusionary environments? Has ADA-mandated access created more possibilities or more struggle?

YES

John Hockenberry

Yes, You Can

Careful! You might miss the light show. If you surrender to any nervousness or caution and avoid looking at me when I roll by in my wheelchair, you'll miss the fireworks in my front wheels: tiny, colored electric lights that blaze out red, blue and green when they turn. That's right. I have electric scooter wheels on my wheelchair, and the greatest thing about them is how they grab the nervous eyes of some folks and pull them in. "Awesome!" people will say to me as I race across the Brooklyn Bridge. "Hey, that's cool!" I'll hear at an airport as I race to catch a plane. "*Really cool.*"

It was two 6-year-old girls who convinced me that high-profile, sparkly wheels were a big improvement over my quiet, in-the-shadows approach to being disabled in public. Those two girls are my oldest twin daughters, Zoe and Olivia. They are almost 7 now, and all of their lives they have ridden on their daddy's lap. Doctors may call me a paraplegic. Strangers might say I am "wheelchair bound." But to my daughters, I have always been a daddy who comes with his own playground apparatus. In their short lives, oblivious of the fears and anxieties of adults, they have known a wheelchair only to represent a warm, safe place.

Going Public

These days, Zoe and Olivia are nearly too big to ride comfortably on my lap anymore, and I will miss them terribly when they stop climbing up altogether. (At least I still have 4-year-old Zach and Regan, our second set of twins!) But I look into the faces of my children and see a sunrise of hope that people with disabilities are experiencing 15 years after the passage of the Americans With Disabilities Act (ADA).

Almost two decades into this landmark civil rights law, people determined to share their distinct talents have begun to take their places in the American mainstream. The signs of their presence go far beyond handicapped parking spaces and wheelchair ramps. Thanks to their persistence, today you are as likely to see a person with a disability on the ski slopes as you are in your workplace. And the momentum is picking up. All across the U.S., people with and without disabilities are bringing about lasting changes in their communities: There are city and state building codes, such as Michigan's, that go

From *Parade*, July 24, 2005, pp. 4–5. Reprinted by permission of John Hockenberry and the Watkins/Loomis Agency.

beyond federal law by mandating that doors, passageways and bathrooms be unobstructed. There is the unique federal and civic partnership that designed and built wheelchair access into Boston's venerated Fenway Park, which for decades was off-limits to the disabled. And there is the Center for Creative Play, a universally accessible indoor playspace in Pittsburgh, Pa., for children of all abilities, which projects such a powerful "Welcome, all!" message that families drive hours just to play there. Taken one at a time, these are small changes you might miss unless you modify old assumptions and look at the world with new eyes.

Strength in Numbers

Even the battles today are different. Fifteen years ago, there might have been a debate over whether someone like Tony Sylvester, a young man born with spina bifida, could even go to a public school. Recently, Tony, 19 and a graduate of Wauwatosa West High School in suburban Milwaukee, Wis., waged a tough campaign for his varsity letter. Tony's a forward for the highly ranked Wheelin' Wizards—a wheelchair basketball team that competes with other disabled athletes, independent of their high schools. To appeal the school superintendent's decision to deny the letter, Tony and his mother, Tish, got advice from a powerful ally—IndependenceFirst, a Milwaukee-based organization that helped them pack a school-board meeting with disabled athletes, coaches, parents and the media. As a result, Tony was awarded his letter—a big W, which he wears proudly.

No doubt, there is strength in numbers—and the numbers are growing. IndependenceFirst, the group that helped Tony and Tish, is just one of about 500 Independent Living Centers across the U.S. that have grown up with the ADA. Typically nonresidential, private and nonprofit (though many are state-supported), these community-based centers provide services and act as advocates for people with disabilities. . . . There also are 10 federally funded ADA & Information Technology centers in the U.S. to help businesses, architects and schools comply with the law by providing information, training and technical assistance. . . .

Clearly, there are fewer excuses today for being inaccessible and indifferent to the disabled. But, in the end, a truly inclusive world will depend on the efforts and courage of those who are not disabled—in a word, society at large. After all, the Civil Rights Act of 1964—which had the backing of the courts, the police and the National Guard—still has not wiped out racism.

It's Up To You, Too

Meanwhile, local victories like Tony Sylvester's boost morale for the bigger struggles that lie ahead. For instance, employment for people with disabilities has not improved significantly since the passage of the ADA. Disabled unemployment has stood near 70% for the past two decades. The ADA itself has suffered setbacks in court decisions and by its own limitations. Businesses can be exempted from the ADA by claiming that compliance is an "undue burden." And houses of worship do not have to comply at all, even though thousands have because it is the right thing to do. Enforcement of the ADA is left to the courts, where the vast majority of lawsuits are thrown out before they ever reach trial.

Perhaps the most significant accomplishment of the Americans With Disabilities Act is that it has widened the expectation that there ought to be some way in for people with disabilities. One telling example is an incident that occurred a few years ago when I was riding on the New York City subway. The train was declared "out of service" and pulled into a station without an elevator—one of many. The conductor ordered all passengers off the train. With the exception of me and a few women with strollers, everyone got off and trudged up the steps to the sidewalk.

When the conductor offered me no help, my only option was to hop out of my wheelchair and lug myself up the filthy subway stairs on my keister. But then one of the stroller women laid into the conductor: "What's your plan for this man? Is he just supposed to stay down here forever? Is that your plan?" She was riled up on my behalf. "We're not stupid people," she continued. "There's a law that says you have to have a plan. Everybody knows that."

We All Benefit

The conductor went from ignoring a solitary man in a wheelchair to being intimidated by a volunteer SWAT team of Brooklyn moms. He told all of us to stay on the train, then drove us to the next elevator station. The stroller mom looked at me and said with a smile, "You're the guy on TV, right? I love your work." I thanked her and left the train in awe of the anonymous outraged lady who had saved the powerless TV star. Her outrage represented something deeper: an expectation that has grown up with the ADA that disabled people have certain rights that cannot be denied. That's what saved me: her expectation— *our shared expectation*—that there is a place for all in America.

It's not like only the disabled benefit from this. Those ladies with their strollers have me to thank for the sidewalk ramps they love. And do you think that young office workers in the gym realize that it is the deaf they have to thank for the captions on the TV screens that allow them to follow their stocks while they huff and puff? Having a place for all is both the American dream and the engine of our success. We've been working on this freedom thing for the past 229 years. As my daughters might say: It's high time for some awesome, sparkly wheels.

What You Should Know

On July 26, 1990, the Americans With Disabilities Act was signed into law, eliminating discrimination in employment, transportation and public accommodations for the nation's 50 million disabled adults and children. Still, to this day, many with physical and mental disabilities do not get their due. To learn more or for technical-assistance materials, . . . call the ADA Information

Line at 1-800-514-0301. (During business hours, specialists help you apply the law to your own situation.) For TTY, call 1-800-514-0383.

- Employers interested in hiring the disabled can consult the Employer Assistance and Recruiting Network (EARN), a free service of the Department of Labor. . . .
- Several states are marking the ADA's 15th anniversary this week with parades and other events. . . .

Patricia Jordan Rea and
Judy Davis-Dorsey

 **NO**

ADA in the Public School Setting: Practitioners' Reflections

The Americans with Disabilities Act of 1990 (ADA) is a sweeping piece of federal legislation enacted with the intention of addressing inequities and correcting segregation and isolation of people with disabilities in a nation that prides itself on equality of opportunity. In the text of this Act are statements indicating that two primary purposes are "to provide a clear and comprehensive national mandate for the elimination of discrimination against individuals with disabilities" and "to provide clear, strong, consistent, enforceable standards addressing discrimination against individuals with disabilities" (42 U.S.C. §12101). Although irrefutable progress has been made in removing discriminatory barriers for people with disabilities since enactment of the Act, equity has not yet been achieved (National Organization on Disability, 1998). Factors that contribute to that inequity include legislative mandates that (a) sometimes compete and conflict with each other, (b) lack clear operational procedures and definitions, and (c) foster myths and misunderstanding rather than supply guidance and support. Attempting to decipher complex legislation, maintain a system of organized and equitable practices, and manage complicated educational programs confounds the persons charged with implementing the Act's requirements.

Public schools provide an interesting setting for examining these complications, because it is in the schools that ADA "meets" the . . . IDEA [which] mandates that special education and related services be provided to students with disabilities. It is based on the premise that "improving educational results for children with disabilities is an essential element of our national policy of ensuring equality of opportunity, full participation, independent living, and economic self-sufficiency for individuals with disabilities" (20 U.S.C. §1400). Based on our experiences as administrators of human resources and student services programs in a school district in Virginia who are striving to implement the provisions of both Acts, we believe that substantial work remains to be done to meet the express purposes of these laws. Despite volumes of technical assistance documents and thousands of pages of training materials published in the wake of passage of the ADA, ambiguity in the text of this legislation, combined with a lack of a clear fit with existing legislation, has led to unintended and, in some instances, undesirable outcomes for persons with disabilities.

From *Journal of Disability Policy*, vol. 15, no. 2, 2004, pp. 66–69. Copyright © 2004 by Pro-Ed, Inc. Reprinted by permission. References omitted.

Before further progress can be made in providing equitable opportunities for people with disabilities, an essential question has to be asked: Does the ADA provide the necessary foundation for meeting the purposes stated within it? Issues related to this question will be explored in the rest of this article.

Lack of Clear Fit

The ADA was intended as companion legislation to the IDEA and Section 504 of the Rehabilitation Act of 1973 (CEC, 1994). The most comprehensive civil rights legislation enacted since the 1960s, the ADA expands the prohibition of discrimination against people with disabilities to the areas of employment, transportation, communications, and public accommodations and reinforces rights guaranteed in earlier pieces of legislation. In addition to the ADA and the IDEA, the Family and Medical Leave Act of 1993, the Civil Rights Act of 1991, and workers' compensation laws promulgated by individual states play significant roles in the workplace. Because public schools are required to implement all of these pieces of legislation, they provide a unique setting for observing the results of the interactions of the various laws. Due to the absence of legislation integrating these laws, employers and service providers are faced with mandates that are often conflicting and that compete for authority in specific cases.

To date, even litigation has failed to offer a clear consensus and definitive answers on the circumstances under which one piece of legislation would supercede the others. One such example is the definition of "essential job functions" as specified in the ADA. These are duties that give the job its character and without which it would be fundamentally changed. For example, school officials must determine if a teacher who cannot teach a full day because of a debilitating health condition is performing the essential functions of teaching. Complicating the situation is the growing number of requests for protection based on disabilities. . . . This is particularly evident in cases of special education paraprofessionals, who are often assigned to provide personal care, such as toileting or mobility assistance, to individual students with physical disabilities in order to allow them to participate in general education classrooms and activities. A clear preference for general education placement is evident in the IDEA. Can a staff member assigned to such duties who has or develops back problems be accommodated in the school setting without placing a negative impact on the delivery of services to students with disabilities?

In this case, the ADA protects both the employee and student, and the IDEA ensures that the student is entitled to the service. In addition to the possible violations of the ADA, the school district is in jeopardy of failing to comply with the IDEA because personnel needed to provide services stipulated in the . . . [IEP] are not available to perform all of their job functions. This relatively common occurrence in the school setting indicates the potential for conflict between competing ADA claims. Not only may the ADA be in conflict with itself, because its provisions cover both student and employee, but it may be in conflict with the IDEA, which guarantees students a free, appropriate public education through the provision of the necessary supplementary aids and support services. Although reassigning personnel is a possible solution in some instances, smaller school districts with a limited pool of employees may not be able to use that strategy. A small district may be forced to reduce educational services to students to avoid possible legal action by the employee. An appropriate, defensible organizational response to this and similar situations remains unclear. Educational administrators cannot predict with an adequate degree of certainty whether their actions will meet expected compliance standards. . . . [Courts] have traditionally required that parents bringing suit against school districts on behalf of their children must exhaust their rights under the IDEA before seeking relief under the ADA. If that relief is determined not to be available under the IDEA, action is possible under the ADA. In such circumstances, both a student and an employee might be seeking corrective action under the same legislation.

Policy and Implementation Ambiguity

Requirements to implement simultaneously these various pieces of legislation in a public school setting leads to considerable confusion and frustration. Although terms such as *qualified individuals, reasonable accommodation,* and *undue hardship* are defined in the law, the lack of a common operational understanding of these terms often puts employers, employees, parents, and students in conflict. Difficulty with definitions thus may lead to adversarial relationships and expensive, protracted procedural exercises or, at worst, legal battles.

For example, a serious breach of trust among parents, students, and school officials may occur in the situation in which a teacher claims that her touching students inappropriately is the result of a disability-related impulsivity. It is proper, and supported by the ADA, to raise questions about this teacher's qualifications for the job and the validity of her claim. This process, which would have been handled through state due process procedures prior to implementation of the ADA, has now become two processes that require a high commitment of human and financial resources. Furthermore, parent and student concern is heightened because the lengthy process may appear to constitute a lack of concern regarding a serious accusation.

Unintended Consequences

Uncertainty and ambiguity have caused organizational stress in public schools. Efforts to implement [these] statutes have produced some unintended consequences, including distraction from the primary mission of educating students, increased isolation and stigmatization of some employees, increased drain of financial resources, and conflict between employer and employee.

In ensuring proper implementation, school personnel become distracted from the legitimate—and critical—issues of simultaneously accommodating employees and appropriately educating students. Dispute resolution processes are cumbersome, unpleasant, and expensive at best and permanently divisive at worst. For example, claims that student injuries occurred in a classroom because the vision and hearing impairments of the teacher prevented him or her from seeing and hearing what students were doing could result in investigatory and resolution processes. Although monitoring students is considered to be an essential job function for a teacher, the level of attention and skill required with different numbers and ages of students varies considerably, making it particularly challenging when an increasingly diverse student population must be served in the classroom.

In the previous example, would an assertion by the teacher that reassignment to small, remedial group instruction is appropriate be "reasonable"? On the surface, it seems plausible that simply moving the teacher to another setting requiring less intensive student monitoring would be the most effective, efficient action. What if, however, a selection process had previously identified another employee as the strongest candidate for the position? Accommodating the employee with a disability would require the reassignment of another employee who had obtained the position through legitimate processes. Further complicating the issue is the possibility that the employee initially given the position and now targeted for transfer from it also has a disability that requires the same accommodation.

One of the original intentions of the ADA was fostering independence and self-reliance among employees with disabilities, who historically had been thought incapable of employment or had been treated patronizingly in the workplace. In reality, however, uncertainly and ambiguity often cause school officials and other employees to err on the side of caution to avoid any action that might reflect poorly on the district and themselves. The logical extension of this type of risk-management strategy is an inappropriate paternalism that may limit opportunities for and choices of people with disabilities in an attempt to avoid legal or political problems. Such a protectionist attitude may result in (a) accommodations that are not reasonable, and therefore not required and expected under the Act, and (b) a loss of the very opportunities for maximum employee functioning intended by the law.

Financial obligations as a result of the ADA are another major consideration for most districts. Data available from the Equal Employment Opportunity Commission (1998) indicate that although between 43 million and 49 million U.S. residents have disabilities, less than 25% of them require accommodations in the workplace, and, furthermore, nearly 70% of those accommodations cost less than $500 per person. Costs are incurred not only for accommodations, however, but also for legal and technical assistance in guiding implementation. . . . Moreover, monetary sanctions for violations can be substantial. In an era of limited public funding for competing political agendas, violations of the ADA are a serious threat to the fiscal operation of a school district. Back pay, attorney's fees, expert witness fees, and fringe benefits, all available to a prevailing employee in a dispute, can quickly diminish the amount of money available to operate a school. Because the ADA includes a complaint-driven accountability process, employee claims of discrimination based on disability are sometimes responses to impending disciplinary action or notification from the employer of changes of employment status or job assignment. When the claim is a response to a disciplinary investigation, the sequence of events described previously is set into motion. If it is a response to a change of employment status or job assignment, there are implications for program staffing patterns and other employees. In this latter situation, would it be appropriate for a middle school teacher identified for transfer to an available high school teaching position to assert that his limited physical stamina requires that he remain at a small middle school building rather than an expansive high school campus? On the surface, keeping this teacher at the middle school may seem to be a reasonable accommodation. It may also mean, however, that no matter how legitimate the selection process for transfer candidates is, how compelling the justification for the teacher's transfer is, or how serious the consequences to colleagues and the school district are, this teacher's claim may prevail.

The purpose of the ADA is elimination of discrimination based on disability through the provision of equitable access to opportunities. This shift requires increased sensitivity to and understanding and appreciation of disability and its meaning and value in the workplace. In reality, the current situation lends itself to potential abuses, such as inappropriate claims for protection and accommodation, an increasing need for stigmatizing labels that reinforce negative stereotypes, and a focus on pathology and human deficiency rather than on individual strengths and talent. The ADA has helped to spawn some myths and misconceptions about people with disabilities, including a perception that anybody can "scream disability" and get preferential treatment. Perhaps more alarming is the development of a subculture in the workforce consisting of individuals with accommodations who are sometimes perceived to be less productive than their nondisabled colleagues. Fortunately, this is rarely the case; however, a lack of clarity concerning the qualifications for the disabled status and subsequent accommodations results in some negative attitudes in the workplace, including the perception that carrying a disability label shields an employee from the consequences of inadequate or inappropriate performance. In order to dispel those myths and misunderstandings, and to ensure fair and just implementation of the ADA, school districts need to provide considerable training for all employees. Sensitivity is developed through awareness, and understanding is developed through education. The level, intensity, and quality of the training necessary for supporting systemic change does not come without a price.

The function of schools can be further skewed when rights and protections afforded to one individual with a disability conflict with those of another and when accommodations intended to improve the situation of one individual create a barrier to access for another. This can occur not only in the areas of service delivery and employment but also in terms of plant and grounds accessibility. For example, the lowered water fountain for the individual in a wheelchair presents a difficulty for someone with a back disorder who cannot bend. Similarly, curb cuts for wheelchairs decrease accessibility for persons with blindness, who need the boundary of the curb as a guide.

Conclusion

Implementation of the ADA in the public school setting has produced many positive outcomes, such as a more diverse workforce; increased accessibility of opportunities, activities, and facilities; increased labor resources; a refreshing call for innovation, creativity, and flexibility; and a new recognition and appreciation of the strengths, contributions, and abilities of people with disabilities. A series of negative consequences, however, need to be acknowledged, reviewed, and addressed in order to remove fully the barriers that prevent people with disabilities from being totally involved in public schools.

Rarely is compliance with the ADA a matter of following step-by-step directions; instead, it is about interpretation, which will occur through administrative hearing and court decisions . . . U.S. Supreme Court decisions [continue] to define the authority and parameters of the ADA. It is possible that school districts, as an arm of the state, will ultimately be granted immunity from the ADA claims. Court decisions are rendered slowly, reinforcing the point that time, energy, and resources go into defining compliance. In any event, it is unlikely that perceived violations would not be challenged while plaintiffs await judicial guidance.

This article reflects the challenges faced by practitioners trying to integrate existing legislation into a coherent set of employment and service delivery practices. It is not our position that these unintended outcomes negate or even diminish the Act's benefits. Our point is that until and unless these issues are resolved in an equitable, logical way, it is unlikely that the ADA will accomplish the outcomes originally intended by its crafters and supporters, that people with disabilities will be able to gain full access to opportunities for success and realize their potential, or that persons without disabilities in the school setting will reap the full benefits of being educated and working with people with diverse characteristics.

POSTSCRIPT

Has the ADA Accomplished Its Goals?

Section 504, IDEA, and the ADA share lofty goals. Each endeavors to expand opportunities for individuals with disabilities to participate fully in our complex society. Although advances have been made, there are differing views on outcomes.

John Hockenberry illustrates the successes of the ADA. Twenty years ago, the idea that a man in a wheelchair could use the subway (much less report from a far-away country) was an unlikely dream. Today, a woman pushing a stroller castigates the subway operator for not considering Hockenberry's needs. The very curb cut that makes Hockenberry's travels possible makes life easier for that stroller-pushing adult.

Writing in *Psychology Today*, Hara Marano (2004) thinks these laws may actually have done their job too well. Marano maintains that parents seeking to ensure success for their children embrace "cleverly devised defects" to secure advantages like untimed SATs. This relentless hunt has created a group of fragile children, unable to resolve their own difficulties.

Rea and Davis-Dorsey agree that sometimes people "scream disabilities" in order to get help, but they are more concerned with situations that impede their ability to create equitable access for all. Specifically, they find obligations to employees and students may conflict. Creating access for one can limit the access of the other. Wheelchair-accessible lower water fountains can be a barrier to someone with a back problem. School personnel overprotect because they cannot predict if their actions will meet compliance standards.

One employer sees things differently. David Morris *(Wall Street Journal,* 2005) is CEO of a global company that has hired large numbers of people with disabilities for 20 years. Morris' experience tells him this just makes good sense. Referencing a number of national studies, Morris finds employees with disabilities resilient, dedicated, and high performing. Noting that most required accommodations are inexpensive, Morris thinks attitudes are larger barriers to overcome.

Morris' conclusions seem supported by the numbers. The 2004 National Organization on Disability/Harris Survey of Americans with Disabilities studied changes in 10 quality-of-life indicators. Two-thirds of respondents said the ADA has improved their lives. Shockingly, only 35 percent of people with disabilities are employed, compared to 78 percent of typical adults. Still, over the life of the ADA, opportunities in four areas demonstrated improvement: education, income, employment, and eating out. People with severe disabilities said the ADA has made their life better than did those with slight disabilities. Could the ADA's success vary by disability?

Editors of the journal *Remedial and Special Education* devoted an entire issue (vol. 24, no. 6, 2003) to adults with learning disabilities. Over half the individuals served by IDEA have been designated as having specific learning disabilities, which is sometimes called an "invisible" disability. Thirty-something adults with learning disabilities attended school fully covered by IDEA and are now active in the workforce. Often, the successes of prominent people with learning disabilities are heralded.

In this journal, Price, Gerber, and Mulligan noted that the ADA ended "years of paternalism" and empowered people with disabilities to participate more fully. This empowerment came with individual responsibilities that are challenging to fulfill. Although barriers to physical access seemed easier to lower, Price et al. uncovered reluctance by adults with learning disabilities to self-disclose their condition and claim accommodations rightfully theirs under the ADA. While this group of individuals did not seem to encounter very many barriers to successful employment, as a result of their reticence, employers were not very knowledgeable about this "invisible" disability.

Paradoxically, Mellard and Lancaster observe that while students with less significant disabilities initially work a large number of hours, their overall pay eventually declines because their peers earn more as a result of postsecondary education and training. Despite 15 years of IDEA emphasis on transition planning, critical linkages may not be made for all.

Other authors in this journal address keys to adult success: speaking up and securing resources. Self-determination—the ability to articulate one's needs and participate in implementing plans and services—is a critical skill (Field, Sarver, Shaw). Mellard and Lancaster emphasize the importance of engaging the resources of community agencies that support adults with disabilities. However, these scarce resources often go to individuals with more significant disabilities.

Commissioned by the second President Bush, the President's Committee for People with Intellectual Disabilities (2003) acknowledged that many strides have been made through IDEA, including the development of self-advocacy skills. However, the committee expressed grave concerns that "faulty attitudes" held by the general public, especially employers, combined with well-intentioned federal policies, have led to a form of "enforced poverty" for individuals with intellectual disabilities (mental retardation). Finding that approximately 90 percent of adults with intellectual disabilities were unemployed, the committee recommended that schools increase transition services. It also advocated for more flexible federal policies among agencies, to ease the way into employment.

IDEA 2004 increases emphasis on transition planning. Beginning with the Individual Education Program (IEP) in place when the student turns 16, educational teams must include postsecondary goals related to training, education, employment, and independent living, where appropriate. Functional, as well as academic, goals must be addressed. An action plan must be created for securing postsecondary services to reach these goals.

Under IDEA, educational options and expectations for individuals with disabilities have expanded. Under the ADA, the reviews seem mixed. For some, especially those with visible disabilities, access to society and work have increased. Some, with less visible disabilities, seem to manage without self-disclosure. Others, with intellectual disabilities, still face limitations and bias. Will new transition efforts under IDEA 2004 result in better outcomes due to increased self-advocacy? How will schools and families balance legal mandates for transition goals and services with the educational pressure for higher academic achievement? Will those who have seen access grow during their education find it easier to facilitate access in the workplace?

ISSUE 2

Does IDEA 2004 Contain Substantial Changes?

YES: H. Rutherford Turnbull III, from "Individuals with Disabilities Education Act Reauthorization: Accountability and Personal Responsibility," *Remedial and Special Education* (November/December 2005)

NO: Tom E. C. Smith, from "IDEA 2004: Another Round in the Reauthorization Process," *Remedial and Special Education* (November/ December 2005)

ISSUE SUMMARY

YES: H. Rutherford Turnbull III, co-founder and co-director of the Beach Center on Disability at the University of Kansas, sees major changes in IDEA 2004. In line with the Bush administration's priorities, Turnbull identifies a shift toward requiring parents and students to take more responsibility for their own behavior and for relationships with schools.

NO: Tom E. C. Smith, professor at the University of Arkansas, focuses his research on disability law and inclusion. Reflecting on IDEA 2004, Smith believes that, although some changes seem significant, they will make little difference in the daily practice of special education.

The first federal special education statute (The Education of All Handicapped Children Act) was passed in 1975. It opened school doors for millions of excluded children with disabilities.

Every 5 years, federal statues undergo a lengthy reauthorization process. Constituent groups identify areas of satisfaction and irritation. Legislators pour over data, searching for patterns of performance, achievement, and financial expenditure to determine whether the intent of the legislation is being realized. Policy analysts reflect on how the statute "fits" within the current administration's goals and priorities.

After all the information is considered, the House and Senate create separate reauthorization bills, which are debated and amended. When passed, a joint conference committee undertakes the daunting task of combining the two versions into one document acceptable to both houses.

Once Congress and the president approve the reauthorized statute, regulations must be formulated to explain how to implement the intent of the statute. These, too, are subject to public comment and further consideration before they become official.

When regulations are issued, state governments align the federal statute with their unique state laws. The latter can exceed, but not fall below, federal standards. After state regulations are formulated, educators and parents know what they must do to comply with the new provisions.

IDEA 97 made some landmark changes to special education law. Perhaps the most earthshaking was the requirement that all students with disabilities participate in state and local assessment systems. Not only were students with disabilities allowed into schools, they now must have access to the general curriculum.

The fifth reauthorization of IDEA began in 2001. It was expected to move quickly. Despite good intentions, the new Individuals with Disabilities Education Improvement Act (still called IDEA), was not signed by President Bush until 2004.

The process to formalize regulations was also expected to move quickly. However, these were not posted in *The Federal Register* until August 14, 2006, after the Education Department considered more than 5500 comments. The regulations became official 60 days later.

Although states were authorized to implement some elements in July 2005, other elements await state response to the final regulations. Current IDEA information is available through your state department of education and/or the federal Web site: http://www.ed.gov/policy/speced/guid/idea/idea2004.html.

This reauthorization was conducted in a highly charged atmosphere. No Child Left Behind (NCLB), holding school districts accountable for the progress of all children, was impacting schools. The Fordham Foundation had just released a comprehensive analysis of the accomplishments and shortcomings of IDEA (*Rethinking Special Education for a New Century*, 2001) as had the President's Commission on Excellence in Special Education (PCESE) (2002). Both called for substantial changes in special education to increase accountability, reduce paperwork, and reign in what each perceived as rampant litigation.

The two articles in this issue contain much information about the changes in IDEA 2004. They differ dramatically in their interpretation of the significance of these revisions.

H. Rutherford Turnbull III believes IDEA 2004 is substantially altered. He finds new provisions substantially increase the responsibilities of parents and students, echoing the Welfare Reform Act of 1996.

Tom Smith predicts that, although a number of the new elements of IDEA 2004 appear substantial, they will have little real impact on the daily practices of school. He sees that the core element of IDEA—providing a free and appropriate public education—remains unchanged.

As you read these articles, consider different perspectives. How will IDEA 2004 affect your life as an educator? What if you are the parent of a student with a disability? What if you were that student?

YES

H. Rutherford Turnbull III

Individuals with Disabilities Education Act Reauthorization: Accountability and Personal Responsibility

It is important at the outset to recognize that law is a form of behavior modification. It regulates the behaviors between the government and the governed, and it shapes the behavior of both. In this respect, the law plays its traditional role of social engineering—shaping the ways that society operates.

Seen in this light, the reauthorized Individuals with Disabilities Education Act (IDEA; 2004) engineers society and shapes behavior in three basic ways. First, it authorizes the expenditure of federal funds and shapes how those funds and the complementary state and local educational agencies' funds are spent, and it aligns those funds and their expenditure patterns with the earlier IDEA (1997) and with the No Child Left Behind Act of 2001 [NCLB]. It continues to be—but becomes more like—a *school reform* law. Second, IDEA grants rights to students and their parents: It continues to be a *civil rights* law. Third, IDEA particularizes the relationships that students and their parents have with local and state educational agencies. It partakes of social reform on a large scale—more like a *"welfare state"* reform law than a civil rights or school reform law.

Taking these three approaches to social engineering as a whole, and based on a close analysis of IDEA's text, it becomes clear that IDEA is more consistent than ever with other federal policies that impose accountability standards and procedures on the beneficiaries of federal largesse. The accountability that IDEA (1997) and NCLB imposed on the schools is now imposed on the students and their parents as well. To support this argument, it is appropriate to begin with analyzing IDEA as an education law, then showing how IDEA retains its basic nature as a civil rights statute, and finally discussing its new accountability and responsibilities provisions, their origins, their relationships to other disability laws, and their implications as welfare law reform.

IDEA as Education Law

When Congress reauthorized IDEA in 2004, it aligned IDEA with the Elementary and Secondary Education Act (ESEA; 1965), as amended by the . . . NCLB.

From *Remedial and Special Education*, vol. 26, no. 6, November/December 2005, pp. 320–326.
Copyright © 2005 by Pro-Ed, Inc. Reprinted by permission. References omitted.

To understand how this is so, it is helpful to describe the six principles that underlie NCLB (Erwin, & Soodak, 2005) and show how IDEA connects to them.

The most obvious and, therefore, the first to be mentioned principle of NCLB is *accountability* for the outcomes (results) of education. NCLB's provisions for the mandatory assessment of student proficiency during the elementary school years are its principal means for ensuring accountability. In 1997, IDEA provided that students with disabilities will have a right to participate in state and district assessments. In 2004, IDEA provides that students will participate, with accommodations and sometimes by alternate assessments, in the NCLB assessments. . . . The significant change is not that the students will engage in the state and district assessments, but that IDEA now references and therefore aligns with NCLB.

To support its accountability principle, NCLB adopts a second principle, the *highly qualified teacher* principle. Without a qualified teacher corps, improved student outcomes will be elusive, and accountability for those outcomes difficult to achieve. Accordingly, IDEA (2004) requires special education staff to be highly qualified. . . . The second principle is a means to achieve the first.

NCLB's third principle is also a means to achieve its ends: The highly qualified teachers will use *scientifically based instruction* (SBI; sometimes called *evidence-based instruction*). IDEA reiterates the SBI requirement through several different provisions:

1. It disqualifies a student from IDEA benefits if the student's educational needs or deficiencies result from "a lack of appropriate instruction in reading, including the essential components of reading instruction," as defined in . . . the Elementary and Secondary Education Act of 1965, as amended by NCLB. . . .
2. It restricts a student from being classified as having a specific learning disability by authorizing an LEA to "use a process that determines if the child responds to scientific, research-based intervention as part of the evaluation procedures.". . .
3. It requires a student's special education, related services, and supplementary aids and services (as set out in the student's . . . IEP) to be "based on peer-reviewed research to the extent practicable." . . .
4. It authorizes the SEA and LEAs to support preservice and professional development (inservice) activities that train educators to use "scientifically based instructional practices.". . .
5. It authorizes "whole-school approaches, scientifically based early reading programs, positive behavioral interventions and supports, and early intervening services" that can prevent students from being classified into special education. . . .
6. It defines "highly qualified" teachers in terms that originate in NCLB. . . .
7. It authorizes the SEA and LEAs to expend Part B money for "early intervening services" that are coordinated with their NCLB activities. . . .
8. It sponsors research, training, demonstration, and other programs that align with NCLB. . . .

NCLB's fourth principle is *local flexibility*, the theory being that too many restrictions are imposed on SEAs and LEAs by too many federal laws and that if the SEAs and LEAs have more flexibility to use their federal funds as suitable to meet their particular needs, they will achieve more acceptable outcomes. Thus, fiscal and programmatic flexibility advances agency accountability, and site-based management is sanctioned. Similarly, IDEA recognizes that SEAs and LEAs have the primary responsibility for educating students with disabilities and that there is a limited role for the federal government (Sec 601)(c)(6)). It is appropriate, then, for IDEA to seek to reduce federal paperwork requirements . . . and to grant SEAs and LEAs more discretion in how they use Part B funds. . . .

NCLB's fifth principle relates to *safe schools,* the theory being that agency accountability and student proficiency are unlikely to be realized when the teaching and learning environment is unsafe. To advance the safe school and acceptable outcome approach, IDEA retains the 1997 provision that allows an LEA to put a student into an interim alternative educational setting for a maximum of 45 days if the student carries weapons or drugs to school or injures others, but it now allows the LEA to take into account any "unique circumstances" relative to that student and his or her conduct. This vague provision is consistent with the flexibility principle, but it targets the discipline issue, not the expenditure issue: The LEA needs to be able to exercise its discretion to carry out the safety principle and thereby advance the accountability principle.

Moreover, IDEA (2004) also makes it more difficult for a student to prove that his or her behavior and disability are causally connected. . . . Under the 1997 law, the student's IEP team had discretion (the statute used the word "may") to conclude that the student's behavior was not a manifestation of his or her disability if (a) the student's IEP and placement were "appropriate," and special education services, supplementary aids and services, and behavior intervention strategies "were provided consistent with" the student's IEP; (b) the student's disability did not "impair" the student's ability to understand "the impact and consequences" of his or her behavior; and (c) the student's disability did not "impair" his or her ability "to control the behavior" for which the school would be disciplining the student.

Under the 2004 reauthorization, however, the discretionary "may" has been deleted. In its place, IDEA (2004) provides that the student's "conduct shall be determined to be a manifestation" of his or her disability under certain conditions. Furthermore, those conditions are more stringent. Instead of the original three conditions, there are now only two, and each is itself more exacting. One is that the student's conduct "was caused by, or had a direct and substantial relationship to" the student's disability. Note the change; "caused" and "direct and substantial relationship" are more immediately connected to the conduct than the two 1997 standards of "did not know" and "could not control." The other condition is that the student's conduct was "the direct result" of the LEA's "failure to implement" the student's IEP. Note again the change: Gone is the 1997 language about services not being provided "consistent with" the student's IEP and placement. "Causation" and "direct relationships" are now clearly more connected to conduct than "consistency" or fidelity of implementation.

NCLB's sixth principle is *parent participation and choice.* This has always been one of IDEA's six principles: the right to be involved in a nondiscriminatory evaluation, to be on the IEP team, to have access to and control over the release of records, and to be eligible for membership on various SEA or LEA advisory boards.

The new IDEA (2004) retains these provisions but clarifies that parents have responsibilities as well. Section 612(a)(10) limits tuition reimbursement and conditions it on the parents' giving an LEA notice and opportunity to cure alleged violations of the student's right to FAPE. Section 614(a)(1)(D) imposes duties on parents with respect to the initial evaluation, and Section 614(c)(3) does the same with respect to reevaluations. Sections 615(b)(5) and (e) make mediation available and create premediation meetings. Section 615(b)(6) creates a 2-year statute of limitations and thus requires parents to complain in a timely way. Section 615(a)(7) obligates parents to notify the LEA concerning "the nature of the problem of the child" and the "proposed resolution" of the problem of the child (not "of the school") and thus imposes on them the duty to specify what is wrong with their child and what the LEA should do for their child. Section 615(c)(E) restricts the parents' (and LEA's) right to amend their due process hearing complaint: The parents have to get their complaint right the first time around, or else the school cannot respond, because it would always be subject to being caught off guard by another and different complaint. Section 615(d)(1)(A) provides that parents may receive the procedural safeguards notice only once a year (with some exceptions), rather than on demand as often as they want it. Section 615(f)(1) requires parents and the LEA to hold a prehearing "resolution session" and to provide sufficient final notice so that the parents' complaint might be resolved before the hearing. Section 615(f)(2) requires the parents to disclose all evaluations and recommendations that they intend to use in the hearing. Section 615(f)(3)(C) creates a 2-year statute of limitations, counting from the time when a parent knew or reasonably should have known that a local educational agency violated IDEA, thus putting the parents to the task of regularly monitoring their child's education. Section 615(i)(3) regulates that award of parents' attorneys' fees and allows a court to charge the LEA's fees to the parents' attorneys if the parents' complaint is frivolous or if the parents do not proceed in good faith during the pendency of any hearing, trial, or appeal.

In summary, the reauthorized IDEA (2004) imposes many new duties on students and their parents, giving them the message that they are personally responsible for their conduct—a point that the following discussion expands.

IDEA as Civil Rights Law

IDEA is still a civil rights law. Section 612(c) parrots the Americans with Disabilities Act (1990; the disability community's civil rights law) by proclaiming that the nation's disability policy consists of ensuring equal opportunity, full participation, independent living, and economic self-sufficiency. The very term *equal opportunity* derives from the equal protection clause of the 14th Amendment (prohibiting a state from denying anyone in its jurisdiction the "equal protection" of the law), and the 14th Amendment itself was the basis on which students with disabilities first gained access to the schools as a matter of constitutional right. More than this, however, IDEA retains the original six principles that endow it as a civil rights law.

Section 612 codifies the *zero rejection* principle by continuing to require that the state plan to provide for the education of *all* students with disabilities and by retaining the "no cessation" provision. Moreover, the Section 615 discipline provisions ensure that students with disabilities will have procedural and substantive protection against discipline that might terminate their right to an education or alter the nature of FAPE for them.

Sections 614(a)–(c) continue the *nondiscriminatory evaluation* principle by retaining the safeguards for nondiscriminatory evaluation. The requirement that the evaluation now must attend to the student's academic, developmental, and functional characteristics simply makes the evaluation more specific. Moreover, the evaluation team still needs to determine the "relative contribution" of "cognitive, behavioral, physical, and developmental factors" to a student's educational needs. Thus, three characteristics, or domains, become the focus of an evaluation under the IEP: academic (consistent with NCLB), developmental, and functional (consistent with the "alternate assessment" provisions of IDEA). The four contributing factors—cognitive (a surrogate for academic), behavioral, physical, and developmental—must be evaluated and taken into account, separately and collectively.

Section 614(d) retains the *appropriate education* principle by setting out the required content of a student's IEP—the theory being that if the content standard is met, the student's education will "benefit" the student and thus meet the *Rowley* definition of "appropriate."

Section 615(f), however, minimizes the "process" component of the *Rowley* definition by providing that a procedural violation constitutes the denial of a free, appropriate public education only if it impedes the student's right to such an education, significantly impedes the parents' opportunity to participate in decision making, or causes a deprivation of educational benefits. This provision seems to codify case law: no significant procedural harm, no substantive foul.

Several sections of the 2004 IDEA restate the *least restrictive environment* principle. Section 612(a)(5) and Sections 614(b)(2)(A) and (c)(1)(B)(iv) continue to ensure that the student may participate and have the opportunity to make progress in the general curriculum. They also retain the requirement that the student's IEP must advance the student's participation in the general curriculum, extracurricular, and other school activities, consistent with the principle of the least restrictive environment.

Likewise, two sections of IDEA (2004) retain the *procedural due process* principle. Section 614 retains the procedural safeguards related to evaluation, program, and placement, and Section 615 retains the procedural due process protections related to grievances, although, as noted earlier, it adds new provisions regarding dispute resolution and mediation and makes it more difficult for a student to resist unilateral placement (see the "unique circumstances" provision) and to prove manifestation of a disability.

Finally, Sections 614 and 615 retain the *parent participation* principle by conferring opportunities on the parents to participate in decisions affecting their child's education.

By retaining its original six principles, IDEA remains a foundation for the 18 core concepts and the related nine overarching principles of disability policy. For example, the zero rejection principle reflects the core concept of *antidiscrimination*. The nondiscriminatory evaluation principle reflects the core concept of *classification*. The appropriate education principle reflects the core concept of *individualized appropriate services.* The least restrictive environment principle reflects the core concept of *integration.* The procedural due process principle reflects the core concept of *accountability.* The parent participation principle reflects the core concept of *empowerment and participatory decision making.*

These core concepts reflect constitutional principles (*life, liberty,* and *equality*) and ethical principles (*dignity, family as foundation,* and *community*). Thus, for example, the NCLB principles of accountability, highly qualified teachers, and scientifically based instruction reflect the core concepts of accountability, professional and system capacity development, and individualized appropriate services, respectively. The principle of local flexibility reflects the core concept of accountability. The principle of safety reflects the core concept of protection from harm. The principle of parental participation and choice reflects the core concept of empowerment and participatory decision making.

The fact that NCLB reflects some of the same core concepts of disability policy as IDEA is significant: It shows how very universalistic and less exceptionalistic IDEA has become. It is "mainstream" disability policy, of course, but it also has become part of the mainstream of education policy.

Two Preludes to IDEA as Accountability Policy

Two reports predicted that the reauthorized IDEA would focus far more on student and parental accountability than it had in the past. The first was *Rethinking Special Education for a New Century.* The second was the report of the President's Commission on Excellence in Special Education (2002). Both reports made similar critiques of special education, and both sought similar improvements to IDEA. Both focused on outcome rather than process, on a model of prevention rather than failure, and on children with disabilities as "general education children first" (President's Commission, 2002). Both reports paid attention to IDEA as an education law but less attention to IDEA as a civil rights law. Most significantly, both reports argued that IDEA leads students with disabilities to have unacceptable outcomes, low expectations, and a diminished sense of personal responsibility.

The point about personal responsibility was made most directly in *Rethinking,* in the chapter by Horn and Tynan, who argued that one of IDEA's "unintended negative consequences" included the "application of an accommodation philosophy to populations better served with prevention or intervention strategies." The "accommodation model," when applied to some "low- and under-achieving students," replaces a goal of "independence" with one of "lifetime dependence on special accommodations, often at tax-payers' expense." The accommodations, and especially the discipline provisions, have been "teaching students in special education that they are entitled to operate under a different set of rules than everyone else." These accommodations constitute "encouragement for special education students to see their disability as rationale for a life-time entitlement to special accommodations." The consequence of these accommodations is that the "end game" of independence has been forgotten: "special education in far too many instances serves to separate, not integrate, through the use of special rules and procedures not available to non-disabled students." Special education "seems focused on encouraging a lifetime entitlement to special accommodations." The "true victims" are the students themselves; they learn that there are "two standards" and they are "encouraged to rely upon special accommodations rather than being challenged to achieve at high levels."

Horn and Tynan's critique has a basic message: IDEA creates dependency. That message is consonant with the messages given by welfare law reform during the last decade, as the following discussion makes clear.

IDEA as Welfare Law

By analyzing the messages that Congress and the Supreme Court have been giving in welfare and disability policy during the past decade, and by bearing in mind Horn and Tynan's critique, it becomes obvious that IDEA extends the basic message of personal responsibility that was the core of welfare reform. This message also relates as much to personal responsibility as it does to social obligations and the social contract.

Congress, the Supreme Court, and the Principle of Personal Responsibility

Congress reformed welfare programs in 1996 by enacting the Personal Responsibility and Work Opportunity Reconciliation Act (PRWORA). This law targeted a subpopulation that allegedly had "learned" to be dependent—namely, families who had been supported by aid-to-dependent-families programs. PRWORA authorized time-limited and conditional cash grants, requiring the head of family to enroll in some educational program or work and entitling the family to receive the grants for only 2 years.

In a nutshell, PRWORA declared an end to learned dependency and imposed responsibilities on heads of families; it taught welfare beneficiaries that they should not continue to expect different treatment from other citizens. It signaled that people should expect less from their government and more from themselves. It proclaimed the renaissance of self-reliance and a work-ethic policy that asserts that everyone has a responsibility to contribute to society.

Similarly, IDEA reflects the theory that special education "teaches" students with disabilities to expect "different" treatment in society. This is a fundamental premise of the Finn et al. report and the Horn and Tynan chapter: The discipline provisions "teach" students with disabilities that they are different, can behave in different (and less acceptable, less conforming) ways and still expect to be treated differently ("no cessation" under Section 612, and special procedural safeguards, including manifestation determinations, under Section 615). The reauthorized IDEA sent a different message, as the many provisions cited earlier demonstrate.

In PRWORA and IDEA, Congress did more than restate the "responsibility" principle. Fundamentally, it restated the quid pro quo of the social contract: Society will do something for you if you cannot do it for yourself, but you first must be responsible for yourself. Self-reliance precedes social support. Personal responsibility precedes social dependency.

The Supreme Court also has advanced the principle of personal responsibility, principally (in its disability-law cases) in *Sutton v. United Air Lines* (1999). In this case, the court held that in determining whether the ADA protects a person, it is permissible to take into account whether the person can or does mitigate his or her disability. If a person's impairment is or can be mitigated, that person does not have a disability. *Sutton's* message and subtext is clear: If you can mitigate your disability, you should, and if you do not, ADA will not cover you.

Following *Sutton,* the Supreme Court made a deliberate effort to reduce the number of people that the ADA covers. The best example is its decision in *Williams v. Toyota.* There, the court declared that the "major life activities" that a person's impairment must significantly limit are performing household chores, bathing, and brushing one's teeth; those activities do not include being able, with accommodations, to perform a particular job. By reducing the number of people who are entitled to accommodations because they have disabilities, the court adopted the premise of *Rethinking* and the President's Commission (2002), namely, that too many people have been included as "disabled" and that it is better social policy to restrict admission to disability entitlements than to allow people to enter the disability category easily. . . .

The Supreme Court's message, then, is congruent with Finn et al., the report of the President's Commission (2002), and the reauthorized IDEA (2004): Disability policy and law should benefit fewer, not more people, and it should teach those who do qualify and those who seek to qualify as having a disability that they have obligations as well as rights and entitlements.

IDEA and the Principle of Personal Responsibility

The reauthorized IDEA (2004) restates the principle of personal responsibility in at least two ways. In this respect, IDEA is consistent with the message that Congress sent in PRWORA and the Supreme Court sent in the ADA employment cases.

First, as noted earlier, IDEA grants a variety of rights to students' parents to participate in decisions about their child's education, but it also imposes duties on them as they do participate. Moreover, IDEA also makes the personal responsibility theme explicit, . . . with respect to the students themselves. Here, Congress declares that students' education can be made more effective when educators have "high expectations" of them and enable them to "meet their developmental goals," to meet the "challenging expectations that have been set for all children," and to "be prepared to lead productive . . . adult lives." . . . Under an analysis of IDEA as welfare law, the provisions about meeting "developmental goals" arguably refer to students' behavior, not just to their academic achievement. Likewise, under the same analysis, the provisions about "lead[ing] productive . . . adult lives" arguably refer to being economically self-sufficient, working and contributing to the nation's economy, or making other socially valued contributions.

Second, as also explained earlier, IDEA allows LEAs to take into account "any unique circumstances on a case-by-case basis" when determining whether to order a change in a student's placement because of conduct that violates school rules. . . . This provision is a Damoclean sword: The "unique circumstances" are a thin hair that can protect the student or, if it is cut, cause the sword of discipline to strike the student. In either event, it permits LEAs to take into account whether the student chose to act responsibly or was incapable of making that choice.

The reauthorized IDEA (2004) also makes it more difficult for students to defend themselves against a disciplinary sanction by alleging "manifestation." As pointed out above, the reauthorized law requires students to prove that their conduct was "caused by" or had a "direct and substantial relationship" to their disability. It also removes the lax standard that the student's services were not delivered "consistent" with the IEP and replaces it with the standard that the LEA must fail to implement the student's IEP and thereby directly cause the student's conduct.

Rights and Responsibilities Within IDEA: Teaching New Lessons

The changes in IDEA's parent participation and student discipline provisions impose a duty of responsibility on parents and students alike. These beneficiaries must either follow new, highly specific procedures and standards or justify why they do not.

The new IDEA, then, teaches parents and students that they have responsibility for their own actions. It intends to shape their behavior by causing them to unlearn their alleged sense of entitlement to act in certain ways. It seeks to reduce their dependency on the schools and to increase their dependency on themselves. It calls on them to be more self-reliant and self-governing. It bears repeating: Section 601(c)(5)(A) proclaims that students' education can be made more "effective" if there are "high expectations" for them (including both behavioral expectations and academic expectations) and ways of "strengthening the role and responsibility of parents." . . .

IDEA, Title I of ESEA, and the New Morbidity

It is not just in its parent and student rights provisions that IDEA reveals that it is a welfare law. There is also a clear line between (a) IDEA and its concern with student outcomes, especially outcomes for ethnically and linguistically diverse students . . . (b) NCLB and the special provisions for Title I schools (i.e., for "poor students" in school); and (c) the "new morbidity." The term *new morbidity* refers to evidence that disability has a positive correlation with poverty and other demographic factors, such as family structure, ethnicity/culture, language, and geography.

IDEA and NCLB focus especially on students whom the new morbidity affects—under IDEA, students from minority populations (Sec. 601(c)(10)–(13)), and under NCLB, the Title I eligible ("poor") students. PRWORA and welfare reform focused on these students' families. Together, IDEA and NCLB continue the PRWORA welfare reform policies passed nearly a decade ago and the *Sutton* line of cases.

Conclusion

It seems unseemly to argue that the reauthorized IDEA is, at its core, part of the reforms that PRWORA and *Sutton* launched more than half a decade before Congress turned its attention to IDEA. Somehow, the notion that students' and parents' rights were sacrosanct had become the conventional wisdom. Yet the transitory nature of "conventional wisdom" is apparent in the very terms that define the concept itself: *Conventional* refers to the conventions, the mores, of a certain time, place, and culture. As our country's history shows, conventions and mores change; the underlying principles (the so-called six principles of IDEA and the so-called core concepts of disability policy) may not have changed, but the ways in which they are expressed in practice and codified in law do.

So it seems to be with the reauthorized IDEA. The conventional notion that rights are paramount now seems to be descendant, not ascendant. At the same time, the notion that rights entail responsibilities is ascendant; this notion does not supersede the importance of rights, but it does assert that, in our society, rights and responsibilities go hand in hand. This is a message of paramount importance to the special education and disability communities. Whether these communities will hear that message—which is sure to be repeated in debates about Social Security, Medicaid, and ADA—and how they will respond to it if they hear it are the stuff of the future.

Tom E. C. Smith  **NO**

IDEA 2004: Another Round in the Reauthorization Process

The Individuals with Disabilities Education Act (IDEA; 1997) has once again been reauthorized. Although the reauthorization was thought to be on a fast track when it was initially begun in 2001, the law was finally passed in November 2004 and signed by President Bush in December 2004. The Individuals with Disabilities Education Improvement Act (2004), still to be referred to as IDEA, contains some significant changes; however, after careful review, the changes may not be as significant as first thought.

Certainly, the lives of children with disabilities in this country have been forever altered as a result of federal legislation. Beginning with the passage of Public Law 94-142, the Education for All Handicapped Children Act, in 1975, federal policies and federal dollars have been an integral component of special education. Overall, there is no doubt that the lives of children with disabilities have improved significantly. Let us review some of the major changes that have resulted from this law; some of the changes made in previous reauthorizations; and finally, some of the major changes associated with IDEA 2004.

Public Law 94-142

When Public Law 94-142 (the Education for All Handicapped Children Act) was passed in 1975, the state of special education was vastly different from what it is today. Prior to its passage, Congress found that up to 1 million of the estimated 8 million children with disabilities in the United States were excluded from public school services, and another 3 million were being served inappropriately. The original four purposes of P.L. 94-142 included

- to assure that all children with disabilities have available to them . . . a free appropriate public education which emphasizes special education and related services designed to meet their unique needs
- to assure that the rights of children with disabilities and their parents . . . are protected
- to assist States and localities to provide for the education of all children with disabilities
- to assess and assure the effectiveness of efforts to educate all children with disabilities

From *Remedial and Special Education,* vol. 26, no. 6, November/December 2005, pp. 314–319.
Copyright © 2005 by Pro-Ed, Inc. Reprinted by permission. References omitted.

Public Law 94-142 resulted in many changes in the way children with disabilities were identified and provided with services. Prior to its passage, special education was a mere footnote in U.S. educational statistics. There were fewer than 3.5 million children with disabilities served in public schools, mostly in isolated, self-contained settings; and teacher preparation for special education was a minor activity. Some of the major requirements of P.L. 94-142 included the following:

- Child Find. Schools were required to locate children with disabilities and initiate the referral process to determine their eligibility for services under this act.
- Individualized Education Program (IEP). Every child served in special education must have an IEP. Although not intending to do so, the IEP requirement resulted in massive amounts of paperwork for special education teachers.
- Least Restrictive Environment (LRE). To the maximum extent appropriate, children with disabilities should be educated with their nondisabled peers. This resulted in "mainstreaming" and the practice of including many students with disabilities in general education settings.
- Nondiscriminatory Assessment. All children must be given a comprehensive assessment prior to determining their eligibility for special education, and this assessment must be administered in such a way as not to discriminate against individuals from different cultural/language groups.
- Related Services. Services that are necessary for a child to benefit from special education, such as physical therapy or transportation, must also be provided.
- Due Process Rights. Children with disabilities, and their parents, must be afforded certain due process rights, including the right of notice and consent prior to actions affecting their child and the right to a due process hearing to resolve complaints and disagreements between parents and the school.
- Funding. Congress said that the federal government would eventually fund up to 40% of the excess costs of educating students with disabilities. Although Congress still has not come close to the 40% level, hundreds of millions of dollars have supported programs under this legislation.
- Free, appropriate public education (FAPE). Schools were required to provide a free, appropriate public education to all students with disabilities. This includes determining the eligibility of children and developing and implementing an IEP for each child. All of the services to children under this act must be provided without cost to the parents.

Although there were many other provisions in the original P. L. 94-142, these were the ones having the greatest impact.

Since P. L. 94-142 was passed, there have been several reauthorizations that have made changes in the law. Although some of these changes have been significant, they have not altered the basic requirements of the original legislation. All children with disabilities must be referred, evaluated, and determined to be eligible or not; all eligible students must have IEPs; and all must be provided with a free, appropriate public education, meaning they must be served in the least

Table 1

Key Components of Reauthorizations of P.L. 94-142/IDEA

Reauthorization	Key components
1983 (PL 98-199)	1. Provided incentives for states to serve preschool children with disabilities.
	2. Required states to collect information and address issues related to students transitioning from school to post-school.
(PL 101-457)	1. Mandated services for children 3–5 lowering all of the requirements of PL 94-142 to include 3–5 year old children.
	2. Provided for attorney's fees in due process or court cases where parents prevailed.
(PL 101-476)	1. Added autism and traumatic brain injury to the list of disabilities covered under IDEA.
	2. Changed the name of the act from the Education for All Handicapped Children Act to the Individuals with Disabilities Education Act.
	3. Required schools to initiate transition services no later than age 16.
1997 (PL 105-17)	1. Required schools to initiate transition planning no later than age 14.
	2. Required schools to include behavior intervention plans for students with behavior problems.

restrictive environment. Some of the major changes associated with successive reauthorizations up to 1997 are included in Table 1.

IDEA 2004

The reauthorization of IDEA in 2004 included a name change: The word "improvement" was inserted, making the official title of the legislation the "Individuals with Disabilities Education Improvement Act." However, the law is still referred to as IDEA. Several significant changes were included in the reauthorization. The following section will describe these changes and discuss the actual implications of the changes.

Highly Qualified Teachers

IDEA 2004 includes a requirement that special education teachers meet the "highly qualified" mandate introduced in the No Child Left Behind Act (NCLB; 2001) legislation. This is the first reauthorization of IDEA that includes any specific requirements related to teacher qualifications. Until this act, determining the qualifications of teachers had always been left to the states. IDEA 2004 now requires teachers to be "highly qualified." Highly qualified means that

1. All special education teachers must be highly qualified under the NCLB definition; also, special education teachers must have a state special education certification; not hold an emergency, temporary, or provisional certification; and have at least a bachelor's degree.

2. Special education teachers who teach content courses and are the teachers of record for those courses must meet the NCLB *highly qualified* requirements. This means that they must be licensed in the subjects taught, similar to general classroom teachers under NCLB.

The ramifications of this addition to the legislation are just now being understood. The Council for Exceptional Children (CEC) has referred to this component of the law as "an extraordinary federal intrusion into what has been the domain of States and the profession." CEC has added that these requirements are bureaucratic, impractical, unsound, and intrusive. Many special education teachers have been involved in providing instruction and support to students in subject areas, especially in middle and high schools. Getting these teachers licensed in these content areas will undoubtedly cause many problems. Teachers are allowed to become licensed through state high objective state standard of evaluation (HOUSSE) options, which is a way states can license teachers under NCLB; however, for the immediate future, these requirements will create problems for many teachers, local districts, and states.

Funding

Finally, more than 30 years since the passage of P.L. 94-142, Congress appears to be ready to meet its promise of full funding for IDEA. P.L. 94-142 said that Congress would fund special education programs under the law at a rate up to 40% of excess costs for educating children with disabilities. Congress has never come close to the 40% level. In fact, federal funding for IDEA has never reached the 20% level. IDEA 2004 lays out a path for full funding. The law authorizes Congress to fund IDEA for $12.36 billion for fiscal year 2005 and an additional $2.3 billion each year through 2011, when full funding will be achieved.

Individualized Education Programs

The level of paperwork associated with special education has increased significantly since the passage of P.L. 94-142. In some cases, special education professionals seem to spend as much time on paperwork as on programs for their students. Excessive paperwork has actually been cited by some teachers as their primary reason for leaving the teaching profession. The 2004 reauthorization has made some changes directly targeting a reduction in paperwork. One of the changes incorporated in IDEA 2004 is deleting the requirement that IEPs include short-term objectives, except for students who are assessed using alternative assessment procedures that are aligned with alternate achievement standards. Eliminating short-term objectives hopefully will not have a negative impact on appropriate programming but will result in a reduction of paperwork.

Another change in IEPs relates to transition requirements. Whereas IDEA 1997 required schools to include transition planning in IEPs when the child reached 14 years of age, IDEA 2004 only requires schools to include a statement of transition goals based on age-appropriate transition assessments beginning with the first IEP that will be in effect when the child reaches 16 years of age.

IDEA 2004 also provides some flexibility in attendance at IEP meetings by permitting team members not to attend if their area of expertise is not needed, as agreed by other team members, and not to attend if they provide written information related to the IEP meeting prior to the meeting, again with team approval. IEPs can also be modified during the year without the entire team being present if the school and parents agree to a written amendment after the original IEP is developed. These provisions should help limit the number of times that complete teams have to get together to develop and modify IEPs. It also keeps some school personnel from having to attend meetings when their expertise is really not needed.

Finally, relative to the IEP, IDEA 2004 has established a 15-state pilot program for multiyear IEPs. States can apply for participation in the pilot program. Under the pilot program, states can develop IEPs for up to 3 years on a trial basis. Whereas students' progress toward achieving their 3-year goals would have to be measured annually, IEPs would not have to be rewritten on an annual basis. This pilot program, advocated by many professionals and some professional organizations, will determine if students can receive FAPE using multiyear IEPs, just as they receive FAPE using annual IEPs. If the results of the pilot program are positive, it is likely that all states will be able to move to multiyear IEPs.

Due Process Requirements

The original P.L. 94-142 included specific due process requirements, including the right to notice and consent and the right to a due process hearing. Parents must give consent prior to the initial evaluation and placement of their child in special education, and they must be notified prior to other actions dealing with their child. IDEA 2004 continues to require that schools obtain consent prior to initial evaluation and placement. If parents refuse their consent for initial evaluation, schools may pursue this denial through due process. However, parental refusal of consent to special education placement may not be pursued by the school through due process. In this situation, the child is not considered a child with a disability under IDEA, and the school district is not responsible for ensuring FAPE for the child.

IDEA 2004 also includes some significant changes related to due process hearings. Parents have been able to recoup attorney fees in situations where they prevailed in due process hearings and court cases, but the schools have not been able to recoup attorney fees in situations where they prevailed. IDEA 2004 enables schools to recoup costs in certain situations from the parents and parents' attorneys.

Specifically, IDEA 2004 says that the court may award fees to the prevailing state education agency (SEA) or local education agency (LEA) against parents' attorneys who (a) file a complaint or other cause of action that is frivolous, unreasonable, or without foundation or (b) continue to litigate after litigation clearly has become frivolous, unreasonable, or without foundation. The prevailing SEA or LEA may also be awarded fees by the courts against the parents' attorney or against the parents if the complaint or subsequent cause of action was presented for any improper purpose (e.g., to harass, cause delay, or increase the cost of litigation).

It is hoped that these provisions will reduce the number of complaints, due process hearing requests, and court actions, unless the situation truly merits those actions. Schools have complained in the past that some parents are filing complaints to retaliate against a school or school personnel and that often parents or their attorneys continue the litigation process to enhance the level of attorney fees. The fact that parents and their attorneys can be held accountable for these fees in situations where the courts think their actions are unwarranted may reduce the level of complaints.

Expulsion and Suspension

Disciplinary procedures for students with disabilities have been a highly debated topic for many years. In fact, disagreements on disciplining students with disabilities have been a major stumbling block in successfully reauthorizing IDEA on several previous occasions. Advocates for children with disabilities have resolutely supported students and opposed disciplinary procedures for this group of children that did not take the effect of the child's disability into consideration. This has resulted, correctly, in schools having to consider the impact of the disability on the behavior. If a suspension was for fewer than 10 days, and the student did not already have a series of suspensions that might add up to 10 days, then the school could suspend the student, similar to suspending any other student. However, if the suspension or expulsion added up to more than 10 days, the schools had to conduct a manifestation determination to determine the relationship, if any, between the disability and the inappropriate behavior. If a relationship was found to exist, then the school could not remove the student. If no relationship was found, the child could be removed from the school but the school had to continue to provide FAPE.

IDEA 2004 makes some changes to the disciplinary procedures for children with disabilities. Similar to IDEA 1997, prior to any suspension or expulsion for more than 10 days, a manifestation determination must be made. If no relationship is found, then the school may suspend or expel the student, similar to a student without disabilities. In this case, however, the school must continue to provide FAPE to the student. If there is a relationship between the disability and the behavior, then the school may not expel or suspend the student. A relationship is found if the behavior was caused by or had a *direct and substantial* relationship to the child's disability, or if the school had failed to implement the child's IEP. IDEA 2004 adds the *direct and substantial* language, possibly making it more difficult to determine that the behavior is related to the disability. If the manifestation determination concludes that there is a relationship between the disability and the behavior, then a functional behavior assessment is conducted and a behavior intervention plan is developed. The child is returned to the original placement unless both parties agree to a change of placement. The parents or the school may appeal a decision. In this case, the student will remain in the alternative placement until appeals are exhausted. An expedited hearing process is held.

In certain instances (e.g., the child has a weapon, is using or in possession of drugs, or inflicts serious bodily injury on someone), the child may be removed for up to 45 school days without regard to whether the behavior is a manifestation of the disability. This action can be taken without a hearing officer's involvement. IDEA 1997 said that a child could be removed for 45 days; by changing this to 45 *school* days, IDEA 2004 in effect allows a substantial increase in the period of time the child can be removed. Again, parents may appeal this decision and have an expedited hearing. While under appeal, the student remains in the placement that resulted from the inappropriate behavior, not the student's placement before the behavior occurred.

Eligibility for Students Classified as Having LD

Overidentification of students as having learning disabilities (LD) has been a concern for many years. Indeed, with more than 50% of all students with disabilities in this classification, many professionals have long been concerned about the use of a discrepancy formula to determine eligibility. Some have agreed that the use of this formula, which requires a severe discrepancy between IQ and achievement scores, has led to overidentification. Although IDEA has never required a discrepancy formula, many states and local education agencies have adopted this model of LD.

IDEA 2004 makes a point that a discrepancy between achievement and aptitude is not required to classify a student as having LD. It further states that schools may use a child's response to intervention as part of their eligibility process. Therefore, a school may choose to implement intervention programs, such as reading programs, and, if a child responds positively to the program, determine that a child is not eligible under IDEA. IDEA 2004 gives schools this flexibility. This language was added to IDEA 2004 in an attempt to limit the number of students identified as eligible for special education services who may simply be experiencing difficulties resulting from inappropriate instruction. If interventions are successful, there is no reason to identify the child as having LD and being eligible for special education.

Other Changes

In addition to the aforementioned changes in IDEA 2004, there are many other changes that schools will be implementing. These include:

- changing definitions of *assistive technology device*
- optional establishment of a risk pool with up to 10% of IDEA funds reserved for state-level activities for high-cost activities and supports
- allowing up to 15% of a school's IDEA funds for prereferral interventions
- flexibility in using Part C funds
- including homeless children in child-find activities
- allowing reevaluations of students not more than once each year and not more than every 3 years, unless school and parents agree it is not necessary
- conducting evaluations in the language or form most likely to yield accurate results, not necessarily in the child's native language

Conclusions

IDEA 2004 includes some significant changes to IDEA 1997; however, in many instances, practices will remain relatively similar. The basic requirement of IDEA— to provide a free, appropriate public education to children with disabilities—has not changed. There are numerous changes, but some of the notable ones include (a) adding NCLB language related to highly qualified special education teachers; (b) increasing funding to the authorized 40% level over a period of years through 2011; (c) changing eligibility for classification as having LD; (d) adding flexibility to attendance at IEP meetings; (e) creating a pilot demonstration for multiyear IEPs; (f) deleting the requirement for short-term objectives on the IEP; and (g) modifying suspension and expulsion requirements.

These notable changes may or may not have a significant impact on schools. Obviously, one change that could negatively affect schools is the requirement that special education teachers meet the NCLB *highly qualified* standard. With special education teachers already in short supply, adding this bureaucratic requirement could only exacerbate the situation, without improving educational opportunities for children with disabilities. Only time will determine the impact of this requirement, as school personnel and professional organizations lobby for a change. Increasing funding for special education could have a dramatic impact on services. However, the first budget proposal from the White House after the passage of IDEA 2004 added only $500 million to the IDEA budget, as opposed to the more than $2 billion called for in the legislation. Therefore, although it initially looked like a movement toward full funding would be made, reality has already set in that the likelihood of such an increase is low.

Changes made in the IEP requirements appear to be major. However, it is unlikely that, previously, all individuals participated in IEP development and changes at every meeting. In practice, IEPs were often developed by one individual or a small number of individuals and were likely changed without a formal IEP meeting. The changes in IDEA 2004 only legitimize those actions. Not having to include objectives might reduce some of the paperwork associated with IEPs; however, there still must be ongoing efforts to ensure that adequate progress is being made toward the student's annual goals. Finally, the multiyear IEP seems to be an idea that could significantly reduce paperwork. However, this is only a pilot program for up to 15 states, and even in schools that participate in the program, school personnel must determine if progress is being made toward the multiyear goals on at least an annual basis.

So, finally, IDEA has been reauthorized once again. Although the 3 years of debate focused on many of the same issues that have been dealt with in each reauthorization—discipline, due process rights, attorney fees, overidentification—the result is similar in many ways to the "old" law. As always, the changes do not satisfy everyone and, in fact, may not satisfy anyone. Hopefully, however, with each reauthorization of IDEA, realizing the original intent of P.L. 94-142 becomes more likely: meeting the needs of each child with a disability in the most appropriate way.

POSTSCRIPT

Does IDEA 2004 Contain Substantial Changes?

Contemplate IDEA 2004 in light of the recommendations of *Rethinking Special Education* (RSE) and the PCESE. As noted, these pre-reauthorization documents called for substantial changes to increase accountability, reduce paperwork, and reign in what each perceived as rampant litigation. What changed?

In today's climate of standards-based assessment, accountability is defined by whether students demonstrate increased academic performance. Writing on IDEA's twenty-fifth anniversary, Katsiyannis, Yell, and Bradley (*Remedial and Special Education*, 2001) declared that IDEA had met its initial goal of providing access to education for students with disabilities. They predicted that future reauthorizations would need to secure increased educational quality to improve achievement. Clearly, IDEA 2004 embraces a results-driven philosophy.

Not everyone is happy with this change. Writing earlier, Turnbull and Turnbull (*Education Next*, 2002) comment that special education addresses more than academics, encompassing efforts to help students succeed in the larger arenas of work, communication, and socialization. They worry that parents might lose confidence in a system that ignores these domains.

Two *RSE* papers (Horn and Tynan, 2001; Lanigan, 2001) maintained that confidence and accountability must be reciprocal. Parents desiring the supports of IDEA must assume personal responsibility in the educational process. According to Turnbull's selection, IDEA 2004 "makes accountability a bilateral concept." Parents and students (as well as schools) must now be more accountable for their actions.

Reactions to these changes are mixed. Some feel the regulations are overly complicated, asking parents to waive rights that help their children (Cleveland, http://www.thearc.org, 2005; Sabia, http://www.ndss.org, 2005). Others, like Peter Wright (http://www.wrightslaw.com/idea/art/goodlaw.optimist.pw.htm, 2005) a high-profile advocate, express no concern about the changes. Wright was actually surprised by his positive response.

Paperwork is the bane of everyone's existence, especially if you would prefer to spend your time teaching. Several contributors to *RSE* noted that special education has become consumed with compliance, documented through reams of paper.

IDEA 2004 seems to take paperwork reduction seriously. Meetings are streamlined; short-term objectives have been eliminated for most students; pilot projects for multiyear IEPs will be funded.

Smith holds out hope that elimination of objectives will stem the paperwork tide. However, he maintains that many other provisions sound more dramatic than they are, and will make little difference in the daily lives of teachers. He is not alone.

Looking at IEP changes, Gartin and Murdick (*Journal of Special Education Leadership*, 2005) feel the elimination of objectives for most students responds to paperwork complaints from both parents and teachers. Simultaneously, they are haunted by the possibility that paperwork may actually increase as teachers document other aspects of IDEA 2004, including agreements for excusing colleagues from team meetings.

Smith's predictions seem fulfilled in other arenas. The heralded multiyear paperwork reduction pilots have hit a snag. Apparently, documenting the efforts of these projects demands manpower exceeding the capacity of any state (Samuels, *Education Week*, 2006). Furthermore, districts must submit "massive" amounts of data documenting progress on issues such as parent involvement and disproportional representation (Samuels, *Education Week*, 2005). If the paperwork burden is shifted from teachers to administrators, not much will have changed (Weatherly, *In CASE*, 2005)—and administrators will have even less time to help teachers meet student needs.

Two final contrasting views complement the main selections: one from parents the other from teachers. From the standpoint of the Center for Law and Education, IDEA 2004 "undermines" hard-won rights, reduces school accountability, and punishes parents for seeking the best for their child (Boundy, http://www.cleweb.org, 2006). Reflecting the teacher's perspective, Pardini's interviewees felt the daily practice of teaching is so far removed from the law, they doubt any changes will make a difference (http://www. rethinkingschools.org, 2002).

Think about the new elements of IDEA 2004—now, and as you learn about the regulations. Will, as Turnbull predicts, the changes in IDEA 2004 be sufficient to modify our behavior or, as Smith says, will the alterations "not satisfy everyone and, in fact, may not satisfy anyone"?

ISSUE 3

Is Eliminating Minority Overrepresentation Beyond the Scope of Public Schools?

YES: M. Suzanne Donovan and Christopher T. Cross, from The Committee on Minority Representation in Special Education, *Minority Students in Special and Gifted Education* (National Academy Press, 2002)

NO: Daniel J. Losen and Gary Orfield, from *Racial Inequality in Special Education* (Harvard Education Press, 2002)

ISSUE SUMMARY

YES: M. Suzanne Donovan and Christopher Cross, researchers representing the findings of a National Research Council (NRC) study on minority students in special and gifted education, believe overrepresentation issues are complex and not easily resolvable. While teachers can make a difference, environmental factors and poverty have a large impact and require interventions beyond schools.

NO: Daniel J. Losen and Gary Orfield, both policy experts, present the results of research commissioned by the Civil Rights Project of Harvard University. While agreeing with some of the NRC recommendations, these findings suggest that patterns will change with stricter enforcement of federal and state regulations.

As far back as 1968, Dunn (*Exceptional Children*, 1968) examined the developing field of special education and voiced concern that African American children were disproportionately placed in special education, re-segregated into substantially separate classes for the mentally retarded.

Researchers and educators sometimes differ about how to calculate special education enrollment statistics. Some compare the percentage of each racial group in the overall school population with their proportion in special education. Others study the racial composition of individual disability categories.

Accurate analysis is complicated by the variable nature of racial designation and of disability definitions. Racial designations are reported by individuals and often governed by the categories provided on official forms. As society becomes more diverse, and more people have a multiracial heritage (think of Tiger Woods, for example), choosing one racial "category" becomes complicated. Furthermore, eligibility qualifications for the disabilities differ across states. Some states use no discrete categories for students.

Whichever method of analysis is applied and despite definitional complications, there is overall agreement that children of color are disproportionately represented in special education. This seems to be especially so in the socially defined disabilities of mental retardation, emotional disturbance, and learning disabilities. IDEA97 attempted to address this imbalance by requiring states to collect and report special education enrollment information by race and ethnicity. IDEA04 requires districts to document their success at reducing overrepresentation.

In 2002, two major reports were issued. Because of their depth, and the differences in their recommendations, they form the readings for this Issue.

M. Suzanne Donovan, a researcher in the areas of education and public policy, and Christopher Cross, who has been active in government and local board of education associations, edited a report representing the work of over a dozen researchers who are members of the National Research Council's (NRC) Committee on Minority Representation in Special Education. Directed by NRC and Congress to update NRC's 1982 study of this same issue, their work was expanded to consider racial under-representation in gifted and talented programs. The committee reviewed existent research studies to determine why disproportionality exists. Their conclusions and recommendations highlight environmental variables, suggesting that there may be reasons for overrepresentation that extend far beyond the school walls.

Daniel Losen and Gary Orfield share a professional commitment to studying the impact of law and public policy on the opportunities available for communities of color. Both have been heavily involved in designing and guiding policy formation, with a particular connection to The Civil Rights Project (CRP) at Harvard University. The impetus for their study was provided by the compelling voices of community leaders concerned about children wrongly placed in special education. To broaden the base of knowledge on the topic, CRP commissioned leading researchers to analyze conditions and contributing factors and to generate solutions. The collective findings led to recommendations that racial disproportionality should become a top school priority, facilitated (if necessary) through federal and state enforcement of school practices.

As you read these articles, discuss the complex issues that are presented. When you compare and contrast the two summaries, what similarities and differences do you find? In assumptions? Methodology? Conclusions and recommendations? Which findings correspond most closely to your own experiences, observations, and the other reading? What is the real problem, and what is the best way to address it?

YES

M. Suzanne Donovan and
Christopher T. Cross

Executive Summary

From the enactment of the 1975 federal law requiring states to provide a free and appropriate education to all students with disabilities, children in some racial/ethnic groups have been identified for services in disproportionately large numbers. Public concern is aroused by the pattern of disproportion. In the low-incidence categories (deaf, blind, orthopedic impairment, etc.) in which the problem is observable outside the school context and is typically diagnosed by medical professionals, no marked disproportion exists. The higher representation of minority students occurs in the high-incidence categories of mild mental retardation (MMR), emotional disturbance (ED), and to a lesser extent learning disabilities (LD), categories in which the problem is often identified first in the school context and the disability diagnosis is typically given without confirmation of an organic cause.

The concern is not new. In 1979 the National Research Council (NRC) was asked to conduct a study to determine the factors accounting for the disproportionate representation of minority students and males in special education programs for students with mental retardation, and to identify placement criteria or practices that do not affect minority students and males disproportionately. Twenty years later, disproportion in special education persists: while about 5 percent of Asian/Pacific Islander students are identified for special education, the rate for Hispanics is 11 percent, for whites 12 percent, for American Indians 13 percent, and for blacks over 14 percent. The NRC, at the request of Congress, has been asked to revisit the issue. In this case, however, the Office for Civil Rights in the U.S. Department of Education extended the committee's charge to include the representation of minority children in gifted and talented programs as well, where racial/ethnic disproportion patterns are, generally speaking, the reverse of those in special education.

Current Context

Since the 1982 NRC report, much has changed in general education as well as in special education. The proportion of minority students in the population of school-age children has risen dramatically—to 35 percent in 2000—increasing the diversity of students and of primary languages spoken in many schools. And state standards have raised the bar for the achievement expected of all students. More than 1 in 10 students is now identified for special education services: in

From *Executive Summary: National Research Council*, 2002, pp. 1–14. Copyright © 2002 by National Academy Press. Reprinted by permission.

the past decade alone, there has been a 35 percent increase in the number of children served under the Individuals with Disabilities Education Act (IDEA). And many more of these students are receiving special education and related services in general education classrooms.

The distribution of students across special education categories has changed as well. Identification rates for students with mental retardation today are about a quarter lower than in 1979. While the decline has applied across racial/ethnic groups, disproportionate representation of black students in that category has persisted. Just over 1 percent of white students but 2.6 percent of black students fall into that category.

Two decades ago, fewer than 3 percent of students were identified with learning disabilities (LD). That number approaches 6 percent of all students today. Only American Indian students are represented in disproportionately large numbers in that category. But for all racial/ethnic groups, the LD category accounts both for the largest number of special education students and for the largest growth rate in special education placements.

While these demographic and policy changes create a somewhat different-context today from that confronting the earlier NRC committee, the problems are conceptually quite similar. At the outset, both committees confronted a paradox: if IDEA provides extra resources and the right to a more individualized education program, why would one consider disproportionate representation of minority children a problem? The answer, as every parent of a child receiving special education services knows, is that in order to be eligible for the additional resources a child must be labeled as having a disability, a label that signals substandard performance. And while that label is intended to bring additional supports, it may also bring lowered expectations on the part of teachers, other children, and the identified student. When a child cannot learn without the additional supports, and when the supports improve outcomes for the child, that trade-off may well be worth making. But because there is a trade-off, both the need and the benefit should be established before the label and the cost are imposed. This committee, like its predecessor, does not view the desirable end necessarily as one in which no minority group is represented in disproportionate numbers, but rather one in which the children who receive special education or gifted program services are those who truly require them and who benefit from them.

Who requires specialized education? Answering that question has always posed a challenge. The historic notion of a child with an emotional or learning disability or a talent conveys a "fixed-trait" model, in which the observed performance is the consequence of characteristics internal to the child. Assessment processes have been designed as an attempt to isolate those children with internal traits that constitute a "disability" or a "gift." And clearly there can be within-child characteristics that underlie placement in one of the high-incidence categories. Neurobiological investigations, for example, reveal different patterns of brain activity in dyslexic and nondyslexic children while reading.

However, in the past few decades a growing body of research has pointed to the critical role that context can play in achievement and behavior. The same child can perform very differently depending on the level of teacher support, and aggressive behavior can be reversed or exacerbated by effective or ineffective classroom management. In practice, it can be quite difficult to distinguish internal child traits that require the ongoing support of special education from inadequate opportunity or contextual support for learning and behavior.

Committee's Approach

The conceptual framework in which the committee considered the issue of minority disproportion in special education and gifted and talented programs, then, is one in which the achievement or behavior at issue is determined by the interaction of the child, the teacher, and the classroom environment. Internal child characteristics play a clear role: what the child brings to the interaction is a function both of biology and of experience in the family and the community. But the child's achievement and behavior outcomes will also reflect the effectiveness of instruction and the instructional environment.

The committee did not view the problem of disproportionate representation in special education as one of simply eliminating racial/ethnic differences in assignment. If special education services provide genuine individualized instruction and accountability for student learning, we consider it as serious a concern when students who need those supports are passed over (false negatives) as when they are inappropriately identified (false positives). Likewise with respect to gifted and talented programs, we consider it a problem if qualified minority students are overlooked in the identification process, but consider it an undesirable solution if minority students are selected when they are not adequately prepared for the demands of gifted and talented programs. The committee's goal, then, was to understand why disproportion occurs. To address our charge, the committee asked four questions:

1. *Is there reason to believe that there is currently a higher incidence of special needs or giftedness among some racial/ethnic groups? Specifically, are there biological and social or contextual contributors to early development that differ by race or ethnicity?*

Our answer to that question is a definitive "yes." We know that minority children are disproportionately poor, and poverty is associated with higher rates of exposure to harmful toxins, including lead, alcohol, and tobacco, in early stages of development. Poor children are also more likely to be born with low birthweight, to have poorer nutrition, and to have home and child care environments that are less supportive of early cognitive and emotional development than their majority counterparts. When poverty is deep and persistent, the number of risk factors rises, seriously jeopardizing development.

Some risk factors have a disproportionate impact on particular groups that goes beyond the poverty effect. In all income groups, black children are more likely to be born with low birthweight and are more likely to be exposed to harmful levels of lead, while American Indian/Alaskan Native children are more likely to be exposed prenatally to high levels of alcohol and tobacco. While the separate effect of each of these factors on school achievement and performance is difficult to determine, substantial differences by race/ethnicity on a variety of dimensions of school preparedness are documented at kindergarten entry.

> 2. *Does schooling independently contribute to the incidence of special needs or giftedness among students in different racial/ethnic groups through the opportunities that it provides?*

Again, our answer is: "yes." Schools with higher concentrations of low income, minority children are less likely to have experienced, well-trained teachers. Per-pupil expenditures in those schools are somewhat lower, while the needs of low-income student populations and the difficulty of attracting teachers to inner-city, urban schools suggest that supporting comparable levels of education would require higher levels of per-pupil expenditures. These schools are less likely to offer advanced courses for their students, providing less support for high academic achievement.

When children come to school from disadvantaged backgrounds, as a disproportionate number of minority students do, high-quality instruction that carefully puts the prerequisites for learning in place, combined with effective classroom management that minimizes chaos, can put students on a path to academic success. While some reform efforts suggest that such an outcome is possible, there are currently no assurances that children will be exposed to effective instruction or classroom management before they are placed in special education programs or are screened for gifted programs.

> 3. *Does the current referral and assessment process reliably identify students with special needs and gifts? In particular, is there reason to believe that the current process is biased in terms of race or ethnicity?*

The answer here is not as straightforward. The majority of children in special and gifted education are referred by teachers. If a teacher is biased in evaluating student performance and behavior, current procedures provide ample room for those biases to be reflected in referrals. Some experimental research suggests that teachers do hold such biases. But whether bias is maintained when teachers have direct contact with children in the classroom is not clear. For example, research that has compared groups of students who are referred by teachers find that minority students actually have greater academic and behavior problems than their majority counterparts.

Once students are referred for special education, they must be assessed as eligible or ineligible. Whether the assessment process is biased is as controversial as the referral process. However research shows that context, including familiarity with test taking and the norms and expectations of school, may depress the scores of students whose experiences prepare them less well for the demands of classrooms and standardized tests.

Whether the referral and assessment of students for special and gifted education is racially biased or not, are the right students being identified—students who need and can benefit from those programs? Here the committee's answer is "no." The subjectivity of the referral process allows for students with significant learning problems to be overlooked for referral, and the conceptual and procedural shortcomings of the assessment process for learning disabilities and emotional disturbance give little confidence that student need has been appropriately identified. Importantly, current procedures result in placements later in the educational process than is most effective or efficient.

>   4. *Is placement in special education a benefit or a risk? Does the outcome differ by race or ethnic group?*

The data that would allow us to answer these questions adequately do not exist. We do know that some specific special education and gifted and talented interventions have been demonstrated to have positive outcomes for students. But how widely those interventions are employed is not known. Nor do we know whether minority students are less likely to be exposed to those high-quality interventions than majority students. What evidence is available suggests that parent advocacy and teacher quality, both of which would be expected to correlate with higher-quality interventions, are less likely in higher-poverty school districts where minority children are concentrated.

At the core of our study is an observation that unites all four questions: *there is substantial evidence with regard to both behavior and achievement that early identification and intervention is more effective than later identification and intervention.* This is true for children of any race or ethnic group, and children with or without an identifiable "within-child" problem. Yet the current special education identification process relies on a "wait-to-fail" principle that both increases the likelihood that children will fail because they do not receive early supports and decreases the effectiveness of supports once they are received. Similarly, the practice of identifying gifted learners after several years of schooling is based on the "wait 'til they succeed" philosophy rather than a developmental orientation.

While this principle applies to all students, the impact is likely to be greatest on students from disadvantaged backgrounds because (a) their experience outside the school prepares them less well for the demands of schooling, placing them at greater risk for failure, and (b) the resources available to them in general education are more likely to be substandard. Early efforts to identify and intervene with children at risk for later failure will help all children who need additional supports. But we would expect a disproportionately large number of those students to be from disadvantaged backgrounds.

The vision we offer in the report is one in which general and special education services are more tightly integrated; one in which no child is judged by the school to have a learning or emotional disability or to lack exceptional talent until efforts to provide high-quality instructional and behavioral support in the general education context have been tried without success. The "earlier is better" principle applies even before the K-12 years. The more effective we are at curtailing early biological harms and injuries and providing children with the supports for normal cognitive and behavioral development in the earliest years of life, the fewer children will arrive at school at risk for failure.

Conclusions and Recommendations

. . . Here we give the conclusions we consider key, along with the recommendations. They are organized here in the following major categories: referral and eligibility determination in special education (SE) and gifted and talented education (GT); teacher quality (TQ); biological and early childhood risk factors (EC); data collection (DC); and expanding the research and development base (RD).

Special Education Eligibility

From our review of the current knowledge base, several important conclusions have led the committee to rethink the current approach to special education:

5. Among the most frequent reasons for referral to special education are reading difficulties and behavior problems.
6. In recent years, interventions appropriate for the general education classroom to improve reading instruction and classroom management have been demonstrated to reduce the number of children who fail at reading or are later identified with behavior disorders.
7. There are currently no mechanisms in place to guarantee that students will be exposed to state-of-the-art reading instruction or classroom management before they are identified as having a "withinchild" problem.
8. Referral "for the high-incidence categories of special education currently requires student failure. However, screening mechanisms exist for early identification of children at risk for later reading and behavior problems. And the effectiveness of early intervention in both areas has been demonstrated to be considerably greater than the effectiveness of later, postfailure intervention.

These findings suggest that schools should be doing more and doing it earlier to ensure that students receive quality general education services to reduce the number of students with pronounced achievement and behavior problems. The committee's proposed alternative would require policy and regulatory changes at both the federal and state levels of government.

Federal-Level Recommendations

Recommendation SE.1: The committee recommends that federal guidelines for special education eligibility be changed in order to encourage better integrated general and special education services. We propose that eligibility ensue when a student exhibits large differences from typical levels of performance in one or more domain(s) and with evidence of insufficient response to high-quality interventions in the relevant domain(s) of functioning in school settings. These domains include achievement (e.g., reading, writing, mathematics), social behavior, and emotional regulation. As is currently the case, eligibility determination would also require a judgment by a multidisciplinary team, including parents, that special education is needed.

The proposed approach would not negate the eligibility of any student who arrives at school with a disability determination, or who has a severe disability, from being served as they are currently. But for children with milder high-incidence disabilities, the implications for referral and assessment are considerable. Assessment for special education eligibility would be focused on gathering information that documents educationally relevant differences from typical levels of performance, and that is relevant to the design, monitoring, and evaluation of treatments.

While eligibility for special education would by law continue to depend on establishment of a disability, in the committee view, noncategorical conceptions and classification criteria that focus on matching a student's specific needs to an intervention strategy would obviate the need for the traditional high-incidence disability labels such as LD and ED. If traditional disability definitions are used, they would need to be revised to focus on characteristics directly related to classroom and school learning and behavior (e.g., reading failure, math failure, persistent inattention and disorganization).

State-Level Recommendations

Regulatory changes would be required in most states for implementation of a reformed special education program that uses functional assessment measures to promote positive outcomes for students with disabilities. Some states have already instituted changes that move in this direction and can serve as examples. These states' rules require a systematic problem-solving process that is centered around quality indicators associated with successful interventions.

Recommendation 5E.2: The committee recommends that states adopt a universal screening and multitiered intervention strategy in general education to enable early identification and intervention with children at risk for reading problems. For students who continue to have difficulty even after intensive intervention, referral to special education and the development of an individualized education program (IEP) would follow. The data regarding student response to intervention would be used for eligibility determination.

Recommendation 5E.3: The committee recommends that states launch large-scale pilot programs in conjunction with universities or research centers to test the plausibility and productivity of universal behavior management interventions, early behavior screening, and techniques to work with children at risk for behavior problems. Research results suggest that these interventions can work. However, a large-scale pilot project would provide a firmer foundation of knowledge regarding scaling up the practices involved.

Federal Support of State Reform Efforts

Recommendation SE.4: While the United States has a strong tradition of state control of education, the committee recommends that the federal government support widespread adoption of early screening and intervention in the states.

Gifted and Talented Eligibility

The research base justifying alternative approaches for the screening, identification, and placement of gifted children is neither as extensive nor as informative as that for special education.

> *Recommendation GT.1: The committee recommends a research program oriented toward the development of a broader knowledge base on early identification and intervention with children who exhibit advanced performance in the verbal or quantitative realm, or who exhibit other advanced abilities.*

This research program should be designed to determine whether there are reliable and valid indicators of current exceptional performance in language, mathematical, or other domains, or indicators of later exceptional performance. Research on classroom practice designed to encourage the early and continued development of gifted behaviors in underrepresented populations should be undertaken so that screening can be followed by effective intervention.

School Context and Student Performance

School resources, class size, and indicators of teacher quality are associated with learning and behavior outcomes. However, their influence is exerted primarily through teacher-student interactions. Moreover, in the prevention and eligibility determination model the committee is recommending, general education assessments and interventions not now in widespread use are proposed as standard practice. Key to our proposals, then, are sustained efforts at capacity building, and sufficient resources, time, and coordination among stakeholders to build that capacity.

State-Level Recommendations

Teacher Quality: General education teachers need improved teacher preparation and professional development to prepare them to address the needs of students with significant underachievement or giftedness.

> *Recommendation TQ.1: State certification or licensure requirements for teachers should systematically require:*
>
> - *competency in understanding and implementing reasonable norms and expectations for students, and core competencies in instructional delivery of academic content;*
> - *coursework and practicum experience in understanding, creating, and modifying an educational environment to meet children's individual needs;*
> - *competency in behavior management in classroom and noninstructional school settings;*
> - *instruction in functional analysis and routine behavioral assessment of students;*

- *instruction in effective intervention strategies for students who fail to meet minimal standards for successful educational performance, or who substantially exceed minimal standards;*
- *coursework and practicum experience to prepare teachers to deliver culturally responsive instruction. More specifically, teachers should be familiar with the beliefs, values, cultural practices, discourse styles, and other features of students' lives that may have an impact on classroom participation and success and be prepared to use this information in designing instruction.*

While a foundational knowledge base can be laid in preservice education, often classroom experience is needed before teachers can make the most of instructional experiences.

- *States should require rigorous professional development for all practicing teachers, administrators, and educational support personnel to assist them in addressing the varied needs of students who differ substantially from the norm in achievement and/or behavior.*
- *The professional development of administrators and educational support personnel should include enhanced capabilities in the improvement and evaluation of teacher instruction with respect to meeting student's individual needs.*

Recommendation TQ.2: State or professional association approval for educator instructional programs should include requirements for faculty competence in the current literature and research on child and adolescent learning and development, and on successful assessment, instructional, and intervention strategies, particularly for atypical learners and students with gifts and disabilities.

Recommendation TQ.3: A credential as a school psychologist or special education teacher should require instruction in classroom observation/ assessment and in teacher support to work with a struggling student or with a gifted student. These skills should be considered as critical to their professional role as the administration and interpretation of tests are now considered.

Federal-Level Recommendations

This committee joins many others at the NRC and elsewhere in calling for improved teacher preparation. How to move from widespread agreement that change is needed to system reform is a challenge that will itself require careful study.

Recommendation TQ.4: The committee recommends that a national advisory panel be convened in an institutional environment that is protected from political influence to study the quality and currency of programs that now exist to train teachers for general, special, and gifted education. The panel should address:

- *the mechanisms for keeping instructional programs current and of high quality;*

- *the standards and requirements of those programs;*
- *the applicability of instructional programs to the demands of classroom practice;*
- *the long-term influence of the programs in successfully promoting educational achievement for pre-K, elementary, and secondary students.*

Direct comparison to other professional fields (e.g., medicine, nursing, law, engineering, accounting) may provide insight applicable to education.

Biological and Social Risk Factors in Early Childhood

Existing intervention- programs to address early biological harms and injuries have demonstrated the potential to substantially improve developmental outcomes. The committee concludes that the number of children, particularly minority children, who require special education can be reduced if resources are devoted to this end. In particular, the committee calls attention to the recommendation of the President's Task Force on Environmental Health Risks and Safety Risks to Children to eliminate lead from the housing stock by 2010.

Federal-Level Recommendations

The committee also looked at social and environmental influences on development with no clear biological basis that might differ by race or ethnicity. Because there is evidence that early intervention on multiple fronts, if *it is of high quality,* can improve the school prospects for children with multiple risk factors and reduce the likelihood that they will require special education, the committee recommends a substantial expansion and improvement of current early intervention efforts. Our recommendation is addressed to federal and state governments, both of whom currently play a major role in early childhood education.

> *Recommendation EC.l: The committee recommends that all high-risk children have access to high-quality early childhood interventions.*
>
> - *For the children at highest risk, these interventions should include family support, health services, and sustained, high-quality care and cognitive stimulation right from birth.*
> - *Preschool children (ages 4 and 5) who are eligible for Head Start should have access to a Head Start or another publicly funded preschool program. These programs should provide exposure to learning opportunities that will prepare them for success in school. Intervention should target services to the level of individual need, including high cognitive challenge for the child who exceeds normative performance.*
> - *The proposed expansion should better coordinate existing federal programs, such as Head Start and Early Head Start, and IDEA parts C and B, as well as state-initiated programs that meet equal or higher standards.*

While much is known about the types of experiences young children need for healthy development, improving the quality of early childhood programs will require refinement of the knowledge base in ways that are directly useful to practice, and bridging the chasm between what is known from research and best practice and is done in common practice. This will require a sustained vision and a rigorous research and development effort that transforms knowledge about what works and what does not work into field-tested program content, supporting materials, and professional development.

> *Recommendation EC2: The committee recommends that the federal government launch a large-scale, rigorous, sustained research and development program in an institutional environment that has the capacity to bring together excellent professionals in research, program development, professional development, and child care/preschool practice for students from all backgrounds and at all levels of exceptional performance.*

Improving Data Collection and Expanding the Research Base

The data documenting disproportionate representation are difficult to interpret in a variety of respects that make them a weak foundation on which to build public policy. Moreover, the data provide little if any insight into factors that contribute to placement or services that students receive.

Federal-Level Recommendations

> *Recommendation DC.1: The committee recommends that the Department of Education conduct a single, well-designed data collection effort to monitor both the number of children receiving services through the Individuals with Disabilities Education Act or through programs for the gifted and talented, and the characteristics of those children of concern to civil rights enforcement efforts.* A unified effort would eliminate the considerable redundancy, and the burden it places on schools, in the current data collection efforts of the Office for Civil Rights and the Office of Special Education Programs.

While a more careful data collection effort of the sort outlined here would improve the understanding of who is being assigned to special education and gifted and talented programs, it would do little to further understanding of the reasons for placement, the appropriateness of placement (or nonplacement), the services provided, or the consequences that ensue.

> *Recommendation DC.2: The committee recommends that a national advisory panel be convened to design the collection of nationally representative longitudinal data that would allow for more informed study of minority disproportion in special education and gifted and talented programs.* The panel should include scholars in special education research as well as researchers experienced in national longitudinal data collection and analysts in a variety of allied fields, including anthropology, psychology, and sociology.

In our study of the issues related to the representation of minority children in special education and gifted and talented programs, the existing knowledge base revealed the potential for substantial progress. We know much about the kinds of experiences that promote children's early health, cognitive, and behavioral development and set them on a more positive trajectory for school success. We know intervention strategies that have demonstrated success with some of the key problems that end in referral to special education. And we know some features of programs that are correlated with successful outcomes for students in special education.

Between the articulation of what we know from research and best practice, and a change in everyday practice, lies a wide chasm. It is the distance between demonstrating that vocabulary development is key to later success in reading, and having every Head Start teacher trained and equipped with materials that will promote vocabulary development among Head Start children. It is the distance between knowing that classroom management affects a child's behavior, and the school psychologist knowing how to help a specific teacher work with a specific child in the classroom context. It is the distance between those who are most knowledgeable and experienced agreeing on what teachers need to know, and every school of education changing its curriculum. Bridging the chasm will require that we become better at accumulating knowledge, extending it in promising areas, incorporating the best of what is known in teacher training efforts and education curricula and materials, and rigorously testing effectiveness. It will require public policies that are aligned with the knowledge base and that provide the support for its widespread application.

Recommendation RD.1: We recommend that education research and development, including that related to special and gifted education, be substantially expanded to carry promising findings and validated practices through to classroom applicability. This includes research on scaling up promising practices from research sites to widespread use.

For medical problems like cancer, federal research programs create a vision, focus research efforts on areas with promise for improving treatments, conduct extensive field tests to determine what works, and facilitate the movement of research findings into practice. If the nation is serious about reducing the number of children who are on a trajectory that leads to school failure and disability identification as well as increasing the number of minority students who are achieving at high levels, we will need to devote the minds and resources to that effort commensurate with the size and the importance of the enterprise.

Daniel J. Losen and
Gary Orfield

Introduction: Racial Inequity in Special Education

Before Congress passed the Education for All Handicapped Children Act—now known as the Individuals with Disabilities Education Act (IDEA)—nearly half of the nation's approximately four million children with disabilities were not receiving a public education. Of the children who were being educated in public schools, many were relegated to a ghetto-like existence in isolated, often run-down classrooms located in the least desirable places within the school building, or sent to entirely separate facilities. Since its passage in 1975, the IDEA has brought tremendous benefits: today, approximately six million children with disabilities enjoy their right to a free appropriate public education. IDEA's substantive rights and procedural protections have produced significant and measurable outcomes for students with disabilities: their graduation rates have increased dramatically, and the number of these students who go on to college has almost tripled since 1978 (though it is still quite low).

Despite these improvements, the benefits of special education have not been equitably distributed. Minority children with disabilities all too often experience inadequate services, low-quality curriculum and instruction, and unnecessary isolation from their nondisabled peers. Moreover, inappropriate practices in both general and special education classrooms have resulted in overrepresentation, misclassification, and hardship for minority students, particularly black children.

A flood of concerns expressed by community leaders about minority children being misplaced in special education prompted The Civil Rights Project at Harvard University to commission the research for [our] book. Since the early 1970s, national surveys by the Office for Civil Rights (OCR) of the U.S. Department of Education have revealed persistent overrepresentation of minority children in certain disability categories. The most pronounced disparities then were black children who, while only 16 percent of the total school enrollment, represented 38 percent of the students in classes for the educationally mentally retarded. After more than twenty years, black children constitute 17 percent of the total school enrollment and 33 percent of those labeled mentally retarded—only a marginal improvement. During this same period, however, disproportionality in the area of emotional disturbance (ED) and the rate of identification for both ED and specific learning disabilities (SLO) grew significantly for blacks.

To better understand this persistent overrepresentation trend, as well as growing reports of profound inequities in the quality of special education, The Civil Rights Project set out to find the best research available. In the original call for papers we asked leading scholars from around the country to document and clarify the issues for minority students with regard to special education. As researchers pursued this task and analyzed possible contributing factors, our fears about the persistence of these problems, the complexities of the contributing factors, and the lack of proven solutions were confirmed.

Our primary purpose in presenting this information is to identify and solve the problem, not to assign blame. This research is intended to inform the debate on special education and racial justice and to provide educators, researchers, advocates, and policymakers with a deeper understanding of the issues as they renew their efforts to find workable solutions. Using national-, state-, district-, and school-level data, these studies document the current trends for minority students regarding identification and restrictiveness of placement. They explore some of the most likely causes, dispel some myths and oversimplified explanations, and highlight the complex interplay of variables within the control of educators at all levels of government. Recognizing the critical role that advocacy has played in securing the rights of all children to educational opportunity, [our] book also provides analysis of the evolving role of the law in stopping inappropriate practices that harm children of color, and in guaranteeing equitable benefits from special education.

The findings [here] point to areas where much improvement is needed and offer an array of ideas for remedies and suggestions for continued research. It is important to recognize that concerns about special education are nested in concerns about inequities in education generally. Special education overrepresentation often mirrors overrepresentation in many undesirable categories—including dropping out, low-track placements, suspensions, and involvement with juvenile justice—and underrepresentation in desirable categories such as gifted and talented. Because special education inequities are often tied to general education issues, remedies should address shortcomings in both special and general education. The recommendations, which are aimed at improving policy and practice, were developed through extensive analysis of the efforts and experiences of educators, policymakers, attorneys, and civil rights enforcement agents. We hope the recommendations will help prevent harmful misidentification and inappropriate placements of minority students, and encourage effective and equitable leadership, enforcement, and distribution of resources to ensure that all children who need special education support receive appropriate and high-quality services.

Issues Explored and Findings

Much of the empirical research . . . explores patterns of overrepresentation of minority children by disability category and whether, once identified, they experience relatively less access to the general education classroom than similarly situated white children. The evidence suggests that black overrepresentation is substantial in state after state. The studies reveal wide differences in disability identification between blacks and Hispanics and between black boys and black girls that cannot be explained in terms of social background or measured ability.

Both the statistical and qualitative analyses . . . suggest that these racial, ethnic, and gender differences are due to many complex and interacting factors, including unconscious racial bias on the part of school authorities, large resource inequalities that run along lines of race and class, unjustifiable reliance on IQ and other evaluation tools, educators' inappropriate responses to the pressures of high-stakes testing, and power differentials between minority parents and school officials.

[We] . . . examine whether the numerous causes of overrepresentation are likely race linked, which is a distinctly different inquiry from whether intentional racial discrimination is the primary cause. Absent a blatantly discriminatory (i.e., illegal as written) policy or practice, to establish that different treatment is purposeful and racist requires specific proof of intent, which is usually discovered through legal enforcement proceedings. The research [here] is obviously not specific enough to explore questions of intent.

Overidentification

On October 4, 2001, the U.S. House of Representatives Committee on Education and the Workforce convened hearings about the overidentification of minority students in special education. In his testimony, Representative Chaka Fattah concluded with the following story of Billy Hawkins:

> For the first fifteen years of his life Billy Hawkins was labeled by his teachers as "educable mentally retarded." Billy was backup quarterback for his high school football team. One night he was called off the bench and rallied his team from far behind. In doing so, he ran complicated plays and clearly demonstrated a gift for the game. The school principal, who was in the stands, recognized that the "retarded boy" could play, and soon after had Billy enrolled in regular classes and instructed his teachers to give him extra help. Billy Hawkins went on to complete a Ph.D. and is now Associate Dean at Michigan's Ferris State University.

Students like Billy Hawkins seldom get the "call off the bench" and an opportunity to shine in front of their principal. Instead, they are removed from the mainstream and never realize their talent. Unfortunately, some in Congress responded to findings we released in earlier reports and to stories like Dr. Hawkins' by opposing efforts to guarantee and fully fund special education at the level Congress originally intended, claiming a need to "fix" special education before providing more funds. [We address] discrete areas of deep racial inequity within a much larger system of special education. It would be wrong to restrict or withhold promised expenditures for all students with disabilities in every state of the nation based on the issues identified in this research.

Of the inequalities in education experienced by minority schoolchildren, those in special education are better documented than most. In 1998, approximately 1.5 million minority children were identified as having mental retardation, emotional disturbance, or a specific learning disability. More than 876,000 of these were black or Native American, and black students were nearly three times as likely as white students to be labeled mentally retarded. Mental retardation diagnoses are relatively rare for all children, and the last twenty years have witnessed a modest decrease in the percentages of students labeled mentally retarded for nearly all racial groups.

Despite this fact, U.S. Department of Education data from 2000–2001 show that in at least thirteen states more than 2.75 percent of all blacks enrolled were labeled mentally retarded. The prevalence of mental retardation for whites nationally was approximately 0.75 percent in 2001, and in no state did the incidence among whites ever rise above 2.32 percent. Moreover, nearly three-quarters of the states with unusually high incidence rates (2.75–5.41%) for blacks were in the South. This is arguably a continuation of the problem as a southern phenomenon that was first observed in the National Research Council's data from 1979, although both then and now many northern states also exhibit remarkably high rates. One positive sign is that southern states exhibited the largest decreases in sheer percentages since 1979.

The data in these studies are generally analyzed in one of three ways. In one, a given minority group's percentage enrollment in the general population is compared to that group's percentage identification in a given disability category. In the second, the actual risk level for a minority group is calculated by dividing the number of students from a given racial group with a given disability by the total enrollment of that racial group. And in the third way, these risk levels are calculated for each minority group and then compared. These comparisons are described as risk ratios and are usually reported in comparison to white children.

. . . Tom Parrish, a senior research analyst with the American Institutes for Research, calculates risk levels using U.S. Department of Education data based on the number of children eligible for special education reported by each state for children between the ages of six and twenty-one in 1998, and compares that with census estimates of children of the same age for each state for the same year. Parrish then calculates the risk ratios for each minority group by cognitive disability category for every state and for the nation.

He finds that black children are 2.88 times more likely than whites to be labeled mentally retarded and 1.92 times more likely to be labeled emotionally disturbed.

Blacks are the most overrepresented minority group in every category and in nearly every state. The gross racial disparities that exist between many minority groups and whites in terms of mental retardation also exist in other cognitive disability categories, but are less pronounced. Nationwide, blacks and Native Americans are less often overidentified for specific learning disabilities (i.e., black children are more than twice as likely as white children to be found to have a specific learning disability in only nine states).

Parrish also shows the extent of overidentification of other minorities in the ED and SLD categories. In the SLD category, for example, only in Hawaii are Asian Americans/Pacific Islanders identified at nearly twice the rate of whites. On the other hand, Native American children in six states are identified at more than twice the rate of whites.

Latinos and Asian Americans are generally underidentified compared to whites in most states and in most categories, raising the possibility of inadequate attention to their special needs; however, the state-level data may underreport the problem for some groups. According to a 1982 National Research Council (NRC) report, district-level data on Hispanics from 1979 suggested that a wide variety of both over- and underrepresentation tended to cancel each other out in aggregate state-level data. Neither the 2002 NRC report, "Minority Students in Special and Gifted Education," nor the studies [here] conducted a district-level analysis with national data comparable to that contained in the 1982 study of Hispanic identification rates. However, Alfredo Artiles, Robert Rueda, Jesus Jose Salazar, and Ignacio Higareda, in their analysis of large urban school districts in California, reveal that disproportionate representation in special education is far more likely for (predominantly Latino) English-language learners in secondary school than in elementary school. Thus, the problem may even be hidden when elementary and secondary school data are aggregated at the district level.

Edward Fierros and James Conroy's research . . . , which does examine district-level data from throughout Connecticut and from selected U.S. cities, suggests that the state data may miss disturbing trends for minority overrepresentation in a given category or educational setting. Generally speaking, the most serious racial disparities (both under- and overrepresentation) become apparent when data on minority children are disaggregated by race/ethnicity subgroups, cognitive disability category, gender, and placement—at least down to the district level.

Educational Placement

Readers should not forget that students with disabilities are entitled to receive supports and services in a setting best suited to their individual needs, and not to be automatically assigned to a separate place, subjected to low expectations, or excluded from educational opportunities. While substantially separate educational environments are certainly best for some individuals, it is equally well established in research that students with disabilities benefit most when they are educated with their general education peers to the maximum extent appropriate, and this is reflected in the law.

Fierros and Conroy's work demonstrates that, once identified as eligible for special education services, both Latinos and blacks are far less likely than whites to be educated in a fully inclusive general education classroom and far more likely to be educated in a substantially separate setting. The data Fierros and Conroy explore show a consistent trend toward less inclusion for minority children at the national, state, and district levels. The relationship between race and greater exclusion, also not examined in the NRC's 2002 report, suggests that, among students with disabilities, black and Latino children with disabilities may be consistently receiving less desirable treatment than white children. Fierros and Conroy further disaggregate the racial data by disability type for the state of Connecticut and find a lower level of inclusion for blacks and Hispanics compared to whites among each of the three disability types examined (students with mental retardation, emotional disturbance, and specific learning disabilities).

The concern with the overrepresentation of minorities would be mitigated if the evidence suggested that minority children reaped benefits from more frequent identification and isolation. But as government officials acknowledge and as data demonstrate, this does not appear to be the case.

Low-Quality Evaluations, Supports, and Services

In their chapter, David Osher, Darren Woodruff, and Anthony Sims illustrate how the issue is often not as simple as the false identification of a nondisabled minority child. Many minority children do have disabilities but are at risk of receiving inappropriate and inadequate services and unwarranted isolation. Osher et al. point out that, for some children, receiving inappropriate services may be more harmful than receiving none at all. For others, not receiving help early enough may exacerbate learning and behavior problems. Both problems are reflected in disturbing statistics on outcomes for minority children with disabilities. As Donald Oswald, Martha Coutinho, and Al Best report in the opening lines of the book's first chapter, there are dramatic differences in what happens to minority students with disabilities after high school:

> In the 1998–1999 school year, over 2.2 million children of color in U.S. schools were served by special education (U.S. Department of Education, 2000). Post–high school outcomes for these minority students with disabilities are strikingly inferior. Among high school youth with disabilities, about 75 percent of African American students, as compared to 47 percent of white students, are not employed two years out of school. Slightly more than half (52%) of African Americans, compared to 39 percent of white young adults, are still not employed three to five years out of school. In this same time period, the arrest rate for African Americans with disabilities is 40 percent, as compared to 27 percent for whites (Wagner, D'Amico, Marder, Newman, & Blackorby, 1992).

In addition to these patterns, Osher, Woodruff, and Sims provide new data depicting substantially higher rates of disciplinary action and placement in correctional facilities for minority students with disabilities still in school. Based on their review of the data and other research, they suggest that investments in high-quality special education and early intervention are sorely needed and could reduce the likelihood that minority students with disabilities will develop serious discipline problems or eventually wind up in correctional facilities.

Racial Discrimination and Other Contributing Factors

In a society where race is so strongly related to individual, family, and community conditions, it is extremely difficult to know what part of the inequalities are caused by discrimination within the school. These studies, however, do uncover correlations with race that cannot be explained by factors such as poverty or exposure to environmental hazards alone. While the scope of this research does not attempt to depict a definitive causal link to racial discrimination, the research does suggest that unconscious racial bias, stereotypes, and other race-linked factors have a significant impact on the patterns of identification, placement, and quality of services for minority children, and particularly for African American children.

The researchers recognize that factors such as poverty and environmenta influences outside of school contribute to a heightened incidence of disability in significant ways. All analysts who attempt to sort out the causes of inequality in U.S. institutions of course face the dilemma that some of the differences in subtracted control variables are themselves products of other forms of racial discrimination. For example, if a researcher determined that 40 percent of the association between race and shorter life expectancy could be explained by poverty, we have to understand that the poverty in question may be influenced by employment discrimination or be due in part to a secondgenerational effect of segregated schooling. Therefore, despite the importance of statistical controls, it is well established that many controls will lower the estimates of the effect of race when race is examined as an isolated variable. What happens in school is only a subset of the far more pervasive impact of racial discrimination that affects minority families and their children.

Even when researchers assume that poverty is independent of race and subtract race and other background variables, many of the trends highlighted by this research appear to contradict the theory that poverty is primarily to blame and that race is not a significant factor. Those trends include the following: (a) pronounced and persistent racial disparities in identification between white and black children in the categories of mental retardation and emotional disturbance, compared with far less disparity in the category of specific learning disabilities; (b) a minimal degree of racial disparity in medically diagnosed disabilities as compared with subjective cognitive disabilities; (c) dramatic differences in the incidence of disability from one state to the next; and (d) gross disparities between blacks and Hispanics, and between black boys and girls, in identification rates for the categories of mentally retarded and emotionally disturbed.

The data on disproportionate representation is compatible with the theory that systemic racial discrimination is a contributing factor where disparities are substantial. Moreover, the trends revealed in [our] book are consistent with the theory that different racial groups, facing different kinds of stereotypes and bias, would experience racial disparities differently. States with a history of racial apartheid under de jure segregation, for example, account for five of the seven states with the highest overrepresentation of African Americans labeled mentally retarded—Mississippi, South Carolina, North Carolina, Florida, and Alabama. This trend suggests that the "soft bigotry of low expectations" may have replaced the undeniable intentional racial discrimination in education against blacks that once pervaded the South. In contrast, no southern state was among the top seven states where Hispanic children deemed mentally retarded were most heavily overrepresented.

The effects of poverty cannot satisfactorily explain racial disparities in identification for mental retardation or emotional disturbance. Regression analysis suggests that race, gender, and poverty are all significant factors. Oswald, Coutinho, and Best specifically asked whether, "taking into account the effects of social, demographic, and school-related variables, gender and ethnicity are significantly associated with the risk of being identified for special education." Their examination of each factor at the district level (based on all of the districts surveyed in OCR's database combined with the National Center for Education Statistics, Common Core of Data) finds that, although disability incidence often increases with poverty, when poverty- and wealth-linked factors are controlled for, ethnicity and gender remain significant predictors of cognitive disability identification by schools. Specifically, wealth-linked factors included per pupil expenditure, median housing value, median income for households with children, percentage of children in households below the poverty level, and percentage of adults in the community who have a twelfth-grade education or less and no diploma.

Most disturbing, was that in wealthier districts, contrary to the expected trend, black children, especially males, were *more likely to be labeled* mentally retarded. Moreover, the sharp gender differences in identification within racial groups, also described in the 2002 NRC report, are not explained by the poverty theory.

Large demographic differences among minority groups are also discussed by Parrish and by Fierros and Conroy, and each confirms that the influence of race and ethnicity is significant, and apparently distinct from that of poverty. For example, Parrish reviews the data for each racial group across all fifty states and finds that, in comparison to whites, each minority group is at greater risk of being labeled mentally retarded as their percentage of the total enrolled population increases.

That poverty does account for some of the observed racial disproportionsin disability identification comes as no surprise. Certain minority groups are disproportionately poor. Logically, one would expect poverty to cause a higher incidence of "hard" disabilities (e.g., blindness and deafness) among members of low-wealth minority groups, due to the impact of poor nutrition and inadequate prenatal care. But the most recent research shows that blacks in any given state are substantially less likely to be overrepresented in these hard categories.

Finally, the theory that poverty and socioeconomic factors can explain all or most of the observed racial disparities fails to account for the extreme differences between black overrepresentation and Hispanic underrepresentation, differences that are even more significant in many states than disparities between blacks and whites. For example, blacks in Alabama and Arkansas are more than seven to nine times as likely as Hispanics to be labeled mentally retarded. Moreover, nationally and in many other states, the disparity in identification rates for mental retardation and emotional disturbance between blacks and Hispanics is greater than the disparity between blacks and whites. Yet Hispanics, like blacks, are at far greater risk than whites for poverty, exposure to environmental toxins in impoverished neighborhoods, and low-level academic achievement in reading and math. Thus, the high variation in identification rates among minority groups with similar levels of poverty and academic failure casts serious doubt on assertions by some researchers that it is primarily poverty and not bias that creates these deep racial disparities.

Multiple Contributing Factors

Most students with disabilities enter school undiagnosed and are referred by regular classroom teachers for evaluations that may lead to special education identification and placement. Therefore, the cause of the observed racial disparity is rooted not only in the system of special education itself, put also in the system of regular education as it encompasses special education. Most students referred for evaluation for special education are deemed in need of services. If differential referral is a key element, then the perceptions and decisions of classroom teachers, as well as school-level policies and practices that have an impact on students in regular classrooms, are, likewise, key elements.

Based on years of research, Beth Harry, Janette Klingner, Keith Sturges, and Robert Moore conclude in their chapter that "[t]he point at which differences [in measured performance and ability] result in one child being labeled disabled and another not are totally matters of social decisionmaking." Special education evaluations are often presented to parents as a set of discrete decisions based on scientific analysis and assessment, but even test-driven decisions are inescapably subjective in nature. The existence of some bias in test *content* is not the primary concern. Harry et al.'s research, for example, describes how subjective decisions creep into all elements of the evaluation *process*, including whom to test, what test to use, when to use alternative tests, how to interpret student responses, and what weight to give results from specific tests. All of these alter the outcomes. As Harry et al. point out, "a penstroke of the American Association on Mental Retardation (AAMR)" lowered the IQ score cutoff point for mental retardation from 85 to 70, "swiftly curing thousands of previously disabled children."

School politics, power relationships between school authorities and minority parents, the quality of regular education, and the classroom management skills of the referring teacher also introduce important elements of subjectivity that often go unrecognized. Other race-linked forces at work include poorly trained teachers who are disproportionately employed in minority schools (some of whom use special education as a disciplinary tool), other resource inequalities correlated to race, beliefs in African American and Latino inferiority and the low expectations that accompany these beliefs, cultural insensitivity, praise differentials, fear and misunderstanding of black males, and overcrowded schools and classrooms that are disproportionately located in school districts with high percentages of minority students. Add to these forces the general phenomenon of white parents' activism, efficaciousness, and high social capital exercised on behalf of their children compared to the relative lack of parent power among minority parents, and one can understand how the combination of regular education problems and the special education identification process has had a disparate impact on students of different races and ethnicities.

Sweeping reforms may also trigger harmful outcomes. For example, Artiles et al.'s preliminary examination of the "Unz Initiative," which eliminated bilingual education in California, suggests that English-language learners whose access to language supports is limited are more likely to be placed in restrictive special education settings. And as Jay Heubert describes in detail in his chapter, over the last ten years the use of high-stakes testing may have disproportionately punished poor and minority students, students with disabilities, and English-language learners: "There is evidence that states with high minority enrollments in special education are also likely to have highstakes testing policies." Heubert goes on to cite evidence that "promotion testing is . . . likely to increase, perhaps significantly, the numbers of students with disabilities and minority students who suffer the serious consequences of dropping out." He points out that the National Research Council has described simple retention in grade as "an ineffective intervention." The aspirational benefits of raising standards aside, Heubert concludes that minority students with disabilities are at "great risk . . . especially in states that administer high-stakes promotion and graduation tests. . . ."

The Status of the Law and Enforcement Policy

Beginning with *Brown v. Board of Education,* litigation and enforcement under civil rights law has been essential to improving racial equity in education. Title VI of the Civil Rights Act of 1964 provided an important lever for racial justice in education that was especially effective when the federal government made enforcement a high priority. Critically important was that, under the Title VI regulations, plaintiffs could use statistical evidence to prove that even a policy that was race neutral on its face had an adverse and unjustifiably disparate impact on children of color in violation of the law. As Daniel Losen and Kevin Welner describe in their chapter, the legal landscape shifted dramatically following the U.S. Supreme Court's 2001 ruling in *Alexander v. Sandoval* which declared that there is no implied private right of action to bring legal challenges under "disparate-impact" theory. Therefore, court challenges that would rely on serious statistical disparities to prove allegations of discrimination are nearly extinguished today. Although the government and individuals filing complaints with government agencies may still use the Title VI regulations to redress the racially disparate impact of neutral policies, enforcement of disparate impact regulations is more vulnerable to an administration's enforcement policy preferences than ever before.

Untouched by *Sandoval* is the potential to challenge policies or practices where the racial disparities in special education identification or placement arise in the context of hearings on school desegregation. For example, in Alabama in 2000, a court review of consent decrees in that state resulted in a settlement yielding comprehensive state- and district-level remedies for overidentification of minorities.

Losen and Welner point out that disability law is becoming a relatively stronger basis for leveraging remedies from states and school districts where overidentification, underservicing, or unnecessarily restrictive placements are an issue. They explain further how systemic legal actions are better suited for seeking effective comprehensive remedies that could address contributing factors in both regular and special education. In her chapter, Theresa Glennon closely examines and evaluates the Office for Civil Rights' enforcement efforts where disability law and Tide VI converge. Glennon's recommendations include better coordinated investigations and interagency information sharing, clearer guidance for schools, and more comprehensive compliance reviews by well-trained investigators.

Sharon Soltman and Donald Moore provide an extensive analysis of how to fashion a remedy through litigation in a case known as *Corey H.* Their thorough chapter combines many years of research on effective practices with models of school improvement. They set forth a roadmap for school district reform to ensure that children with disabilities in Illinois be educated in the least restrictive environment as required by law. The multitiered *Corey H.* remedy entails a ten-year process for change, in one set of schools each year. The plaintiffs also won a large infusion of state funding to make implementing the *Corey H.* requirements a fully funded mandate. Further research on the efficacy of the court-ordered remedy should prove extremely useful to policymakers and others seeking to guarantee that minority children with disabilities have appropriate educational opportunities.

The only study in this volume that explores restricting federal funds as a remedy does so in the context of analyzing the viability of the Department of Education's Office for Special Education Programs' (OSEP) enforcement mechanisms for redressing racial disproportionality. In that study, Thomas Hehir argues forcefully for more frequent exercise of partial withholding by enforcement agents that is narrowly targeted to leverage compliance by specific states or districts in certain areas. As Hehir points out, partial withholding would allow OSEP to ratchet up its enforcement efforts without wholesale withdrawal of federal funds, which would heighten the risk of political backlash and have a negative impact on students in properly run programs. Likewise, federal policymakers should improve IDEA implementation and civil rights enforcement without imposing wholesale limitations on federal special education funding, which would have a negative impact on children with disabilities nationwide. Of course, there may be extreme cases in noncompliant districts where the only way to end serious violations is to cut off general funds, which proved very effective in spurring the desegregation of southern schools.

Moreover, Tom Parrish's research suggests that some state funding formulas are contributing to problems of overidentification. Some of these formulas fail to follow the federal model, which relies on U.S. Census data to determine allocations. The most problematic state formulas instead channel funds by disability identification and/or program and are suspected of creating incentives for overidentification.

Recommendations

Theses studies and the NRC's 2002 report both suggest that special education issues faced by minority children often begin with shortcomings in the realm of general education well before teachers or parents seek an evaluation for special education eligibility. Therefore, policy solutions that fail to consider the connection with general education classrooms will unlikely bring about significant change.

A New Federal Initiative With Implications for State Accountability

Our nation's education policy is at a crossroads. Leaders demand an end to the "soft bigotry of low expectations" and our government has promised to improve the achievement of all children in 2002 through the new education reform act, known as the No Child Left Behind Act. Racial equity is rooted in the commitment to teach all children well, with particular attention to meeting the needs of minority children.

To tackle racial disparities in achievement and graduation rates, the president and Congress embraced three reform approaches: public reporting, accountability at all levels (school, district, and state), and mandatory enforcement. These three reform approaches could be used to address the gross racial disparities in special education identification, restrictiveness of placement, and quality of services.

For policymakers, there is no need to pinpoint a specific cause or allege race discrimination in order to achieve racial equity. Scholars report that many schools today still operate under a deficit model, where school authorities regard students with disabilities as the embodiments of their particular disability and ask only *what the special educators are required to do in order to accommodate the student's problem.* A universal commitment to equity in special education would help erode this deficit model by shifting the focus to *what all public educators should do to improve educational opportunities and outcomes for all children.*

There is bipartisan acknowledgement that special education issues faced by minority children need a federal legislative response. This apparent consensus holds promise for effective federal reform. Reform attempts in the recent past can be improved upon. In 1997 the IDEA was amended to require states to collect and review data on racial disproportionality in both identification and placement and to intervene where disproportionality is significant. Before that, in 1995, the Office for Civil Rights made racial disproportionality in special education a top priority. The persistence of this problem suggests that states' legal obligations under IDEA and our civil rights enforcement priorities have not been met.

OCR was once a major force in the effort to desegregate our nation's schools, suggesting that the agency's efficacy is related to political will as much as it is to resources. It is apparent that there is a glaring need for stepped-up enforcement and oversight by both federal and state agencies. These actions must be geared toward encouraging the active participation of educators at all levels if there is to be any hope of meaningful and lasting improvement. Most important, aggressive efforts to remedy these issues are only the starting point. The efficacy of enforcement interventions and attempted reforms must be evaluated in terms of the outcomes for minority children.

Both general and special education teachers and administrators need better training to deliver effective instruction in the least restrictive, most inclusive environment appropriate. Meeting this need, along with the need for better data collection on racial and ethnic disparities and enhanced civil rights enforcement, would require an infusion of special education funds, which could be expected to result in net gains in education outcomes and savings in juvenile justice expenditures in the long term. By increasing federal oversight and by encouraging states to intervene where appropriate, the federal government could help improve the quality of instruction, supports, and services received by minority students in both regular and special education.

Although OCR still does not collect national data to determine racial disparities in the educational environment, the 1997 IDEA amendments obligate the states to collect sampled data. If the government required every state and school district to collect disaggregated data by race with disability category and educational setting (all three together), research on overrepresentation would benefit tremendously.

Moreover, much general education reform law is predicated on the concept that public pressure at the local level from parents and community stakeholders will stimulate meaningful improvements. To generate local reform pressure, the Bush education program requires public reporting of test achievement by a number of student subgroups, including disability status and major racial and ethnic subgroups. Policymakers could likewise stimulate meaningful improvements in special education by amending the IDEA to require public reporting of racial disparities in special education identification and placement.

IDEA should also require states to intervene under specified circumstances (they now have complete discretion) and to provide technical assistance to effect reforms. Such required intervention and assistance would likely foster greater self-reflection and improvement at the district level. While adopting mandatory interventions would be helpful, given the context of shrinking state education budgets, an emphasis on rewards and continued supports to foster successful efforts must be an integral part of any new enforcement efforts.

Finally, new mechanisms for minority children to exercise their rights under IDEA, including legal services support, would help considerably.

Toward Comprehensive Solutions to Systemic Problems at the District Level

The research and analysis presented in [the] volume are intended to serve educators, advocates, and policymakers alike. In addition to raising awareness of the issues, suggesting changes in legislation, and improving the enforcement of existing requirements, much can be accomplished with greater determination by school leadership.

For communities of color, disproportionate representation in special education is just one facet of the denial of access to educational opportunity. Denial begins in the regular education setting with school segregation, low tracking, test-based diploma denial and retention, overly harsh discipline, less access to programs for the gifted, and resource inequalities that have a distinctly racial dimension. Education leaders who suspect a problem at their school can accomplish a great deal by clearly stating that this problem is one that they and their staff can do something about, and that it has a racial dimension. By squarely shouldering responsibility and resolving to improve outcomes for all children as they tackle the racial disparities, school leaders can also reduce racial tensions among staff and in their school community and recover lives and talents that would otherwise be wasted. Tackling these issues should be a shared responsibility, not the duty of the principal or special education administrator alone. Furthermore, technical assistance can be sought from state and federal agencies, including OCR and OSEP, without triggering legal action. School leaders concerned with the issues raised above can also renew their efforts to involve parents and community in innovative ways. Some suggested methods include entering into partnerships with community organizations in order to boost minority parent involvement, and engaging school-based councils that would share decisionmaking power, working more closely with social service agencies to ensure that at-risk students receive high-quality services and that social workers and teachers are collaborating effectively, and increasing direct outreach to families.

Moreover, teachers need support to change their practice and improve classroom outcomes. In many cases regular classroom teachers have received little or no training in working with students from diverse backgrounds or with special education students, or have had little practicum experience in inclusive classrooms. Similarly, many special education teachers have not had the degree of training in the core curriculum or on how to work in a full-inclusion setting. Without both academic and multicultural training and time for special education and regular education teachers to collaborate, it is unrealistic to expect significant improvement.

Protecting the civil rights of all students benefits society at large. Obviously, it is much better if this problem is solved within the school than through external enforcement. Strong leadership at all levels could make an important difference. There is a great deal of work that can and should be done by schools, by districts, by states, and by federal lawmakers and enforcement agents that would improve educational opportunities for minority children in general, and make tremendous progress in solving the specific problems highlighted [here].

There are no quick fixes. The problems [we explore] have many roots, and creating better outcomes requires difficult changes at many levels. Far more research is needed on the practices that produce inequality and the reforms that can successfully correct them. We need to reach the point at which every child is treated as if he or she were our own child, with the same tirelessly defended and protected life possibilities. In schools where we can predict the racial makeup of a special education class before we open the door, we must have leadership, if possible, and enforcement, if necessary, to ensure that each child receives the quality academic support and special services he or she truly needs without diminishing any of the opportunities that are any child's right in American society. We hope [our] book will contribute to that dream.

POSTSCRIPT

Is Eliminating Minority Overrepresentation Beyond the Scope of Public Schools?

Although these selections are larger than most in this book, they provide only a glimpse into the projects they represent. Reading both reports in their entirety delivers a much more textured appreciation of their extensiveness.

The studies share common ground in their concern about the issues surrounding overrepresentation. Their opening words, however, set the tone for their differences. Donovan and Cross endeavor not necessarily to end disproportionate representation, if it serves a purpose and delivers a benefit. Losen and Orfield would like to end disproportionality in special education, asserting that minority children with disabilities have not received much benefit.

In their literature review, Donovan and Cross find there may be some grounds for overrepresentation. Citing risks that come from poverty and environmental hazards, they conclude that children who have encountered these conditions come to school at greater risk. While experience is not unalterable, they say, there are actual differences in school readiness. Schools can address student performance, but environmental issues are matters of "political priority."

Losen and Orfield agree that environmental circumstances affect school-readiness and performance, but raise two compelling puzzles. First, if environmental issues are causal, why is there not overrepresentation in every disability category? Second, why is it that Hispanic children, who generally share economic status with African Americans, experience less overrepresentation?

Both studies agree that general education programs are critical. Indeed, while doctors identify the most visible disabilities, the majority of children in special education are referred by their classroom teachers. To what extent is overrepresentation affected by poor schools with inexperienced teachers and principals?

Racial bias is hard to evaluate, say the authors. The NRC study notes that the effects of prejudice are often subtle and intangible. Losen and Orfield comment that it is difficult to determine whether disproportionality results from intentional, biased behaviors, but describe what happens in school as a "subset" of the racial impacts in society. Both sets of researchers agree educators must re-examine an evaluation process that can be subjective and influenced by cultural differences.

Many others have explored the issues surrounding disproportionality. Looking at environmental issues, Ness (*Rethinking Schools Online,* 2003) refers to the deleterious effects of lead toxins as "environmental racism," which results in lower school performance in children of poverty, many of whom are also children of color.

Artiles, Harry, Reschly, and Chinn (*Multicultural Perspectives,* 2002) explored a range of forces that impact disproportionality, including poverty, instructional and assessment factors, and cultural discontinuity. While concluding that many are "beyond the workscope" of schools, they believe that educators can draw attention to problems and strive to make positive changes.

Cultural and linguistic barriers that can affect the educational experience of African American children are discussed by Obi and Obiakor (*The Western Journal of Black Studies,* 2001). Since society is likely to become increasingly diverse, they emphasize the need for all educators to become more sensitive and responsive to linguistic and cultural differences.

Is disproportionality an issue for schools to solve, or is it a broader societal challenge? If society committed resources to address environmental problems and poverty, what differences would we see? Can communities and schools implement early intervention systems that would prevent referrals? Will the uniform expectations and accountability of No Child Left Behind ensure that everyone attends to the needs of all children, rather than succumb to "the soft bigotry of lowered expectations"? Or is the answer to be found in stricter governmental oversight? These are not simple questions to ponder, much less answer. But they must be raised and addressed, for the benefit of all children.

ISSUE 4

Do Funding Systems Create a Perverse Incentive to Place Students in Special Education?

YES: Jay P. **Greene and Greg Forster,** from *Effects of Funding Incentives on Special Education Enrollment* (Center for Civic Innovation at the Manhattan Institute, December 2002)

NO: Kanya **Mahitivanichcha and Thomas Parrish,** from "Do Non-Census Funding Systems Encourage Special Education Identification? Reconsidering Greene and Forster," *Journal of Special Education Leadership* (April 2005)

ISSUE SUMMARY

YES: Jay P. Greene, senior fellow, and Greg Forster, senior research associate, both with The Manhattan Institute for Policy Research, assert that the number of students identified as disabled is increasing at an excessive rate, especially in states where funding systems provide a "perverse incentive" in favor of placement.

NO: Kanya Mahitivanichcha, research analyst, and Tom Parrish, managing director for the Education and Human Development Program, both at the American Institutes for Research, maintain that funding formulas are only one reason behind increases in special education placement.

Thirty years ago, approximately 8 percent of school children were in special education. Thousands more lived in institutions, spent their days at home, or struggled in school with little, if any, assistance. Today, approximately 13 percent of school-age children are enrolled in special education across the nation.

The percentage of children in special education has risen consistently over time. Curiously, there is enormous variation among states, ranging (in 2000-01) from 9.4 percent in California to 17.8 percent in Rhode Island (Mahitivanichcha and Parrish).

Thirty years ago, legislators knew that establishing and maintaining programs for students with disabilities would cost money. No one knew how much or approached an accurate prediction. Passage of the first special education law came with Congress' promise to pay up to 40 percent of the cost of educating children with disabilities. Annually determined through Capital Hill negotiations, the actual amount appropriated has never come close to this promise. From 1998 to 2003, the federal share rose from 8 percent to 13 percent of the spending.

Once budget wrangling ends, checks are sent to each state. Since FY 2000, this allocation has been determined primarily by the state's school-aged population, with an additional factor reflecting the state's relative poverty. After retaining some funds for the operation of its own special education activities, each state disperses the remaining federal money among school districts.

To qualify for these funds, districts maintain detailed records documenting compliance with special education laws and regulations. Students are counted annually, along with the extent of their time in special education. These figures are reported to the state and then to the U.S. Department of Education.

Two types of funding systems exist. Census-based mechanisms distribute money in accordance with the overall number of children in a district. Another option is a weighted strategy, allotting funds based on the number of children receiving special education services. While states alter their funding mechanisms periodically, most are currently using weighted systems.

Jay Greene and Greg Forster are troubled by the continuing increase in the percentage of children receiving special education services. Rejecting competing explanations, they hold that schools are responding to the "bounty" provided by weighted systems for placing children in special education. Results of their analyses maintain that using census (or lump sum) mechanisms would save $1.5 billion annually.

Kanya Mahitivanichcha and Thomas Parrish share the concern about rising special education numbers, but disagree that census-based funding mechanisms are the clear solution. Their own analyses doubt the magnitude of Greene and Forster's findings and point to more complex interactions.

As you read these articles, note that both studies consider expenditures for children from ages 6 to 21. Many districts serve children as young as age 3; at least one state extends services to the twenty-sixth birthday. Ask yourself whether funding formulas are "culprits," encouraging schools to increase the number of children in special education. How does anyone determine the "right" number of children who deserve these services?

YES

**Jay P. Greene and
Greg Forster**

Effects of Funding Incentives on Special Education Enrollment

... Over the past decade, the U.S. special education enrollment rate has increased from 10.6% of all students to 12.3%. The rate of growth is accelerating and shows no sign of slowing down, and policy makers are anxious to determine why. Critics of the U.S. special education system argue that it creates perverse financial incentives to label children as disabled. School districts have traditionally received state funding based on the size of their special education programs, so in effect they receive a bounty for each child they place in special education. Critics claim that this rewards schools for placing students in special education unnecessarily. Some defenders of the system argue that special education enrollment is growing because the real incidence of disabilities in children is growing, but this explanation does not withstand scrutiny very well. A number of researchers are now pointing towards still another culprit: perverse incentives arising not from funding systems but from high-stakes testing. When schools are held accountable for students' performance on standardized tests, they have an incentive to remove the lowest-scoring students from the testing pool by placing them in special education, where they will be exempt from testing requirements.

Several states, struggling to cope with the ever-accelerating growth of special education, have adopted new funding systems that eliminate the bounty for new special education students. An even larger number of states have adopted high-stakes testing, in the hope that it will improve education outcomes. However, no national statistical studies have attempted to measure what effect these new lump-sum funding and high-stakes testing policies are having on special education enrollment.

This study finds that funding systems have a dramatic effect on special education enrollment, while high-stakes testing has no significant effect. We estimate that in the states that adhere to the traditional bounty system, over the last decade the rate of special education enrollment grew a total of 1.24 percentage points more than it would have if these states had lump-sum funding systems, accounting for a full 62% of these states' total increase in special

From *Civic Report,* no. 32, December 2002, pp. 1–9. Copyright © 2002 by Jay P. Greene, Ph.D. Reprinted by permission. Notes omitted. References omitted.

education enrollment. This represents approximately 390,000 extra students placed in special education because of the bounty system, resulting in additional spending of over $2.3 billion per year. Using another method that is more sensitive to the timing of changes in states' funding systems, we estimate that if all bounty system states had switched to lump-sum systems in the 1994-95 school year, their special education enrollments in the 2000-01 school year would have been lower by an average of 0.82 percentage points. This margin represents a difference of roughly 258,000 students and over $1.5 billion per year in extra spending. In light of these findings, reforms that would remove the perverse incentives of bounty funding systems—such as switching to lump-sum systems or offering private school scholarships to disabled children—are urgently needed.

Previous Research

Enrollment in special education has been growing steadily for decades, and the rate of growth has been accelerating for the past ten years. Already high—over 10% of the student population—at the beginning of the 1990s, special education enrollment is now approaching 13% and shows no sign of slowing down. Since special education students are a significantly greater burden on schools than regular students because of the individual attention and specially trained staff they require, this expansion of the special education population is becoming a more and more urgent concern for U.S. education. Indeed, the percentage of students in special education has been going up at a time when the average cost of special education per student has also been rising, exacerbating the problem further.

Unfortunately, any effort to address this problem must first overcome sharp disagreement over what is causing it in the first place. At least three different culprits have been identified: greater real incidence of disabilities, the advent of high-stakes testing, and the financial incentives created by special education funding.

Defenders of the U.S. special education system argue that the growth of enrollment in special education reflects growth in the real incidence of disabilities in children. According to this explanation, there are simply more disabled students than there used to be, and those students have more costly disabilities. . . . Berman, . . . Davis, . . . Koufman-Frederick, and . . . Urion argue that increases in special education enrollment and spending "have been primarily due to the increased numbers of children with more significant special needs who require more costly services." They attribute this alleged growth in student disabilities to social forces over which schools have no control, pointing to three factors in particular: improvements in medical technology, deinstitutionalization of children with serious difficulties, and increases in childhood poverty.

However, this account is not consistent with the facts. The authors argue that there are now more children with mental retardation because improved medicine saves more low-birth-weight babies. While it is true that the number of such babies expected to exhibit retardation has grown, the actual number of students classified as mentally retarded has dropped remarkably—from about 961,000 in 1976–77 to about 599,000 in 2000–01. Improvements in prevention of mental retardation have more than offset any growth in mental retardation caused by increased numbers of surviving low-birth-weight babies. As a general matter, while medical improvements will certainly cause some number of children to survive with disabilities where in a previous era they would have died, it will also cause other children to avoid developing disabilities where in a previous era they would have become disabled. From improved prenatal medicine to safer child car seats to reductions in exposure to lead paint, medical improvements have saved untold thousands of children from disabilities. Furthermore, the decline in the number of students with mental retardation, as well as those with other severe types of disability, also disproves the argument that deinstitutionalization of students with severe problems is driving increases in special education enrollment. As for childhood poverty, it hasn't actually increased. For children under 6, it was 17.7% in 1976 when federal law first required special services for disabled students, and it was 16.9% in 2000. Even that understates the case, since the standard for what counts as "poverty" goes up over time as society gets richer.

If the real incidence of childhood disabilities isn't going up, then more students are being classified as disabled when there has been no change in the number of students who actually are disabled. Some of this change may be caused by improved diagnosis of existing disabilities. For example, growth in the number of students classified as autistic may be attributable to improved diagnosis. Likewise, growth in the number of students placed in special education under the category of "other health disorders" may be attributable to more widespread recognition and diagnosis of attention-deficit disorder and related disorders—though most students with such disorders are not placed in special education, some students with severe cases are.

But it is extremely unlikely that improved diagnosis is the most important cause of the last decade's overall growth in special education. Autism represents only a tiny fraction of total special education enrollment, and the category of "other health disorders," though larger, is not large enough to even come close to explaining the explosive growth in special education enrollment. As for other categories, we have no reason to believe that between 1990 and 2000 schools dramatically improved their ability to accurately identify students with most types of disabilities.

This leaves us with a less benign explanation—that schools are increasingly diagnosing students as disabled and placing them in special education for reasons unrelated to those students' genuine need for special education services. This would help explain not only the growth of special education enrollment, but also the recent increase in graduation rates for special education students—if more students who aren't truly disabled are being placed in special education, we would expect to see improvements in the academic performance of students in special education.

Why would schools place more students in special education when they didn't truly need it? Some researchers are now identifying high-stakes testing as a possible cause. More and more states have adopted test-based accountability programs in which significant consequences, such as student promotion and graduation or school funding cuts, are attached to performance on a standardized test. The goal of such programs is to provide schools with a firm incentive to improve performance—if students do poorly on the test, schools can be held accountable. But these programs can also create a perverse incentive: an incentive to game the system by getting low-performing students out of the testing pool altogether. By labeling such students as disabled and placing them in special education, schools can exempt them from mandatory testing. In some states, special education students who are considered testable are included in mandatory testing, but schools could still game the system by labeling special education students untestable (that is, too disabled to take the test). When low-performing students are exempt from testing, schools' average test scores go up, which makes the schools look better.

Examining a high-stakes statewide test in Texas, Deere and Strayer found that students who failed the test in one year were more likely to be classified as exempt from the test (either as special education students or limited English proficient students) the next year; that schools were more likely to classify minority students as exempt if this would reduce the number of minority students tested to a low enough level that the school's minority test scores would not be reported; and that when the state started counting the scores of special education students who did take the test towards schools' accountability ratings, the percentage of special education students who were classified as exempt from the test went up, reversing a downward trend. Figlio and Getzler, examining a high-stakes test in Florida, found that special education enrollment went up after the introduction of the test, that students in tested grades were more likely than students in untested grades to be placed in special education, that lower-scoring students were more likely to be placed in special education, and that severe disability categories did not rise after the introduction of the test. Jacob, studying Chicago schools, found that the percentage of students exempted from testing through special education rose faster after the introduction of high-stakes testing, and most quickly among lower-scoring students.

These findings are limited to various extents by research methodology. Most obviously, all these studies are confined to one state or city. None of them attempts to control for the national trend in special education enrollment, or otherwise compare states with high-stakes testing to states without high-stakes testing (although a few of the findings do compare students who are and are not subject to high-stakes testing within the same state). Special education enrollment was increasing nationwide throughout the 1990s, and the nationwide rate of growth increased as the decade progressed. Thus, finding that special education enrollment in a state or city grew faster after it adopted high-stakes testing does not, in itself, prove that high-stakes testing caused faster growth; it only proves that the state or city in question behaved in a manner consistent with the national trend.

Likewise, correlations between low test scores and special education enrollment are of limited value. If low-performing students are more likely to be enrolled in special education programs, it may well be that schools are pushing those students into special education to remove them from the testing pool. But it is also possible that those students' low test scores are indicative of genuine disabilities, for which they were subsequently diagnosed and enrolled in special education. Deere and Strayer try to account for this by comparing more than one set of paired years—that is, they look not only at whether students are more likely to be enrolled in special education one year after performing poorly on the test, but also at whether they are more likely to be enrolled in special education after two or three years of performing poorly. However, this does nothing to overcome the problem; it only proves that when schools put low-performing students into special education, they do not always do so after only one year of low performance. In fact, this is exactly what schools are supposed to do—they are not supposed to put students into special education based solely on a low test score. Deere and Strayer's finding is simply a multi-year correlation between low test scores and special education enrollment, which is still just as easily attributable to real disabilities in low-performing students as it is to schools' desire to remove those students from the testing pool.

Hanushek and Raymond conducted the only prior national study of high-stakes testing and special education enrollment, covering 1995–2000. They looked only at states with high-stakes testing, but they controlled for the national trend in special education enrollment. This control serves to implicitly compare states with high-stakes testing to states without high-stakes testing, a significant advantage over previous research. They found that when the control for the national trend was applied, the significant statistical relationship between high-stakes testing and special education enrollment disappeared entirely.

In explaining surging enrollment in special education, there is another possible culprit besides high-stakes testing. School districts have traditionally received state funding for special education, which makes up the bulk of all special education funding, in such a manner that they receive more money if their special education programs are larger. This provides school districts with a financial reward—a bounty, so to speak—for placing students in special education. Critics of the U.S. special education system have long argued that this creates a perverse financial incentive to put as many students as possible into special education.

Defenders of the system often argue that funding for special education cannot create perverse incentives because placing a student in special education creates costs at least equal to the new funding it generates. This misrepresents what truly is and is not a "cost" of placing a child in special education. A true cost is an expenditure that the school would not have made otherwise. Some services that a school would have provided to a particular child no matter what can be redefined as special education services if the child is placed in special education; these services are not truly special education costs because they would have been provided anyway. For example, if a school provides extra reading help to students who are falling behind in reading, the school must bear that cost itself. But if the same school redefines those students as learning disabled rather than slow readers, state and federal government will help pick up the tab for those services. This is financially advantageous for the school because it brings in new state and federal funding to cover "costs" that the school would have had to pay for anyway. Furthermore, there are many fixed costs associated with special education that do not increase with every new child. For example, if a school hires a full-time special education reading teacher, it will pay the same cost whether that teacher handles three students a day or ten. However, the school will collect a lot more money for teaching ten special education students than it would for teaching three.

Although there have been no national statistical studies of this question, and in particular no studies directly comparing states with and without bounty system funding, there has been a study of the relationship between financial incentives and special education enrollment. Cullen studied how school districts in Texas responded to changes in financial incentives arising from court-mandated restructuring of the state education financial system. She found that after the court order took effect, in districts where the amount of money provided for placing a student in special education went up, special education enrollment also went up. Specifically, she found that a 10% increase in the bounty for placing a student in special education could be expected to produce a 1.4% increase in a district's special education enrollment rate. The relationship between changes in financial incentives and changes in special education enrollment was strong enough that Cullen found it explained 35% of the growth in special education in Texas from the 1991–92 school year through the 1996–97 school year.

Method

To perform the study, we needed two types of enrollment data for each state: enrollment of students served in special education under . . . [IDEA] and total public school enrollment during the school years from 1991–92 through 2000–01. We obtained special education enrollment data from the Annual Report to Congress on the Implementation of the Individuals with Disabilities Education Act, published each year by the U.S. Department of Education's Office of Special Education Programs. We obtained total enroll-ment data from the Digest of Education Statistics, published by the U.S. Department of Education's National Center for Education Statistics. All these figures included students between the ages of 6 and 21. For each state in each year, we divided special education enrollment by total enrollment to determine the special education enrollment rate.

To obtain information on special education funding systems, we con-tacted each state's education department and asked three questions: what kind of funding system was in place, whether the system had been changed since the 1991–92 school year (and if so, when and from what kind of system), and whether there had been any other major changes in special education funding since 1991. For each state, we classified the funding system as a bounty system if it caused state funding to vary significantly by the size of each district's spe-cial education program. This included systems that distributed funds accord-ing to the number of special education students in each district, the number of special education staff in each district, or the level of special education spend-ing in each district. Systems that did not cause state funding to vary signifi-cantly by the size of each district's special education program, which typically distributed funds according to the total student population in each district, were classified as lump-sum systems.

We also collected information on high-stakes testing in each state. A test was considered high-stakes if any of the following depended upon it: student promotion or graduation, accreditation, funding cuts, teacher bonuses, a published school grading or ranking system, or state assumption of at least some school responsibilities. . . .

Our first method of analysis was a linear regression. To provide a measurement of growth in special education enrollment to serve as the dependent variable, we plotted each state's special education enrollment rates for the years included in the study, fitted a line to these data points using the ordinary least squares (OLS) method, and determined the slope of the line. The OLS line represents the closest possible approximation of the state trend in special education enrollment; the slope of the OLS line serves as a measurement of the rate at which special education enrollment grew during the study period. The independent variables in our analysis (that is, factors that might explain growth in special education enrollment rates) were both binary measurements: whether or not the state had a lump-sum system during the study period, and whether or not the state had a high-stakes test.

This regression analysis has the advantage of identifying the difference in the rates of special education growth in states with different funding systems. However, it is not sensitive to when changes in funding systems occurred during the study period. Of the states that had lump-sum systems in the 2000-01 school year, only a few had those systems since the 1991-92 school year; the rest switched from a bounty system to a lump-sum system at some point in between. The regression analysis counts all of these states as lump-sum states; it does not differentiate between states that had lump-sum systems for the whole decade and states that had lump-sum systems for only part of that period.

To capture the difference that changes in state funding systems may have made during the study period, we performed another analysis using a method that keeps track of which states had lump-sum systems in each specific year. First, we determined that the average school year in which states adopted lump-sum systems (counting the four states that had always had such systems during the study period as if they had switched in 1990-91) was 1994-95. In that year, seven states had lump-sum systems, a sufficiently large number for meaningful analysis. For each year from 1994-95 onward, for all states that had lump-sum systems in that year we subtracted that state's special education enrollment rate for the previous year from its special education enrollment rate in that year. For example, for each state that had a lump-sum system in 1994-95 we subtracted that state's special education enrollment rate in 1993-94 from its enrollment rate in 1994-95. This gave us the change in enrollment rate for each state with a lump-sum system in each year. We then calculated the average change in enrollment rate for all lump-sum system states in each year.

Turning to the remaining states—those that had bounty systems for the entire study period—we took each state's special education enrollment rate in

1993–94 and added the average change in enrollment rate for lump-sum states in 1994–95. This gave us projected values for the enrollment rates that those bounty states would have had in 1994–95 if they had switched to lump-sum systems in that year. We then added the average change for lump-sum states in 1995–96 to get a projected value for that year, and so on through 2000–01. This gave us projected values for the enrollment rates that bounty states would have had in 2000–01 if they had switched to lump-sum systems in 1994–95. By subtracting each state's projected 2000–01 rate from its actual 2000–01 rate and taking the average difference for all bounty states, we were able to estimate the average effect it would have had if all bounty states had switched to lump-sum systems in 1994–95.

Results

. . . Four states had lump-sum systems for the entire study period, twelve states began with bounty systems and switched to lump-sum systems during the study period, and 33 states (plus the District of Columbia) had bounty systems for the entire study period. Twenty-nine states (plus the District of Columbia) had high-stakes testing and 21 states did not. By far the most common type of high-stakes testing was a requirement that students pass a certain test to be promoted to the next grade or graduate from high school.

Hawaii and the District of Columbia each have only one school district. Rather than classifying them according to the system by which funds are distributed to school districts, we classified them according to the system by which the school district distributes funds to individual schools. Though the incentives are at a different organizational level, they work the same way.

One state, New Hampshire, did not have any state-level funding of special education until 1999. In that year, to comply with a court order, it created a new state program that funds special education by a bounty system. To prevent distortion of our results by this unusual case in which there was no state funding system of any kind for many years, we excluded New Hampshire from all calculations.

The national special education enrollment rate is shown in Figure 1. It grew from 10.6% of all students in the 1991–92 school year to 12.3% in the 2000–01 school year. The rate of growth has accelerated consistently during the past decade.

Figure 2 shows the special education enrollment rate over the same period, with figures separated into enrollments under lump-sum systems and bounty systems. Special education enrollment under lump-sum systems grew from 10.5% in the 1991–92 school year to 11.5% in the 2000–01 school year, an increase of one percentage point. Meanwhile, special education enrollment under bounty systems grew from 10.6% to 12.6% in the same period, an increase of two percentage points.

In interpreting Figure 2, we must bear in mind that it represents enrollments under the two types of funding systems rather than enrollments in two fixed sets of states. Enrollment figures in states that changed from bounty to lump-sum systems during the study period were included in the "bounty system" set for years before the state changed, and in the "lump-sum system" set for years

Figure 1

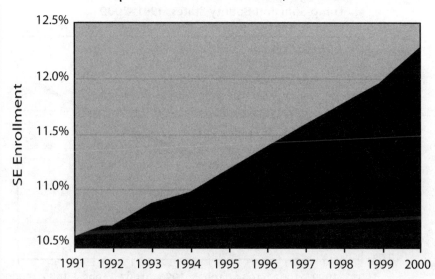

Figure 2

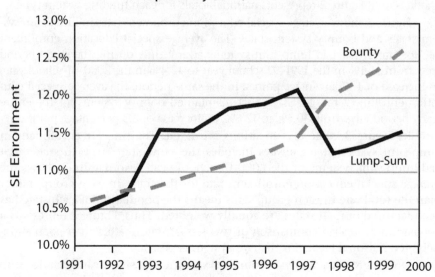

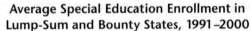

Figure 3

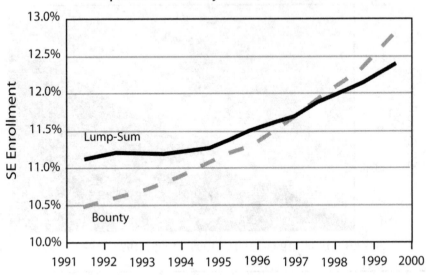

after the change. The line for enrollment under lump-sum systems includes four states in 1991–92, but this rises to 16 states by 2000–01.We must also bear in mind that these rates are based on total figures rather than averages, so they are population-weighted. The 1998 funding system change in California will produce a much larger impact on these figures than the 1995 funding system change in Rhode Island. Figure 2 represents national totals for each funding system type.

Figure 3 shows average special education enrollment rates in lump-sum system states and bounty system states. The average special education enrollment rate for states that had lump-sum systems at any time during the study period grew from 11.1% in the 1991–92 school year to 12.4% in the 2000–01 school year, an increase of 1.3 percentage points. In the same period, the average special education enrollment rate for states that maintained bounty systems for the entire study period grew from 10.5% to 12.8%, an increase of 2.3 percentage points.

In Figure 3, state classifications are fixed. The line for enrollment in lump-sum system states always includes the same states: the 16 states that had lump-sum systems in the 2000–01 school year. Also, Figure 3 shows the average special education enrollment rate for the states in each group, rather than the total rate in each group. This means the population of each state has been factored out; all states are equally weighted. Thus, Figure 3 represents a population-controlled comparison of two sets of states, rather than population-weighted national totals for the two system types.

Our regression analysis found a statistically significant relationship between a state's special education enrollment rate and whether or not that state had a lump-sum system during the study period. The regression coefficient for funding systems was 0.124. This means that every year, bounty system states experienced 0.124 more percentage points of growth in special education enrollment than they would have experienced if they had lump-sum systems. Over a ten-year period this adds up to 1.24 percentage points of additional special education enrollment because of the bounty system. The 33 states (plus the District of Columbia) that adhered to the bounty system saw special education enrollment grow by two percentage points over the study period, so a full 62% of that growth can be attributed to the effects of the bounty system. Also, 1.24% of total enrollment in bounty states in 2000–01 represents 390,000 extra students placed in special education because of the bounty system, resulting in additional spending of over $2.3 billion per year.

As for high-stakes testing, not only did the regression analysis find that the relationship between special education enrollment and high-stakes testing was not statistically significant, the regression coefficient for high-stakes testing was negative. That is, states with high-stakes testing actually had lower rather than higher rates of special education enrollment, although not so much so that we can be highly confident that this reflects a real relationship between high-stakes testing and special education enrollment. This study cannot tell us why there isn't a statistically significant relationship between high-stakes testing and higher special education enrollment, but one possible explanation is that states may be anticipating perverse incentives from high-stakes testing and taking preventative measures against them, but not taking similar measures against perverse incentives from funding special education by the bounty system.

. . . [Our] second analysis . . . [compared] actual and projected average special education enrollment rates in the states that stuck to the bounty system. The projected rate estimates the average special education enrollment these states would have had if they had switched to lump-sum systems in the 1994–95 school year. The difference between the actual and projected rates represents the average extra enrollment in these states attributable to the bounty system. In the 2000–01 school year this difference is 0.82 percentage points. In these states, 0.82% of total enrollment in 2000–01 represents roughly 258,000 additional students in special education, which would generate over $1.5 billion per year in extra spending.

Conclusion

State funding systems are having a dramatic effect on special education enrollment rates. In states where schools had a financial incentive to identify more students as disabled and place them in special education, the percentage of all students enrolled in special education grew significantly more rapidly over the past decade. By contrast, high-stakes testing appears to be having no significant effect on special education enrollment. This is contrary to the findings of previous studies that have looked only at individual cities or states and have not controlled for national trends, but agrees with the finding of the only previous national study.

The ever-accelerating growth of special education enrollment is becoming an urgent problem for American education, drawing off more and more billions of dollars that could otherwise be spent on better education for all students. The finding that state funding systems are responsible for the bulk of the past decade's growth in special education enrollment suggests how this problem could be curtailed. The most obvious policy solution would be for bounty system states to adopt lump-sum funding systems, removing the perverse financial incentive to place students in special education. However, state funding reform is not the only way to remove that incentive.

There are several ways in which the federal government could help alleviate the problem of perverse funding incentives. One approach would be to provide private school scholarships to all special education students, on the model of Florida's popular McKay Scholarship Program. This would mitigate perverse incentives from state special education funding, since placing a student in special education would not automatically bring more money into a school district's budget. It would also have the advantage of potentially providing the other benefits of school choice to families with disabled students, such as the ability to choose for themselves which school will provide the best education for their children.

If full-scale private school scholarships are not politically feasible, there are several smaller steps that could be taken in this direction. For example, existing federal IDEA funding could be made portable. Under such a system, families could choose either to continue receiving special education services from their public school, in which case federal money would continue to go to that school, or to take their federal dollars to another service provider of their choice. In cases where only limited special education services are needed, families choosing to seek services elsewhere could even leave their children in public school for regular educational services.

Another way to combat the effects of perverse state funding incentives would be to begin federal auditing of special education placements. The federal government could identify districts with especially high or especially low rates of special education placement, either generally or for certain groups. Other districts could be chosen for audits at random. Independent experts could then make their own diagnoses of students in special education in those districts, to determine how frequently students have been misdiagnosed. This would serve to expose to the public the true extent to which students without disabilities have been placed in special education; at the very least, such exposure would generate much stronger political pressure for reform of the system.

Finally, Congress could redirect its spending priorities when considering how new IDEA funds should be structured. Giving higher financial priority to types of disability that have more clearly objective diagnostic standards—such as autism, visual impairments, and hearing impairments—would send a clear message to states that the federal government will not provide infinite amounts of money for out-of-control special education programs. It would also have the beneficial effect of directing new federal money towards disability categories that place larger financial burdens on schools.

Kanya Mahitivanichcha
and Thomas Parrish

 **NO**

Do Non-Census Funding Systems Encourage Special Education Identification? Reconsidering Greene and Forster

Over the past 25 years, special education as a percentage of total enrollment has risen significantly across the nation. In 1975–76, special education made up about 8% of the school-age population. This figure rose to 10.6% in 1991–92, and was 12.2% by 2001–02. Rising enrollments have led to increased spending, with an estimated national expenditure of $50 billion on special education services during the 1999–2000 school year.

These growing numbers have garnered increased public attention and raised questions as to whether the type of special education funding formula used by states may be affecting rising special education identification rates. One perspective is that the same federal provisions govern special education identification throughout the country, and that each identified student undergoes extensive scrutiny by a multidisciplinary team of professionals prior to being deemed eligible for special education. These professionals often have no knowledge of underlying fiscal provisions, so their professional eligibility decisions would not be affected by them.

On the other hand, in 2000–01 the percentage of students identified for special education services in Rhode Island (17.8%) was nearly twice the identification rate for California (9.4%). Why are one state's identification criteria and procedures for students in special education so different from another? As the same federal provisions, the Individuals with Disabilities Education Act (IDEA), pertain, what combination of state policies and circumstances result in such broad variation? What role might the state's type of special education funding formula play, if any?

One analysis that was fairly widely publicized concluded that the nation could save over $1.5 billion per year in special education spending if all states were to adopt funding formulas free of fiscal incentives to identify additional special education students. A savings of this magnitude appears to be counter to the prevailing, but also fairly limited, research previously conducted on this topic. While other studies, some of which are briefly described in this article, have found evidence of the effects of funding incentives on special

From *Journal of Special Education Leadership*, vol. 18, no. 1, April 2005, pp. 38–45. Copyright © 2005 by the Journal of Special Education Leadership. Reprinted by permission. Notes omitted. References omitted.

education practice, most have concluded that fiscal provisions are just one set of a complex array of factors explaining the large range in identification rates across states. No prior report reveals the type of unequivocal relationship that Greene and Forster claim to have found, or suggests the extensive changes in practice and resultant savings that would result from adopting what they refer to as an "incentive-free" approach to special education funding.

Rather than favoring one type of funding formula over another, this article argues that incentive-free approaches to special education funding do not exist, since all formulas place fiscal premiums on some behaviors over others. The real question addressed by this article is the extent to which evidence can be found that special education providers actually alter behavior in response to these fiscal incentives. This article briefly explores existing research about the relationship between alternative types of funding systems and special education identification rates, re-examines the analysis and findings of Greene and Forster, and provides some independent analyses related to the possible impact of special education fiscal incentives.

To the degree that fiscal incentives impact policy and practice, the questions addressed in this article are important. According to a survey on state special education funding systems conducted by the Center for Special Education Finance (CSEF) in 1999–2000, more than half of the responding states (28 of 46) said they had altered the way they fund special education since 1994–95. Additionally, almost half of the responding states said they were considering further changes. These findings point to the dynamic nature of the mechanisms through which states allocate special education funds and the ongoing opportunity to inform policy. If $1.5 billion can be saved per year, as claimed by Greene and Forster, all states should adopt the type of funding system they advocate.

Fiscal Incentives in the Context of Special Education Funding

Greene and Forster argue that all states should adopt the special education funding systems that are based on the total number of children living in a state or the total number of students enrolled in a district. These formulas are not directly related to special education enrollments or the types or levels of service provision. However, they may be adjusted to reflect variations in measures of student need that cannot be directly affected by district practice, such as student poverty (as found in the federal special education formula), or an external estimate of student severity (as used in California). These formulas are sometimes referred to as "census-based" or "population-based." Such formulas are used by the federal government in allocating a growing portion of IDEA funds, as well as by states such as Pennsylvania, Massachusetts, and California.

A second category of formulas, which is more predominant across the states, is based on some measure of special education provision. Examples include formulas in which the amount of state aid is based on varying funding "weights" (or amounts) associated with each special education student, formulas where districts are reimbursed for a certain percentage of their special education expenditures, or formulas in which funding is based on the allocation of specific special education resources such as classroom units or teachers.

The major distinction between these two categories of formulas is that under non-census systems, the amount of funds allocated is based on some measure of the degree of special education services provided, while under census systems they are not. Greene and Forster posit that the non-census systems create incentives to identify more students for special education than the census-based approaches. They further claim that their analyses strongly confirm the hypothesis that higher special education identification rates occur under non-census types of formulas.

Review of the Prior Literature

Although there has been much speculation regarding fiscal incentives in special education, relatively few studies have directly examined the association between fiscal incentives and special education identification rates. Among the most recent is the work of Cullen, in which the author utilized data from Texas from the early- to the mid-1990s to quantify the relationship between changes in fiscal incentives and student disability rates. According to these findings, fiscal incentives explained about 40% of the increase in disability rates among school districts in Texas during the study's period.

In a study by Kane and Johnson, the authors evaluated the first three years of implementation of Act 230 in Vermont. Under Act 230, the special education funding system was changed so that the block grant portion was based on total student membership rather than special education enrollment. Act 230 also included other changes in the funding system that increased flexibility and decreased incentives to identify children as disabled. The authors found that special education enrollment in Vermont over the first three years of implementation of Act 230 decreased by over 17%.

Thus, these two studies did find a relationship between fiscal incentives and special education identification patterns in Texas and Vermont. In Pennsylvania, Hartman also initially found evidence that the shift to a census funding formula appeared to slow special education identification across the state. In contrast with nationwide trends throughout the 1990s, Pennsylvania actually experienced initial decreases in special education as a percentage of total public school enrollment. However, this series of decreases in Pennsylvania was followed by increases in the mid- to late-1990s. By the 2000–01 school year, Pennsylvania's special education percentage was once again slightly above the national average.

Other studies, however, have pointed to the complexity of these relationships and the need to also consider the influence of such factors as the organizational structure, program constraints and regulations, characteristics of advocacy groups, commitment and leadership of staff, legal requirements, and variation in funding from other sources that are available to states and school districts. Such factors may interact with fiscal incentives created by funding formulas, resulting in behaviors and responses that are much less predictable.

Magnetti found relationships between governing agencies, such as the collaboration between special education programs and welfare services, affect special education identification. Weikart found that variables such as the organization of the state department of education, priorities of state leadership, and the relative effectiveness of federal monitoring influence the placement patterns of students in special education.

In his paper examining issues of reliability, validity, and usefulness of disability assessments on special education identification and classification, Reschly pointed out that disability classification is not uniform across states. Assessing disabilities is a complex task, and professional judgment may vary across districts and states. Identical characteristics may be interpreted and classified differently depending on the state in which the student resides.

In summary, although research evidence can be found that funding formulas may create fiscal incentives that sometimes influence the provision of special education services, the literature also suggests that these incentives need to be understood in conjunction with other factors such as the historical context, impact of advocacy groups, organizational structure, professional judgment, program constraints, and government regulations.

Reconsidering Greene and Forster

In examining the association between fiscal incentives in funding mechanisms and special education enrollment, Greene and Forster classified state funding systems into the census and non-census categories previously described. Figure 1 replicates their analysis showing enrollment figures under the two funding systems over ten years. It is important to note that each point on the chart represents a weighted average of the percentage of students in special education across all the states having one type of funding system as opposed to another in

Figure 1

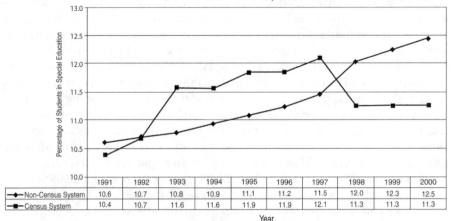

Replication of Greene and Forster's Population-Weighted Analysis

Special Ed Enrollments Under Non-Census
and Census Systems, 1991-2000

	1991	1992	1993	1994	1995	1996	1997	1998	1999	2000
Non-Census System	10.6	10.7	10.8	10.9	11.1	11.2	11.5	12.0	12.3	12.5
Census System	10.4	10.7	11.6	11.6	11.9	11.9	12.1	11.3	11.3	11.3

Year

Greene and Forster's estimates: 1991 = NC(10.6), C(10.5); 2000 = NC(12.6), C(11.5).

—◆— Non-Census System —■— Census System

Figure 2

Modification of Greene and Forster's Population-Weighted Analysis Without California

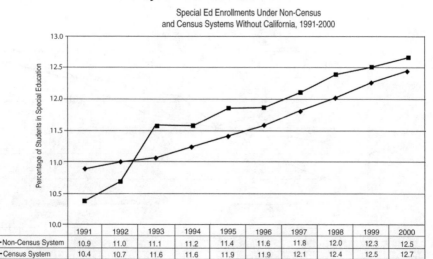

Special Ed Enrollments Under Non-Census
and Census Systems Without California, 1991-2000

	1991	1992	1993	1994	1995	1996	1997	1998	1999	2000
Non-Census System	10.9	11.0	11.1	11.2	11.4	11.6	11.8	12.0	12.3	12.5
Census System	10.4	10.7	11.6	11.6	11.9	11.9	12.1	12.4	12.5	12.7

Year

Greene and Forster's estimates: 1991 = NC(10.6), C(10.5); 2000 = NC(12.6), C(11.5).

━◆━ Non-Census System   ━■━ Census System

a given year. This type of weighted approach results in very large states having a vastly larger impact than very small ones. The resulting averages are, therefore, much more susceptible to what happens in a few large states as opposed to reflecting a true average of 50 varying state experiments regarding the relationship between funding policies and special education enrollments. It is also important to note that the states included in each category of funding differ across the years as they change from one type of funding system to another.

For example, California had a non-census system up until 1998, and therefore is included in the non-census averages shown in Figure 1 from 1991-97. After changing its funding policy in 1998, California is reflected in the figures representing the census system. Given this change and the fact that the weight generated by a single state with a very large student enrollment has the capacity to substantially alter aggregate trends, it is important to question whether the sudden drop shown for 1998 in Figure 1 is simply a result of California's shift from a non-census to a census system during that year. As California represents one-eighth of the nation, this state alone may have driven the observed aggregate trend, which Greene and Forster cite as evidence that census funding systems result in lower special education identification rates.

Figure 2 ... is a replication of the same chart with California removed from the analysis. As can be seen, without California the trends in total special education enrollment rate representing each funding system look quite different. Greene and Forster concluded from Figure 1 that the states with a non-census system exhibit an

Figure 3

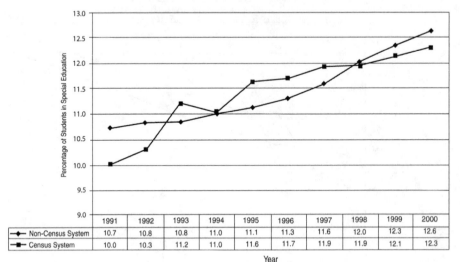

Unweighted Analysis of States in Non-Census and Census Systems

Special Education Under Non-Census and Census Systems, 1991-2000
(Unweighted)

	1991	1992	1993	1994	1995	1996	1997	1998	1999	2000
Non-Census System	10.7	10.8	10.8	11.0	11.1	11.3	11.6	12.0	12.3	12.6
Census System	10.0	10.3	11.2	11.0	11.6	11.7	11.9	11.9	12.1	12.3

Year

increase in special education enrollment rate of about 1.9 percentage points over the ten-year period, while the census system saw an increase of about 0.9 percentage points. With the removal of California, Figure 2 . . . tells a different story: The non-census states now show an increase of about 1.6 percentage points over the ten-year period, while the census states saw an increase of 2.3 percentage points over the ten-year period. Hence, the trends reverse when removing the "California effect."

A further argument against the Greene and Forster approach shown in Figure 1 is that the trends associated with the two funding systems are more appropriately examined through the calculation of unweighted averages, treating each state as an independent experiment regarding the relationship between state funding policies and special education identification rates. The results of such analyses are shown in Figure 3. . . . With each state weighed equally, the non-census states saw an increase of 1.9 percentage points over the ten-year period, while those designated as using a census system saw an increase of 2.3 percentage points. On the other hand, the non-census states showed slightly higher identification rates over the past few years. Overall, however, the relationship observed from tracking the two lines in Figure 3 is far from stable, and does not appear to warrant any clear conclusions about the impact of one type of funding system over another on special education enrollments.

Regression Analysis

Greene and Forster also used Ordinary Least Squares (OLS) analyses to test their basic premise regarding the impact of alternative funding systems. They used special education growth from 1991–92 to 2000–01 as the dependent variable. From these analyses, they reported a statistically significant, positive correlation between non-census funding and growth in special education enrollment. According to the authors, these systems were associated with an additional increase of 1.24 percentage points in special education enrollment over this ten-year span. They also concluded from these findings that disability rates would be lower by an average of 0.82 percentage points if states with non-census systems were to switch to census formulas.

To test these results, using the same data as Greene and Forster we first ran similar analyses, only modifying the independent (predictor/explanatory) variables somewhat. We retained the variable indicating whether the state had a census system at any point in time during the study period. However, we replaced their independent variable indicating whether the state had a "high stakes" testing system with the poverty rate among children in each state Greene and Forster's rationale for including the "high stakes" testing variable was that special education identification rates might be affected by the existence of "high stakes" testing (i.e., there may be an incentive for placing low-performing students in special education to avoid exposure to the tests that may pull down average district or state test scores). However, their analyses showed this variable to be statistically insignificant in explaining growth in special education enrollment. Hence, we replaced this variable with a poverty measure to reflect the established relationship between poverty and the need for special education services. Indeed, we found poverty to be a significant predictor of special education identification rate.

Table 1 compares regression results from Greene and Forster with two alternative model specifications. Model 1 shows that after controlling for poverty, the differential effect on identification rates associated with the two

Table 1

Replication and Modification of Greene and Forster's OLS Regression: Funding Formulas and other Variables as Predictors of Growth in Special Education Enrollment over the Ten-Year Period (N = 51)

	Replication of Greene & Forster	Model 1	Model 2
Census	−0.122*[a] (0.040)	−0.090* (0.039)	—
Five-Year Census	—	—	−0.080 (0.044)
High Stakes	−0.066 (0.038)	—	—
Poverty	—	0.006* (0.003)	0.007* (0.003)
Adjusted R-sq.	0.146	0.177	0.145

*p < 0.05, standard errors in parentheses.
[a]Greene and Forster's estimate = −0.124*

types of funding formulas becomes less pronounced, with the estimated effects on special education enrollment growth associated with census systems dropping from 1.24 to 0.9 percentage points ($p < 0.05$). However, the difference between our estimate in Model 1 and that of Greene and Forster is not statistically significant.

Model 2, as shown in Table 1, includes a different definition for determining whether a state is classified as census or non-census in the analysis. In this case, states were only classified as census if they had such a system in place for at least five years during the study period. This contrasts with Greene and Forster's approach, which designated states as census if they had a census formula in place in any single year over this ten-year span. This modification was based on the assumption that if a state had nine years of non-census funding and one year of census funding, it made little sense to include them in the census grouping. Assuming that some period of implementation would be needed before any program effect would occur, a state was labeled as census or non-census, based on the prevailing system through the ten-year period.

Using this revised definition of census states and poverty as predictors (see Model 2 in Table 1), the census variable shows up as statistically insignificant. In other words, the analysis suggests that there are no statistically reliable correlations between states' special education growth rates and states' having census systems for at least five years. Estimates on the poverty variable, however, showed up as statistically significant in both Models 1 and 2.

In deciding how to classify states in our regression models, we also used a model in which states were classified as having a census system if they had a census system in place for three years or more. The resulting estimates were identical to those reported by Greene and Forster, because all states with a census system in place at any point in time had had it for at least three years. In an attempt to further test the resiliency of the relationship between the funding system and identification rates, we applied the five-year definition, whereby only states that have had the census system for at least five years were categorized as having a prevailing census system. The rationale is that if an influence is seen under the census system, the longer it is in place the more pronounced the effect should be. However, as shown in Model 2, we found that the relationship seemed to disappear when we applied the five-year test. This suggests that with the small sample size (limited by the number of states), the results are more a reflection of how states are classified, than a measure of any relationship between the census funding systems and special education identification rates.

An Alternative Regression Analysis

In addition to re-examining Greene and Forster's methodology, an alternative regression approach for considering the relationship between funding systems and special education identification was applied. Specifically, a repeated measures regression analysis was conducted, using special education enrollment rates for each of the ten years across 50 states and the District of Columbia, resulting in 510 cases (see Table 2).

Table 2

Repeated Measures Analysis: Funding Formulas and Poverty as Predictors of Special Education Enrollment over the Ten-Year Period (N = 51)

Variables	Estimated Coefficients on Special Education Enrollment Rate
Census	−0.00082 (0.002699)
Year	0.00223** (0.000081)
Census × Year	−0.00059* (0.000201)
Poverty	0.000018 (0.000459)

*p < 0.05.
**p < 0.01, standard errors in parentheses.

Repeated measures analysis takes into consideration that the observations across years for each state may be correlated with one another and account for such intrastate dependence. The predictor variables in this analysis include a poverty measure; a continuous year variable (to reflect special education enrollment growth over the ten-year period); a binary variable classifying whether the state has a census system for each respective year; and an interaction term, "census × year." This interaction term captures average growth (per year) in special education enrollment over the ten-year period associated with the census system relative to the non-census system.

Applying this repeated measures regression model, the estimate on the census variable shows up as statistically insignificant. This suggests that states with census systems do not have significantly lower special education enrollment rates relative to states with non-census systems, after filtering out the effects of poverty. However, the interaction term shows up as significant (p < 0.01). That is, the average growth (per year over the ten-year period) in special education enrollment rate in a census system is 0.06% lower than in a non-census system. This finding is consistent with, but considerably less pronounced, than that of Greene and Forster.

Implications for Policymakers

What are the policy implications of these varying results? As mentioned earlier, a number of states, as well as the federal government, have altered the basis on which special education funds have been allocated over the past ten years. In addition, the Center for Special Education Finance reports continuing evidence that future changes are likely. States report that one factor driving change is concern about rising special education enrollments and costs. As states continue to actively consider future funding provisions, it is important for policymakers to understand the possible program implications of alternative funding policies.

All of the formula options from which policymakers may choose contain fiscal incentives in relation to one another. Census formulas, which do not base funding received on any measure of special education provision, contain a fiscal incentive to identify fewer students for special education and to provide lower levels of service as compared to non-census formulas in which the allocation of funds is clearly based on these factors.

Some states may adopt census-based systems specifically in an attempt to dampen growing special education enrollments. There are also many other reasons why a state may wish to choose one type of formula over another. Thus, in considering the relative merits of alternative formulas, perhaps the operative question is not whether varying fiscal incentives for special education identification are contained in them, but whether these incentives have any effect on practice. Greene and Forster seemed to extend a clear call to action by arguing that the nation could save over $1.5 billion per year in special education spending if all states were to adopt census-based funding formulas.

After a review of prior research in this area, a re-examination of Greene and Forster's methods and results, and an attempt at a more rigorous empirical examination of this question, there appears to be mild evidence that the choice of a census-based funding system alone may have a slight affect on future special education enrollments. However, little evidence is found that this relationship is as clear or close to the magnitude claimed by Greene and Forster. Rather, the findings in this paper seem to substantiate evidence from the prior literature that fiscal provisions are among many factors that appear to affect varying patterns of special education enrollment.

POSTSCRIPT

Do Funding Systems Create a Perverse Incentive to Place Students in Special Education?

Special education costs stimulate many heated arguments. Everyone agrees it would be better not to have such high expenses.

Many parents struggle to have their children qualify for special education, convinced that intensive academic attention is essential for their success. Many say their struggle is due to districts' reluctance to spend money on services. Everyone agrees it would be better if their children learned effortlessly and did not require supports.

All four authors agree that special education numbers are rising. They all use complex statistical analyses to discover the "culprit." They disagree about what fuels the growth.

Greene and Forster staunchly believe that funding systems are to blame. Maintaining that even 10% of children in special education is too many, they provide powerful illustrations of how state expenses have changed. Their models suggest that impressive savings could be easily realized by implementing systems that do not tempt districts.

Mahitivanichcha and Parrish analyze the data differently and reach other conclusions. Removing "California effect" of size, they found smaller discrepancies between the funding systems. Additionally, although agreeing that special education numbers in census-based states are slightly lower, they present evidence that poverty is a compelling element affecting these enrollments.

Competing demands for funds always cause financial tension between general and special education. The *Journal of Special Education Leadership* *(JSEL)* focused its entire April 2005 issue on this topic. The centerpiece was the recently released Special Education Expenditure Project (SEEP). Mandated by IDEA 97, SEEP was conducted by the American Institutes for Research (http://csef.air.org), with which Mahitivanichcha and Parrish are affiliated.

Initial SEEP analyses made an unexpected discovery (Chambers, Perez, Harr, and Shkolnik, *JSEL*, 2005). While expenditures varied widely, the last comprehensive study, conducted in 1985-86, calculated the annual expense of educating a child in special education to be 2.28 times that of educating a typical child. SEEP, using data from the 1999-2000 school year, found that ratio had fallen to 1.90:1. This amount is lower than the 1.92:1 figures gathered in 1968-69.

Special education costs have increased (108 percent). General education costs have risen even more (110 percent). Agreeing with all of this issue's authors, SEEP finds that larger expenditures are due to added numbers of students with mild needs.

Harr and Parrish (*JSEL*, 2005) echo Parrish's statement—every funding system contains incentives. Census-based systems reward districts for identifying fewer students. Weight-based systems reward identification. Which preference will result in better outcomes for all our students?

In the same issue, Brian Benzel, superintendent of the Spokane (WA) public schools, notes that his district has rising special education numbers despite a funding ceiling. Although proud of his district's attention to students, he worries about how to afford services. One of his suggestions is a funding system based on a defined set of services that could be standardized across the country. This, and fulfillment of the federal funding promise, would help Spokane.

Are there ways to determine a standard level of services in special education? What about general education? Is it possible that increased numbers in special education are driven by fewer services available to all children?

There is agreement that special education numbers are rising and that services to these children are costly. Is this controversy about the number of children in special education, the cost to educate these children, or the limited resources for all of education?

ISSUE 5

Does School Choice Open Doors for Students With Disabilities?

YES: Lewis M. Andrews, from "More Choices for Disabled Kids," *Policy Review* (no. 112, 2002)

NO: Barbara Miner, from "Vouchers: Special Ed Students Need Not Apply," *Rethinking Schools Online* (Winter 2003)

ISSUE SUMMARY

YES: Lewis M. Andrews, executive director for the Yankee Institute for Public Policy, reviews the experiences of a number of countries with considerable school choice experience. He maintains that children with disabilities will find unexpected opportunities in choice-sponsored schools.

NO: Barbara Miner, a freelance writer and former managing editor of *Rethinking Schools*, explores experiences with the pioneering Milwaukee voucher system and discusses exclusionary policies and practices that limit access for students with disabilities.

School choice, a major component of education reform, offers parents alternatives to their neighborhood school. Intradistrict options range from open-enrollment programs to magnet schools focusing on thematic education. Charter schools, which operate within the public school structure, are funded by direct transfers of funds from public schools. Dependent on state law, charter schools can be created from the ground up or converted from existent public schools. Finally, voucher programs grant families an amount of money that they can use across district lines to enroll in a suitable program, even in a private school. The goal of each of these options is to offer unique programs to children, stimulate creativity in public schools, and increase academic achievement.

Charter and private schools are exempt from many of the rules that structure (some say bind) public schools. Freedom from union contracts and many state rules and regulations—together with strict accountability for student performance—will, it is hoped, result in creative, innovative, nontraditional programs that offer more desirable alternatives for all children rather than bureaucracy-ridden, neighborhood public schools. In turn, the possibilities created by choice schools will hopefully stimulate public schools to move beyond their traditions and become creative in their own right.

The vast majority of states have some sort of school choice structure. No Child Left Behind (NCLB) expands the options further by mandating a range of interventions when a child's own school does not demonstrate sufficient progress toward meeting Adequate Yearly Progress. Many of the remedies open to parents include services outside the public school. Sometimes this can be enrollment in another school, which could be private. Sometimes the remedy can be supplemental services from a private provider.

While privately funded and charter schools are free from many regulations, including union contracts, they are required to abide by federal laws, including those governing the education of students with disabilities. Lively discussions have emerged about whether or not students with disabilities are welcome in the world of charter schools—and whether or not they are well served there.

Lewis M. Andrews acknowledges a frequently heard criticism, that school choice options will "skim" away the best students ("the cream") from public schools, leaving only those who have the most trouble learning. Lewis reviews the educational systems of the Netherlands, Sweden, and Denmark to demonstrate his contention that this is a baseless prediction.

Barbara Miner investigated voucher schools in Milwaukee and cites evidence that all is not rosy in the world of school choice—especially for students with disabilities. She talked with parents and researchers who found that many voucher schools find reasons not to be available to students with disabilities.

As you read the following selections, consider the alternatives open to all students. Are school choice options in the United States too new to have opened all the doors? Or are the doors to choice schools not open enough to the full range of children and their needs?

YES

Lewis M. Andrews

More Choices for Disabled Kids

If the opponents of school choice could have their way, the national debate over the use of public money to subsidize private schooling would turn on the subject of special education. With research demonstrating the overall success of school voucher programs in Milwaukee and Cleveland, and with the constitutional issue of public funding of religiously affiliated schools headed for resolution in a seemingly God-tolerant Supreme Court, defenders of the educational status quo have been reduced to fanning fears that government support of greater parental choice would transform public schools into dumping grounds for difficult-to-educate students.

Sandra Feldman, president of the American Federation of Teachers, repeatedly warns that, with private education more accessible to the poor and middle class, good students will "flee" to independent and parochial schools, leaving behind those kids who are physically and emotionally handicapped, are hyperactive, or have been involved with the juvenile justice system. "[P]rivate schools ... don't have to take [the learning-disabled]," agrees Tammy Johnson of the liberal activist group Wisconsin Citizen Action, so public schools would be left "to deal with those children." Even if private schools were required to take a certain percentage of disabled students, adds *Rethinking Schools*, an online publication of teachers opposed to school choice, they "tend not to provide needed services for children with special education needs or for children who speak English as a second language." NAACP president Kweisi Mfume predicts that the true cost of private education will always exceed what the government can afford to cover, so "those in the upper- and middle-income brackets will be helped the most ... as long as their kids don't have personal, behavioral, or educational challenges that cause the private school to pass them by."

Given the large number of parents who have come to rely on special education services provided through America's public schools, this strategy of conjuring a worst-case scenario for learning-disabled students would at first appear a promising one. According to the *Seventeenth Annual Report to Congress on the Implementation of the Individuals with Disabilities Education Act*, over 5.37 million children—97 percent of American students diagnosed with "special needs"—currently participate in public school special education programs; their parents, many of whom have become adept at using the legal

From *Policy Review*, no. 112, April/May 2002. Copyright © 2002 by Policy Review. Reprinted with permission system to access an estimated $32 billion in annual services, are a potent political force. The vast majority of these parents have come to believe that their own son or daughter benefits most from being educated in the same classes as normal students—a remedial philosophy known as "inclusion"—and would vigorously oppose any policy that threatens to isolate special-needs children in separate schools for the learning-disabled.

The argument that school choice must inevitably create special education ghettos would appear to have been strengthened by the recent adoption of market-based education reforms in New Zealand. In the late 1980s, that country's Labour government undertook a sweeping reorganization of its highly centralized education system, replacing the Department of Education and its 4,000 employees with a new Ministry of Education staffed by only 400 people and putting each local school under the control of a community board of trustees. At the same time, the government abolished school zoning, allowing children to transfer freely between schools, even to private schools, at state expense.

A recent book on these New Zealand reforms by school choice opponents Edward Fiske and Helen Ladd, *When Schools Compete: A Cautionary Tale*, makes much of a flaw in the initial legislation, which permitted the more popular public schools to reject students who would be costly to educate or whose disabilities might drag down the test averages. The authors argue that this "skimming" or "creaming" of the better students—which did happen in some cases—is an inevitable consequence of any school choice program, a conclusion widely publicized in the United States by our teachers union.

Yet a closer look at how learning-disabled students are actually faring under a variety of school choice programs worldwide suggests that the special education card may not play out exactly as the opponents of market-based education reform are hoping. Take the case of New Zealand itself, which has largely remedied its original legislation with two amendments: a 1999 supplemental voucher program targeted at the country's indigenous population, the Maori, and a law requiring all schools accepting state funds to adopt a non-discriminatory admissions policy. Under the new Special Education 2000 policy, schools also receive supplemental funding for each learning-disabled child they take in; principals are free to spend the money on what they and the child's parents determine are the most appropriate services. And if the special-needs child leaves the school for any reason, the supplemental funding follows the child to his or her new placement. As a result of these modifications to the initial law, school choice now enjoys nearly universal public support, says Roger Moltzen, director of special education programs in the Department of Education at New Zealand's University of Waikato, and "is unlikely to be repealed."

The Dutch Experience

To see more clearly the impact of school choice on the treatment of learning disabilities, it is useful to compare the experience of three northern European countries: the Netherlands, Sweden, and Denmark. Each has adopted school choice as part of its national education policy, but with very different provisions in the area of special education. Consider first the Netherlands, where public funding of parental choice has been national policy since 1917 and where almost two-thirds of Dutch students attend private schools.

Until about 15 years ago, universal school choice for mainstream students coexisted with a separate, complex, and cumbersome arrangement for educating the learning-disabled. The Dutch had actually maintained 14 separate school systems, each geared to a particular learning disability—deafness, physical handicaps, mild mental retardation, severe mental retardation, multiple disabilities, and so on—and each mimicking as closely as possible the grade levels of conventional public and private schools.

This separate-but-parallel system did employ private providers; it also tested children regularly to determine whether any might be eligible for transfer to mainstream schools. But by the late 1980s the Dutch began to notice a disturbing increase in the percentage of pupils classified as learning-disabled. (The number of learning-disabled students actually remained constant, but this represented a sharp percentage increase, given the steady decline in the total number of school-age children.) There was widespread concern that the special education bureaucracy was expanding its services at the expense of children with mild-to-moderate learning problems, who were not being adequately integrated into mainstream society. The key to reform, many believed, was to create a financial structure that gave parents of special-needs children the same educational choices as other parents.

Under a "Going to School Together" policy adopted by the Netherlands in 1990, it became the stated intention of the Ministry of Education that parents of children with disabilities should . . . be able to choose between [any] ordinary or a special school for their child." Children who required additional services for serious learning disabilities were awarded "a personal budget," which under Dutch law parents could spend at either a special or a mainstream school. To ensure equality of opportunity for all students, supplemental funding was provided to both public and private schools in economically depressed districts, where the percentage of learning-disabled students tends to be higher.

Today the Dutch educational structure enjoys strong support from all political quarters, but especially from advocates of greater inclusion for the learning-disabled. Already the number of separate special school systems has been reduced from 14 to only four.

The Swedes and the Danes

Compare the evolution of special education services in the Netherlands with Sweden, which in March 1992 adopted a "Freedom of Choice and Independent Schools" bill. It gave parents "the right and opportunity to choose a school and education for one's children" by granting all independent schools a municipal subsidy equal to 85 percent of the public school per-pupil cost multiplied by that private or parochial school's enrollment. Independent schools that received this funding were free to emphasize a particular teaching method, such as Montessori, an ethnic affiliation, or even a religious affiliation—but all had to be licensed by the national authority, Skolverket.

Like the Dutch, the Swedes had adopted a universal choice policy, but with one important limitation: The parents of special education students were not effectively granted the same freedom as parents of normal children. This omission was due in large part to Sweden's long history of pedagogic paternalism, which for decades had lowered testing standards, altered textbooks, and micromanaged both classroom and extracurricular activities—all in an effort to avoid making the learning-disabled feel in any way inferior. ("A handicap," according to official publications of the Swedish National Agency for Special Needs Education, "is not tied to an individual but is created by the demands, expectations, and attitudes of the environment.") When the Swedes finally adopted school choice for mainstream children, they were reluctant to risk letting learning-disabled students "flounder" in this new, more competitive educational marketplace.

The result today is that the majority of Sweden's deaf students are still educated in separate institutions. Other special-needs students, who supposedly have been integrated into the educational mainstream, continue to suffer under a centrally managed system in which support services are negotiated between school principals and municipal finance officers, with parents having little input. In theory, all conventional schools are supposed to have an action plan outlining a program of support for their special-needs students. According to a 1998 study by Sweden's National Agency for Education (NAE), however, only half of the country's schools maintain any such plans and fewer than 20 percent of affected parents feel they are able to participate.

One interesting consequence of this lingering paternalism is that the percentage of Swedish children classified as needing special education services is high relative to other industrialized countries and continues to grow at a disproportionate rate. Between the school years 1992–93 and 1996–97, according to the NAE, the number of students registered in schools for the mentally impaired rose by one-fifth. Furthermore, the severity of disabilities tends to be ranked higher within categories. For example, only 25 percent of Sweden's mentally retarded are considered mild cases, while 75 percent are labeled "moderate-to-severe." In the United States, by way of contrast, the proportions are exactly reversed. To what extent this reflects the failure of Sweden's centralized management of special education—or simply the tendency of a large bureaucracy to expand its client base—is unclear at present, but the failure of Sweden to make school choice truly universal has clearly undermined the government's stated goal of promoting greater inclusion.

Finally we come to Denmark, where political support for private education dates back to 1899 and where 11 percent of students attend more than 400 private schools with municipal governments covering 80–85 percent of the cost. Compared to Sweden and the Netherlands, the Danish education ministry has the longest history of, in its own words, letting "resources follow the [special-needs] child." Parents normally have the final say over what school their learning-disabled son or daughter attends, and if an independent school is chosen, the Ministry of Education pays a sum per pupil to the receiving school, with the student's hometown ultimately reimbursing the ministry. The Ministry of Education provides supplemental resources—such as classroom aids, extra courses, and after-hours tutoring—through special grants on a case-by-case basis.

The startling result is that only 0.7 percent of Denmark's 80,000 learning-disabled students are confined to specialized institutions—as compared to five times that percentage in the United States. The Paris-based Organization for Economic Cooperation and Development (OECD), which tracks special education statistics internationally, has praised the Danes for their exceptionally "strong commitment to inclusive education" and for years has held up Denmark's approach to schooling as a model to the rest of the world.

One obvious conclusion to be drawn from the three-way comparison of the Netherlands, Sweden, and Denmark—as well as from the experience of New Zealand—is that inclusion is not only possible under school choice, but with the right policy adjustments, may succeed to an extent not even imagined by American educators. The critical variable appears to be the willingness of legislators to extend freedom of choice to all parents, including the parents of the learning-disabled. In Australia, a school choice country where supplemental funding to support special education is provided to both private and public schools by the national government—but where individual territories have wide discretion in directing how the money is spent—those regions which provide the most flexibility to parents of the learning-disabled also have the best record of mainstreaming. From 1990 to 1995, the percentage of special-needs students successfully integrated into schools in New South Wales more than doubled, while the number of Schools for Special Purposes (the Australian euphemism for segregated special-needs schools) declined sharply. By contrast, West Australia retained most of its separate schools during that same period.

It is also worth noting that, regardless of the degree to which choice has been offered to parents of the learning-disabled, the subsidy of private education in foreign countries has not turned government schools into the "special education ghettos" American critics have predicted; rather it has led to a general increase in standards for all schools. According to studies by the European Agency for Development in Special Needs Education (EADSNE), the choice of an independent school in countries subsidizing private education is based far less on academic status than on a school's denominational affiliation, its political or social leanings, and, in some cases, the school's mix of instructional languages.

In a recently published review of education in Denmark, the Netherlands, and Sweden, EADSNE notes that private schools in these countries are "not generally considered elite" and that attending one confers "no added status or advantages." It is true in the case of the Netherlands that private schools have the legal right to impose admissions criteria, but in practice the vast majority follow an unrestrictive admissions policy. Sweden has seen a large increase in its number of private and religious schools since legalizing choice—an average annual growth of 15 percent—but this is from an extraordinarily low base created by a steeply progressive tax code that, prior to 1992, had made private education prohibitively expensive for all but the wealthiest families. Australia has a number of elite private boarding schools, which cater to parents of children from Hong Kong, Singapore, and Malaysia; but the domestic reality is that nearly half the enrollment in Australia's non-government schools is from families with a combined income of less than $27,000 (U.S.). In none of the 18 countries that in any way subsidize private or parochial education could the increase in the number of independent schools be described as a "massive flight" of the most capable students from public education.

Upon thoughtful consideration, the failure of school choice policies abroad to harm public education is not surprising. In the United States the concept of public funding of private education has become synonymous with the idea of a voucher system whereby parents receive a tuition coupon from the government for each of their children, which they are free to redeem at a school of their choosing. This equivalence between choice and vouchers in the American mind has allowed opponents of school choice to conjure up fearful scenarios in which wealthier families combine vouchers with their own resources to bid up and buy out limited slots at the most prestigious private schools.

Even if we put aside the appropriate counterargument—namely, that a free education marketplace would create as many good private schools as the public demanded—we have already seen that there are many ways other than vouchers to finance school choice, with as many protections for the poor and disabled as the state is willing to entertain. In Australia, where school choice was actually adopted as a populist reform in 1973 by a liberal-leaning Labor government, subsidies for private education are based on what is called a Social Economic Status (SES) model. Students attending private schools from wealthy towns receive assistance amounting to less than 25 percent of tuition, while students from poorer areas in the western part of the country can be reimbursed up to 97 percent. Technically speaking, school choice refers only to a method for making educators more accountable to parents—by empowering parents to choose their children's schools—not to any ideological bias involved in selecting among them any options for financing this method.

If there is a cautionary lesson to be learned from the experience of foreign countries, it comes from the United Kingdom, where in 1981 the parliament adopted the Assisted Places Scheme with the aim of providing private school tuition scholarships to 11-, 12-, and 13-year-old children from low-income families. By 1992 there were more than 26,000 voucher students attending almost 300 independent schools throughout England and Wales—and a separate parallel system had been established in Scotland.

Yet in spite of the program's apparent success, the annual enrollment cap of 5,000 was not raised, nor was there a serious effort to include children in their younger, more formative years. Instead, in 1988, Parliament enacted a more limited form of school choice, very similar to what Connecticut Sen. Joseph Lieberman and other Democrats are now advancing in the United States as a "moderate" alternative to a freer education marketplace. Under this "open enrollment" system all students were allowed to transfer between government-run schools on a space-available basis, but no funding could follow a student to private (what the English call "public") or religious schools, thus inhibiting the ability of education entrepreneurs to offer students real academic options.

The result of Britain's attempt to limit parental choice to government schools has been to create the very special education ghettos that opponents of school reform say they are against. "Popular schools in wealthy communities have devised many subtle ways to keep out expensive-to-educate students," observes Philip Garner, research professor in special education at Nottingham Trent University. Children with learning disabilities "are confined to failing schools in poorer districts, such as Liverpool, Tower Hamlets, and Hackney." In a telling indication of popular dissatisfaction with England's "moderate" approach to choice, the number of appeals brought before that country's special education tribunal reached 3 per week in the school year 1995–96. It was not until just before the last election, with polls showing a growing public anger over declining social services, that Parliament finally passed legislation allowing private companies and foundations to take over management of what the tabloids were calling "Britain's sink schools."

Inclusion and Achievement

So far we have seen that school choice is not only compatible with inclusion but may, under the right circumstances, be the most effective means of implementing it. Yet social inclusion is not a synonym for academic achievement. How, we must also ask, does a more competitive educational marketplace affect the intellectual development of learning-disabled students?

One clue comes from, of all places, the United States, where the same administrators who oppose choice for mainstream and moderately impaired children in their own schools tend overwhelmingly to favor private placements over public institutions for their towns' most difficult-to-educate students. According to Department of Education statistics, over 2 percent of the nation's learning-disabled population—100,700 students—are contracted out by local school boards to independent institutions, many operated by Catholics, Jews, Mennonites, Quakers, Lutherans, Baptists, Methodists, Presbyterians, and Episcopalians. Ironically, the states that rely most on private providers to teach the severely disabled have been among the staunchest opponents of market-based education reform: California, Connecticut, Illinois, Maryland, Massachusetts, New Jersey, New York, and Rhode Island.

American public school administrators are far less inclined to use private providers to teach students within their own walls; yet when they do, the results are instructive. In the school year 1999–2000, the school board of Hawthorne, California, hired Sylvan Learning Systems to offer remedial reading services to its learning-disabled students, while continuing to tutor normal children with regular teachers. According to the Hawthorne district's own standardized test, the special education students exceeded the gains of the non-special education students by five points for a total Normal Curve Equivalent (NCE) gain of nine. (NCEs are a common standard for measuring student progress in reading.)

Special education students who completed a similar program in Compton, California, during the same school year made similar gains.

The overall academic success of special-needs students in school choice countries has led the European Agency for Development in Special Needs Education to conclude that the policy mechanisms for providing services to the learning-disabled may be just as important to their intellectual and social development as any teaching technique. In its recently published *Seventeen Country Study of the Relationship Between Financing of Special Needs Education and Inclusion,* EADSNE found that monopolistic public school systems characterized by "direct input funding"—that is, upping the budget for every increase in the number of learning-disabled students—produced the least desirable outcomes. Conversely, school systems characterized by multiple service providers, decentralization, accountability to parents, and an emphasis on teaching over such bureaucratic procedures as diagnosis and categorization "seem to be the most successful" at helping the learning-disabled to grow into happy, productive adults.

Again, it is useful to consider specific countries. In Sweden—where, as we have seen, choice is encouraged only for mainstream students—a telling split has developed in measures of parental satisfaction with the educational system. In 1993, a poll conducted by Sweden's National Agency of Education concluded that "85 percent of Swedes value their new school choice rights," a clear indication that parents of mainstream children were pleased with the academic results. On the other hand, studies by the same agency showed that the confidence of parents of learning-disabled children in Sweden's special education services was eroding at a rapid pace. It is "alarming," concluded the NAE in its 1998 report, *Students in Need of Special Support,* "that parents of more than 100,000 schoolchildren feel that the school system does not have the means to give their children the support they may need."

Halfway around the world in New Zealand, where exceptional efforts have been made in recent years to ensure that special-needs students benefit from school choice, experts such as Dr. David Mitchell of the School of Education at the University of Waikato record significant progress in the treatment of learning disabilities. Over the past three years, he notes, New Zealand's special education system has moved "from being relatively ad hoc, unpredictable, uncoordinated, and nationally inconsistent to being relatively coherent, predictable, integrated, and consistent across the country. It is moving away from ... seeing the reasons for failure at school as residing in some defect or inadequacy within the student to seeing it as reflecting a mismatch between individual abilities and environmental opportunities."

In Australia, a 1998 study funded by the national Department of Education, Training, and Youth Affairs found that many intellectually and physically disabled students who received an inclusive education under the nation's school choice program were "achieving in literacy and [math skills] at the same levels as their peers and, in some cases, much better than their classmates." Because the overwhelming percentage of non-government schools in that country are religiously affiliated, the internationally respected Schonell Special Education Research Centre at the University of Queensland has begun a previously unthinkable study to determine the extent to which faith improves academic achievement in the learning-impaired.

Current Dissatisfactions

All of which suggests that the more American parents of learning-disabled children become knowledgeable about the benefits of school choice around the world, the more the advocates of the status quo may regret ever trying to exploit the issue of special education in the first place. After all, notes Thomas B. Fordham Foundation president Chester E. Finn, it's not as if parents of learning-disabled children are anywhere near being satisfied with the services public schools now provide. "America's special education program has an urgent special need of its own," he writes. "It is, in many ways, broken." Jay Matthews, education reporter for *The Washington Post*, agrees, noting that journalists, himself included, "have done a terrible job telling this story. Special education systems are often too confusing, too bureaucratic and too bound by privacy rules to yield much useful information." What research is available, he adds, "suggests that the special education system has led to widespread, if well-intentioned, misuse of tax dollars and has failed to help kids."

To appreciate the unexpected way in which parental dissatisfaction with current services may shape domestic education policy, consider the surprising evolution of the "A+ Plan," the statewide voucher program adopted by the Florida legislature in 1999. Although initially regarded by some as a muted reform because children were not entitled to a private education unless their public school had failed to meet minimum academic standards in only two of four years, the law did authorize a sweeping pilot program for learning-disabled students in Sarasota County. Under this test project, the only requirement for a special-needs child to transfer to a private school was that his parents express dissatisfaction over his progress at meeting the goals of his individualized instructional plan.

So popular was the pilot program that just one year later, state senator John McKay was able to pass an amendment to the original A+ Plan, allowing the Sarasota County provision to apply to the entire state. According to the new law, known as the McKay Scholarship Program, private schools taking on a special-needs child could recover from the government from $6,000 to $20,000, depending on the severity of the child's disability. The only caveat was that any school wanting to participate in the program had to accept all learning-disabled applicants. In the school year 2000–01, 105 private schools in 36 of Florida's 67 districts signed up to enroll more than 900 special education students. Over the current academic year (2001–02), Florida state officials estimate the number of learning-disabled students receiving assistance will quadruple to 4,000, while the number of participating schools will triple to more than 300.

Although researchers have yet to identify the precise reasons the expansion of the McKay Scholarship Program had such easy political sailing, anecdotal evidence suggests strong backing from the largest group of eligible families: those with moderately disabled children who, while continuing to be promoted with their classmates, were nevertheless floundering academically. "My child needed a choice, an alternative. [She] was lost in middle school," says the mother of a scholarship recipient from the western part of the state. "She was held back early on, and the district did not want to keep holding her back, so even though she was not learning, she was moved along." Black clergy from Florida's cities, where the percentage of fourth-graders unable to read can soar as high as 60 percent, were also outspoken advocates of the McKay Scholarship Program.

Interestingly, a similar alliance of middle-class parents and minority clergy seems to have coalesced behind President Bush's recently enacted "No Child Left Behind" education bill. While stripped of its initial tuition voucher proposal for mainstream schools, the legislation nevertheless retained its "supplemental services" provision, which makes parents at over 3,000 poorly performing schools nationwide eligible for federal funding of remedial tutoring at an independent school or even a private company of their choice. Essentially a remedial education voucher program, it lets parents decide how and where the funds will be used.

While the prospect of advocates for the learning-disabled leading the charge for school choice here in the United States will doubtless come as a shock to the teachers unions and their political allies, it is hardly without precedent. Much of the shift toward the privatization of public education in Europe and elsewhere has come from political activism on behalf of special-needs students.

Indeed, it can be argued that opponents of school choice and parents of the learning-disabled were never very likely to stick together in the first place. Unlike mainstream students, most of whom can survive one bad year of mediocre instruction, a special-needs child can be permanently damaged by a single incompetent teacher, whose tenured position is protected by the current public school monopoly. In the end, the parents of learning-disabled students have the same goal as all market-oriented school reformers: to make every educator accountable to the highest possible standards.

Barbara Miner  **NO**

Vouchers: Special Ed
Students Need Not Apply

Susan Endress is into her second decade of demanding, cajoling, threatening, and doing whatever it takes to ensure that Milwaukee schools honor the rights of special education students.

On a recent afternoon, she shakes her head in weary frustration as she reads a summary of the special ed services provided (or, more likely, not provided) by Milwaukee voucher schools that receive public dollars yet operate as private schools.

"What do they mean, they can't serve children more than a year below grade level?" she says of one school's description. "That's terrible."

"Oh, here's a good one," she says as she continues reading. "'We cannot serve wheelchair-bound students.' And look at this one, it cannot serve 'students who are unable to climb stairs.'" She turns to a young man in a wheelchair working in the office with her at Wisconsin FACETS, a special education advocacy and support group for families. "Make sure you're bound to your wheelchair," she tells him good-naturedly. "And better learn to climb stairs."

Her moment of humor over, Endress turns serious again.

"You have to remember, it's only been a little over 25 years that special needs children have even had the right to attend a public school," she says. "And here we're moving backwards with the voucher schools, not forward. I'm personally scared to death of where this might lead."

Milwaukee's voucher program, the country's oldest, has long been seen as a prototype for what, in essence, is a conservative strategy to privatize education under the guise of "choice." With the U.S. Congress poised to start the first federally funded voucher program... in the Washington, D.C., schools, vouchers have once again jumped to the fore of educational debate.

Although Milwaukee's voucher schools receive tax dollars, they operate as private schools and thus can ignore almost all of the requirements and accountability measures that public schools must follow. They do not, for example, have to hire certified teachers, nor administer the same tests as public schools, nor report their students' academic achievement.

Nor do they have to provide the special education services required of public schools. While voucher supporters portray vouchers as a new Civil Rights Movement, disability activists see a different reality.

From *Rethinking Schools Online*, vol. 18, no. 2, Winter 2003. Copyright © 2003 by Rethinking Schools, Ltd. Reprinted by permission of the author.

Jim Ward, president of ADA Watch and the National Coalition for Disability Rights in Washington, D.C., warns that voucher programs threaten the rights of students with special needs. He cites a 1998 survey by the U.S. Department of Education that between 70 and 85 percent of private schools in large inner cities would "definitely or probably" not participate in a voucher program if required to accept "students with special needs such as learning disabilities, limited English proficiency, or low achievement." Among religious schools, the figure was 86 percent.

"The Supreme Court's 1954 *Brown vs. Board of Education* decision struck down 'separate but equal' schools, but voucher programs threaten to usher in a new form of segregation," Ward warns.

Milwaukee's voucher program shows that Ward's fears are well-founded. At a time when the percentage of special education students in the Milwaukee Public Schools (MPS) hovers around 16 percent and is projected to reach 19 percent by 2007, voucher schools are not legally obliged to provide special education services to their students.

The only official data on special ed and Milwaukee voucher schools is from a 2000 report by the Wisconsin Legislative Audit Bureau. It found that only 3 percent of the students in voucher schools in 1998-99 had previously been identified as needing special education services. It also noted that voucher schools likely served children with "lower-cost" needs such as speech, language, and learning disabilities.

Current data is sketchy, at best, because voucher schools do not have to collect or release information. The little information that's available paints a bleak picture.

A voluntary, unaudited survey by the Public Policy Forum in October 2002 found that almost half of the voucher schools provide no special ed services, even for students with mild learning disabilities. A significant number reported programs such as "Title I" or "smaller classes" that are generally not considered special education services. Some note that they work with MPS, which provides the special education services. One school said that special needs students are served through its "Jesus Cares Ministry."

A look at a website hosted by the University of Wisconsin-Milwaukee (www.uwm.edu/EPIC) is even more revealing. The site has information on most Milwaukee schools, private and public, and has a section where schools report on "categories of students which the school cannot serve." Some voucher schools do not report anything. Or, like Marquette University High School, they say the information is "n/a."

Many voucher schools succinctly note that they cannot serve "LD, ED, children with physical disabilities"—referring to learning disabled (LD) and emotionally disabled (ED). Some explanations are more elaborate. Blessed Sacrament, for example, says: "We believe that students who are 2-3 years below grade level cannot be realistically brought up to grade level because we do not have a tutorial/learning center to accommodate their needs. Students who have severe emotional or behavioral problems need specific programs to assist them—we do not have a counselor or social worker."

Some schools send mixed messages. St. Adelbert says: "We do not have specific services for ED students though we do have ED students. We do not have an elevator. However, we do have physically disabled students. We do have sight- and hearing-impaired students. We cannot service severe MR [mental retardation]."

A few voucher schools note they provide some special ed services, in particular for children with mild learning or physical disabilities. St. Gregory the Great, for instance, says, "We are able to accommodate most children with learning disabilities."

Services for special education students seem to be particularly limited at voucher high schools. Messmer, which had 398 voucher students last year, specifically notes on the EPIC website that it has "no special [ed] classes." Learning Enterprise, which had 175 voucher students, likewise said it cannot serve special education students. Pius XI, meanwhile, with 199 voucher students last year, is making an effort. While it says it cannot serve ED or EMR [educable mentally retarded] students, it provides services for LD students.

The Milwaukee voucher program is expected to cost about $76 million in taxpayer dollars this year, bringing the total to almost $350 million since its inception in 1990. This year it will serve almost 13,000 students, providing up to $5,882 for each child.

Funding Special Ed

Voucher proponents sometimes argue that voucher schools do not provide special education services because they do not get money to do so. But Endress of Wisconsin FACETS doesn't buy the money argument, whether it comes from public schools, charter schools, or voucher schools.

She understands why all schools may not be equipped to deal with students needing a full-time aide, such as medically fragile students or those with multiple physical, emotional, and medical needs. But such students are the exception, she says. Most special education students can be served without extraordinary accommodations.

"The main thing they have to do is have a teacher on staff that is licensed in special education that is cross categorical," she says. "There is no reason why these voucher schools can't have just one teacher. Think of all the support they could provide not just the students but also other teachers. To me, it just makes good educational sense."

The money argument assumes that public schools receive adequate funding for special education. But they don't. In MPS, for example, special ed spending is about $164 million this year, according to Michelle Nate, director of finance. Since the state and federal governments reimburse only 66 percent of that money, MPS must take $55 million from its overall budget to fund special education.

The Milwaukee Archdiocese, which oversees the largest bloc of voucher schools, does not have figures on special education. Nor does the Archdiocese provide special education teachers for its schools. Dave Prothero, superintendent for the Milwaukee Archdiocesan schools, says special education issues are dealt with at the school level. "Any parent that calls and says that their child has special needs, the response will be, 'Please come in to the school and talk about the specific needs of your child to see if we can meet those needs.'"

Special education experts, based on anecdotal evidence, say this often means that special ed children are "counseled out" of applying, or encouraged to leave if already enrolled, on the grounds that the school is not a good match.

"I think they are oftentimes discouraged from the very beginning," says Dennis Oulahan, an MPS teacher who provides special education assessments for bilingual children in both private and public schools. "The message might be, 'Don't apply.'"

Voucher schools are legally prohibited from discriminating in admissions against children with special needs and are only required to provide services that require "minor adjustments." Until the definition of "minor adjustments" is tested in the courts, it is doubtful that voucher schools will significantly change their practice.

As Oulahan notes, "Voucher schools don't have to deal with special ed. They are private schools. And as long as they don't have to deal with it, I don't think they are going to volunteer."

POSTSCRIPT

Does School Choice Open Doors for Students With Disabilities?

Project SEARCH, a three-year qualitative study of school choice policies and practices in 15 states (Rhim and McLaughlin, 2001), discovered that the inventiveness encouraged in charter schools can create an environment in which some students with some mild to moderate disabilities will flourish. However, sometimes this very focus can create "intentional and unintentional barriers."

Competing legislation complicates the situation. IDEA mandates that public schools adapt curriculum and instruction to ensure the meaningful participation of every child with a disability. School choice laws charge alternative programs to create break-the-mold structures and prove their success through solid test scores. One entity must be flexible to all students; the other must focus on results (Howe and Welner, 2002). Can both mandates be satisfied in any one school?

Lewis notes that parents of students with disabilities have long sought unique programs. He asserts that often, responsive options have been found in private special education schools—resulting in de facto segregation from typical schools. The choice between separation for special schooling and inclusion with typical peers is difficult. In fact, he predicts that these parents, who often find fault with their own district's education, will be major forces in extending the boundaries of both school choice and inclusion.

Miner also brings compelling experiences to light. She cites how one city's choice options do not extend to students who need specialized instruction or attention. And she sees dangerous echoes of the way schools were before special education law, when parents could be told that there was no place for their child in the educational system.

The Enrollment Options Project has been studying Minnesota's school choice experiences (Lange and Lehr, 2000). Parents of students with disabilities expressed pleasure with their child's charter school, citing the extensive series available. The only catch is that directors of these very same schools reported offering fewer services than the public schools. Is it possible that the environment counted as a "service," creating opportunities for success and support?

The challenge of understanding the "real story" is also evident in a 1998 publication from the U.S. Department of Education Office of Educational Research and Improvement. *Charter Schools and Students With Disabilities: Review of Existing Data* presents an extensive compilation of studies and reports, along with the caveat that the authors do not claim to evaluate or substantiate the validity of the referenced articles. Few compare practices across states. Many findings are contradictory. While one study maintains that students with disabilities are underenrolled in charter schools, another counters that they are simply undercounted or underreported. While some papers mention special education costs as prohibitive, the authors find no evidence that such expenses have ever threatened the financial existence of a school. They do, however, note that some charter school administrators are not skilled in seeking the federal funds to which they may be entitled. On still another front, some studies mention parental satisfaction with the responsiveness of charter schools, while others find that a single instructional approach may not respond to the needs of diverse learners.

The only clear answer is that there are many answers. And many questions. Will school choice creators and parents of children with disabilities discover creative ways to teach children? Will the corporate owners of private programs enforce admissions criteria so they can demonstrate increased test scores? Will students with unique and significant special education needs find themselves unable to access options that are open to their "typical" peers, or will their current access to a range of placement options be broad enough?

ISSUE 6

Do Students with Disabilities Threaten Effective School Discipline?

YES: Kay S. Hymowitz, from "Who Killed School Discipline?" *The City Journal* (Spring 2000)

NO: James A. Taylor and Richard A. Baker, Jr., from "Discipline and the Special Education Student," *Educational Leadership* (January 2002)

ISSUE SUMMARY

YES: Kay S. Hymowitz, a regular contributing editor to *The City Journal* (published by The Manhattan Institute), cites inclusive educational programming for students with disabilities and the legal limitations of IDEA as primary contributors to the destruction of effective discipline in today's schools.

NO: James A. Taylor and Richard A. Baker, Jr., president and vice president of Edleaders.com, respectively, believe that school administrators who design and implement an effective disciplinary code that applies to all students, including those with disabilities, can create a more orderly environment for everyone.

Barely a week goes by without reading about violence in schools. Politicians, school boards, teachers, and parents are all concerned. If there hasn't been a recent incident, then the media cover efforts to anticipate and prevent violence: more metal detectors, recent lock-down drills, and strengthened zero-tolerance policies.

When the local press covers an incident that has affected a community, it is not unusual to hear that the students involved experienced different consequences. Frequently, there is a comment that some of the youngsters are covered by special education and are remaining in school pending further evaluations, while their peers are given suspensions. Or that some suspensions have been revoked while parents seek evaluations to see if a disability could have caused the offending behavior. These situations elicit feelings of frustration, unfairness, and confusion.

IDEA97 significantly changed the procedures administrators have to follow in disciplining students with disabilities. The changes attempted to address two goals: (1) to mesh special education laws with the Gun Free Schools Act, designed to protect against weapons in schools, and (2) to ensure that, while doing so, those with documented disabilities are not ejected from school because of behavior beyond their control, thereby losing access to the free and appropriate public education to which they are entitled.

Despite the opinions of some, IDEA does not prohibit disciplining students with disabilities. IDEA does require specific actions. If behavior problems are part of a student's disability, the IEP must include services geared to improve this area. If a student's disability impacts her ability to adhere to the behavior code (perhaps because the child has significant cognitive limitations and simply cannot comprehend some of the standards), alternate disciplinary expectations and interventions need to be stipulated.

If punishable behavior occurs repeatedly, educators must conduct a functional behavioral assessment (FBA) to determine the cause of a behavior. Specific steps to address this behavior must be included in the IEP. Most importantly, if long-term suspensions are considered, the school must conduct a manifestation determination to learn if the behavior is a direct result of the disability, and thus, outside the student's control. If this is the case, appropriate changes in the educational program must be made.

Kay S. Hymowitz, an author who frequently writes about public policy issues in New York, laments that such legalistic processes have turned principals into "psychobabble-spouting" bureaucrats, incapable of preventing harm or maintaining the most basic order in schools.

James A Taylor and Richard A. Baker, Jr. assert that such beliefs are in error. They maintain that principals who understand the law, and implement an effective disciplinary code, will foster an improved climate for all students. With such standards in place, administrators actually have a broad array of actions at their disposal.

As you read these articles, think about situations that have occurred in your own school or town. Do teachers and principals think that all students must follow the same behavior standards, or do they think there must always be special treatment for students with disabilities? Seek out schools with reputations for differing climates. Talk to the teachers. Do you observe differences in the way behavioral expectations are communicated? Are all students treated fairly?

YES

Kay S. Hymowitz

Who Killed School Discipline?

Ask Americans what worries them most about the public schools, and the answer might surprise you: discipline. For several decades now, poll after poll shows it topping the list of parents' concerns. Recent news stories—from the Columbine massacre to Jesse Jackson's protests against the expulsion of six brawling Decatur, Illinois, high school students to the killing of one Flint, Michigan, six-year-old by another—guarantee that the issue won't lose its urgency any time soon.

Though fortunately only a small percentage of schools will ever experience real violence, the public's sense that something has gone drastically wrong with school discipline isn't mistaken. Over the past 30 years or so, the courts and the federal government have hacked away at the power of educators to maintain a safe and civil school environment. Rigid school bureaucracies and psychobabble-spouting "experts" have twisted such authority as remains into alien—and alienating—shapes, so that kids today are more likely than ever to go to disorderly schools, whose only answers to the disorder are ham-fisted rules and therapeutic techniques designed to manipulate students' behavior, rather than to initiate them into a genuine civil and moral order. What's been lost is educators' crucial role of passing on cultural values to the young and instructing them in how to behave through innumerable small daily lessons and examples. If the children become disruptive and disengaged, who can be surprised?

School discipline today would be a tougher problem than ever, even without all these changes, because of the nationwide increase of troubled families and disorderly kids. Some schools, especially those in inner cities, even have students who are literally violent felons. High school principal Nora Rosensweig of Green Acres, Florida, estimates that she has had 20 to 25 such felons in her school over the last three years, several of them sporting the electronic ankle bracelets that keep track of paroled criminals. "The impact that one of those students has on 100 kids is amazing," Rosensweig observes. Some students, she says, find them frightening. Others, intrigued, see them as rebel heroes.

But today principals lack the tools they used to have for dealing even with the unruliest kids. Formerly, they could expel such kids permanently or send them to special schools for the hard-to-discipline. The special schools have largely vanished, and state education laws usually don't allow for permanent expulsion. So at best a school might manage to transfer a student felon elsewhere in the same district. New York City principals sometimes engage in a black-humored game of exchanging these "Fulbright Scholars," as they jokingly call them: "I'll take two of yours, if you take one of mine, and you'll owe me."

Educators today also find their hands tied when dealing with another disruptive—and much larger—group of pupils, those covered by the 1975 Individuals with Disabilities Education Act (IDEA). This law, which mandates that schools provide a "free and appropriate education" for children regardless of disability—and provide it, moreover, within regular classrooms whenever humanly possible—effectively strips educators of the authority to transfer or to suspend for long periods any student classified as needing special education.

This wouldn't matter if special education included mainly the wheelchair-bound or deaf students whom we ordinarily think of as disabled. But it doesn't. Over the past several decades, the number of children classified under the vaguely defined disability categories of "learning disability" and "emotional disturbance" has exploded. Many of these kids are those once just called "unmanageable" or "antisocial": part of the legal definition of emotional disturbance is "an inability to build or maintain satisfactory interpersonal relationships with peers and teachers"—in other words, to be part of an orderly community. Prosecutors will tell you that disproportionate numbers of the juvenile criminals they now see are special-ed students.

With IDEA restrictions hampering them, school officials can't respond forcefully when these kids get into fights, curse teachers, or even put students and staff at serious risk, as too often happens. One example captures the law's absurdity. School officials in Connecticut caught one student passing a gun to another on school premises. One, a regular student, received a yearlong suspension, as federal law requires. The other, disabled (he stuttered), received just a 45-day suspension and special, individualized services, as IDEA requires. Most times, though, schools can't get even a 45-day respite from the chaos these kids can unleash. "They are free to do things in school that will land them in jail when they graduate," says Bruce Hunter, an official of the American Association of School Administrators. Laments Julie Lewis, staff attorney for the National School Boards Association: "We have examples of kids who have sexually assaulted their teacher and are then returned to the classroom."

⋅❀⋅

Discipline in the schools isn't primarily about expelling sex offenders and kids who pack guns, of course. Most of the time, what's involved is the "get your feet off the table" or "don't whisper in class" kind of discipline that allows teachers to assume that kids will follow the commonplace directions they give hundreds of times daily. Thanks to two Supreme Court decisions of the late 1960s and the 1970s, though, this everyday authority has come under attack, too.

The first decision, *Tinker v. Des Moines School District*, came about in 1969, after a principal suspended five high school students for wearing black armbands in protest against the Vietnam War. *Tinker* found that the school had violated students' free-speech rights. "It can hardly be argued," wrote Justice Abe Fortas for the majority, "that students or teachers shed their constitutional rights to free speech or expression at the schoolhouse gate." Schools cannot be "enclaves of totalitarianism" nor can officials have "absolute authority over their students," the court solemnly concluded.

Quite possibly the principal in *Tinker* made an error in judgment. But by making matters of school discipline a constitutional issue, the court has left educators fumbling their way through everyday disciplinary encounters with kids ever since. "At each elementary and middle school door, you have some guy making a constitutional decision every day," observes Jeff Krausman, legal counsel to several Iowa school districts. Suppose, says Krausman by way of example, that a student shows up at school wearing a T-shirt emblazoned WHITE POWER. The principal wants to send the kid home to change, but he's not sure it's within his authority to do so, so he calls the superintendent. The superintendent is also unsure, so he calls the district's lawyer. The lawyer's concern, though, isn't that the child has breached the boundaries of respect and tolerance, and needs an adult to tell him so, but whether disciplining the student would violate the First Amendment. Is this, in other words, literally a federal case?

And that's not easy to answer. "Where do you draw the line?" Krausman asks. "Some lawyers say you should have to prove that something is "significantly disruptive." But in Iowa you might have a hard time proving that a T-shirt saying WHITE POWER or ASIANS ARE GEEKS is significantly disruptive." Meanwhile, educators' power to instill civility and order in school dissolves into tendentious debates over the exact meaning of legal terms like "significantly disruptive."

In 1975, the Supreme Court hampered school officials' authority yet further in *Goss v. Lopez*, a decision that expanded the due-process rights of students. *Goss* concerned several students suspended for brawling in the school lunchroom. Though the principal who suspended them actually witnessed the fight himself, the court concluded that he had failed to give the students an adequate hearing before lowering the boom. Students, pronounced the court, are citizens with a property right to their education. To deny that right requires, at the least, an informal hearing with notice, witnesses, and the like; suspensions for longer than ten days might require even more formal procedures.

Following *Tinker's* lead, *Goss* brought lawyers and judges deeper inside the schoolhouse. You want to suspend a violent troublemaker? Because of Goss, you now had to ask: Would a judge find your procedures satisfactory? Would he agree that you have enough witnesses? The appropriate documentation? To suspend a student became a time-consuming and frustrating business.

Students soon learned that, if a school official does something they don't like, they can sue him, or at least threaten to do so. New York City special-ed teacher Jeffrey Gerstel's story is sadly typical. Last year, Gerstel pulled a student out of his classroom as he was threatening to kill the assistant teacher. The boy collided with a bookcase and cut his back, though not badly enough to need medical attention. Even so, Gerstel found himself at a hearing, facing the student's indignant mother, who wanted to sue, and three "emotionally disturbed adolescents"—classmates of the boy—who witnessed the scuffle. The mother soon settled the dispute out of court and sent her son back to Gerstel's classroom. But by then, Gerstel had lost the confidence that he needed to handle a roomful of volatile teenagers, and the kids knew it. For the rest of the year, they taunted him: "I'm going to get my mother up here and bring you up on charges."

In another typical recent case, a Saint Charles, Missouri, high schooler running for student council handed out condoms as a way of drumming up votes. The school suspended him. He promptly sued on free-speech grounds; in previous student council elections, he whined, candidates had handed out candy. Though he lost his case, his ability to stymie adults in such a matter, even if only temporarily, could not but give him an enlarged sense of his power against the school authorities: his adolescent fantasy of rebellion had come true.

These days, school lawyers will tell you, this problem is clearing up: in recent years, they point out, the courts have usually sided with schools in discipline cases, as they did in Missouri. But the damage done by *Tinker, Goss,* and their ilk isn't so easily undone. Lawsuits are expensive and time-consuming, even if you win. More important, the mere potential for a lawsuit shrinks the adult in the child's eyes. It transforms the person who should be the teacher and the representative of society's moral and cultural values into a civil servant who may or may not please the young, rights-armed citizen. The natural relationship between adult and child begins to crumble.

The architects of IDEA, *Tinker,* and *Goss,* of course, thought of themselves as progressive reformers, designing fairer, more responsive schools. Introducing the rights of free speech and due process, they imagined, would ensure that school officials would make fewer "arbitrary and capricious" decisions. But lawmakers failed to see how they were radically destabilizing traditional relations between adults and children and thus eroding school discipline.

•◦⟨◉⟩◦•

School bureaucracies have struggled to restore the discipline that the courts and federal laws have taken away, but their efforts have only alienated students and undermined adult authority even more. Their first stratagem has been to bring in the lawyers to help them craft regulations, policies, and procedures. "If you have a law, you'd better have a policy," warns Julie Lewis, staff attorney for the American School Boards Association. These legalistic rules, designed more to avoid future lawsuits than to establish classroom order, are inevitably abstract and inflexible. Understandably, they inspire a certain contempt from students.

Putting them into practice often gives rise to the arbitrary and capricious decisions that lawmakers originally wanted to thwart. Take "zero tolerance" policies mandating automatic suspension of students for the worst offenses. These proliferated in the wake of Congress's 1994 Gun-Free Schools Act, which required school districts to boot out for a full year students caught with firearms. Many state and local boards, fearful that the federal law and the growing public clamor for safe schools could spawn a new generation of future lawsuits, fell into a kind of bureaucratic mania. Why not require suspension for *any* weapon—a nail file, a plastic Nerf gun? Common sense went out the window, and suspensions multiplied.

Other districts wrote up new anti-weapon codes as precise and defensive as any corporate merger agreement. These efforts, however, ended up making educators look more obtuse. When a New York City high school student came to school with a metal-spiked ball whose sole purpose could only be to maim classmates, he wasn't suspended: metal-spiked balls weren't on the superintendent's detailed list of proscribed weapons. Suspend him, and he might sue you for being arbitrary and capricious.

Worse, the influence of lawyers over school discipline means that educators speak to children in an unrecognizable language, far removed from the straight talk about right and wrong that most children crave. A sample policy listed in "Keep Schools Safe," a pamphlet co-published by the National Attorneys General and the National School Boards Association (a partnership that itself says much about the character of American school discipline today), offers characteristically legalistic language: "I acknowledge and understand that 1. Student lockers are the property of the school system. 2. Student lockers remain at all times under the control of the school system. 3. I am expected to assume full responsibility for my school locker." Students correctly sense that what lies behind such desiccated language is not a moral worldview and a concern for their well-being and character but fear of lawsuits.

⋅⟨◉⟩⋅

When educators aren't talking like lawyers, they're sounding like therapists, for they've called in the psychobabblers and psychologists from the nation's ed schools and academic departments of psychology to reinforce the attorneys in helping them reestablish school discipline. School bureaucrats have been falling over one another in their rush to implement trendy-sounding "research-based programs"—emotional literacy training, anti-bullying workshops, violence prevention curriculums, and the like—as "preventive measures" and "early interventions" for various school discipline problems. Of dubious efficacy, these grimly utilitarian nostrums seek to control behavior in the crudest, most mechanical way. Nowhere is there any indication that adults are instilling in the young qualities they believe in and consider integral to a good life and a decent community. Kids find little that their innate sociality and longing for meaning can respond to.

Typical is "Second Step," a widely used safety program from a Seattle-based nonprofit. According to its architects, the goals of "Second Step" are "to reduce impulsive and aggressive behavior in children, teach social and emotional skills, and build self-esteem." Like many such therapeutic programs, it recommends role-playing games, breathing exercises, and learning to "identify feelings," "manage anger," and "solve problems." The universal moral values of self-control, self-respect, and respect for others shrink to mere "skills," as scripted and mechanical as a computer program.

In this leaden spirit, the National Association of School Psychologists newsletter, *Communiqué*, proposes a "Caring Habit of the Month Adventure," a program now in use in Aliquippa Middle School near Pittsburgh. Each month, school officials adorn school hallways with posters and stickers that promote a different caring habit or "skill." The skittish avoidance of moral language is a giveaway: this is a program more in love with behavioral technique than inducting children into moral consciousness. It's not surprising to find that *Communiqué* recommends dedicating a month to each "skill," because "[r]esearchers say a month is about the length of time it takes to make a habit out of consistently repeated action."

The legal, bureaucratic, and therapeutic efforts make up what Senator McCain would call an "iron triangle," each side reinforcing the others. Consider the fallout from last year's Supreme Court decision *Davis v. Monroe County School District*, which held that school districts could be liable for damages resulting from student-on-student sexual harassment. Now every school district in the country is preparing an arsenal to protect itself against future lawsuits: talking to lawyers, developing bureaucratic policies, and calling in therapeutic consultants or even full-time "gender specialists" to show a "proactive" effort to stamp out harassment. Experts at universities across the U.S. are contentedly churning out the predictable curriculums, with such names as "Flirting and Hurting" and "Safe Date," as cloying and suspect to any normal adolescent as to a grownup.

❦

The full consequence of these dramatic changes has been to prevent principals and teachers from creating the kind of moral community that is the most powerful and dependable guarantor of good discipline ever devised. When things work as they should—in the traditional manner familiar all over the world and across the ages—principals forge a cohesive society with very clear shared values, whose observance confers a sense of worth on all those who subscribe to them. People behave morally primarily because they assent to the standards of the group, not because they fear punishment. A community of shared values cannot be legalistic or bureaucratic or based on moronic behavior exercises; it must be personal, enforced by the sense that the authority figure is protective, benevolent, and worthy of respect.

That's why good principals have to be a constant, palpable presence, out in the hallways, in the classrooms, in the cafeteria, enforcing and modeling for students and staff the moral ethos of the school. They're there, long before the school day begins and long after it ends; they know students' names, joke with them, and encourage them; and they don't let little things go—a nasty put-down between students, a profanity uttered in irritation, even a belt missing from a school uniform. They know which infraction takes only a gentle reminder and which a more forceful response—because they have a clear scale of values and they know their students. They work with their entire staff, from teachers to bus drivers, to enlist them in their efforts.

For such principals, safety is of course a key concern. Frank Mickens, a wonderful principal of a big high school in a tough Brooklyn neighborhood, posts 17 staff members in the blocks near the school during dismissal time, while he sits in his car by the subway station, in order to keep students from fighting and bullies from picking on smaller or less aggressive children. Such measures go beyond reducing injuries. When students believe that the adults around them are not only fair but genuinely concerned with protecting them, the school can become a community that, like a good family, inspires affection, trust—and the longing to please.

◄◉►

But how can you create such a school if you have to make students sit next to felons or a kid transferred to your school because he likes to carry a box cutter in his pocket? June Arnette, Associate Director of the National School Safety Center, reports that, after Columbine, her office received numerous e-mails from students who said they wouldn't bother reporting kids who had made threats or carried weapons because they didn't think teachers or principals would do anything about them. A number of studies show that school officials rarely do anything about bullies.

How can you convince kids that you are interested in their well-being when from day one of the school year you feel bureaucratic pressure to speak to them in legalistic or quasi-therapeutic gobbledygook rather than a simple, moral language that they can understand? How can you inspire students' trust when you're not sure whether you can prevent a kid from wearing a WHITE POWER T-shirt or stop him from cursing at the teacher? It becomes virtually impossible, requiring heroic effort. Even when good principals come along and try to create a vibrant school culture, they are likely to leave for a new job before they have been able to effect any change.

Since heroes are few, most principals tend to become what John Chubb and Terry Moe in *Politics, Markets and American Schools* call "lower level managers," administering decisions made from above. Teachers often grumble that principals, perhaps enervated by their loss of authority, retreat into their offices, where they hold meetings and shuffle papers. It's not that they don't make a show of setting up "clear rules and expectations," as educators commonly call it, but they are understandably in a defensive mood. "Don't touch anyone. Mind your own business," was the way one New York City elementary school principal summed up her profound thinking on the subject.

In tough middle and high schools presided over by such functionaries, this defensive attitude is pervasive among teachers. "Protect yourself," one New York City high school teacher describes the reigning spirit. "If kids are fighting, stand back. Call a supervisor or a security guard. Don't get involved."

That teachers are asked to rely for the safety of their students on security guards—figures unknown to schools 30 years ago—says much about the wreckage of both adult-child relations and of the school as a civil community. It also serves as a grim reminder that when adults withdraw from the thousand daily encouragements, reminders, and scoldings required to socialize children, authoritarian measures are all that's left.

The effect of the collapse of adult authority on kids is practically to guarantee their mistrust and alienation. Schools in this country, particularly high schools, tend to become what sociologist James Coleman called an "adolescent society," dominated by concern with dating, sex, and consumerism. The loss of adult guidance makes it certain that adolescent society—more powerful than ever, if we're to believe TV shows like *Freaks and Geeks* and *Popular*—will continue in its sovereignty. Quaking before the threat of lawsuits and without support from their superiors, educators hesitate to assert the most basic civic and moral values that might pose a challenge to the crude and status-crazed peer culture. When they do talk, it is in a language that doesn't make any sense to kids and cannot possibly compel their respect.

◄◉►

Though under the current system it's easy to lose sight of this truth, there's nothing particularly complex about defining moral expectations for children. At one successful inner-city middle school I visited, a sign on the walls said, WORK HARD, BE KIND; BE KIND, WORK HARD: and if the school can instill just those two values, it will have accomplished about all we could ask. Educators who talk like this grasp that a coherent and meaningful moral environment is what socializes children best. Paul Vallas, CEO of the Chicago public schools, has introduced character education, community service requirements, and a daily recitation of the Pledge of Allegiance. "It's the Greek in me," explains Vallas. "I take Aristotle's approach to education. We are teaching kids to be citizens." Two and a half millennia later, Aristotle's approach remains a surer recipe for disciplined schools than all the belawyered conduct codes and all the trendy life-skills programs that the courts and the bureaucrats have given us.

James A. Taylor and
Richard A. Baker, Jr.

 **NO**

Discipline and the Special Education Student

John is a special education student who attends only one resource class each day. Otherwise, he participates in regular education classes. During English class, the teacher corrects him for disruptive behavior, but he continues to make inappropriate comments. The teacher asks him to step into the hallway so that she can address his behavior privately. As she begins speaking to him, he walks away, then turns to her and says, "Shut up, you bitch." The teacher submits a referral to the assistant principal, who consults the district handbook and recommends that John spend three days in the supervised suspension center.

Because of John's status as a special education student, however, personnel at the district level—without conducting a hearing or a meeting with John's individualized education program (IEP) team—allow John to spend the three days at home. The district's concern is with John's protections under the Individuals with Disabilities Education Act. But is the district's action in compliance with federal law?

The general belief among teachers and administrators is that the Individuals with Disabilities Education Act insulates special education students from experiencing consequences for their disciplinary infractions and sets them apart from the school's regular disciplinary procedures. Horror stories abound about students whose behavior, like John's, threatens the safety of staff and students, disrupting learning for themselves and other students.

The misperception that educators are supposed to tolerate such behavior is largely the result of the unclear administrative procedures outlined under the Education for All Handicapped Children Act of 1975 (Public Law 94-142) and the Supreme Court decision in *Honig v. Doe* (1988). Aware of these unclear procedures and educators' common misunderstanding of the law, the U.S. Congress took care, when reauthorizing the Education for All Handicapped Children Act as the Individuals with Disabilities Education Act in 1990 (Public Law 101-476) and 1997 (Public Law 105-17), to address the issue of appropriate disciplinary procedures for special education students. Educators need to know the provisions of the current law as they develop schoolwide discipline plans and the individualized education programs required for special education students.

From *Educational Leadership*, December 2001/January 2002, pp. 28-30. Reprinted with permission of the Association for Supervision and Curriculum Development (ASCD). © 2001 by ASCD. All rights reserved.

The 1997 Individuals with Disabilities Education Act amendments clarify that the only disciplinary procedure that applies exclusively to special education students is the determination of a long-term change of placement—that is, a long-term suspension or removal to an alternative school setting. If the disciplinary measure for behavior infractions lasts for 10 or fewer days, and 45 or fewer days for weapon or drug infractions, the special education student receives the same treatment that students without disabilities receive. If, however, the special education student's suspensions are recurrent and add up to more than 10 days in a school year or more than 45 days for a serious infraction, the local education agency must conduct an assessment of the student's behavior and implement an intervention plan to address the student's behavior problems.

After conducting classroom observations and closely examining the evaluation of the student's disability and the implementation of the student's individualized education program, a committee designated by the local education agency must decide whether or not the student's behavior is a manifestation of the student's disability. If the committee determines that it is, the student's IEP team must immediately rewrite the student's program to correct the behavior. If the committee determines that the behavior is not a manifestation of the disability, the child must be disciplined "in the same manner . . . applied to children without disabilities" (Individuals with Disabilities Education Act, 20 U.S.C. § 1415 [k][5]).

In the case of John, the district should have applied the same disciplinary measures that it applies to students without disabilities. If the district plans to treat John differently, or if the behavior is recurrent and disciplinary measures have exceeded 10 days, the district must hold a meeting with the IEP team to determine whether this behavior is a manifestation of John's disability. If the team decides that it is not a result of the disability, the district must assign the same disciplinary consequences to John that it assigns to students without disabilities.

A Discipline Policy for All Students

To meet the federal standard, schools need a humane and just administration of discipline that respects and protects all students' rights to a free and public education. Comprehensive discipline guidelines must cover the treatment of students with and without disabilities. Moreover, the discipline plan must do more than take corrective action for offenses; it must also prevent discipline problems and support positive behavior (Charles, 1999).

As administrators and IEP teams develop behavioral intervention plans for students with disabilities, they should keep in mind the overall goal of implementing a schoolwide discipline system that is more than merely corrective. Special education students must understand that they are subject to the same disciplinary measures as other students. Such practices as before-school and after-school detentions, weekend detentions, additional written work, or required community service, commonly found in school discipline plans, do not create a change in special education placement and may serve as corrective measures for disciplinary infractions that are not directly related to the safety of fellow students or disturbance of the learning environment. Integrating these alternatives into behavioral intervention plans for special education students reminds them of the consequences of their choices. The discipline plan for all students should also incorporate preventive and supportive discipline measures.

Preventive Discipline

Preventive discipline promotes behaviors that are beneficial to the learning environment. By affirming and practicing them and reflecting on their meaning, everyone can practice showing concern, modeling courtesy, and supporting one another. Translating classroom rules and procedures into affirmative "we" statements to which the students and teachers commit themselves helps to identify good behaviors and strengthens the sense of belonging that both learners and adults need.

For example, Mr. Boudreaux has taught 7th graders for several years and knows that they will enter the classroom in an energetic, boisterous manner. Without a preventive discipline plan, the students will take a long time to settle down and focus on the lesson. Mr. Boudreaux, however, meets the students at the door and requires them to enter according to a specific procedure. First, he says, we enter in silence, then go to the materials shelf, read the assignments on the board, and assemble our materials. Instruction begins within three minutes of classroom entry, with all students having materials in place. In this way, Mr. Boudreaux meets all students' need for structure, limits, and routine.

Learning experiences that are worthwhile and enjoyable provide the foundation of a quality preventive discipline plan. Three elements—fun, focus, and energy—are essential components of a preventive discipline plan (Taylor & Baker, 2001), particularly for students with disabilities, whose classes and activities are often unchallenging and devoid of opportunities for creative expression.

Supportive Discipline

Supportive discipline helps students channel their own behaviors productively. As a weight lifter needs a spotter to provide support during a challenging lift, students need positive intervention. The teacher and students need a set of common signals so that either can ask for or offer assistance without judgment or confrontation. Such agreed-upon techniques as "eye drive" (a deliberate look that signals affirmation or correction), physical proximity, silent signals, and head movement can communicate the need for a refocus to productive behavior.

The teacher's goal is not to control the students but rather to support students as they learn to control themselves. A supportive disciplinary action is an offer to help, not a judgment or imposition of will. To minimize the need for corrective discipline, educators need to explain the supportive elements of this approach to students with disabilities and to their parents.

Several supportive techniques have been developed by Mr. Boulanger, an 8th grade teacher. His signals remind students that they are responsible for controlling themselves. When he stands in front of the room and looks intently from student to student, they understand and respond to his signal by focusing on the task at hand. Through routine and consistent reinforcement, each student learns that the purpose of these signals is to help them achieve the level of excellence they desire.

Corrective Discipline

Even the best preventive and supportive approaches sometimes fail, at which point corrective action becomes necessary. Educators must administer corrective discipline expeditiously, invoking well-known guidelines about consequences for certain kinds of behavior. The purpose of corrective discipline is not to intimidate or punish but to provide natural consequences for disciplinary infractions that disrupt the learning environment.

The person in authority must never ignore disruptive behavior. One helpful technique for remaining calm is to administer corrective action in a matter-of-fact manner, adopting the demeanor of a state trooper. "May I see your driver's license, insurance card, and automobile registration? You were traveling 50 miles per hour in a 35 miles per hour zone."

Invoke the insubordination rule when necessary. Use a predetermined plan to command assistance if it is necessary to correct the situation. The behavior intervention plan that the Individuals with Disabilities Education Act regulations now require must include clear corrective procedures.

For example, Mrs. Thibodaux has developed a set of consequences for the most common infractions. Each student knows that being late to class will mean a period of after-school detention for a certain number of school days. Each knows that repeated failure to complete assignments will result in a telephone conference with a parent during work hours. Educators must work out these corrective measures ahead of time. Although the measures are not harsh or excessively punitive, they should be consistently inconvenient for the students and parents.

The U.S. Congress has now made it clear that schools should not allow children with disabilities to disrupt learning environments. All students need guidance to become respectful, responsible citizens who enjoy and effectively exercise their rights. If educators make excuses for special education students' behaviors, they deny them the benefits contained in the laws. All students deserve well-disciplined learning environments that are fun, focused, and full of creative energy. Developing discipline systems that combine preventive, supportive, and corrective measures for all students will move our schools toward that ideal.

POSTSCRIPT

Do Students with Disabilities Threaten Effective School Discipline?

Many people agree with Kay Hymowitz that too much of the behavior seen in schools hurts the overall learning climate. Conflicting laws dealing with freedom of speech, as well as disabilities, can dominate the thinking of administrators and teachers who should be focusing on teaching and learning.

Responses from a survey of middle and high school parents and teachers (Teaching Interrupted; Public Agenda, 2004) revealed behavior as a major concern to both groups. Teachers and parents agree that a few persistent students create the most trouble. Teachers report that documentation requirements are overwhelming. Surprisingly, the majority of teachers and parents believe that the primary problem is that parents do not teach discipline to their children. They believe that this, in combination with a "culture of disrespect" and overcrowded classrooms, results in behavior problems. Additionally, teachers report that lack of parental support and fear of lawsuits impact the kind of behavior they tolerate.

IDEA acknowledges that issues are complex. Its provisions specifically encourage schools to develop and communicate clear behavioral expectations for all students; to ensure that faculty respond consistently to misbehavior, and to treat students fairly. Taylor and Baker describe a system where these practices create an orderly climate in which students meet the expectations that are set for them. Individualized responses can be crafted for students who need specialized instruction to learn how to abide by these expectations.

The ramifications of IDEA are wide-ranging. Schools must walk a fine line between managing effective disciplinary practices and upholding legal rights based on disabilities (Yell, Katsiyannis, Bradley, & Rozalksi, *Journal of Special Education Leadership,* 2000). While the requirements of the law may be clear, the practices of implementation are sometimes cloudy.

IDEA04 seems to have set firmer limits. Schools have broader latitude to send students with disabilities to short-term alternate facilities. There is a heightened standard for determining whether the behavior is a manifestation of the student's disability. If so, schools must conduct a functional behavioral assessment and implement a behavioral intervention plan. Parents now bear the burden of proof if they disagree with the school's determination regarding manifestation.

In this time of research-based practice demands, two of these practices have been questioned by credible researchers. Sasso, Conroy, Stichter, and Fox (*Behavioral Disorders,* 2001) acknowledge that although functional assessments are a fine tool with individuals with retardation, it may not yet be possible to determine the function of a behavior demonstrated by students with emotional and behavioral problems.

Similarly, Katsiyannis and Maag (*Exceptional Children,* 2001) believe that currently there are no valid tools to help a school decide if a particular behavior is a manifestation of a disability. They suggest the key questions to answer include whether the student has the skills to engage in appropriate behavior, to analyze situations and craft acceptable responses, and to interpret a situation accurately.

There is no doubt that some children with disabilities exhibit significant behavior problems. There is also no doubt that some typical children do as well. Are students with disabilities being targeted as the cause of school disciplinary problems when the real issue is much broader? Will increased school-wide positive behavioral supports reduce this stress? Do IDEA's requirements support students with disabilities or overwhelm educators and provide excuses for some students? Will the tougher standards of IDEA04 result in tighter discipline, but more parent-initiated litigation?

ISSUE 7

Will More Federal Monitoring Result in Better Special Education?

YES: National Council on Disability, from *Back to School on Civil Rights: Advancing the Federal Commitment to Leave No Child Behind* (January 25, 2000)

NO: Frederick M. Hess and Frederick J. Brigham, from "How Federal Special Education Policy Affects Schooling in Virginia," in Chester E. Finn, Jr., Andrew J. Rotherham, and Charles R. Hokanson, Jr., eds., *Rethinking Special Education for a New Century* (Thomas B. Fordham Foundation & Progressive Policy Institute, 2001)

ISSUE SUMMARY

YES: The National Council on Disability (NCD) is an independent federal agency composed of 15 members appointed by the president and confirmed by the U.S. Senate, dedicated to promoting policies, programs, practices and procedures that guarantee equal opportunity and empowerment for all individuals with disabilities. NCD found all 50 states to be out of compliance with special education law, a condition that must be remedied by increased federal attention.

NO: Frederick M. Hess, assistant professor of education and government at the University of Virginia, and Frederick J. Brigham, assistant professor of education at the same school, share Virginia's experience that increased federal monitoring will only deepen the separation between general and special education, drawing resources away from true educational excellence for all.

Federal and state laws regarding special education were written to compel school districts to design and deliver education to students with disabilities. The rules and regulations for IDEA, the federal special education law, can be found in full at http://www.ed.gov/policy/speced/guid/idea/idea2004.html. Hard copies of the regulations fill over 100 pages of the Federal Register, in very tiny type. These regulations translate IDEA into operational elements, ranging from definitions of terms to the contents of an IEP to the substance, form, and timelines of communications with families to reporting responsibilities to federal agencies. In short, the regulations guide the daily practices of schools.

Comparable regulations exist for Section 504 of the Rehabilitation Act of 1973, designed to eliminate discrimination on the basis of disability in any program or activity that receives federal funds.

Beyond these, each state has its own specific statutes and accompanying regulations governing the education of typical children and those with disabilities. While there is much similarity between state and federal requirements, states are free to exceed federal requirements and to add unique local expectations.

Interpreting and implementing these layers of laws and regulations is not a one-time task. Changes in any of these laws mean changes in school practice. Parents who do not believe the rights of their children are being preserved may seek resolution through administrative hearings or action before a state or federal court. As legal cases clarify the meaning of any of these laws, schools adjust to these interpretations.

As with most situations when the weight of law is used to force action, the process of ensuring compliance is complicated and detailed. Each state is audited by the federal government on a periodic basis. In turn, states evaluate the performance of each school district. Some oversight takes place in regular reports of practices and finances. Periodically more extensive study occurs in on-site visits to districts, which include record review and interviews with educators and parents. States and districts that refuse to correct identified faults run the risk of losing federal special education funds.

In an extensive study of federal monitoring and enforcement of elements of IDEA, the National Council on Disability (NCD) finds that, despite more than 20 years of effort, there is not one single state that fully and accurately complies with IDEA's requirements. The Executive Summary of "Back to School on Civil Rights" delineates how the promises of IDEA—and the educational rights of children with disabilities—remain unmet by weak oversight procedures, poor follow-through and lack of consequences for repeated failings. The report recommends changes necessary to ensure the civil rights of children with disabilities and a strong special education system.

Frederick Hess and Frederick Brigham, reflecting on the impact of federal regulations in Virginia, believe that the current emphasis on compliance forces districts to focus more on procedures than children. Filling out forms according to regulation takes precedence over ensuring good programs for children. Money spent on compliance details reduces money spent on services for children. They hold that strict adherence to rigid procedures creates an adversarial system that engenders distrust between families and educators and unnecessary divisions in school districts.

As you read these articles, ask yourself whether meeting the letter of the law prevents meeting the spirit of the laws. Does holding states and districts to exacting standards help or hinder the implementation of an effective educational program?

YES

National Council on Disability

Back to School on Civil Rights

Executive Summary

Twenty-five years ago, Congress enacted and President Gerald Ford signed the Education for All Handicapped Children Act, one of the most important civil rights laws ever written. The basic premise of this federal law, now known as the Individuals with Disabilities Education Act (IDEA), is that all children with disabilities have a federally protected civil right to have available to them a free appropriate public education that meets their education and related services needs in the least restrictive environment. The statutory right articulated in IDEA is grounded in the Constitution's guarantee of equal protection under law and the constitutional power of Congress to authorize and place conditions on participation in federal spending programs. It is complemented by the federal civil rights protections contained in section 504 of the Rehabilitation Act of 1973, as amended, and Title II of the Americans with Disabilities Act.

This report, the second in a series of independent analyses by the National Council on Disability (NCD) of federal enforcement of civil rights laws, looks at more than two decades of federal monitoring and enforcement of compliance with Part B of IDEA. Overall, NCD finds that federal efforts to enforce the law over several Administrations have been inconsistent, ineffective, and lacking any real teeth. The report includes recommendations to the President and the Congress that would build on the 1997 reauthorization of IDEA. The intent is to advance a more aggressive, credible, and meaningful federal approach to enforcing this critical civil rights law, so that the nation's 25-year-old commitment to effective education for all children will be more fully realized.

Background

In 1970, before enactment of the federal protections in IDEA, schools in America educated only one in five students with disabilities. More than 1 million students were excluded from public schools, and another 3.5 million did not receive appropriate services. Many states had laws excluding certain students, including those who were blind, deaf, or labeled "emotionally disturbed" or "mentally retarded." Almost 200,000 school-age children with mental retardation or emotional disabilities were institutionalized. The likelihood of exclusion

From National Council on Disability, *Back to School on Civil Rights: Advancing the Federal Commitment to Leave No Child Behind*, (January 25, 2000). Washington, D.C.: U.S. Government Printing Office, 2000. Notes omitted.

was greater for children with disabilities living in low-income, ethnic and racial minority, or rural communities.

In the more than two decades since its enactment, IDEA implementation has produced important improvements in the quality and effectiveness of the public education received by millions of American children with disabilities. Today almost 6 million children and young people with disabilities ages 3 through 21 qualify for educational interventions under Part B of IDEA. Some of these students with disabilities are being educated in their neighborhood schools in regular classrooms. These children have a right to have support services and devices such as assistive listening systems, braille text books, paraprofessional supports, curricular modifications, talking computers, and speech synthesizers made available to them as needed to facilitate their learning side-by-side with their nondisabled peers. Post-secondary and employment opportunities are opening up for increasing numbers of young adults with disabilities as they leave high school. Post-school employment rates for youth served under Part B are twice that of older adults with disabilities who did not benefit from IDEA in school, and self-reports indicate that the percentage of college freshmen with a disability has almost tripled since 1978.

Findings

As significant as the gains over time are, they tell only part of the story. In the past 25 years states have not met their general supervisory obligations to ensure compliance with the core civil rights requirements of IDEA at the local level. Children with disabilities and their families are required far too often to file complaints to ensure that the law is followed. The Federal Government has frequently failed to take effective action to enforce the civil rights protections of IDEA when federal officials determine that states have failed to ensure compliance with the law. Although Department of Education [DoED] Secretary Richard W. Riley has been more aggressive in his efforts to monitor compliance and take formal enforcement action involving sanctions than all his predecessors combined, formal enforcement of IDEA has been very limited. Based on its review of the Department of Education's monitoring reports of states between 1994 and 1998, NCD found:

- Every state was out of compliance with IDEA requirements to some degree; in the sampling of states studied, noncompliance persisted over many years.
- Notwithstanding federal monitoring reports documenting widespread noncompliance, enforcement of the law is the burden of parents who too often must invoke formal complaint procedures and due process hearings, including expensive and time-consuming litigation, to obtain the appropriate services and supports to which their children are entitled under the law. Many parents with limited resources are unable to challenge violations successfully when they occur. Even parents with significant resources are hard-pressed to prevail over state education agencies (SEAs) and local education agencies (LEAs) when they or their publicly financed attorneys choose to be recalcitrant.

- The Department of Education has made very limited use of its authority to impose enforcement sanctions such as withholding of funds or making referrals to the Department of Justice, despite persistent failures to ensure compliance in many states.
- DoED has not made known to the states and the public any objective criteria for using enforcement sanctions, so that the relationship between findings of noncompliance by federal monitors and a decision to apply sanctions is not clear.

DoED Monitoring Model

The oversight model adopted by the Department of Education is multitiered and multipurpose. The Office of Special Education Programs (OSEP) distributes federal IDEA funding to the states and monitors the SEAs. The SEAs in turn monitor the LEAs to make sure they are in compliance with IDEA. In this tiered oversight model, the same Department of Education office (OSEP) distributes federal funds, monitors compliance, and enforces the law where violations are identified. The politics and conflicts inherent in administering these three disparate functions have challenged the Department's ability to integrate and balance the objectives of all three.

Data Sources and Summary of Analyses

As mentioned above, NCD found that the most recent federal monitoring reports demonstrated that every state failed to ensure compliance with the requirements of IDEA to some extent during the period covered by this review. More than half of the states failed to ensure compliance in five of the seven main compliance areas. For example, in OSEP's most recent monitoring reports, 90 percent of the states (n = 45) had failed to ensure compliance in the category of general supervision (the state mechanism for ensuring that LEAs are carrying out their responsibilities to ensure compliance with the law); 88 percent of the states (n = 44) had failed to ensure compliance with the law's secondary transition services provisions, which require schools to promote the appropriate transition of students with disabilities to work or post-secondary education; 80 percent of the states (n = 40) failed to ensure compliance with the law's free appropriate public education requirements; 78 percent of the states (n = 39) failed to ensure compliance with the procedural safeguards provisions of the law; and 72 percent of the states (n = 36) failed to ensure compliance with the placement in the least restrictive environment requirements of IDEA. In the two remaining major compliance areas, IEPs [individual education programs] and protection in evaluation, 44 percent of the states (n = 22) failed to ensure compliance with the former and 38 percent of the states (n = 19) failed to ensure compliance with the latter.

Enforcement Authority

Currently, the U.S. Department of Education has neither the authority nor the resources to investigate and resolve individual complaints alleging noncompliance. The Department does consult with and share some of its enforcement authority with the U.S. Department of Justice (DOJ), which has no independent litigation authority. Yet between the date it was given explicit referral authority in 1997 and the date this report went to the printer, DoED had not sent a single case to DOJ for "substantial noncompliance," and had articulated no objective criteria for defining that important term. The Department of Justice, whose role has been largely limited to participation as an amicus in IDEA litigation, does not appear to have a process for determining what cases to litigate.

Overall Enforcement Action

Despite the high rate of failure to ensure compliance with Part B requirements indicated in the monitoring reports for all states, only one enforcement action involving a sanction (withholding) and five others involving imposition of "high risk" status and corrective action as a prerequisite to receiving further funds have been taken. The only withholding action occurred once for a temporary period and was overruled by a federal court. Overall, the DoED tends to emphasize collaboration with the states through technical assistance and developing corrective action plans or compliance agreements for addressing compliance problems. There appear to be no clearcut, objective criteria for determining which enforcement options ought to be applied and when to enforce in situations of substantial and persistent noncompliance.

Recommendations for Strengthening Federal Enforcement

NCD makes the following recommendations to strengthen the capacity of both the Department of Education and the Department of Justice to more effectively enforce IDEA:

- Congress should amend IDEA to create a complaint-handling process at the federal level to address systemic violations occurring in a SEA or LEA. Congress should designate the Department of Justice to administer the process and allocate adequate funding to enable the Department to take on this new role. This new federal complaint process should be designed to complement, not supplant, complaint procedures and the due process hearing at the state level. The federal process should be simple to use and easy to understand by parents and students.
- Congress should amend IDEA to provide the Department of Justice with independent authority to investigate and litigate cases brought under IDEA. The Department of Justice should be authorized to develop and disseminate explicit criteria for the types of alleged systemic violation complaints it will prioritize given its limited resources.
- Congress should include in the amendment that the Department of Education and the Department of Justice shall consult with students with disabilities, their parents, and other stakeholders to develop objective criteria for defining "substantial noncompliance," the point at which a state that fails to ensure compliance with IDEA's requirements will be referred to the Department of Justice for legal action.
- Congress should ask the General Accounting Office (GAO) to conduct a study of the extent to which SEAs and LEAs are ensuring that the

requirements of IDEA in the areas of general supervision, secondary transition services, free appropriate public education, procedural safeguards, and placement in the least restrictive environment are being met. In addition, the DoED Office of Inspector General (OIG) should conduct regular independent special education audits (fiscal and program). The purpose of the audits would be to examine whether federal funds granted under IDEA Parts B and D (State Program Improvement Grants) have been and are being spent in compliance with IDEA requirements. These audits should supplement OSEP's annual compliance-monitoring visits, and the audit results should be in DoED's annual report to Congress. To the extent that the DoED OIG lacks the subject-matter expertise to conduct program audits under IDEA, the OIG should contract with independent entities having such expertise when a program audit is necessary.

- The Department of Education should establish and use national compliance standards and objective measures for assessing state progress toward better performance outcomes for children with disabilities and for achieving full compliance with Part B.

- The Department of Education should consult with students with disabilities, their parents and other stakeholders in developing and implementing a range of enforcement sanctions that will be triggered by specific indicators and measures indicating a state's failure to ensure compliance with Part B.

- When Congress and the President approve an increase in the funding to be distributed to local schools under Part B, Congress and the President should appropriate at the same time an amount equal to 10 percent of the total increase in Part B funding to be used to build the Department of Justice's and the Department of Education's enforcement, complaint-handling, and technical assistance infrastructure to effectively enable the federal agencies to drive improvements in state compliance and ensure better outcomes for children.

Personnel Training Needs

Regular and special education teachers in many states are frustrated by the mixed messages regarding compliance from school administrators, local special education directors, state oversight agents, school district attorneys, and federal oversight agents. Teachers ultimately bear the responsibility to implement interventions and accommodations for students with disabilities, often without adequate training, planning time, or assistance. They must function within an educational system that often lacks adequate commitment, expertise, or funding to deliver appropriate services to every child who needs them. School administrators, special education directors, school principals, and agents of federal, state, and local governments must stop working at cross purposes and commit to working together to resolve, not conceal or ignore, these very real problems. If the Federal Government continues to refrain from taking enforcement action in the face of widespread failures to ensure Part B compliance, this atmosphere of questionable commitment to the civil rights of students with disabilities will continue.

Advocacy Service Needs

Pervasive and persistent noncompliance with IDEA is a complex problem with often dramatic implications on a daily basis for the lives of children with disabilities and their families. Too many parents continue to expend endless resources in confronting obstacles to their child's most basic right to an appropriate education, often at the expense of their personal lives, their financial livelihoods, and their careers. Students are frustrated—their skills undeveloped and their sense of belonging tenuous. When informal efforts have failed to end unnecessary segregation or inappropriate programming for individual children, many have used the rights and protections afforded by IDEA to successfully challenge these injustices. Advocacy and litigation have been essential to ending destructive patterns of recurring noncompliance. Litigation has resulted in important victories for the children involved and better outcomes for other students with disabilities by exposing and remedying systemic noncompliance with IDEA. Yet legal services are often far beyond the financial reach of many families of students with disabilities.

Children with disabilities and their families are often the least prepared to advocate for their rights in the juvenile justice, immigration and naturalization, and child welfare systems when egregious violations occur. Children with disabilities and their families who are non-English speaking, or who live in low income, ethnic or racial minority, and rural communities, are frequently not represented as players in the process. These individuals must be included and given the information and resources they need to contribute and advocate for themselves.

Recommendations for Training and Advocacy

Accordingly, NCD makes the following recommendations:

- When Congress and the President approve an increase in the funding to be distributed to local schools under Part B of IDEA, Congress and the President should appropriate at the same time an amount equal to 10 percent of the total Part B increase to fund free or low-cost legal advocacy services to students with disabilities and their parents through public and private legal service providers, putting competent legal assistance within their financial reach and beginning to level the playing field between them and their local school districts.

- The Department of Education should give priority support to the formation of a comprehensive and coordinated advocacy and technical assistance system in each state. The Department should develop a separate OSEP-administered funding stream to aid public and private advocacy entities in each state in collaborating to expand and coordinate self-advocacy training programs, resources, and services for students with disabilities and their parents throughout the state. Elements of the coordinated advocacy and technical assistance systems should include:

  —The availability of a lawyer at every state Parent Training and Information (PTI) Center, a protection and advocacy agency, legal services, and independent living center to provide legal advice and representation to students with disabilities and their parents in advocating for their legal rights under IDEA.

—Self-advocacy training programs for students with disabilities and their parents focused on civil rights awareness, education and secondary transition services planning, and independent living in the community.

—The establishment of a national backup center with legal materials, training, and other supports available for attorneys working on IDEA cases and issues at the state level.

—Expansion of involvement by the private bar and legal services organizations in providing legal advice to students with disabilities and their parents in advocating for their legal rights under IDEA.

—Training in culturally sensitive dispute resolution to meet the needs of growing populations of citizens from racial and ethnic backgrounds having diverse traditions and customs. Multiple language needs and communication styles must be accommodated in all training.

Full compliance with IDEA will ultimately be the product of collaborative partnership and long-term alliances among all parties having an interest in how IDEA is implemented. For such partnerships to be effective, all interested parties must be well prepared to articulate their needs and advocate for their objectives. To that end, coordinated statewide strategies of self-advocacy training for students with disabilities and their parents are vital. To make this happen, NCD recommends the following:

- The Department of Education should fund additional technical assistance, training, and dissemination of materials to meet continuing needs in the following areas:

—Culturally appropriate technical assistance, which should be available to ensure that American Indian children with disabilities, their families, tribal leaders, and advocates in every interested tribe can participate as full partners in implementing IDEA in their communities. Culturally appropriate training and technical assistance should be developed and delivered through the satellite offices of newly created disability technical assistance centers (DBTACs) managed and staffed primarily by Native Americans that serve American Indian communities around the country.

—Training to enhance evaluation skills for parents to assess the effectiveness of their states' IDEA compliance-monitoring systems.

—Training of the appropriate agents (officials, advocates, and other stakeholders) in the immigration and naturalization and child welfare systems in IDEA's civil rights requirements.

—Training of the appropriate agents (officials, advocates, and other stakeholders) in the juvenile justice system in IDEA's civil rights requirements, how they apply within the juvenile justice system, and ways the law can be used to help minimize detention of children with disabilities in the juvenile justice system.

A Six-State In-Depth Sample

NCD looked in depth at a sampling of six states, using the last three monitoring reports to assess the compliance picture in those states over time. The first two of the monitoring reports for these six states (covering a period from 1983–1998) included failure to ensure compliance with a total of 66 Part B requirements. Only 27 percent (n = 18) of the 66 violations had been corrected by the time of the third report. Based on the reported data, in 73 percent (n = 48) of the 66 violations, either the six states still failed to ensure compliance or no compliance finding was reported at all in the last monitoring report.

To date federal compliance-monitoring and enforcement efforts have not fully dealt with the root causes of widespread noncompliance, and children with disabilities and their parents have suffered the consequences. This report details NCD's findings and recommendations for improving the effectiveness of federal efforts to ensure state compliance with IDEA and related legislation. NCD calls on Congress and the President to work together to address the inadequacies identified by this report so that children and families will have an effective and responsive partner in the Federal Government when they seek to ensure that IDEA's goals of enhanced school system accountability and improved performance outcomes for students with disabilities move from the language of the law to the reality of each American classroom.

IDEA mandates that school systems respond to the needs of individual children with disabilities, making education accessible to them, regardless of the severity of their disabilities. Teachers today know that education tailored to individual needs and learning styles can make all the difference in the quality of a child's learning, whether or not she has a disability. Very few public schools consistently and effectively deliver this individualized approach for all children. Accordingly, many children fall through the cracks, as performance on achievement tests across the nation demonstrates. Alternatives to traditional public education such as charter and private schools, as well as political calls for vouchers, indicate growing public dissatisfaction with schools that do not educate all children effectively. IDEA calls for a responsive public education system that meets the individual learning needs of students with disabilities. It also contains a blueprint for the future of public education—where no child is left behind, and all children have an equal opportunity to gain the knowledge and skills they need to fulfill their dreams.

Ultimately, the enforcement of the civil rights protections of IDEA will make a difference to every child, not only children with disabilities. At the national summit on disability policy hosted by NCD in 1996, more than 350 disability advocates called for a unified system of education that incorporates all students into the vision of IDEA. NCD's 1996 report, *Achieving Independence*, presents the outline of a system in which every child, with or without a disability, has an individualized educational program and access to the educational services she or he needs to learn effectively. IDEA leads the way in reshaping today's educational system from one that struggles to accommodate the educational needs of children with disabilities to one that readily responds to the individual educational needs of all children.

Frederick M. Hess and
Frederick J. Brigham

 **NO**

How Federal Special Education Policy Affects Schooling in Virginia

Federal special education legislation has an honorable heritage and a laudable purpose. Unfortunately, the manner in which Congress and the executive branch have pursued that purpose now impedes the ability of state school systems to serve children in both general and special education.

The current system of oversight and resource allocation focuses less on educational attainment and more on procedural civil rights. Problems result from the federal government's use of this legalistic approach. In most areas of education, Washington offers supplementary funding as a carrot to encourage desired state behaviors. The challenge of compelling states to abide by federal dictates in special education, however, has produced a reliance on procedural oversight with deleterious effects for the federal-state partnership in education.

Under the present system, educators are restricted in their ability to make decisions regarding how best to assist children with disabilities. Instead, in response to federal dictates, states press school districts toward a defensive posture in which educators may spend more time attending to procedural requirements than to students' instructional and behavioral needs. Most discussions of reforming special education at the federal level ask what policy changes would alleviate this problem of excessive proceduralism. We suggest that such an approach is too narrow, that over-reliance upon procedural regulation actually arises from Washington's attempt to compel behaviors with insufficient incentives or guidance.

While seeking to get states to do its bidding with respect to children and youths with disabilities, Congress has provided neither inducements for them to cooperate nor flexibility in how they comply with federal direction. Lacking the capacity to implement special education policy on its own—considering that it does not operate public schools or employ their teachers—Washington has instead relied upon micro-managing state procedures and using the threat of legal action as a primary enforcement tool.

Lacking explicit federal direction or support, state officials cope by crafting their own muddled guidelines. This permits the state, like the federal government, to forestall messy conflict over details regarding program eligibility and services by pushing such questions down to districts and schools. Principals

From Frederick M. Hess and Frederick J. Brigham, "How Federal Special Education Policy Affects Schooling in Virginia," in Chester E. Finn, Jr., Andrew J. Rotherham, and Charles R. Hokanson, Jr., eds., *Rethinking Special Education for a New Century* (Thomas B. Fordham Foundation & Progressive Policy Institute, May 2001). Copyright © 2001 by The Thomas B. Fordham Foundation. Reprinted by permission. Notes omitted.

and teachers complain that the nested levels of governance deepen the confusion as the rules grow more convoluted and cumbersome at each stage. . . .

The Federal Role in Special Education . . .

The IDEA [Individuals With Disabilities Education Act]

In making special education law, Congress and the executive branch have relied heavily upon judicial precedents rooted in the Equal Protection and Due Process Clauses of the 14th Amendment. Whereas most federal legislation is framed as a compromise between competing interests and claims, this more absolutist orientation means that special education policies turn on endowing claimants with an inviolable set of rights. That mindset is illustrated by the "inclusion" proponent who prominently argued, "It really doesn't matter whether or not [full inclusion] works . . . even if it didn't work it would still be the thing to do."

Under the IDEA, a satisfactory program is defined as one that adheres to due process, regardless of its results. Critics suggested that this orientation fed lower expectations for students with disabilities. In response, the 1997 IDEA reauthorization sought to emphasize academic performance by insisting upon "meaningful access to the general education curriculum to the maximum extent possible" for students with special needs. . . .

Section 504

In theory, states are free to disregard the IDEA. The only federal sanction is the ability of the Office of Special Education Programs (OSEP) to withdraw IDEA grants. These grants amount to less than ten percent of state special education spending. This apparent freedom is illusory, however, because any state that fails to comply with the IDEA's requirements would still be liable under Section 504 of the Rehabilitation Act of 1973. Section 504 is designed . . . "to eliminate discrimination on the basis of handicap in any program or activity receiving Federal financial assistance." Although it supplies no funding, Section 504 applies to any entity receiving any federal funding, meaning that all states must abide by its directives. . . .

Although the IDEA offers guidelines regarding various disability conditions, the provisions of Section 504 are so nebulous that it becomes extremely difficult to distinguish students entitled to special education services from those not entitled. As one administrator said, "In my opinion, IDEA is much more precise, much more specific. . . . 504 is the same as saying, 'you have a problem here.' [Anybody can identify some problem] 'substantially limits' [a life activity]. . . . What's the line there? So you're wide open."

Special Education in Virginia

Special education comprises a substantial share of Virginia's K–12 educational expenditures. Between 1995 and 1998, special education students made up 13 percent to 14 percent of the state's student population, while the special education budget consumed 23 percent to 25 percent of the state's education budget. . . .

In Virginia, federal special education directives are interpreted and implemented by a designated group of professionals in the state Department of Education (DOE). Within the larger DOE, headed by the state Superintendent of Education, is a directorate for special education headed by a Director of Special Education and Student Services (SESS). Historically, the directorate for Special Education did nothing else. In 2000, DOE merged "Special Education" with "Student Services," the unit responsible for activities such as school health and safety. Despite this reorganization, Special Education remains relatively isolated from the other areas of the DOE. In January 2001, SESS included 23 positions devoted to oversight of special education. These individuals include specialists in learning disabilities, emotional disturbance, mental retardation, early childhood, and severe disabilities. Not one member is explicitly charged with coordinating policy with the other parts of the DOE.

Virginia's DOE essentially runs parallel school systems, one staffed by special educators for students with disabilities, the second staffed by general educators for everyone else. Each side exhibits distrust and frustration with the other. A local special education administrator observed, "People in general education don't listen to us or even ask us about the kids in our caseloads." A state-level administrator said, "We have consistent problems with some of our districts," explaining that the state deals with such challenges by using legal and administrative sanctions to coerce general educators into "playing ball." General educators voice reciprocal concerns. One administrator spoke for many, saying, "I have all I can handle right now without attending to students with wildly varying educational and behavioral needs." . . .

The current structure ensures that special education policy decisions are mostly made by people removed from actual school practice and from the general decisionmaking process for K–12 curriculum and instruction. This makes it less likely that services for students with special needs will be integrated or coordinated with the larger educational program. . . . The structure of the DOE helps to divide general and special education personnel, while encouraging professionals to think differently about different categories of children, despite Congress' insistence that its goal is to eliminate distinctions among students.

Special Education Litigation

Despite the visibility of special education cases that reach the courts, such actions are relatively rare in Virginia. The most common legal or quasi-legal actions are complaints and due process hearings. The Commonwealth devotes considerable time and energy to these. Due process hearings are a quasijudicial, adversarial procedure overseen by part-time hearing officers trained by the DOE.

Between 1992–93 and 1999–2000, 799 due process requests were filed with the DOE. . . . All such requests require formal notification to the Department that the plaintiff is exercising his right to a due process hearing. Ninety-three percent of these requests were filed by parents. The remaining 7 percent were filed by school districts, usually when the district was concerned that parents were refusing to allow it to provide the services it deemed appropriate. These figures indicate that formal legal proceedings may be less of an issue than critics sometimes fear.

Of these 799 cases filed, 586 were resolved in the same year. Of the 586, 176 (30 percent) led to decisions by a hearing officer while the rest ended through withdrawal of the complaint or settlement prior to a hearing. Of the 176 decisions rendered, three-quarters were resolved wholly in favor of the school district. The other 25 percent either favored the parent or split the difference between parent and district.

There are at least two ways to interpret these outcomes. One is that a substantial percentage of the requests filed lack merit. A second is that some schools respond to parental concerns only when faced with the threat of legal sanctions. A significant number of hearing requests are withdrawn after districts make concessions. . . .

The larger problem is not the number of formal complaints or their resolution, but the incentives that this legalistic mechanism creates for local educators. Presently, the desire to avoid legal sanctions and officer-ordered costs and services is the clearest incentive for schools to make extraordinary efforts to serve students with disabilities. Such efforts may cause the district to divert resources from other worthy purposes. Educators have cause to focus on what services and accommodations will forestall complaints, rather than on which are cost-effective and educationally appropriate. The result is that districts are caught between a desire to "cut corners" on special education expenditures and the impulse to provide services in order to avoid the threat of legal action. By encouraging schools and parents to adopt adversarial roles, the legalistic emphasis makes cooperative solutions more difficult and shifts the focus of decision-making from educational performance to the avoidance of potential liability.

The Institutional Shape of Special Education

Here we examine three key program dimensions used by the federal government to define special education and to ensure that it is delivered in an acceptable manner. . . .

FAPE and LRE

The key IDEA mandates affecting instruction and student placement are FAPE (free appropriate public education) and LRE (least restrictive environment). FAPE addresses the elements of a student's education program, although LRE addresses the integration of disabled students into the general education system. Often, the two mandates embody contradictory impulses. Legal scholar Anne Dupre has observed, "The friction between 'appropriate' education and 'appropriate' integration has baffled the court and led to a confusing array of opinions on inclusion." While educators must attend to both considerations, in Virginia it appears that the balance is tipped in favor of inclusion, even at the cast of effective education. An attorney who often represents parents of children with disabilities said, "[t]he intensity of the programs offered for students with mild disabilities fell after the push for more inclusion. Now we more often have to pursue formal action to get these students the services they need."

The most difficult aspect of FAPE involves the meaning of "appropriate," which is clearer for some disabilities than others. Few question the need for Braille tests for students who are blind or ramps for those with limited mobility. For students with less obvious disabilities, however, program appropriateness ought to take into account curricular demands on the student as well as the larger educational context of the school. . . .

Although the challenge of validating the appropriateness of a given student's educational program is daunting, it is overshadowed by the problems surrounding the LRE requirement. Few areas of special education are as controversial. Much effort is invested in determining the LRE for individual students, closely watched by a group of educators and advocates who call for "full inclusion" of disabled youngsters in regular education classes. . . .

In Virginia, as a result of the push for "inclusion," many of the services formerly available to students with mild disabilities . . . have been cut back or eliminated. Such programs frequently have been replaced by "collaborative" or "consultative" models, in which students with special needs are enrolled full-time in general education classrooms. One result has been that a continuum of placement options has been replaced with a starker choice between intensive (for example, self-contained) classes and limited services (for example, enrollment in general education programs). This shift has left both general and special education teachers with fewer ways to respond to the needs of students, which reduces their ability to make effective professional judgments about what works for children in their schools. . . .

The current approach to FAPE and LRE fails to resolve the tension between maximizing achievement and maximizing integration, leaving these competing desiderata to be worked out by administrators, teachers, and parents without clear guidelines. Yet educators are blocked from using their professional judgment in weighing these two imperatives and are subjected to administrative or judicial review and sanction if deemed to have proceeded in an inappropriate manner. In other words, district officials are granted an ambiguous autonomy and expected to make appropriate decisions but are prevented from relying upon their professional determinations of efficiency and efficacy in reaching those decisions. The system is faintly redolent of a star chamber in which one is not sure the criteria to which one is being held.

Funding

One of most significant impacts of FAPE is on state education funding. Because Congress has imbued disabled children with particular rights, the state is legally required to give budgetary priority to their needs. States are legally vulnerable to charges that they have failed to provide adequately for students with special needs, while parents of general education students cannot make similar claims. The consequence is that states have a difficult time making the case against the provision of even very expensive special education services and tend to fund these by dipping into the pool that would otherwise fund general education. . . .

Monitoring Special Education

In theory, federally inspired monitoring ensures that special education programs provide an appropriate education to all eligible students. In reality, the monitoring focuses more on procedural compliance than on either the appropriateness or effectiveness of the education being delivered. Given the lack of evidence that procedural compliance equates to more effective services, it is not clear that federal monitoring is effectively promoting quality special education. Moreover, such an emphasis undermines teacher professionalism by forcing educators to invest significant time in managing procedures and documenting processes, rather than on instruction.

OSEP's policy, adopted after the 1997 IDEA amendments, monitors states predominantly by requiring them to conduct self-studies. A key problem in this process is that the reporting requirements are both complex and vague. For example, the phrase "free appropriate public education" sounds straightforward and easily implemented, but a closer look proves otherwise.

Assuming that "free" means no cost to the parents, interpreting this part is straightforward. But, what does "appropriate" mean? In order to define this term, one must first determine the goals of the education program and ask the question, "Appropriate for what?" The IDEA is silent on that point, meaning that this question must be revisited in the case of each student. OSEP plainly is unable to monitor the "appropriateness" of a given decision in the case of a particular child. Therefore, it winds up monitoring processes and procedures—for example, the way that the decision was made. In practice, the guidelines are daunting, elaborate, and time-consuming even for many special education professionals—let alone the parents and students they are intended to protect. As one state official commented, "Monitoring used to be a part of my job, now it's all I do. Running the monitoring program has become my whole job."

Virginia's SSEAC [State Special Education Advisory Committee], which is supposed to identify critical issues and advise DOE on carrying out special education programs, scrapped its entire agenda for 2000–2001 in order to concentrate on the issue of program monitoring. The state DOE has had to add additional staff to handle these responsibilities.

In early January 2001, the SSEAC met to discuss the self-study that comprises the initial stage of Virginia's federal monitoring. At the beginning of the meeting, a facilitator asked each committee member why he or she had given up the time to attend this particular meeting. The most common response was to attain closure on the process. The facilitator pointed out that the federal monitoring process, being continuous, could never result in closure.

Reports were presented regarding programs for both school-aged and preschool children. Each report was several hundred pages long. After the meeting, several parent representatives remarked that they saw little connection between the activities conducted through the federal monitoring and discernible improvements in the educational services offered to their children. The best that can be said of the self-study is that it allows parents and special educators to voice their concerns. However, there is little reason to suspect that this unfocused airing of grievances is likely to produce substantive improvements in special education. More likely, because the state officials who led the self-study procedure were diverted from their responsibilities to monitor and support local education agencies (LEAs), the federal monitoring program is likely to result in decreased attention to the problems faced by children and youths with disabilities, their families, and the schools that serve them.

The Practice of Special Education . . .

IEPs

As originally conceived, IEPs were to be a flexible tool for creating specialized programs responsive to student needs as well as parental and school concerns. However, Virginia practice emphasizes *pro forma* compliance with IEPs in order to protect educators from administrative and legal actions. A typical IEP form offers 45 boxes for committees to check off before they even begin to describe the student's own education program. Rather than a flexible pedagogical tool, the IEP is often a ritualized document. As one special education administrator said, "Of course, all of our special ed students have IEPs. But how relevant are [the IEPs] to what our teachers are doing on a day-to-day basis? Not very."

Parents are not alone in their dissatisfaction. Teachers often complain that IEPs do little but absorb time and repeat platitudes. . . .

IEPs have historically reflected a given student's particular instructional regimen, rather than provided a road map for helping that child accomplish the general education goals promulgated by the school or state. A result is that they are often written with little input from general education teachers and scant regard for the standards of general education programs. . . .

The 1997 amendments required that general education teachers be included in IEP meetings and that IEPs yield "meaningful access to the general education curriculum." Unfortunately, both changes appear to hold only limited promise. So long as special education policy is driven by rights and legalisms, inserting general education teachers into IEP planning sessions is unlikely to produce significant changes in practice. As for "meaningful access to the general education curriculum," the phrase is so nebulous as to serve no real purpose, while creating yet one more interpretive minefield for school personnel.

The trouble with most efforts to improve IEPs is that they fail to address the contradiction at the heart of the process. On the one hand, professional educators are charged with designing flexible programs that respond to the needs of each student with disabilities. On the other hand, these plans are devised and implemented in a context shaped by compliance-based rules and marked by legal peril. The result is that IEPs cease to be useful pedagogical tools.

Discipline Policy

The IDEA requires the development of distinct disciplinary policies for students with disabilities. Some of these distinctions make sense. It is unreasonable to discipline a wheelchair-bound student for failing to stand during the national anthem. The IDEA prevents schools from punishing students in such situations (although we see no evidence that Virginia schools, left to their own judgment, would engage in such practices). The IDEA requires a "zero reject" model that extends special education services to *all* students with disabilities. Under this logic, schools may not interrupt or withhold services for any such students save for infractions involving guns or possession of drugs. Such interruption of services has been deemed to violate the IDEA's procedural safeguards. . . .

IDEA regulation of discipline may serve a legitimate purpose. It is well established that students with disabilities are frequently "over-punished" for behavior infractions. Many parents of children with disabilities report that their children feel singled out by school officials for behavior that rarely leads to sanctions for other students. . . .

Unfortunately, the IDEA also has a number of undesirable disciplinary consequences. School officials must determine the extent to which an act of misbehavior results from a disability. Judgments regarding the motivation of a specific act have eluded philosophers and psychologists through the ages, yet are required by the IDEA. Such deliberations are bound to yield variable results, even as they consume substantial time. Effective disciplinary procedures require that acts and consequences be closely linked in time and consistent over time if they are to have the desired effect. The IDEA's procedural mandates make such practices doubly difficult when the child has any sort of disability.

Despite the frequent voicing of such concerns, the IDEA constraints do not actually result in many disciplinary measures being challenged or overturned in Virginia. . . . Still, the fear of such a challenge reportedly causes many teachers and administrators to shy away from punishing students with disabilities for infractions for which others would be disciplined. . . . The perception in Virginia that the IDEA creates a class of students licensed to "terrorize schools and teachers" undermines public trust in school safety and support for special education.

State Education Standards

. . . Much special education practice draws heavily on the philosophy of progressive education, emphasizing notions of personal relevance more heavily than traditional academic skills and knowledge. . . . The IDEA's ethos of individualized instruction is at odds with systems of standards-based accountability that seek to improve education by requiring all students to perform at a measurably high level on a specified set of objectives.

In the past, this conflict was often accommodated by exempting special education students from standardized assessments. In the 1990s, however, special educators began to assert that such policies caused disabled students to be denied effective and equitable instruction. Consequently, the 1997 IDEA amendments mandated that students with disabilities be included in testing programs to the maximum feasible extent. As a result, students with special needs now participate in Virginia's SOL [Standards of Learning] testing regime.

This change places schools and districts in an awkward position, as the state simultaneously asks them to raise test results and to include students who have shown historically poor performances on standardized assessments. The IDEA requires educators to take greater responsibility for the achievement of students with disabilities. However, the law can also encourage educators to look for loopholes to relax the standards for students who are unlikely to fare well on high-stakes assessments. An example of this tendency was the SSEAC recommendation in early 2000 that the state extend the category of "developmental disabilities" up to the federal maximum age of nine so that more students would be afforded special accommodations on the SOL tests. The nature of this request suggests the fundamental tension between special education provisions and the push toward high uniform standards. . . .

Perhaps the central dilemma for states pursuing high-stakes accountability is how best to serve those students with mild disabilities who find attaining acceptable levels of performance a daunting challenge. On the one hand, it is sensible to hold these students and their teachers to the same high level of expectations to which we hold others. On the other hand, these students may find assessments frustrating or insurmountable and may drop out of school altogether. This bifurcation is partly a function of the Virginia SOL's virtually exclusive focus on academic preparation. Although this emphasis is understandable, it leads to de-emphasis of programs such as vocational education and the arts that can provide other forms of useful instruction and skill-based learning for students with mild or moderate disabilities.

Conclusion

Surveying the six dimensions of policy and practice in which special education poses significant challenges, we can see that the key problems have much in common. FAPE and LRE demand that educators abide by open-ended and ill-defined directives, even as the court-enforced right of a select group of children to "free and appropriate education" prohibits measured decisions regarding the allocation of resources. The monitoring of special education relies upon documentation and paper trails, requiring much time and effort and forcing educators to base program decisions upon procedures rather than determinations of efficiency or effectiveness. IEPs intended as flexible instruments of learning have evolved into written records of compliance with formal requirements. In the area of school discipline, protections afforded to special education students have caused educators to look askance upon these children and have made it more difficult to enforce clear and uniform standards in schools. And in jurisdictions such as Virginia, which have moved to a standards-based curriculum and a results-based accountability system, the question arises of how to track the progress of disabled students and whether they will be treated as part of the reformed education system or (reminiscent of pre-IDEA discrimination) as a separate educational world.

Reformers have sought to tackle one or another of these issues in isolation, acting in the belief that incremental policy shifts could remedy the particular problem. For example, the 1997 IDEA reforms sought to emphasize outcomes by requiring schools to test all students and enhancing schools' ability to discipline disabled students who misbehave. Such efforts have not worked very well, however, because they fail to recognize that the enumerated problems are symptomatic of a deeper tension at the heart of the federal-state relationship.

In sum, special education policy today is unwieldy, exasperating, and ripe for rethinking. Congress has demanded that states and schools provide certain services, but it has refused to pay their costs. States are obliged to deliver special education, yet lack substantive control over its objectives and policy design and the nature and shape of its services. But Washington does not actually run the program, either. Instead it tells states, albeit in ambiguous terms, what they must do, no matter whether these requirements are in the best interests of children, schools, or the larger education enterprise. Whatever the cost of compliance, states and districts are obliged to pay it, regardless of the effect on other children, programs, and priorities. The result is a hybrid reminiscent of the "push-me, pull-you" that accompanied Dr. Doolittle in Hugh Lofting's legendary children's tales. Like that mythical two-headed creature, the special education system is constantly tugged in opposite directions. To compel state cooperation with its directives, Washington relies upon a rights-based regimen of mandated procedures and voluminous records, enforced by the specter of judicial power. Yet because states and districts end up paying most of the bill for special education, Congress is hesitant to order the provision of particular services or to demand specific results. The consequence is that educators must interpret vague federal directives while operating under the shadow of legal threat.

Arguably, this produces the worst of two very different policy regimes. If special education were an outright federal program, like the National Park Service, the Weather Bureau, or Social Security, Washington would run it directly, in uniform fashion, with all bills being paid via Congressional appropriation. If it were a state program, Congress might contribute to its costs but states would determine how best to run it. Today, however, it is neither, and the result is not working very well.

These are two obvious solutions. The first is for Congress to pay for the special education services that it wishes to provide disabled children. The second is for Washington explicitly to decentralize special education, granting substantive authority to states, districts, and schools.

Either remedy, of course, would bring its own new problems. Full federal funding, for example, may encourage local overspending. Similarly, decentralization raises the likelihood that substantial variation will occur between states.

Yet these problems are likely to be less vexing than those we now face and apt to be more amenable to solution. The intergovernmental confusion would diminish. Those setting policy would be directly in charge of those delivering services. And a shift away from today's emphasis on rights and procedures will increase flexibility and foster innovations responsive to the distinctive needs of individual students, the judgments of expert educators, the preferences of parents, and the priorities of communities. This, we believe, would be good for children. And that, we believe, is the main point.

POSTSCRIPT

Will More Federal Monitoring Result in Better Special Education?

A frequently heard comment is that IDEA is the "full employment for attorneys" act. Sometimes it feels that way. There is a long distance between the dream of helping all children learn and the reality of legal time deadlines, shifting interpretations, and confusing terminology.

In writing "Back to School on Civil Rights," the NCD authors interviewed 14 parents from nine states, each of whom trusted that their children would receive an appropriate education in the least restrictive environment. Each shared the disillusionment and distrust that resulted from finding their rights side-stepped or ignored. NCD found substantiation in their review of monitoring activities. Without increased federal attention to legal detail and requirements, the authors worry that schools will continue to evade meeting the requirements of the laws. In the full report, NCD is dismayed that education reform efforts and budgetary cutbacks have siphoned away state funds that could have been used for compliance monitoring. They urge restoration of these moneys so that no more ground (or time) is lost.

In sharp contrast, Hess and Brigham believe that much ground has been too easily surrendered because districts fear costly litigation, which might find them out of bureaucratic compliance with special education laws. The impact of individual challenges to school performance provides the protection that a global state audit could not—perhaps preventing educators from selecting effective practices that could benefit the whole school. Unfortunately, according to the authors, the confusing tangle of regulations often prevents schools from focusing on the more appropriate target of accountability for the progress of all children.

IDEA97 made a shift from compliance to accountability, requiring that all students have access to the general curriculum and participate in the large-scale testing that is part of education reform. Regretting a lost opportunity, Wolf and Hassel (Finn, Rotheram, & Hokanson, 2001) find that this change has succeeded only in adding another layer of bureaucratic responsibilities while reducing none.

Providing the perspective of attorneys who have represented both parents and schools, Lanigan, Audette, Dreier, and Kobersy (Fordham, 2001) see the situation this way:

> Special education staff members in the public schools devote their professional lives to educating children with disabilities, are truly dedicated to the endeavor, and genuinely want to provide appropriate special education and related services to the students they are charged with educating. Yet

150

school resources are not unlimited, budget pressures are real, and the IDEA allows districts to take program costs into account only so long as they still are meeting the FAPE requirement. This is the fundamental source of school district conflict with parents.

Parents (and other guardians) who devote their lives to raising children with disabilities genuinely want to make sure that their children receive at least appropriate special education and related services. In truth, however, what these parents *really,* want—indeed what *all* parents want—is an education that will allow their children to maximize their potential. The IDEA does not require this. This is the fundamental source of parents' conflict with school officials.

Does monitoring of complex federal regulations waste time and resources that could be devoted to the education of children? Do these very regulations protect the rights of children with disabilities to an equitable education? Is it possible that well-meaning people can interpret the law in two different ways and yet both care deeply about the children they share? If so, how can they resolve their differences? How do your local educators view the controversy? What do they do now because of oversight? What would they do better if there were closer scrutiny? What would they do if no one checked to see if they were complying—would students with disabilities benefit from creative new programs, or would options be foreclosed because no one was watching?

Internet References . . .

Circle of Inclusion

This Web site, funded by the U.S. Office of Special Education Programs, is targeted to providing information and resources about the effective practices of inclusive educational programs for children from birth through age eight. Links to additional resources and videoclips can be found on the home page.

http://www.circleofinclusion.org/

National Center on Educational Outcomes

The National Center on Educational Outcomes (NCEO), based at the University of Minnesota, is a primary research site for the participation of students with disabilities in large-scale testing. This Web site contains current resources on the status of testing in all statues as well as information on the ways in which students with disabilities participate. Links include numerous printable NCEO publications.

http://education.umn.edu/nceo/

National Dissemination Center for Children with Disabilities (NICHCY) Research Center for Children with Disabilities

A new resource for educators and parents of students with disabilities, this site provides comprehensive information on the research process. One element, The NICHCY Research-to-Practice Database, enables readers to access research about techniques and practices that might be useful in their work with children with disabilities. An update feature announces added topics or updated pages

http://nichcy.org/

No Child Left Behind

Use this U.S. Department of Education Web site to learn everything you want to know about No Child Left Behind. Information encompasses the following: text of the statute, updates on hearings, notices of changes in the regulations, and resources for teachers. A newsletter is also available to deliver information as soon as it becomes available.

http://www.ed.gov/nclb/landing.jhtml

What Works Clearinghouse

The What Works Clearinghouse was established in 2002 by the U.S. Department of Education's Institute of Education Sciences to provide educators, policymakers, researchers, and the public with a central and trusted source of scientific evidence of what works in education.

http://www.whatworks.ed.gov/

PART 2

Access and Accountability

*T*hirty *years ago, special education was concerned with getting students with disabilities into schools. Next, the conversation turned to opening classroom doors so students with disabilities had access to typical peers and were included in school experiences. Now discussions revolve around access to the general curriculum—the real work of schools. With access has come accountability. Now that the doors are open, we all must be accountable for the learning that goes on inside. As this new step in inclusionary practice takes shape, we want to retain the careful attention to individuals that is the hallmark of special education.*

- Does NCLB Leave Some Students Behind?

- Will NCLB Requirements Produce Highly Qualified Special Education Teachers?

- Can Scientifically Based Research Guide Instructional Practice?

- Can One Model of Special Education Serve All Students?

- Is Full Inclusion the Least Restrictive Environment?

- Should Students with Disabilities Be Exempt from Standards-Based Curriculum?

- Have Schools Gone Too Far in Using Accommodations?

- Should Students with Cognitive Disabilities Be Expected to Demonstrate Academic Proficiency?

ISSUE 8

Does NCLB Leave Some Students Behind?

YES: Jennifer Booher-Jennings, from "Rationing Education in an Era of Accountability," *Phi Delta Kappan* (June 2006)

NO: U.S. Department of Education, from "Working Together for Students with Disabilities: Individuals with Disabilities Education Act (IDEA) and No Child Left Behind Act (NCLB)," http://www.ed.gov/admins/lead/speced/toolkit/index.html (December 2005)

ISSUE SUMMARY

YES: Jennifer Booher-Jennings, a doctoral candidate at Columbia University, finds the accountability pressures of No Child Left Behind are leading some administrators to advise teachers to focus only on those children who will improve their school's scores; other students don't count much.

NO: The U.S. Department of Education FAQ Sheet on IDEA and NCLB advises readers that the link between these two statutes is sound, emphasizing how they work together to ensure that every student's performance and needs receive appropriate attention.

The No Child Left Behind (NCLB) Act of 2001, a reauthorization of the Elementary and Secondary Education Act (ESEA), has changed the vocabulary and practice of educators in every publicly funded school in America.

ESEA, more familiarly known as Title I, has long provided funds to districts to improve the educational performance of children from low-income families. In the reauthorization now known as NCLB, the federal government demands a return on its investment.

Four key principles form the foundation of NCLB:

- Schools must be accountable for student performance and teacher qualifications.
- States and districts must set growth targets and have the latitude to achieve them.

- Parents must have more information about their schools and broader educational options if their schools do not reach growth targets.
- Schools must use research-based instructional strategies.

The principle most on the minds of educators is accountability. NCLB mandates that all children be proficient in math and reading/language arts by 2013–2014. States determine their own educational standards, as well as specific benchmark goals, staged to reach the proficiency target.

Regular testing determines if a school is making adequate yearly progress (AYP) toward the target: Students must be assessed in reading/language arts and math annually in grades 3–8, and at least once in grades 9–10. Beginning in 2007–08, students must be assessed in science at least once in grades 3–5, 6–9, and 10–12.

Some schools appear to be successful, but small groups within their walls do markedly less well than others. To hold schools accountable for the achievement of *all* students, NCLB identifies particular subgroups, including students from low-income families, students from major racial and ethnic groups, those with limited English proficiency, and those with disabilities. Unless each subgroup makes AYP, a school is deemed not making total adequate yearly progress.

Schools that do not make AYP are subject to an array of interventions. Their leadership must take actions to improve. Parents must be notified of the status and have the option of transferring to higher-performing schools. Supplemental educational services must be available. In the extreme, schools are subject to "corrective actions" under the guidance/supervision of external experts.

These expectations and consequences are taken seriously by all educators. While striving to meet them, some wonder if all students will be part of the race or if some, especially students with disabilities, will be left behind.

Jennifer Booher-Jennings, after studying NCLB implementation in one Texas school, found teachers were being encouraged to focus their attention on "the kids who count" because their improvement could increase school scores. Since students with disabilities didn't "count," or because they were "hopelessly" unlikely to do well, they were not deemed worthy of teacher energy.

The U.S. Department of Education, in responses to frequently asked questions, maintains that NCLB and IDEA work in concert to ensure that every child with a disability reaches high standards. The FAQ notes that most children with disabilities are in general education placements and are already participating in high numbers. The information gleaned from frequent assessments should "shine a light on student needs and draw attention to how schools can better serve (them)."

NCLB says it is committed to helping all students reach proficiency by 2014, but does "all" really mean "all"? As you read these articles, ask yourself how the schools in your neighborhood are implementing NCLB. Are all subgroups participating meaningfully, or are some more important than others?

YES

Jennifer Booher-Jennings

Rationing Education in an Era of Accountability

Meet Mrs. Dewey, 46 years old and a veteran fourth-grade teacher at Marshall Elementary School. Mrs. Dewey entered the teaching profession in the wake of *A Nation at Risk* and has weathered the storm ever since. For the last 20 years, she has survived the continuous succession of faddish programs that has characterized American education reform. Year after year, administrators have asked Marshall teachers to alter their practice to conform to the latest theory. Mrs. Dewey's colleagues, frustrated by the implementation of such silver-bullet approaches, have often flouted the administrative directives and chosen instead to serve as the sole arbiters of their classroom practice.

But it is the newest of the new solutions that worries Mrs. Dewey most. The language of accountability is swift and uncompromising: hold educators responsible for results. Identify those teachers who, as President Bush says, "won't teach." Fair enough, Mrs. Dewey thinks. The consummate professional, Mrs. Dewey always looks for the silver lining.

Like other reforms, accountability requires teachers to embrace a new strategy. Data-driven decision making, a consultant told the faculty at a professional development session, is the philosophy Marshall teachers must adopt. The theory is simple. Give students regular benchmark assessments; use the data to identify individual students' weaknesses; provide targeted instruction and support that addresses those areas. Mrs. Dewey remembers nodding approvingly. After all, this approach—gathering textured information on each student to guide instructional activities—was one she had been using for 22 years.

The consultant moved on. "Using the data, you can identify and focus on the kids who are close to passing. The bubble kids. And focus on the kids that count—the ones that show up at Marshall after October won't count toward the school's test scores this year. Because you don't have enough special education students to disaggregate scores for that group, don't worry about them either." To make this concept tangible for teachers, the consultant passed out markers in three colors: green, yellow, and red. Mrs. Dewey heard someone mutter, "What is this? The traffic light theory of education?"

"Take out your classes' latest benchmark scores," the consultant told them, "and divide your students into three groups. Color the 'safe cases,' or

From *Phi Delta Kappan*, June 2006, pp. 756–761. Copyright © 2006 by Jennifer Booher-Jennings. Reprinted by permission. References omitted.

kids who will definitely pass, green. Now, here's the most important part: identify the kids who are 'suitable cases for treatment.' Those are the ones who can pass with a little extra help. Color them yellow. Then, color the kids who have no chance of passing this year and the kids that don't count—the 'hopeless cases'—red. You should focus your attention on the yellow kids, the bubble kids. They'll give you the biggest return on your investment."

As the bell tolls a final warning to the boisterous 9-year-olds bringing up the rear of her class line, Mrs. Dewey stares blankly into the hallway. Never did she believe that the advice offered by that consultant would become Marshall's educational mantra. Focus on the bubble kids. Tutor only these students. Pay more attention to them in class. Why? It's data-driven. Yet this is what her colleagues have been doing, and Marshall's scores are up. The community is proud, and the principal has been anointed one of the most promising educational leaders in the state. At every faculty meeting, the principal presents a "league table," ranking teachers by the percentage of their students passing the latest benchmark test. And the teachers talk, as they always do. The table makes perfect fodder for faculty room gossip: "Did you see who was at the bottom of the table this month?"

Mrs. Dewey has made compromises, both large and small, throughout her career. Every educator who's in it for the long haul must. But this institutionalized policy of educational triage weighs heavily and hurts more. Should she focus only on Brittney, Julian, Shennell, Tiffany, George, and Marlena—the so-called bubble kids—to the exclusion of the other 17 students in her class? Should Mrs. Dewey refuse to tutor Anthony, a persistent and eager little boy with no chance of passing the state test this year, so that she can spend time with students who have a better shot at passing? What should she tell Celine, a precocious student, whose mother wants Mrs. Dewey to review her entry for an essay contest? Celine will certainly pass the state test, so can Mrs. Dewey afford the time? What about the five students who moved into the school in the middle of the year? Since they don't count toward Marshall's scores, should Mrs. Dewey worry about their performance at all?

In her angrier moments, Mrs. Dewey pledges to ignore Marshall's approach and to teach as she always has, the best way she knows how. Yet, if she does, Mrs. Dewey risks being denounced as a traitor to the school's effort to increase scores—in short, a bad teacher. Given 22 years of sacrifices for her profession, it is this reality that stings the most.

Mulling over her choices, Mrs. Dewey shuts her classroom door and begins her class.

Unintended Consequences of Accountability Systems: Educational Triage

Test-based accountability systems aim to direct the behavior of educators toward the improvement of student achievement. The No Child Left Behind (NCLB) Act codified accountability as our national educational blueprint, requiring schools to increase test scores incrementally so that all students are proficient in reading and math by 2014. Yet, despite the stated intent of NCLB to improve outcomes for all students, particularly those who have been historically neglected, educators and others may adopt a series of "gaming" practices in order to artificially inflate schools' passing rates. Such practices include giving students a special education classification to exclude them from high-stakes tests, retaining students in grade to delay test-taking, diverting attention away from subjects not evaluated on high-stakes tests, teaching to the test, and cheating.

In what follows, I discuss two of the dilemmas presented by a less-well-known gaming practice: educational triage. The insights offered here derive from an ethnographic study of an urban elementary school in Texas, to which I have assigned the pseudonym "Beck Elementary." Educational triage has become an increasingly widespread response to accountability systems and has been documented in Texas, California, Chicago, Philadelphia, New York, and even England. By educational triage, I mean the process through which teachers divide students into safe cases, cases suitable for treatment, and hopeless cases and ration resources to focus on those students most likely to improve a school's test scores. The idea of triage, a practice usually restricted to the direst of circumstances, like the battlefield or the emergency room, poignantly captures the dynamics of many schools' responses to NCLB. In the name of improving schools' scores, some students must inevitably be sacrificed. And the stakes are high—for schools, which face serious sanctions for failing to meet adequate yearly progress targets; for students, who increasingly face retention if they do not pass state tests; and for teachers, who are judged by the number of students they "save."

Dilemma 1.   *Data can be used to improve student achievement, but they can also be used to target some students at the expense of others.* Data-driven decision making has become something of a sacrosanct term in education policy circles. Who could be against it? The public face of data-driven decision making—identifying the needs of each individual child and introducing interventions to remediate any learning difficulties—is sensible and beyond question.

But the Achilles' heel of education policy has always been implementation. When I listened closely to the conversations that educators at Beck Elementary School had about "being data-driven," the slippage between evaluating the individual needs of every student and deciding which students to target to maximize school performance quickly became evident. As I moved closer and closer to the classroom, the administrators' ideal version dissipated and gave way to a triage-based understanding of data-driven decision making. Teachers were most attuned to the chasm between administrators' theoretical proclamations and how the same administrators expected them to operate: teachers understood that the bottom line in this numbers game was the percentage of students who passed. Because of the unrelenting pressure to increase test scores, one mode of using data became dominant at Beck: the diversion of resources (e.g., additional time in class; enrichment sessions with the literacy teacher; and after-school, Saturday, and summer tutoring) to students on the threshold of passing the test, the "bubble kids."

All my questions about which students received extra help were met with the deferent maxim, "It's data-driven." When I asked one teacher how the school allocated additional services to students—for example, the reading specialist or after-school and Saturday tutoring—she provided the following response:

It's all data-driven. . . . We do projections—how many of them do you think will pass, how many of them do you think will need more instruction, how many teachers do we have to work with, what time limit do we have. Based on that, who are we going to work with? It comes down to that. . . . We really worked with the bubble kids . . . that's the most realistic and time-efficient thing we can think of.

In this conception of data-driven practice, the choice to privilege one group of students over another is viewed as neutral and objective. The decision to distribute resources to those most advantageous to the school's pass rates is not understood as a moral or ethical decision. Instead, it is seen as a sterile management imperative. Protected by its scientific underpinnings, the data-driven focus on the bubble kids is difficult for teachers to attack. In sum, at Beck Elementary, the invocation of the phrase "data-driven" obscures, neutralizes, and legitimates a system of resource distribution that is designed to increase passing rates rather than to meet the needs of individual students.

The blunt vocabulary of triage infiltrated every corner of Beck. The tenor of the phrases used to describe students—"the ones who could make it" and "hopeless cases"—speaks not only to the perceived urgency to improve test scores but also to the destructive labeling of those children who find themselves below the bubble. Driven by the pressure to increase the passing rate, teachers turned their attention away from these students. As one teacher related in an interview:

I guess there's supposed to be remediation for anything below 55%, but you have to figure out who to focus on in class, and I definitely focus more attention on the bubble kids. If you look at her score [pointing to a student's score on her class test-score summary sheet], she's got a 25%. What's the point in trying to get her to grade level? It would take two years to get her to pass to the test, so there's really no hope for her. . . . I feel like we might as well focus on the ones that there's hope for.

To say that hope is absent for a 10-year-old child is a particularly telling comment on how dramatically the accountability system has altered the realm of imagined possibility in the classroom. Now, with an unforgiving bottom line for which to strive, teachers can retain hope only for those perceived as potential passers. To assert that students below the bubble are just too low-performing to help establishes that the only worthwhile improvement in this brave new world is one that converts a nonpasser to a passer.

The problem is that those students who arrive at school as the most disadvantaged are often the lowest scoring. And since the focus on the bubble kids at Beck Elementary begins not in the third grade—the first year that students take state tests—but the moment students enter kindergarten, they are branded as "hopeless cases" from the very first days of their schooling.

An important shift occurs in a system focused on the percentage of students above a particular threshold. When a low-performing student enters a teacher's classroom, he or she is seen as a liability rather than as an opportunity to promote individual student growth. As Michael Apple trenchantly wrote, the emphasis changes "from student needs to student performance, and from what the school does for the student to what the student does for the school."

Certainly one can imagine uses of data that could turn attention to the individual needs of each and every student. However, the current monolithic discourse on data-driven decision making begs for a discussion of unintended consequences. Data can be used to target some students at the expense of others, and it is happening today.

When we blindly defer to "the data," we abdicate responsibility for tough decisions, all the while claiming neutrality. But data are not actors and cannot do anything by themselves. Data do not make decisions; people make decisions that can be informed by data. Decisions about resource allocation are ethical decisions with which educators and communities must grapple and for which they must ultimately take responsibility.

What we need above all is a sustained discussion among educators and the broader polity about the very real tradeoffs involved in schools' responses to accountability systems. If schools adopt the practices of educational triage in response to NCLB, the consequence may be suboptimal outcomes for students "below the bubble," as well as for their peers who are mid-level and high-achieving students. And all of these unintended consequences can happen while official pass rates increase.

Dilemma 2.   *It is unfair to hold schools accountable for new students or for subgroups that are too small to yield statistically reliable estimates of a school's effectiveness; however, the consequence of excluding some students may be to deny them access to scarce educational resources.* Educational triage does not end with the diversion of resources to the "bubble kids." Because of the fine print in NCLB, all students are not equally valuable to a school's test scores. Subgroups are not disaggregated if the number of test-takers does not meet a minimum size requirement, and students are not counted at all in a school's scores if they are not enrolled in a school for a full academic year. For example, in Texas, the scores of students who arrive at the school after the end of October do not count toward schools' scores. Such a definition is logical, for it attempts to isolate the impact of schools on students. Including students who have not attended the school for a reasonable period of time might bias estimates of the school's quality and unfairly penalize schools serving more mobile students.

However, if resources flow only toward those students who affect a school's outcomes, students who do not "count" may be denied access to scarce educational resources. I found that another pithy term, "the accountables"—those students who count toward a school's scores—was incorporated into the lexicon of Beck educators. Teachers engaged in a second kind of educational triage by focusing resources on the "accountables," to the virtual exclusion of students who "did not count." In accountability's ultimate contradiction, the protean word "accountable" retained only a semblance of its intended meaning—taking responsibility for each and every student.

How many students are affected by the mobility provisions of NCLB? Take the Houston Independent School District as an illustrative example. Serving 211,157 students, this district is the largest in Texas and the seventh largest in the nation. The average Houston school excludes 8% of its students from its "accountables." Almost one-third of Houston schools (31%) exclude more than 10% of their students from scores used for accountability. By any measure, this is not an insignificant number of students. Moreover, because mobility is not uniformly distributed across the population, some demographic groups have much higher numbers of mobile—and thus unaccountable—students. In Houston, an average of 16% of special education students and 11% of African American students are not counted in schools' scores because they have not been enrolled in a school for a full academic year. Ironically, the very students NCLB was designed to target are often those least likely to be counted.

A second way that students may "not count" stems from states' definitions of the subgroup size required for disaggregation. If states define subgroup size expediently, the scores of various subgroups will continue to be buried in schoolwide averages. Again, Texas is a good example of artful definition of subgroup size. Under the Texas state accountability system, subgroups must include at least 30 students and account for at least 10% of all students—or include 50 or more students—to be evaluated. Under Texas' NCLB implementation plan, subgroups must include at least 50 students and make up at least 10% of all students—or include 200 or more students—to be evaluated. Under the state system, 82% of Houston schools with African American test-takers disaggregate scores for African American students, while for the purposes of NCLB, only 66% do.

Though Texas does not include a special education subgroup in its state system, the impact of using the 50 and 10% or greater than 200 definition rather than the lower threshold is significant. Shifting the definition upward reduces the percentage of Houston schools that disaggregate scores for special education from 55% to 24%. Other states have similarly gamed the subgroup-size provision of the law. In 2005, the U.S. Department of Education allowed Florida to change its minimum subgroup size to 30 students who also make up 15% of test-takers. Because special education students rarely account for more than 15% of a school's population, very few schools in Florida will be required to disaggregate scores for these students.

There is an irreconcilable tension between accurately measuring school effects and forestalling the potential negative consequences of excluding some students from accountability calculations. If accuracy of measurement is privileged, some students will necessarily be excluded from accountability calculations. In order to best estimate school effects, a school should not be responsible for students who attend it for a short period of time. Similarly, small subgroups may yield statistically unreliable estimates of the school's efficacy with a particular group of students. Moreover, mainstream state tests may be inappropriate measures for some English-language learners or special education students. In other words, there are valid reasons, from a measurement perspective, for excluding students from schools' scores. On the other hand, the consequence of excluding these students may be to deny them access to scarce educational resources.

Better Choices?

So Mrs. Dewey can choose to teach all of her students, regardless of their potential contribution to her school's bottom line, or she can participate in educational triage. If she refuses to focus her time and attention on those students most likely to raise the school's scores, she risks not only the school's survival but her professional reputation as a good teacher and, potentially, her job.

Mrs. Dewey should not be asked to make such choices, and it is unconscionable to question her ethics when she does what she has little choice but to do. Systems of public policy cannot be designed solely for those with the moral certitude to qualify them for sainthood.

Educators will respond to systemic incentives, and NCLB's current incentives structurally induce behaviors that are inimical to broader notions of equity and fairness. In many cases, these perverse incentives turn educators' attention away from NCLB's intended beneficiaries. Until these issues are addressed, we can expect to see educational triage practices flourish across the country.

Working Together for Students with Disabilities: Individuals with Disabilities Education Act (IDEA) and No Child Left Behind Act (NCLB)

1. Are *NCLB* and *IDEA* in conflict with each other?

No. Both laws have the same goal of improving academic achievement through high expectations and high-quality education programs. *NCLB* works to achieve that goal by focusing on school accountability, teacher quality, parental involvement through access to information and choices about their children's education, and the use of evidence-based instruction. *IDEA* complements those efforts by focusing specifically on how best to help students with disabilities meet academic goals.

NCLB aims to improve the achievement of all students and recognizes that schools must ensure that all groups receive the support they need to achieve to high standards. That is why *NCLB* requires that schools look at the performance of specific subgroups of students, including students with disabilities, and holds schools accountable for their achievement. By including students with disabilities in the overall accountability system, the law makes their achievement everybody's business, not just the business of special education teachers. Shining the light on the needs of students with disabilities draws attention to the responsibility of states, districts, and schools to target resources to improve the achievement of students with disabilities and to monitor closely the quality of services provided under *IDEA*.

2. If *NCLB* focuses on school performance while *IDEA* focuses on individual students, how can a student's individual rights not be compromised under *NCLB*?

The requirements of *NCLB* do not infringe on the rights of students with disabilities under *IDEA*.

IDEA requires that schools provide special education and related services to meet the individual needs of each student with a disability. To

From http://www.ed.gov/admins/lead/speced/toolkit/index.html, December 2005.

provide these services, a team of educators and parents develop a plan (referred to as an "Individualized Education Program," or IEP) for each student with a disability that maps out what achievement is expected and what services are needed to help the student meet these expectations. With the appropriate supports and services, students with disabilities can and should be held to high standards.

NCLB is designed to ensure that schools are held accountable for educational results so that each and every student can achieve to high standards. Setting the bar high helps all students, including students with disabilities, reach those standards. The expectation of *NCLB* is that students with disabilities can achieve to high standards as other students, given the appropriate supports and services.

3. Was *NCLB* the first federal law to require states to include students with disabilities in the state's assessment system?

NCLB is the first law to hold schools accountable for ensuring that all students participate in the state assessment system, but it is built on earlier law. The 1997 amendments to the *IDEA* required that students with disabilities participate in state and district assessments and that their results be reported publicly in the same way and with the same frequency as those of other students. The federal law that preceded *NCLB*, the *Improving America's Schools Act of 1994*, required schools to include the assessment results of students with disabilities in accountability decisions for Title I schools. *NCLB* and the 2004 *IDEA* amendments strengthened a commitment to this requirement, and now all states are paying attention to testing students with disabilities and are using those results to hold schools accountable for the performance of these students.

Data indicate that participation and achievement levels are rising each year. Data from the National Council on Educational Outcomes (NCEO) show that in 2003, most states had 95 percent to 100 percent participation in state math and reading assessments by students with disabilities in elementary school, middle school, and high school. By including students with disabilities in the assessment and accountability systems, we raise our expectations for them while giving schools the data they need to help all of their students to be successful. *NCLB* is helping special education programs and each child's IEP team know what academic goals children need to achieve so that they are given the appropriate supports and services. *NCLB* tells us what we're working towards, while *IDEA* brings to bear multiple resources and services to help students attain the learning standards.

4. My school did not make Adequate Yearly Progress (AYP) because students with disabilities did not score well on the state test. Is that fair?

Only by holding schools accountable for *all* students will the spotlight of attention and necessary resources be directed to those children most in need of assistance and most often left behind academically.

Schools need to be accountable for all students. To achieve that goal, AYP is intentionally designed to identify those areas where schools need to improve the achievement of their students. What we are learning is that some schools perform well on average, but they may miss their AYP goals as a result of the student achievement of one or a few groups of students. The requirement for states, districts, and schools to disaggregate their data (i.e., separate their assessment data by the results of the different subgroups of students) is one of the fundamental principles of *NCLB*. This ensures that all schools and districts are held accountable for the performance of subgroups of students, not just the school as a whole.

The Department recognizes the challenges educators face in helping all children achieve to high standards. But allowing overall school performance to mask the lower performance of particular groups of students who need additional academic assistance would be *unfair* to those struggling groups of students.

5. **Why should students with disabilities be tested and included in accountability systems?**

Students with disabilities deserve the same high-quality education as their peers. Ever since Congress enacted the 1997 amendments to the *IDEA*, the nation has been working to improve the participation of students with disabilities in state assessments and provide students with disabilities with access to the general education curriculum. Many states have been committed to this goal for an even longer period of time. The purpose of requiring participation in assessments is to improve achievement for students with disabilities. As Secretary Spellings has said on more than one occasion, "What gets measured gets done." Too often in the past, students with disabilities were excluded from assessments and accountability systems, and the consequence was that they did not receive the academic attention and resources they deserved.

Students with disabilities, including those with the most significant cognitive disabilities, benefit instructionally from such participation. One state explains the instructional benefits of including students with the most significant cognitive disabilities in its assessment system in the following way: "Some students with disabilities have never been taught academic skills and concepts, for example, reading, mathematics, science, and social studies, even at very basic levels. Yet all students are capable of learning at a level that engages and challenges them. Teachers who have incorporated learning standards into their instruction cite unanticipated gains in students' performance and understanding. Furthermore, some individualized social, communication, motor, and self-help skills can be practiced during activities based on the learning standards."

To ensure that adequate resources are dedicated to helping these students succeed, appropriate measurement of their achievement needs to be part of school and district accountability systems. Furthermore, when students with disabilities are part of the accountability system, educators' expectations for these students are more likely to increase. In such a system, educators realize that students with disabilities count and that they can learn to high standards, just like students without disabilities.

6. Is it fair to make students with disabilities take a test that they cannot pass?

For too long in this country, students with disabilities have been held to lower standards than their peers and unjustly routed through school systems that expected less of them than of other students. Several states have found that once students with disabilities are included in the assessment system and expected to achieve like other students, performance improves. In 2005, for example, 60 percent of fourth-graders with disabilities in Kansas were proficient in reading. This represented an increase over 2003, when 51 percent of students with disabilities were proficient.

Students with disabilities can achieve at high levels. That is why *NCLB* requires states and school districts to hold all students to the same challenging academic standards and have all students participate in annual state assessments. We test students to see what they are learning, identify academic needs, and address those needs. The purpose is not to frustrate children. Rather, it is to shine a light on student needs and draw attention to how schools can better serve their students.

If students are excluded from assessments, they are excluded from school improvement plans based on those assessment results. If all students are to benefit from education reforms, all students must be included. Only by measuring how well the system is doing will we clearly identify and then fill the gaps in instructional opportunities that leave some students behind.

We do, however, need to improve tests for students with disabilities. We need tests that measure what students know and can do without the interference of their disability. The Department is currently looking at ways to make tests more accessible and valid for a wider range of students so that all students can participate and receive meaningful scores. For more information about this work, please refer to item 13 of this document and to the proposed regulation that was released in December 2005. . . .

7. Why can't a student's Individualized Education Program (IEP), instead of the state assessment, be used to measure progress?

There are several reasons why IEPs are not appropriate for school accountability purposes. In general, IEP goals are individualized for each student and may cover a range of needs beyond reading/language arts and mathematics, such as behavior and social skills. They are not necessarily aligned with state standards, and they are not designed to ensure consistent judgments about schools—a fundamental requirement for AYP determinations. The IEP is used to provide parents with information about a student's progress and for making individualized decisions about the special education and related services a student needs to succeed. Assessments used for school accountability purposes must be aligned to state standards and have related achievement standards.

8. **Students in special education get extra privileges in taking the state tests. Some of them get more time and get tested by themselves or in small groups. Isn't this unfair?**

These "privileges" are called "accommodations." Accommodations are changes in testing materials or procedures, such as repeating directions or allowing extended time, that, by design, do not invalidate the student's test score. In other words, accommodations help students access the material but do not give students with disabilities an unfair advantage. These accommodations instead help level the playing field so that a test measures what the student knows and can do and not the effect of the child's disability. It is not unfair to allow valid accommodations during a test because these accommodations allow a test to measure the student's knowledge and skills rather than the student's disability.

The state is responsible for analyzing accommodations to determine which are acceptable on the basis of the test design. It is important for the state to make sure that students use only those accommodations that result in a valid score. For example, if the assessment is supposed to measure how well a student decodes text, reading the test aloud to the student would result in an invalid score.

9. **Isn't it unrealistic to expect *all* students with disabilities to meet grade-level standards? Students are in special education for a reason.**

Students receive special education services for a reason. They are in special education because a team of professionals has evaluated the child using a variety of assessment tools and strategies to gather relevant functional, developmental, and academic information about the child, including information provided by the parent, and determined that the child has a disability and needs special education services. Their achievement on grade-level standards is only part of the picture. It does not determine whether or not they need services. Assessments and other evaluation materials include those tailored to assess specific areas of education need. The child must be assessed in all areas related to the suspected disability including, if appropriate, health, vision, hearing, social and emotional status, general intelligence, academic performance, communicative status, and motor abilities. The impression that students are receiving special education services because they cannot pass a state test is a misunderstanding of what it means to be eligible for *IDEA* services.

Being in special education does not mean that a student cannot learn and reach grade-level standards. In fact, the majority of students with disabilities should be able to meet those standards. Special education provides the additional help and support that these students need to learn. This means designing instruction to meet their specific needs and providing supports, such as physical therapy, counseling services, or interpreting services, to help students learn alongside their peers and reach the same high standards as all other students.

10. **What about students with significant cognitive disabilities? Is it realistic to expect them to meet the same level of achievement as all other students?**

The expectation of *NCLB* is that the majority of students with disabilities can and should participate in and achieve proficiency on state assessments. We understand, however, that there is a small percentage of students with disabilities who may not reach grade-level standards, even with the best instruction. These are students with the most significant cognitive disabilities (about 10 percent of all special education students). The Title I regulations allow these students to take an alternate assessment based on alternate achievement standards that is less difficult and more tailored to their needs. Their proficient scores can be counted in the same way as any other student's proficient score on a state assessment. The Department has developed certain safeguards around this policy to help prevent students from being placed in an assessment and curricula that are inappropriately restricted in scope, thus limiting their educational opportunities (see item 11).

11. **It seems like the Department has said the following: "Only 1 percent of students with disabilities can take an alternate assessment based on alternate achievement standards." Is this true?**

The Department has not made such a statement. In fact, it reflects several common misunderstandings about federal education policy. Current Title I regulations permit a student's proficient score on assessments based on alternate achievement standards to count the same as any other student's proficient score on a state assessment, subject to a 1.0 percent cap at the district and state levels. If more than 1.0 percent of proficient scores come from such assessments, then the state must establish procedures to count those scores as non-proficient for the purposes of school accountability.

MYTH.   The Department expects that only 1 percent of students with disabilities should take a test based on alternate achievement standards (1 percent cap).

FACT.   The 1.0 percent cap reflects the following: 1 percent of *all* students represents about 10 percent of students with disabilities. While all children can learn challenging content, evaluating that learning through the use of alternate achievement standards is appropriate only for a small, limited percentage of students who are within one or more of the existing disability categories under the *IDEA* (e.g., autism, multiple disabilities, traumatic brain injury), and whose cognitive disability prevents them from attaining grade-level achievement standards, even with the very best instruction. The 1 percent cap (or approximately 10 percent of students with disabilities) is based on current incidence rates of students with the most significant cognitive disabilities, allowing for reasonable local variation in prevalence.

MYTH. IEP teams are limited in the number of students with disabilities that they may determine need an alternate assessment based on alternate achievement standards.

FACT. The cap is a limit on the number of proficient scores that may be included in AYP decisions at the district and state levels. The cap is not a limit on the number of students who may take such an alternate assessment based on alternate achievement standards.

FACT. IEP teams must make informed and appropriate decisions for each individual student, based on each student's unique needs. If more than 1 percent of all students in a district need to take an assessment based on alternate achievement standards, then all such students may take them. To protect students from inappropriate, low standards, however, districts and states are limited in the use of proficient scores based on alternate achievement standards in making AYP decisions.

FACT. Alternate assessments based on alternate achievement standards must only be given to students with the most significant cognitive disabilities. States must develop guidelines to help IEP teams determine which assessment is most appropriate for a student with a disability to take. If those guidelines are appropriately developed and implemented, IEP teams should be making the right decisions for their students.

12. Don't such "caps" interfere with IEP decisions?

No. The policies on including students with disabilities in assessment and accountability systems do not affect the IEP teamís role in making specific individual decisions about how to best address the needs of children with disabilities. The policies do not restrict the number of students who can participate in an alternate assessment. Instead, the policy restricts, solely for purposes of calculating AYP for school accountability, the number of scores that can be counted as proficient or advanced based on alternate achievement standards on alternate assessments.

13. How will the Department's recent proposed regulations change the policy on assessing and including students with disabilities in school accountability?

Since the regulation permitting a state to develop alternate achievement standards for students with the most significant cognitive disabilities was issued, information and experience in states, as well as important recent research, indicate that there may be an additional number of students who, because of their disability, have significant difficulty achieving grade-level proficiency, even with the best instruction, within the same time frame as other students.

The best available research and data indicate that this group of students comprises about 2 percent of the school-age population (or approximately 20 percent of students with disabilities). The progress of these students with disabilities in response to high-quality instruction, including special education and related services designed to address the students' individual needs, is such that the students are not likely to achieve grade-level proficiency within the school year covered by the students' IEPs.

The Department is publishing proposed regulations to address how these students may be included in a state's assessment and accountability systems. The proposed regulations would permit a state to (1) develop modified achievement standards, that is, standards that are aligned with the state's academic content standards for the grade in which a student is enrolled, but may reflect reduced breadth or depth of grade-level content; (2) develop assessments to measure the achievement of students based on such modified achievement standards; and (3) include the proficient and advanced scores based on modified achievement standards in determining AYP for school accountability purposes only, subject to a cap of 2.0 percent at the district and state levels.

The goal of the proposed regulations is to recognize, based on research, the specific needs of an additional group of students with disabilities while ensuring that states continue to hold schools accountable for helping these students with disabilities meet challenging standards that enable the students to approach, and even meet, grade-level standards. The proposed regulations would require certain safeguards, such as requiring that modified achievement standards provide access for students with disabilities to grade-level curricula and do not preclude a student from earning a regular high school diploma. They would also require a state to develop clear and appropriate guidelines for IEP teams to apply in determining which students should be assessed based on modified achievement standards and to ensure that parents are informed that their child's achievement will be measured on those standards. The proposed regulations would also permit a state, in determining AYP for the students with disabilities subgroup, to include, for a period of up to two years, the scores of students who were previously identified as having a disability but who are no longer receiving special education services.

The proposed regulation affects both *IDEA* and *NCLB* by ensuring that the requirements for participation in state assessment systems are the same. With this proposed change, students with disabilities must participate in an assessment that results in a valid score.

14. How will *IDEA* and *NCLB* work together for students with disabilities in the future?

IDEA and *NCLB* reinforce and strengthen the goal of accountability for all children. Both laws require states to include students with disabilities in state assessments and to report publicly the achievement of students with disabilities. In addition, state performance goals under the *IDEA* must be aligned with the state's definition of AYP. Such consistency across these two laws will facilitate greater collaboration between special education and general education teachers and realize the goal of considering children with disabilities as general education students first. One of the ways that *IDEA* supports this effort is through new provisions added by the 2004 reauthorization of the *IDEA* that allow local education agencies (LEAs) to use federal special education funds to provide early intervention services for students who are at risk of later identification and placement in special education. (There is nothing precluding state funds from also being used for this purpose.) This provides an opportunity for educators to work together to implement scientifically based instructional practices like curriculum-based measurement to identify and address academic problems early.

POSTSCRIPT

Does NCLB Leave Some Students Behind?

"Mrs. Dewey" dislikes being told to focus on students whose performance will lead to higher scores; this contradicts her professional ethics. Yet, she worries that teaching every child brands her as not contributing to the school's targets.

Secretary Spellings' words would puzzle 'Mrs. Dewey': "Special education is no longer a peripheral issue. IDEA and NCLB have put the needs of students with disabilities front and center. We've torn down the final barrier between special and general education. And now everyone in the system has a stake in ensuring students with disabilities achieve high standards" (Spellings, 2005). If so, "Mrs. Dewey" might ask, "Why is my group of students with disabilities too small to matter?"

Subgroups, and their sizes, engender much discussion. Scores from a very small number of students may not be statistically valid or reliable. Additionally, with small subgroups, privacy can be compromised when scores become public. These issues are particularly relevant in small and/or rural schools (McLaughlin, Embler, Hernandez, and Caron, *Rural Special Education Quarterly*, 2005).

Under NCLB, states set their own minimum subgroup size. If a subgroup falls below the minimum size, it is considered as having met AYP, regardless of student scores.

An extensive study on subgroup size and confidence intervals (another statistical tool for evaluating scores) found subgroup sizes vary widely nationwide, from 10 to at least 80 (Simpson, Gong, and Marion, http://www.nciea.org, 2005). Sometimes different subgroups had different minimums. The authors noted that larger minimum subgroup sizes mask the performance of students with disabilities. Schools meet their targets without being accountable for these students.

Diverse groups have signified strong opposition to this practice (*Joint Organizational Statement on NCLB*, http://www.fairtest.org, 2004; National Conference of State Legislatures, 2005; Commission on No Child Left Behind, 2006). It continues. Does it lead to statistically accurate results or deny access to some students?

Authors of the Department of Education FAQ sheet might say schools who manipulate subgroup sizes violate the spirit of NCLB. The FAQ sheet would advise Mrs. Dewey's administrators to believe their students with disabilities can meet high expectations and to use assessment results and services to pursue that target. In support, the Commission on No Child Left Behind (2006) found that disability subgroup scores were "very often not the sole reason a school is identified as not making AYP."

Yell, Katsiyannis, and Shiner (*TEACHING Exceptional Children,* 2006) express confidence that NCLB provides tools and guidance to meet its ambitious challenge. Inspired by its belief in students and educators, Faust (*In CASE,* 2006) finds "kernels of gold" in NCLB: opportunities for systemic change and growth.

Most people agree that students with disabilities should be included in education reform. Few would like to see these students relegated to shabby classrooms with outdated books. One quote (Petrilli, *The Education Gadfly,* 2005) strikes a jarring note:

> Nobody thinks kids with significant cognitive disabilities should be expected to reach the same standards as everyone else; it's hard if not impossible to find anyone in the Administration or on Capitol Hill who claims credit for the idea of including special education students as an NCLB subgroup in the first place. Once it was embedded in the law, however, special ed advocates seized on its potential, making it impossible to move. Spellings—and Secretary Paige before her—have been carefully walking federal policy back from this brink since the Act's ink was dry.

Is it possible that NCLB targets were painted with little thought of students with disabilities?

Is NCLB a leap forward, holding schools accountable for the performance of *all* students? Or does NCLB represent a step backward; creating loopholes (alternate and modified standards, alternate assessments, safe harbor provisions) that exclude students whose parents and teachers believed the promise that no child would be left behind? NCLB faces reauthorization in 2007. How, if at all, will it change?

ISSUE 9

Will NCLB Requirements Produce Highly Qualified Special Education Teachers?

YES: Rod Paige, from Remarks at the Education Department's First Annual Teacher Quality Evaluation Conference, http://www.ed.gov/print/news/speeches/2002/06/061102.html (June 11, 2002)

NO: James McLeskey and Dorene D. Ross, from "The Politics of Teacher Education in the New Millennium: Implications for Special Education Teacher Educators," *Teacher Education and Special Education* (Fall 2004)

ISSUE SUMMARY

YES: Rod Paige, then-Secretary of the U.S. Department of Education, and former Houston, Texas, superintendent, believes the promise of No Child Left Behind can be realized by mandating that every teacher be highly qualified by increasing their focus in the content areas they teach and decreasing time spent on pedagogical skills.

NO: James McLeskey and Dorene D. Ross, teacher education faculty at the University of Florida, present competing views of what constitutes "highly qualified" special education teachers, one based on deregulation and one based on professionalization; they encourage ongoing consideration to determine the value and impact of each.

The No Child Left Behind Act of 2001 (NCLB) holds high expectations for student achievement. Every child must be proficient in reading and math by 2014. To help each student reach that goal, NCLB also sets high expectations for teachers.

The first selection is the speech made by then-Secretary of the U.S. Department of Education Rod Paige that accompanied the release of his first Secretary's Annual Report on Teacher Quality (2002, http://www.title2.org). With affection and passion, Paige acknowledges the critical role teachers play in the lives of their students. With equal passion, Paige laments the current quality of teachers and teacher-education programs. His vision of a highly qualified teacher has spent many educational hours studying fields of concentration (what to teach) and very little time on theory and pedagogy (how to teach).

NCLB requires that all teachers must be highly qualified. To be considered as such, teachers must have a bachelor's degree, hold full state certification or licensure, and demonstrate competence in each subject they teach. The latter can be done by either a graduate degree or a "rigorous" test. Elementary teachers can demonstrate content competence through a "rigorous" test. Both new and veteran teachers must be highly qualified.

These requirements were relatively easy to understand as they applied to secondary teachers assigned to a specific subject area. Less clear was how special education teachers would be deemed highly qualified, especially those responsible for teaching an array of subjects to groups of middle/secondary students with significant disabilities.

Striving for consistency with NCLB, IDEA04 requires that the highly qualified special education teacher providing consultative services or support services possess at least a bachelor's degree and hold full state certification in special education. However, a special education teacher responsible for primary instruction in any core academic subject (English, reading or language arts, math, science, foreign languages, civics and government, economics, arts, history and geography) must also demonstrate competence in each subject area taught. Competence could be established through any of the methods available to general education teachers. This requirement extends to special education teachers in substantially separate settings for students with complex disabilities.

In this issue's second selection, James McLeskey and Dorene D. Ross, who study programs of teacher preparation, as well as teach in them, discuss two competing perspectives about the kind of training that leads to a well-qualified special education teacher. Those favoring deregulation, including NCLB proponents, have little use for traditional courses of study that highlight adaptations and/or strategies addressing student behavior and learning patterns. In contrast, numerous professional associations call for rigorous standards that include content, but also stress the critical importance of demonstrated teaching practices that respond to the unique needs of students with disabilities. While McLeskey and Ross favor the professionalization argument, they maintain there are insufficient research findings to enable us to embrace either one of these perspectives to the exclusion of the other.

As you read these articles, consider whether you think the increased emphasis on subject area content is a wise direction for special education teachers. Should time developing teaching skill be replaced by courses in content areas to enhance access to the general curriculum? Will a highly qualified special education teacher be highly competent to address the learning and behavior needs of students for whom learning poses significant challenges?

YES

Rod Paige

Education Secretary Paige Addresses First Annual Teacher Quality Evaluation Conference

I want to thank all of you for coming and for being a part of this, the first annual Teacher Quality Evaluation Conference.

For those who have come from out of town, I hope you get a chance to visit some of our national treasures and see for yourself what an incredibly beautiful and vibrant place our nation's capital is.

More than a year later, I am still in awe seeing Lincoln and Jefferson in the early morning light—or Lady Freedom standing sentry on the Capitol dome. There is a special feeling when you pass the White House and see families peering through the fence, hoping for a glance of their president or first lady or first dogs.

Every day I'm reminded what an honor it is to live here and to serve as U.S. Secretary of Education.

One of the things you learn right off the bat is that children are going to write and ask for favors. Three of the most popular requests are: shorter school days, less homework and better cafeteria food.

Some write to ask me to come visit their schools and *to please bring the president with me!*

But most of their letters include well-thought out questions—like the one from a New Jersey eighth grader named Brianna who wrote to ask: "What do you believe are the most important issues facing elementary or high school education in the United States today?"

That's a great question—in fact, it goes to the very heart of our new education reforms signed into law by President Bush on January 8.

I believe the *No Child Left Behind* Act of 2001 will go down in history as the key piece of public policy that finally slammed close the achievement gap between those who have and those who don't—between those who are hopeful and those who are hopeless.

Our nation has been called to commit itself to a bold goal—the goal of creating an education system that insists on accountability, results, teacher quality and reading programs that work so all children in our public schools get the excellent education their parents sent them there for. And it all started

From http://ed/gov/print/news/speeches/2002/06/061102.html, June 11, 2002.

because we have a president who believes that the most sacred duty of government is to educate its children. They are our future.

Yet national report cards in recent years show we are destroying that future—one child at a time.

- Two out of three fourth-graders can't read proficiently
- Seven out of 10 inner-city and rural fourth graders can't read at the most basic level
- Nearly a third of college freshmen need remedial classes before they can handle entry level courses
- America's twelfth graders rank among the lowest in math and science achievement among their counterparts in other industrialized nations

These are more than just statistics. They are a grim picture of the human toll of an education system that is failing too many African-American, Hispanic and low-income children in our nation's classrooms.

Soon after President Bush took office, he called on Congress to fundamentally change the structure of education—and enact the most sweeping change in education in 35 years.

Never before have we as a nation made the commitment to all children in our public schools that every one of them can and will learn. *Every single child*. Regardless of race, income or zip code.

The *No Child Left Behind* law also recognizes that just throwing money at a problem won't make it go away. Over the last half-century local, state and federal taxpayers have spent more than $10 trillion on our public schools. $10 trillion.

And what have we got to show for it?

Every year we did the same thing: spent more money. And every year we got the same result: mediocre student performance—or worse.

It was Albert Einstein who said insanity is "the belief that one can get different results by doing the same thing."

It doesn't take an Einstein to see the truth is that all the money in the world won't fix our schools if your *only* plan is to throw more money at the problem.

To solve the problem, you must first create a framework for change.

And our new education reforms provide that framework by insisting on accountability and results; by providing local control and flexibility; by empowering parents to take a lead in their children's education; and by insisting on teaching methods that work.

The basics work. Research-based reading programs work. Testing works.

Defenders of the status quo hate the idea of testing. But parents don't. Recent polls show the American people standing shoulder to shoulder with the president on annual testing. Moms and dads want the best for their children. They understand that the only way to know if teachers are teaching and their children are learning is to measure for results—and to hold schools accountable.

Their own children agree. A Public Agenda poll shows 95 percent of students are not obsessing over the idea of tests.

No Child Left Behind provided the framework for change. And it provided historic levels of funding to get the job done—including the largest education budget for disadvantaged children in U.S. history.

The big difference now is that taxpayers know what they're getting for their money. And parents know if their children are learning.

And if a school is failing its mission, moms and dads no longer have to helplessly stand by and watch every last spark of curiosity die in their children's eyes.

Thanks to *No Child Left Behind* they can choose one-on-one tutoring, or after-school help or enroll their children in a better public school.

Our new education reforms depend on high standards and accountability—and teaching every child to read. Most of all, our new education reforms depend on who's standing at the front of the classroom teaching.

Most of us can remember a favorite teacher. President Bush loved teachers so much he married one.

I had two favorite teachers: my parents. By day, they taught other children in Monticello, Mississippi. But on nights and weekends, they taught me and my sisters and brothers.

Books filled our house, and so did love—for learning, for our faith, for our country and for each other. Their example inspired me to become a teacher as well.

And it was while working in the classroom that I discovered the truth in the words of World War II General Omar Bradley when he said: "The teacher is the real soldier of democracy. Others can defend it, but only he can make it work."

Very few people have the influence over our lives that teachers do. And that is why the president, the Congress and I are determined to meet the goal of a quality teacher in every classroom by 2006.

Today, I am sending Congress a report on the state of teacher quality in America that spells out the challenges states face in achieving this goal. And we have a few:

- Too many teachers are not qualified in the subject they're teaching
- Too many states do not test to make sure teachers know what they're teaching
- Too many states that do test set the bar for passing way too low
- Too many education programs require too much focus on theory and pedagogy, and too little focus on fields of concentration—like math, history or science.
- Too many barriers are built into the system that keep talented people out of the classroom and force districts to fill vacancies with teachers on waivers

Clearly, there is much work to do.

Fortunately, we have a growing body of scientific research that tells us what it takes to be an effective teacher, and we must listen.

And we must do several things:

First, we must strengthen academic standards for teachers.

Research confirms that the most effective teachers are those who are smart and who know the subject they're teaching—inside and out. How much teachers know determines how well students learn.

Yet academic standards for teachers are low. Not all states test potential teachers on content knowledge. And many states that do test use tests that are not rigorous enough.

California, for example, requires teachers to take the California Basic Educational Skills Test that is set at roughly the 10th grade level.

Other states set the bar so low that even teachers who scored in only the 20th percentile passed certification.

Sadly, it's the children who need help most—those in inner-city and rural schools—who are *least* likely to have well-prepared teachers.

- 43 percent of math teachers in high poverty schools have neither majored nor minored in math-related fields, compared to 27 percent of middle class schools
- 25 percent of disadvantaged children are taught English by teachers who don't have a degree in English, compared to only 11 percent of middle class children.

Not only is this troubling to me. It's troubling to teachers.

Some months back, Mrs. Bush held a White House conference on teacher preparation. At that conference, Sandra Feldman, the president of the American Federation of Teachers, said: "Good teachers need to be really well educated . . . They need to know—deeply—the subject they teach. Prospective teachers should complete an academic major and have a solid foundation in the liberal arts. You can't teach what you don't know well."

Some states have embraced meaningful standards—I think of Pennsylvania and Virginia.

But *all states* need to take a hard look at how they decide who's qualified to teach and who's not.

Which brings me to my second point: we must tear down barriers preventing talented men and women from entering the teaching profession.

At a time when we desperately need strong teachers in our classrooms, we should be doing all we can to attract and keep the best and the brightest candidates. A good place to start is by drawing from nontraditional sources.

For example, Teach For America is a program that recruits gifted and talented students from our nation's college campuses to teach in inner-city schools.

Transition to Teaching matches talented mid-career professionals with schools with the greatest need.

And Troops to Teachers is a program that taps retired service men and women for the classroom—people like Army Sgt. Art Moore.

Sgt. Moore served our country for 21 years. When he retired, he wanted to keep serving. So he contacted Troops to Teachers about alternative certification. And for the past seven years, Sgt. Moore has been a special education teacher in Baltimore.

Another teacher who took a different route to the chalkboard is Col. Chauncey Veatch.

After 25 years serving our country, Col. Veatch left the Army to teach children of migrant workers in California.

In April, President Bush and I had the honor of joining Chauncey in the Rose Garden as he was named the 2002 National Teacher of the Year.

We must streamline the process to encourage more people like Art and Chauncy to help fill the need in our nation's classrooms.

Finally, states must improve the quality of teacher education programs to ensure that new teachers are prepared to be effective in the classroom.

I've been a dean of a school of education. And I know the special problems these schools face and the responsibilities they bear.

But I am also mindful of what Diane Ravitch of New York University said during the White House conference on teachers. She said the original idea behind colleges of education was to create rigorous professional training for teachers—just like doctors and lawyers.

Yet here we are—a century later—with research showing many teachers fresh out of college lack what they need to meet the challenges of the classroom. More than one in five will give up and leave the profession within their first three years.

In one study, less than 36 percent surveyed said they felt "very well prepared" to teach and help their students meet performance standards. Less than 20 percent said they felt prepared to meet the needs of diverse students or those with limited English proficiency.

Despite this, many schools of education have continued, business-as-usual—focusing heavily on pedagogy—how to be a teacher—when the evidence cries out that what future teachers need most is a deeper understanding of the subject they'll be teaching—of how to monitor student progress and of how to help students who are falling behind.

It got so bad in the Elk Grove school district in California, that its Superintendent—David Gordon—took the matter into his own hands. David is with us today. Where are you David?

Working with a local university that was willing to "think outside the box", David started a fast-track teacher credential program called the Teacher Education Institute. They set high standards for prospective teachers and then provided intensive training to meet those high standards.

You know what happened? Even though he raised the bar for achievement for both students and teachers—and even though a teacher shortage loomed—Elk Grove schools began filling its classrooms with top-quality and well-trained people who were up to the challenge of the rigorous curriculum.

Student achievement soared. And the number of college-bound students has more than doubled.

Future teachers certainly need to learn the basics of teaching and managing a classroom, but that should not be the main focus of teacher preparation.

We must be open to innovative approaches and rethink traditional methods that may not work anymore.

There is no doubt that we ask a lot of our teachers—and we owe them something in return. We owe them our respect for the professionals they are. We owe them our support. And we owe them the training and tools to succeed.

The *No Child Left Behind* Act gives schools greater flexibility to use federal funds where the local need is greatest: to recruit new teachers, to improve teacher training, or to increase teacher pay in critical need areas.

President Bush's 2003 budget calls on Congress to:

- Increase funding for teacher development to help teachers succeed
- Increase funding to train and recruit teachers in math and science
- Provide tax relief to help teachers defray expenses
- Expand loan forgiveness for those who teach in high need schools

President Bush's $2.85 billion Teacher Quality Initiative represents the largest and most comprehensive federal investment in preparation, training and recruiting teachers and principals.

These resources—and the ideas I've laid out—will help states as they work to ensure a highly qualified teacher in every classroom, and to implement our new education reforms.

Some defenders of the status quo are resisting our new education reforms. And, frankly, I don't understand that.

How can they possibly argue with a plan that says we want to provide more resources and better instruction for disadvantaged children?

Maybe the critics are like those people Sam Rayburn used to talk about when he said, "Any jackass can kick over a barn. It takes a carpenter to build one."

We're talking about helping children so far down on the achievement scale they're not even a blip on the radar.

We're talking about helping children who show up in national report cards that say 40 percent of white fourth graders can read while only 12 percent of black fourth graders can read.

In the 19 years since *A Nation at Risk* set off a wave of well-intentioned school reform efforts, we still have too many children—mostly urban and mostly African American—falling through the cracks.

The reforms of *No Child Left Behind*, when implemented, will provide a safety net to catch these children and get them back on track academically.

To be sure, there are pockets of excellence all around our country. As I travel our country I see many inspiring examples of schools and teachers and students rising to the challenges, of moms and dads getting involved in their children's schools.

No Child Left Behind is not just a law, it's a revolution. A profound moment of change. And all of us—as educators, policymakers, community leaders and those of us in public life—have a role to play.

Years from now, people will look back and say: That's when they raised the bar and student achievement began to soar. That's when leadership triumphed over politics and no child was left behind. That's when the American people realized they could create great schools worthy of a great nation.

God bless you all. And God bless America.

James McLeskey and
Dorene D. Ross

 **NO**

The Politics of Teacher Education in the New Millennium: Implications for Special Education Teacher Educators

O ver the last several years, teacher education has become a 'front burner' political issue in Washington, DC and in most statehouses. This new found status has resulted largely from the wide spread agreement that highly qualified teachers make a significant difference in the academic achievement of students. The National Commission on Teaching and America's Future has argued that what teachers know and do makes a difference in their impact on students and student learning. Research by Sanders and Horn provides robust evidence to support this claim. Specifically, Sanders and Horn found that over a period of years, the quality of the teacher contributes more to student achievement than any other factor, including class size, class composition, or student background. This research, coupled with calls at the federal level and in most states for 'tougher academic standards', led to the inclusion of the mandate in the recently passed No Child Left Behind (NCLB) Act that all content area teachers in Title I schools be "highly qualified" by 2005-06. . . . [A] similar mandate will be included in the next reauthorization of the Individuals with Disabilities Education Act (IDEA), requiring that all special education teachers be highly qualified.

The current highly politicized context for teaching and teacher education creates both challenges and opportunities for teacher educators. Two questions emerge as central in this debate: (1) What is the definition of "highly qualified" teacher? (2) What are the characteristics of high quality teacher education which produce highly qualified teachers? Although educational researchers have frequently engaged these questions, the distinction in today's context is that each issue is being debated and defined within a highly charged political context. Acknowledging and understanding the implications of the way these issues are being defined and the potential solutions that are being proposed is critical to the work of teacher educators over the next decade. . . .

From *Teacher Education and Special Education*, vol. 27, no. 4, 2004, pp. 342–349. Copyright © 2004 by Council for Exceptional Children. Reprinted by permission. References omitted.

What Is the Definition of "Highly Qualified Teacher"?

While all agree on the need for highly qualified teachers, there is disagreement about what 'highly qualified' entails. Two camps control the discussion regarding this issue. One group is calling for the deregulation of teacher education, while a second group argues for the professionalization of teaching. Both of these positions exert considerable pressure on state departments of education and teacher education programs and have a significant influence on who enters the classroom as a beginning teacher. . . .

The leading advocate to deregulate teacher education has been Rod Paige, former Superintendent of the Houston (TX) Independent School District, and current Secretary of the U.S. Department of Education. In a paper addressing the need for highly qualified teachers, the Secretary made his position clear by stating that "rigorous research indicates that verbal ability and content knowledge are the most important attributes of highly qualified teachers. In addition, there is little evidence that education school course work leads to improved student achievement." This perspective on teacher quality is reflected in [NCLB], which provides alternate definitions for "highly qualified teachers", including an option to fully certify as "highly qualified" those who (a) complete a bachelor's degree and pass a test of subject knowledge (for middle and secondary level teachers) or (b) complete a bachelor's degree and pass a test or tests of subject knowledge and teaching skills (elementary teachers). In this way NCLB gives the force of law to alternative certification routes currently in place in many states which do nor hold participants to the same high standards as other state approved teacher education programs . . . that are typically based in Institutions of Higher Education. . . .

Much of the support for the 'deregulation' position has come from the work of private foundations. . . . In a position paper that provided the basis for the Secretary's position, the Abell Foundation contended that there is no research to support the perspective that teacher certification leads to improved student outcomes. Furthermore, in this report Walsh contended that teacher certification requirements are unnecessary regulatory hurdles that prevent many potentially well-qualified individuals from becoming teachers. Similar to NCLB, the Abell Foundation recommended that "the only fixed requirement (for teacher certification) should be a bachelor's degree and a passing score on an appropriate teacher's exam." Chester Finn and colleagues from the Heritage and Fordham Foundations took similar positions, and also called for a dramatic increase in alternate routes to certification, which circumvent the regulatory hurdles that exist for traditional preparation programs.

The positions taken by Secretary Paige and others cited above lead to the conclusion that the image they have of a 'highly qualified' teacher is "a technician who faithfully implements the highly sequenced instructional techniques stipulated in government-approved texts and materials, which are based on the results of 'scientific research'." This contrasts sharply to the perspective taken by those who support the professionalization of teaching and a broadened and more complex definition of "highly qualified teacher".

Professional education groups, including the National Council for the Accreditation of Teacher Education (NCATE), the National Board for Professional Teaching Standards (NBPTS), the American Association of Colleges for Teacher Education (AACTE), the Interstate New Teacher Assessment and Support Consortium (INTASC), and the Council for Exceptional Children (CEC), among many others, are major representatives of those who seek to professionalize teaching. The most influential of these groups has been the National Commission on Teaching and America's Future (NCTAF). . . . This group has called for more rigorous standards for teachers. These standards have been produced by the NBPTS and INTASC, and incorporated into teacher education program approval by NCATE and CEC. While these standards include and emphasize knowledge of subject matter, as the deregulationists recommend, they also include knowledge of teaching and demonstration of this knowledge through teacher performance in the classroom. These groups advocate the use of high, national standards for the preparation and certification of teachers, is well as uniform assessments to ensure that teachers can demonstrate mastery of these standards through classroom performance.

Research to support the professionalization agenda has primarily been reviewed by Darling-Hammond and Wilson. These investigators . . . concluded that pedagogical preparation enhances teacher quality and results in increased student achievement. These investigators also reported a significant relationship between teacher certification and student achievement. Finally, while these investigators conclude that research supports the importance of subject matter preparation for teachers, they did not find that subject matter preparation was more important than knowledge of how to teach as a factor influencing student achievement.

The image of a teacher that emerges from the perspectives taken by those who seek to professionalize teaching contrasts sharply with those who seek to deregulate teaching. This image reflects the perspective that the teacher "knows subject matter (what to teach) and pedagogy (how to teach) but also knows how to learn and how to make decisions informed by theory and research from many bodies of knowledge and also is informed by feedback from school and classroom evidence in particular contexts."

What Are the Characteristics of High Quality Teacher Education Which Produces Highly Qualified Teachers?

For teacher educators, among others, it follows logically that the quality of a beginning teacher is influenced by her or his teacher education program. However, this has not been the conclusion reached by all, as the contrasting definitions of "highly qualified" teacher reveal, Indeed, the simultaneous calls for deregulation and increased professionalization in teaching and teacher education have played out in state departments of education across the U.S. in two distinctive ways. First, the deregulation movement has resulted in a range of alternative teacher preparation programs in every state. In some instances these alternative certification programs are held to the same standards as . . . teacher education programs . . . based in Institutions of Higher Education . . . , while in others they are not held to these same high standards. The most extreme example of lowering standards has been the option of becoming certified through receipt of a bachelor's degree with any major, and subsequently passing a test of content and/or instructional knowledge, as proposed in NCLB. . . . At least one state currently has a test-based alternative to traditional certification (Florida), and a national test is being developed for this purpose by the American Board for Certification of Teaching Excellence.

In many of the same states that have lowered standards through alternative paths to teacher certification, departments of education have responded to the professionalization of teaching agenda by changing and often raising standards for traditional, Institution of Higher Education . . . based teacher preparation programs. For example, in Florida, more specific requirements for general education course work have been added to teacher education requirements, along with specific course requirements in classroom management, assessment, reading, and ESOL. In addition, rigorous outcomes measures, which must be demonstrated through course work and in field experiences, have been added. . . .

The major weakness in the arguments made by advocates for both sides of this debate is the lack of definitive research evidence to guide decision making about how best to prepare and credential teachers. Rice noted that the current debate is largely ideological, because there is so little robust research to guide policy decisions. It is important to acknowledge that teacher education is still a relatively new research field, and therefore it is hardly surprising that we lack definitive answers to the many important questions that would allow an informed response to the professionalism/deregulation debate.

As is characteristic of many emerging fields, the very nature of our research questions has progressed over time as we have gained knowledge about teaching and teachers. Cochran-Smith provides a brief review of the history of teacher education research, noting that we have moved from research on the attributes of good teachers (1950s and 1960s), to research about the kinds of instructional strategies used by good teachers (1960s to mid-1980s), to syntheses that focused on the domains of knowledge essential for good teaching (1980s to 1990s), to research about the outcomes of teacher education and the links to student learning (1990s to today). While one might wonder why we have not yet developed strong linkages between teacher education and student outcomes, it is important to remember that such studies require longitudinal cross-institutional research and access to student achievement data bases in ways that link achievement data to specific teachers. Unfortunately, until recently there has been little funding for this kind of evaluative research, nor has there been the availability of and access to databases needed to conduct such studies.

At present, teacher education researchers are working to distill from available, peer-reviewed research clear conclusions about the impact of the full range of teacher preparation programs or paths and, more specifically, the impact of components of teacher education programs on teacher quality and student outcomes. . . . (Researchers are working to determine what we KNOW about the practices most likely to prepare high quality teachers.)

While Rice finds sufficient research to conclude that "there is no merit in large-scale elimination of all credential requirements," Shulman has pointed out that neither teacher education nor certification can be considered a variable, because both are ill-defined and vary from setting to setting. Instead, he argues that teacher education researchers need to document the impact of various components of teacher education on both teacher and student learning. Thus, the most important question for teacher education researchers is, "What components of teacher education programs (whether traditional or alternative) are critical to produce highly qualified teachers?"

Recent reviews of available research in both general and special education teacher education suggest that currently available research provides more questions than answers. At this point, the available research evidence suggests:

- Content knowledge is important for teachers, particularly those in secondary education. However, developing subject matter knowledge is more complex than completing a major in one's discipline or taking some specified number of courses. Research does not tell us how much content preparation is sufficient or whether certain courses provide better preparation than others. Additionally, most content related studies have been done in the areas of math and science, and provide little guidance related to teachers in other content areas, or in elementary or special education.
- Pedagogical preparation strengthens the skills of teachers. In fact, Goldhaber an Brewer found that pedagogical preparation of teachers had a larger impact on student achievement in math and science than content preparation. Similarly, Rice concludes that "it appears that having subject matter expertise is necessary but not sufficient. A number of Studies . . . suggest that teachers must learn and practice how to apply that knowledge in classroom settings, implying an important role for pedagogical training." However, studies of this issue do not tell us how much or what kinds of pedagogical preparation teachers need, nor do they tell us whether pedagogical knowledge is better developed in a general course (e.g. an instructional strategies course), or as part of content specific courses. Available research suggests that subject specific preparation is of critical importance for high school mathematics teachers, but the impact of subject specific pedagogical preparation for other content areas, elementary education, or special education is less apparent, and in some cases even negative.
- Preservice teachers learn more from focused, well-structured clinical experience than from other kinds of field experiences. . . . While available research provides evidence that field experience provides opportunity to "learn the profession" and reduces the anxiety of beginning teachers we know little about the impact of different forms of clinical experience on the practice of novice teachers and the learning of their students. In addition, we know little about the contribution of fieldwork versus the contribution of course work on the development of knowledge and skills in novice teachers.

Clearly, our knowledge about the components of effective teacher education is still emerging. One of the challenges to further developing this area of research is that there are few cross-institutional studies available and that the studies that do exist seldom link findings to future classroom practice or to subsequent student outcomes. . . .

What Are the Implications of the Current Political Climate for Teacher Education and Special Education?

The national discussions regarding the definition of a "highly qualified" teacher and what constitutes high quality teacher preparation have significant implications for special education. Recent research indicates that the shortage of fully certified teachers in special education is greater than in any other area, including mathematics, science, and foreign language. Currently, 47,532 or 11.4% of all special education teachers in the U.S. lack full certification for their current teaching assignment. These teachers provide instruction for 800,000 students with disabilities. Thus, the greatest shortage of 'highly qualified' teachers is in the area where students have the greatest need for teachers with the most expertise, special education.

To address this severe shortage of special education teachers, some states have lowered standards for obtaining certification in keeping with NCLB, to allow anyone who has a bachelor's degree and can pass a test to be certified. Moreover, many states have approved quick, alternative paths to certification via routes that do not meet the standards of traditional teacher education programs or the characteristics of intensive, high quality alternative routes to licensure. These actions will result in the placement of many teachers into special education classrooms who are called "highly qualified', yet in many instances lack the most basic preparation for successfully teaming students with disabilities. Furthermore, these actions may well exacerbate shortages in special education, as the attrition rates for graduates of short-cut routes to certification are significantly higher (up to three times greater) than those of graduates from traditional teacher education programs.

At the same time that states have lowered requirements for certification via some routes, the movement toward demanding increasingly higher standards for all students, coupled with the professionalization movement in teacher education has resulted in increasing requirements for traditional . . . program approval in these same and many other states. These higher requirements will likely result in *fewer* prospective teachers in traditional teacher education programs, as these candidates seek out alternative paths to certification that are less time-consuming and less demanding.

With these ideas in mind, it seems highly likely that the reform agendas that are currently playing out in Washington and in statehouses across the U.S. will result in *fewer* special education teachers who have the qualifications to successfully teach students with disabilities, rather than more 'highly qualified' teachers. . . .

While teaching and teacher education have always been influenced by national policy and legislation, many educators currently contend that the controls set by policymakers are both more intrusive and more troubling than has ever been the case. Special educators do not have a long history of research in teacher education. In fact most research in special education has focused on the nature and impact of specific interventions on the learning or behavior of children. Clearly, this research has been and continues to be highly important. However, if we are to have an impact on policy related to teacher education, which is setting (and will continue to set for the foreseeable future) policy that will shape the nature and training of teachers in special education classrooms, it is time for more special educators to study the education of our teachers, so that we will have research based evidence to influence these policy decision.

POSTSCRIPT

Will NCLB Requirements Produce Highly Qualified Special Education Teachers?

The call for highly qualified special education teachers comes at a time of a serious teacher shortage. A comprehensive study revealed that a nationwide scarcity of special education teachers has existed for 15 years and is greater than shortages in mathematics and science (McLeskey, Tyler, and Flippin, *The Journal of Special Education*, 2004). How will NCLB requirements impact this shortage?

Unease about this predicament comes from several fronts. Margaret Spellings, Paige's successor, noted that staffing problems in self-contained special education classes remain among the most persistent (*Key Policy Letter*, October 2005). Her concern is echoed by administrators in both rural (Hardman, Rosenburg, and Sindelar, *Rural Special Education Quarterly*, 2005) and urban (Nagle and Crawford, *Journal of Special Education Leadership*, 2005) settings. In its fourth report studying NCLB implementation, the Center on Education Policy (http://www.cep-dc.org, 2006) found states cite finding highly qualified special education teachers as their biggest challenge.

In his *Second Annual Report on Teacher Quality*, Paige (2003) advocated a "high standards, low barriers" approach to improving teacher quality. Acknowledging particular staffing stresses in urban and rural areas, Paige encouraged alternative preparation programs to offer streamlined paths to the classroom. These would attract non-traditional candidates who bring content expertise with them.

McLeskey and Ross emphasize that alternative routes are often held to looser standards than are traditional programs. They are concerned that a bachelor's degree and a passing test score will not guarantee someone capable of successfully teaching students with disabilities. Similar concerns are expressed by other researchers (Gelman, Pullen, & Kauffman, *Exceptionality*, 2004; Torff, *Phi Delta Kappan*, 2005).

Others are troubled about the highly qualified expectations themselves. Describing the regulations as nothing more than pretense, Rebell and Hunter (*Phi Delta Kappan*, 2004) find NCLB's intentions weakened because state licensing standards differ widely. They observe that NCLB does not require anyone to demonstrate that they can "translate their academic knowledge into effective instruction for even the easiest-to-educate students." And yet, they note that the groups most targeted by NCLB—including students with disabilities—demand the most skillful instruction.

McCormick (*TEACHING Exceptional Children,* 2005) concedes that experienced chemists might transfer their knowledge to advanced high school students. However, he objects strenuously to reducing elements of strong traditional programs: provide training to assess students with disabilities, modify learning environments, adapt curricula, and select and implement appropriate behavioral supports. He is concerned that a shift in emphasis sacrifices the essence of special education, leading to distrust and litigation.

Viewing highly qualified teacher requirements from their legal perspective, Jameson and Huefner (*Journal of Law and Education,* 2006) hypothesize that current tensions between teacher quality, student achievement, and educational placement might ultimately be resolved through litigation. Several court cases have supported education in the least restrictive environment. Will parents prefer supported inclusive environments or those with the most content-trained teachers? If parents pursue a combination of opportunities, will a new model of inclusion be ordered—successfully blending the content expertise of a general education teacher with the instructional expertise of a special educator?

Perhaps general education teachers will need more competence in special education knowledge and strategies. A noted scholar of special education teacher attrition and retention, Billingsley (*Journal of Special Education Leadership,* 2005) observes that principals must actively support meaningful, effective collaboration between general education and special education teachers through consistent planning time and mentoring.

Will there be enough highly qualified special education teachers? Can alternative programs fill the need? Can co-teaching teams blend the talents of two highly qualified teachers to create ideal programs? Or will NCLB's content emphasis create special education teachers unable to deliver the specially designed instruction that is the hallmark of IDEA?

ISSUE 10

Can Scientifically Based Research Guide Instructional Practice?

YES: Samuel L. Odom, Ellen Brantlinger, Russell Gersten, Robert H. Horner, Bruce Thompson, and Karen R. Harris, from "Research in Special Education: Scientific Methods and Evidence-Based Practices," *Exceptional Children* (Winter 2005)

NO: Frederick J. Brigham, William E. Gustashaw III, Andrew L. Wiley, and Michele St. Peter Brigham, from "Research in the Wake of the No Child Left Behind Act: Why the Controversies Will Continue and Some Suggestions for Controversial Research," *Behavioral Disorders* (May 2004)

ISSUE SUMMARY

YES: Samuel L. Odom, Ellen Brantlinger, Russell Gersten, Robert H. Horner, Bruce Thompson, and Karen R. Harris, all college faculty members and educational researchers, begin their article with definitive support for research-based methodology. They herald proposals for quality indicators, to establish rigor in an array of research methods that can identify effective educational practices.

NO: Frederick J. Brigham, associate professor at the University of Virginia, Charlottesville; William E. Gustashaw III and Andrew L. Wiley, both doctoral candidates at the University of Virginia, Charlottesville; and Michele St. Peter Brigham, a special education practitioner, believe that disagreement, mistrust, and the shifting general education environment preclude the usefulness of scientifically based research to guide daily instruction.

Dismayed by decades of flat results on the National Assessment of Educational Progress, the framers of No Child Left Behind (NCLB) emphatically state that educators must use interventions based on scientifically based research "that involves the application of rigorous, systematic, and objective procedures to obtain reliable and valid knowledge" (NCLB, 2001). Interventions encompass educational practices, strategies, curriculum, and programs.

A profusion of educational materials now claim to be scientifically based. Close comparison with NCLB requirements may reveal that, although some may rely on the research done by others, they do not measure up to NCLB standards. This issue explores the controversy swirling around the application of these standards.

Two resources are available to assist educators in understanding the meaning and application of scientifically based research: *Identifying and Implementing Educational Practices Supported by Rigorous Evidence: A User Friendly Guide* (Institute of Educational Sciences, 2003) and the What Works Clearinghouse (http://www. whatworks.ed.gov). A third resource, the NICHCY's Research Center (http://research. nichcy.org) debuted in February 2006, focusing solely on special education.

Noting that many educational practices have been supported by "poorly-designed studies and/or advocacy-driven studies" (p. iii), the authors of *Identifying and Implementing* "seek(s) to provide educational practitioners with user-friendly tools to distinguish practices supported by rigorous evidence from those that are not" (p. iii).

This useful guide begins by defining NCLB's "gold standard" of evidence: randomized controlled trials (RCT), which are "studies that randomly assign individuals to an intervention group or to a control group, in order to measure the effects of the intervention" (p. 1). Briefly, students, similar on critical variables, are randomly assigned into two groups. One receives the intervention; the other does not. If the first group significantly outperforms the second, the intervention can be said to be effective. Similar students ensure that no other factors could account for the results. Random assignment of these students ensures that no bias differentiated the groups.

The What Works Clearinghouse (WWC), an online resource, "collects, screens, and identifies studies" on topic areas such as middle school mathematics, and reports "on the strengths and weaknesses of those studies against the WWC Evidence Standards so that you know what the best scientific evidence has to say." In addition to using RCT, the strongest evidence comes from studies that have lasted at least a semester, have outcome measures, and have been published in peer-reviewed journals.

Educational researchers have risen to this challenge. A number of prominent research-based journals have published thematic issues on the topic of scientifically based methodologies.

Our first selection is the lead article in one of these thematic issues. Odom, Brantlinger, Gersten, Horner, Thompson, and Harris review the considerable history of special education research. Embracing the use of scientific data to guide practice, Odom et al. discuss research stages, each of which requires specific methods to identify scientifically supported interventions.

In the second selection, Brigham, Gustashaw, Wiley, and Brigham argue that even gold-standard evidence will not resolve the controversies surrounding practices in special education. They believe competing motives, perspectives, and goals will not be eliminated by evidence. They also wonder if today's research findings will be relevant in the rapidly changing schools of tomorrow.

As you read these articles, ask yourself if the methods used in your school could stand up to gold-standard scrutiny. Can the assistance of *The User Friendly Guide* and WWC help you make better choices? Will parents, teachers, and administrators agree on the choices? What happens if they disagree?

YES

Samuel L. Odom et al.

Research in Special Education: Scientific Methods and Evidence-Based Practices

Should science guide practice in special education? Most individuals would say "Yes." However, the "devil is in the details." Major initiatives in other disciplines such as medicine, the allied health professions, and psychology are attempting to identify and disseminate practices that have scientific evidence of effectiveness. In education, national policies such as the No Child Left Behind Act (NCLB) require that teachers use scientifically proven practices in their classrooms. Yet, there is concern about the quality of scientific research in the field of education and disagreement about the type of scientific information that is acceptable as evidence. An oft-cited report from the National Research Council (NRC) states that science in education consists of different types of questions and that different methodologies are needed to address these questions. In contrast, other agencies and research synthesis organizations (e.g., the What Works Clearinghouse [WWC]) have focused primarily on the question of whether a practice is effective and proposed that the "gold standard" for addressing this question is a single type of research methodology— randomized experimental group designs (also called randomized clinical trials or RCTs).

In January 2003, the Council for Exceptional Children's (CEC) Division for Research established a task force to address these devilish details as they apply to special education. The operating assumptions of this task force were that different types of research questions are important for building and documenting the effectiveness of practices, and that different types of methodologies are essential in order to address these questions. The task force identified four types of research methodologies in special education: (a) experimental group, (b) correlational, (c) single subject, and (d) qualitative designs. The task force was to establish quality indicators for each methodology and to propose how evidence from each methodology could be used to identify and understand effective practices in special education. . . .

This article provides a context and rationale for this endeavor. We begin with a discussion of the importance of multiple scientific methodologies in special education research. Next, we examine efforts to identify high-quality

From *Exceptional Children*, vol. 71, no. 2, Winter 2005, pp. 137–148. Copyright © 2005 by Council for Exceptional Children. Reprinted by permission. References omitted.

research methodology and then examine initiatives in the fields of medicine and education to identify evidence-based practice. In conclusion, we propose that research and development on effective practices in special education exists on a continuum, with each methodology matched to questions arising from different points of the continuum. Also, it is important to acknowledge that although basic research serves as the foundation for the development of effective practices and is critically important for our work in special education, the issues addressed in this article will be most relevant for applied research.

Rationale for Multiple Scientific Research Methodologies in Special Education

The rationale for having different research methodologies in special education is based on the current conceptualization of research in education and the complexity of special education as a field. The history and tradition of special education research, when employing multiple methodologies, has resulted in the identification of effective practices.

Current Conceptualization of Research in Education

A primary emphasis in education policy today is to improve the quality of education for all of America's children. This policy, exemplified by NCLB, compels educators to use "teaching practices that have been proven to work." However, a general concern has been voiced about the quality of research in education. To address this concern, the National Academy of Sciences (NAS) created a committee to examine the status of scientific research in education. An operating assumption of this committee was that research questions must guide researchers' selections of scientific methods. The NAS committee proposed that most research questions in education could be grouped into three types: (a) description (what is happening?); (b) cause (is there a systematic effect?); and (c) process or mechanism (why or how is it happening?). The committee conveyed two important points about these types of research and their associated questions. First, each type of question is scientific. Second, the different types of questions require different types of methodologies. It follows that each type of methodology that empirically, rigorously, and appropriately addresses these questions is also legitimately scientific. Scientists and social philosophers as diverse as B. F. Skinner, John Dewey, and J. Habermas have emphasized that the appropriate match between question and methodology is an essential feature of scientific research.

Complexity of Special Education as a Field

In his commentary on the NAS report on scientific research in education and the policy emphasizing use of RCTs implied by NCLB, Berliner noted that such a conceptualization of science is based on hard sciences, such as physics, chemistry, and biology. He proposed that science in education is not a hard science but it is the "hardest-to-do science." Berliner stated,

We [educational researchers] do our science under conditions that physical scientists find intolerable. We face particular problems and must deal with local conditions that limit generalizations and theory building—problems that are different from those faced by the easier-to-do sciences [chemistry, biology, medicine].

Special education research, because of its complexity, may be the hardest of the hardest-to-do science. One feature of special education research that makes it more complex is the variability of the participants. The Individuals with Disabilities Education Act (IDEA) identifies 12 eligibility (or disability) categories in special education (Office of Special Education and Rehabilitation Services [OSERS]), and within these categories are several different identifiable conditions. For example, in addition to "typical" learning disabilities, attention deficit/hyperactive disorder is often subsumed under the Specific Learning Disabilities category. Autism is now widely conceptualized as a spectrum consisting of four disorders. Mental retardation varies on the range of severity. Emotional and behavioral disorders consist of externalizing and internalizing disorders. Visual and hearing impairments range in severity from mildly impaired to totally blind or profoundly deaf. Physical impairment can be exhibited as hypotonia or hypertonia. Other health impaired may incorporate health conditions as distinct and diverse as asthma, epilepsy, and diabetes. Adding to this variability is the greater ethnic and linguistic diversity that, unfortunately, occurs in special education because of overrepresentation of some minority groups.

A second dimension of complexity is the educational context. Special education extends beyond the traditional conceptualization of "schooling" for typical students. Certainly many students with disabilities attend general education classes. However, the continuum of special education contexts is broader than general education. At one end of the chronological continuum, infants, toddlers, and many preschoolers receive services in their home or in an inclusive child care setting outside of the public school settings (e.g., Head Start Centers). For school-age students with disabilities, placement sometimes occurs in special education classes or a combination of special education and general education classes. For adolescents and young adults with disabilities, special education may take place in community living or vocational settings in preparation for the transition out of high school and into the workplace.

Complexity in special education has several implications for research. Researchers cannot just address a simple question about whether a practice in special education is effective; they must specify clearly for whom the practice is effective and in what context. The heterogeneity of participant characteristics poses a significant challenge to research designs based on establishing equivalent groups, even when randomization and stratification is possible. Certain disabilities have a low prevalence, so methodologies that require a relatively large number of participants to build the power of the analysis may be very difficult or not feasible. In addition, because IDEA ensures the right to a free appropriate public education, some research and policy questions (e.g., Are IEPs effective in promoting student progress?) may not be addressable through research methodologies that require random assignment to a "nontreatment" group or condition. Last, in special education, students with disabilities are often "clustered" in classrooms, and in experimental group design, the classroom rather than the student becomes the unit on which researchers base random assignment, data analysis, and power estimates.

History of Special Education Research

Special education research has a long history in which different methodologies have been employed. In the early 19th century beginning with Itard's foundational work, *The Wild Boy of Aveyron,* there was a tradition of discovery, development, experimentation, and verification. Initially, the research methods employed in the field that was to become special education research were derived from medicine. Many of the early pioneers in services for individuals with disabilities (Itard, Seguin, Montessori, Fernald, Goldstein) were physicians. Similarly, early services for individuals with disabilities occurred in residential facilities and training schools, which were based on the medical tradition of care.

As psychology, sociology, and anthropology became academic disciplines, they provided methodological tools for research in special education. For example, Skeels's and Kirk's works, respectively, on early experiences and preschool education for infants and young children with mental retardation employed experimental and quasi-experimental group designs prominent in psychology. Edgerton's research on individuals with mental retardation who left institutions and moved to the community, drew from methods in sociology and anthropology. In academic instructional studies, Lovitt and Haring based their methodology on the then newly created single-subject design methodology of the time. Farber's important early work on families of children with disabilities and continuing through work by Blacher and Dunst had its roots in family sociology. Many of the current special education research tools now frequently employed, such as sophisticated multivariate designs, qualitative research designs, and program evaluation designs, have their roots in general education and educational psychology. Today a range of methodological approaches are available to researchers in special education as a result of this rich history.

More than One Research Methodology Is Important in Special Education Research

A current initiative of the U.S. Department of Education is to improve the quality of research in the field of education, with the rationale that improved research will lead to improved practice. A major effort to improve quality has come through the establishment in 2003 of the Institute of Education Sciences (IES), whose mission is to expand fundamental knowledge about education. A central theme advocated by IES is to focus research on the questions of effectiveness and to employ high-quality research methods to address these questions. The gold standard for research methodology that addresses these issues is the use of RCT methodology. The IES acknowledges that different methodologies are important for addressing different questions.

The increased use of RCT methodology, when conducted well, will undoubtedly enhance the quality of research in education and special education. Rigorously conducted RCT studies have greater capacity to control for threats to internal validity than do quasi-experimental designs that are often used in special education. Because of this greater experimental control, Gersten et al. propose that random assignment to experimental groups is one indicator of high-quality group design research. The IES and Department of Education policy of encouraging RCT studies may well move the field closer to the goal of identifying evidence-based special education practices. But again, there are devilish details that challenge the near exclusive use of this methodology for investigating effective practices in special education.

In special education, other methodologies, such as single-subject designs, are experimental and may be a better fit for some research contexts and participant characteristics. Powerful correlational methodologies may suggest causal relationships by statistically controlling for competing hypotheses and may be essential for addressing causal-like questions when researchers are not able to conduct experimental group or single-subject design studies. The discovery and development of new effective practices may require researchers to work in naturalistic contexts where they may not be able to exert experimental control and/or in design experiments, or where they have the flexibility of changing certain elements of an intervention based on students' responses. Such descriptive and process-oriented research may require the use of qualitative methods. Educational researchers have acknowledged the value of mixing methodologies to provide a complementary set of information that would more effectively (than a single method) inform practice.

Quality Indicators of Research Methodology

Quality indicators are the feature of research that represents rigorous application of methodology to questions of interest. They may serve as guidelines for (a) researchers who design and conduct research, (b) reviewers who evaluate the "believability" of research findings, and (c) consumers who need to determine the "usability" of research findings. High-quality research is designed to rule out alternative explanations for both the results of the study and the conclusions that researchers draw. The higher the quality of research methodology, the more confidence the researcher and readers will have in the findings of the study.

Textbooks on educational research describe the methodology that investigators should follow, but they usually do not provide a succinct or understandable set of indicators that are useful for individuals who lack graduate training on research methodology. Several professional organizations have developed standards for describing and, in some cases, evaluating research. Division 16 of the American Psychological Association (APA) and the Society for the Study of School Psychology have established criteria for evaluating group design, single-subject design, and qualitative methodology used in research on practices in school psychology. Similarly, APA Division 12 Task Force on Psychological Interventions has established criteria primarily for experimental group designs studies used to provide support for therapies in clinical psychology and clinical child psychology. The CEC Division for Early Childhood (DEC) created procedures for describing research methodology for studies using group, single-subject, and qualitative research methodology, which they used to determine recommended practices for early intervention/ early childhood special education. These standards have been used to determine the quality of research methods employed; however, they have not been published as quality indicators that other researchers could use.

In their work on summarizing evidence for effective practices, which will be described in the next section, some research synthesis organizations have established evaluation criteria and methods for determining the quality of research. For example, the WWC created an evaluation instrument, called the Design and Implementation Assessment Device (DIAD), with which a rater could conduct an extremely detailed evaluation of a research article. At this writing, a DIAD has only been created for experimental and quasi-experimental group design, but the WWC reports that DIADs are also being constructed for single-subject and qualitative group designs. Other research synthesis organizations, such as the Campbell Collaboration and the Evidence for Policy and Practice Information Centre (EPPIC), have somewhat similar research evaluation procedures.

Efforts described here illustrate the progress that professional and governmental organizations have made toward establishing standards for quality in research. To date, however, such quality indicators have not been identified specifically for research in special education. As noted, the purpose of the work conducted by this task force was to establish a set of quality indicators that were clearly stated, understandable, and readily available for use as guides for identifying high-quality research in special education. These quality indicators are presented in the articles appearing in this special issue.

Evidence-Based Practice

The type and magnitude of evidence needed to verify a practice as evidence-based is a prominent issue in the discussion of scientific research and effective educational practices. These devilish details are critical for policymakers, practitioners, educational researchers, and consumers. Current endeavors to establish standards for evidence-based practice as well as to identify the evidence-based-practices themselves, are occurring through two different, but related, initiatives. In this section, we describe briefly the history of identifying effective practices first in medicine and then other social science fields, efforts by professional organizations to identify effective practices, and similar efforts being conducted by research synthesis organizations.

Identifying Evidence-Based Practice

Like the evolution of special education research methods noted previously, the search for evidence-based practice originated in the field of medicine. Although the practice of evidence-based medicine extends back to the mid 19th century, the modern era of evidence-based practice emerged in the early 1970s and 1980s and came into fruition in Great Britain in the early 1990s. Cutspec tracked the evolution of evidence-based medicine from a movement that began with the intent to address the gap between research and practitioners' provision of medical care, moved to the use of the literature to inform practice decisions, and then became an approach to practicing medicine. Evidence-based practice is now a central part of medical education, education in allied health professions such as nursing, and counselor education.

General and special education have followed suit in adopting scientific evidence as the appropriate basis for selecting teaching practices. The impetus for the current evidence-based movement in education is similar to that in medicine: A concern that effective educational practices, as proven by research, are not being used in schools. This current concern reflects a long-standing discussion in the field of special education regarding the distance between research and practice. In response, a large number of initiatives have been established to identify practices that will generate positive outcomes for children. Two types of groups are sponsoring these initiatives: research synthesis organizations and professional associations that propose standards for practice.

Research Synthesis Organizations.   Research synthesis organizations systematically evaluate and aggregate findings from the research literature in order to inform practitioners. Perhaps the largest and longest standing synthesis organization is the Cochrane Collaboration . . . , located in Great Britain and founded in 1963. This organization, which focuses on medical and health research, consists of over 50 collaborative review groups and has completed over 1,300 reviews. Following this model, the Campbell Collaboration . . . was established in the United States in 1999 to assist individuals in education and the social sciences to make informed decisions about what works based on high-quality research and reviews. In Great Britain, EPPIC at the University of London Institute of Education . . . was created in 1993 to conduct systematic reviews of research on social interventions. This organization was recently funded to conduct reviews specifically on educational practices, which it plans to make available through their Research Evidence in Education Library. . . .

In the United States, the IES has established the WWC . . . , which is jointly managed by the Campbell Collaboration and the American Institutes for Research. WWC conducts reviews of educational practices supported by high-quality research and makes this information available to practitioners through Web-based databases. The U.S. Department of Education funds the Research and Training Center on Early Childhood Development (CED) . . . , which is conducting a set of practice-sensitive research syntheses on the effectiveness (and ineffectiveness) of practices for infants and young children with disabilities and their families. Whereas other organizational efforts primarily provide evidence that a practice is effective, the CED has created a more functional operational definition by stating that evidence-based practices are "informed by research, in which the characteristics and consequences of environmental variables are empirically established and the relationship directly informs what a practitioner can do to produce the desired outcome.

To examine the effectiveness of programs for children with autism, a committee formed by NAS established guidelines for the strength of evidence provided by individual studies. The dimensions of the studies evaluated were internal validity, external validity, and generalization, with strength of evidence (i.e., from I to IV) evaluated for each.

A key feature in these research synthesis initiatives is the methodological criteria established to select or exclude research studies for the synthesis. Most organizations confined evidence of effectiveness to research studies that have employed RCT methodology or rigorously constructed quasi-experimental designs. The CED researchers took a broader view of the empirical linkage between a practice and an outcome and looked for descriptions of the process of the intervention practices that led to the outcome. The leadership of the WWC has noted that qualitative research may provide information about the ways in which interventions work and can be used to substantiate "promising practices" in education, although they proposed that clearly efficacious practices would require verification through RCTs. For the EPPIC, Oakley reported that they incorporated qualitative research in their reviews, but they had encountered multiple problems in their evaluation of qualitative studies.

Professional Associations.   Professional associations and groups have also examined the literature to determine effective practices. These groups have often established the level of evidence needed to identify a practice as effective. For example, the Child-Clinical Section of Division 12 of the APA established the Task Force on Empirically Supported Psychosocial Interventions for Children. They proposed the types and amount of evidence needed to identify a practice as (a) well-established (i.e., two well-conducted group design studies by different researchers or nine well-conducted single-subject designs); or (b) "probably efficacious" (i.e., two group design studies by same investigator or at least three single-subject design studies).

The Division for Early Childhood of CEC established a process for identifying recommended practices that incorporated evidence from the research literature. Mentioned previously, DEC conducted an extensive literature review to identify support for recommended practices and also to incorporate information from focus groups of experts, practitioners, and family members in the final identification of practices. The level or type of evidence needed to support a recommended practice was not identified.

The American Speech-Language-Hearing Association (ASHA) proposed that different types of evidence may be important for different clinical activities. For questions of treatment efficacy, they propose that different frameworks are available for evaluating the level of evidence that documents efficacy. They provide as an example one such framework developed by the Oxford Centre for Evidence-based Medicine. This system could be used to classify practices according to four levels of evidence:

- Level I evidence derives from meta-analyses including at least one randomized experimental design or well-designed randomized control studies.
- Level II evidence includes controlled studies without randomization and quasi-experimental designs.
- Level III consists of well designed nonexperimental studies (i.e., correlational and case studies).
- Level IV includes expert committee report, consensus conference, and clinical experience of respected authorities.

The ASHA policy emphasizes that other frameworks are currently available or evolving ansd could be useful for specific questions related to treatment efficacy.

To date, the special education community has yet to develop systematic guidelines for specifying the types and levels of evidence needed to identify a practice as evidence-based and effective. The Division for Learning Disabilities (DLD) and the Division for Research (DR) jointly published a document entitled *Alerts,* in which an expert from the field reviews the literature relevant to a specific practice and describes the evidence or lack of evidence that underlies the practice. These alerts, however, have been based on individual authors' reviews of the literature and, although quite useful, different authors may well be using different criteria for the evidence they include. The second goal of the current DR Task Force, therefore, was to describe the types of results generated by each research methodology and to recommend guidelines for using the results as evidence of effectiveness, or lack of effectiveness, of practices in special education.

Where Do We Go From Here?

The Department of Education is under pressure to prove to Congress that there are educational practices that have evidence of effectiveness and that supporting educational research is a good investment of public funds. In specifying RCT methodology as the gold standard for research, the Department of Education is investing the bulk of research funding in addressing the question of effectiveness, which is clearly important. However, Berliner urges us to avoid confusing science with a specific method or technique. It is more important to look at the broader goal of using science to improve education for all children.

To accomplish such a goal, educational science might be more appropriately seen as a continuum rather than a fixed point. Levin, O'Donnell, and Kratochwill suggest that a program of educational research might be thought of as occurring in four stages. The first stage would involve observational, focused exploration and flexible methodology, which qualitative and correlational methods allow. Stage 2 would involve controlled laboratory or classroom experiments, observational studies of classrooms, and teacher-researcher collaborative experiments. Design experimentation involving qualitative methodology, single-subject designs, quasi-experimental and/or RCT design could be useful at that stage. stages to design well-documented interventions and "prove" their effectiveness through well-controlled RCT studies implemented in classroom or naturalistic settings by the natural participants (e.g., teachers) in the settings. We propose that single-subject design studies could also accomplish this purpose.

If research ended here, however, the movement of effective, evidence-based research into practices that teachers use on Monday morning would likely fail. A further step in the development process (Stage 4) would be to determine the factors that lead to adoption of effective practices in typical school systems under naturally existing conditions. That last step would require research into organizational factors that facilitate or impede adoption of innovation in local contexts. The research methodologies that would generate this information are more likely qualitative, correlational, and mixed methods, as well as RCT and large-scale, single-case designs. Researchers may well draw from such disciplines as sociology, political science, economics, as well as education, in this research. Research at this stage may best occur though a partnership among researchers from education, researchers from other disciplines, local education agencies, and teachers. Indeed, an initiative is emerging from another panel convened by the NRC, which is proposing a broad federal initiative that would create just such a partnership.

Conclusion

If different methodologies are appropriate for addressing important questions in special education, then we, as a field, need to be clear about (a) the match between research questions and methodology, (b), the features of each methodology that represent high quality, (c) and the use of research findings for each methodology as scientific evidence for effective practices in special education. To date, we have numerous texts and papers that describe each methodology, but they are not a coordinated, clear index of how each contributes to the present research-to-practice challenge. . . .

Frederick J. Brigham et al.  **NO**

Research in the Wake of the No Child Left Behind Act: Why the Controversies Will Continue and Some Suggestions for Controversial Research

The unique and sometimes competing interests of key stakeholders, which often drive the development of educational policy, may lead to misunderstanding and confusion. For example, policies espoused by educational advocates and the pragmatic management procedures of educational administrators are sometimes difficult to understand for educators who advocate the adoption of scientific practices. This is because science and advocacy have different traditions and purposes. Scientists begin from a position of doubt and collect evidence, whereas advocates are more likely to begin from a position of certainty. A different point of view yet is held by administrators and policymakers, who must work within the political system and deal with the realities of compromise and communication that affect policy development.

Given the differing perspectives and traditions of the stakeholders in educational reform, it is unlikely that any major educational policy will be without controversy. However, if a coherent educational policy is to be developed, controversial issues must be decided according to some framework. Failure to adopt a coherent position is likely to lead to a hodge-podge of competing initiatives rather than a broadened range of educational opportunities.

In 2001, the interests of various stakeholders were brought together in the passage of the No Child Left Behind (NCLB) Act. A crucial component of NCLB was the requirement that educators use practices that are validated through scientific research. This presents a useful opportunity for individuals concerned with the education of children with emotional or behavioral disorders (E/BD) to introduce scientifically validated practices into the classroom and collect data related to a number of important questions—mainly questions regarding better ways of providing instruction in academic skills. However, the history of educational practice suggests that consensus will be elusive at best, even with the soundest of scientific evidence. With this in mind, in this article we (a) describe reasons why educational practices will remain controversial even with the call for scientifically validated procedures and (b) suggest areas of research opportunities that NCLB may provide.

From *Behavioral Disorders*, 29(3) May 2004, pp. 300–310. Copyright © 2004 by CCBD Publications. Reprinted by permission. Notes omitted.

Policies, Science, Uncertainty, and Justification

To withstand debate, policies must often be crafted in such a way that people with different perceptions and purposes can recognize their interests in them. One way of creating such policies is to make the wording vague and, therefore, its meaning elusive. As a result, a variety of interpretations and actions are likely to follow from policy statements crafted into law. No Child Left Behind is no exception. For example, according to the U.S. Department of Education, "Under *No Child Left Behind,* states and school districts have unprecedented flexibility in how they use federal education funds, in exchange for greater accountability for results." Whether the flexibility provided by NCLB is real or illusory is debatable. It is clear, however, that this law, like most other policies, is open to a number of conflicting interpretations except for the bottom line—academic accountability.

One way of dealing with the uncertainty that accompanies large-scale policies is to analyze them with respect to a particular philosophical orientation. For example, the impetus for initiatives such as inclusion or whole language can be viewed as primarily philosophical rather than scientific because they are based not on data but on a sense of what should be. From this perspective, actions in violation of a philosophical orientation are irresponsible. Regrettably, acting according to philosophical principles has led to some unfortunate and ludicrous behaviors. For example, consider the behaviors exhibited by virtually any cult. The philosophic stances proclaimed by some cult leaders have led to mass suicides, killings, or other atrocities, often in the name of justice. In education, the whole language movement is probably the best known of the failed philosophies. However, movements such as facilitated communication and full inclusion are better seen as philosophical rather than scientific and empirical in their orientation. Although the evidence in support of these activities is lacking, proponents claim that they are worth implementing because they are consistent with their beliefs. However, in a zero-sum environment such as education, funds devoted to one thing are necessarily diverted from other options. Spending money on disproven programs such as facilitated communication is simply folly. A philosophical orientation, while important, is insufficient to protect the field from folly.

Scientists are more likely to endorse the position that it is foolish to act in a manner that fails to conform to the available data. This position is far from invulnerable to failure and unfortunate outcomes. Fortunately, science possesses a self-correcting mechanism that, over time, eliminates wishful thinking, self-serving bias, and erroneous beliefs from the body of accepted scientific belief. Although it has become fashionable in some circles to decry science as merely a sociopolitical activity, such a position drastically underestimates the power of science to serve society and, just as dramatically, overestimates the alternative approaches to guide decisionmaking.

The social aspects of scientific inquiry are actually a major part of science's self-correcting mechanism. The self-correcting mechanism is the major component that unifies all forms of scientific inquiry. This self-correcting mechanism limits the amount of effort expended on ideas that are unlikely to be productive and also limits the lifespan of ideas that do not produce consistent results. For example, through the self-correcting mechanism of science, strong genetic and environmental positions with regard to human behavior have given way to a more balanced interactionist perspective that accommodates both positions. In academic instruction, the idea that children would improve their spelling by drawing boxes around words and examining their shape has virtually disappeared from serious educational literature because the evidence failed to support it.

As Shermer put it:

> Science is a social process, where one is trained in a certain paradigm and works with others in the field. A community of scientists reads the same journals, goes to the same conferences, reviews one another's papers and books, and generally exchanges ideas about the facts, hypotheses, and theories in that field. Through vast experience they know, fairly quickly, which new ideas have a chance of succeeding and which are obviously wrong. Newcomers from other fields, who typically dive in with both feet without the requisite training and experience, proceed to generate new ideas that they think—because of their success in their own field—will be revolutionary. Instead, they are usually greeted with disdain (or more typically, ignored) by the professionals in the field. This is not because (as they usually think is the reason) insiders don't like outsiders (or that all great revolutionaries are persecuted or ignored), but because in most cases those ideas were considered years or decades before and rejected for perfectly good reasons.

Although the data are not always conclusive and the implications of data in social science are not always readily apparent, the absence of scientifically collected data fails to absolve policymakers and administrators from the need to act. In the absence of scientific advice, however, policymakers, administrators, practitioners, and other concerned parties often turn to influences such as tradition, currently popular ideas, ideas that are expedient at the moment, and various philosophical positions that they may hold. Sometimes the actions taken are counterproductive and actually undermine the responsible and ethical intentions of the policymakers.

If it were easy to undo these counterproductive actions and change course, we could chalk it up to learning through experience. When such policies are in place, however, they are very difficult to change even if they turn out to be unworkable. There are several reasons for this, including the following two: First, certain stakeholders have vested interests in keeping the policies intact. Second, people tend to develop justifications for their actions. Reasoning that has the appearance of rational scientific discourse is often used toward that end. In other words, it is common to find irrational actions supported by seemingly rational justifications. Thus, individuals are unlikely to engage in behavior that works contrary to their own interests (e.g., support a teacher licensing bill that would eliminate their jobs), and they are quite likely to develop elaborate ideational schemes to justify self-interested action as actually pursuant to larger and more noble motives.

Shermer provided an analysis of the ways in which people justify beliefs in "weird things." He defined weird things as:

(1) a claim unaccepted by most people in that field of study,

(2) a claim that is either logically impossible or highly unlikely, and/or

(3) a claim for which the evidence is largely anecdotal and uncorroborated

It is clear that people who are superstitious, foolish, or desperate are especially vulnerable to beliefs that fit these criteria. However, they are not the only people who fall victim to such beliefs. Smart people can also hold irrational beliefs and behave in a stupid manner. Shermer suggested that "smart people believe weird things because they are skilled at defending beliefs they arrived at for non-smart reasons." He proposed two forms of biased thinking—attribution bias and confirmation bias—that are primarily responsible for the maintenance of irrational beliefs by ostensibly rational individuals.

Attribution Bias

Attribution bias occurs when a behavior exhibited by both oneself and another person, even though identical, is suggested to have occurred for different reasons. Most often attribution bias is self-serving. That is, individuals perceive their own actions to have been for good and just reasons, whereas the same actions taken by others are dismissed as unjust and unjustifiable. Areas in which attribution bias have been noted include religious beliefs, vigilante behavior, interpersonal aggression, aggressive acts between nations, and even interpersonal relations among scientists. Ironically, even though science is described as having a major social component, Kramer found that scientists ascribed trustworthy and collegial intent to their own efforts to share resources, data, and the like with others but often believed that attempts to obtain resources, data, and the like by others were the result of untrustworthy and sinister motives.

Attribution bias in relation to NCLB is likely to result in proponents of any action being viewed with suspicion, even by others who support similar ideas. For example, suggestions that students should be excused from the state-wide and district-wide assessment requirements of both NCLB and the 1997 reauthorization of the Individuals with Disabilities Education Act (IDEA) may be viewed as serving the interests of a child by one group and as an attempt to inflate a school's test scores by another. Whereas the extreme positions are easily identified, the likelihood is that the truth lies somewhere between these polar opposite.

We suggest that the production of scientific data is the best way to identify the most probable location of the truth between the self-serving poles of any debate. It must be noted, however, that scientific data can be determined as good or useful only in relation to a specific purpose or set of purposes. Therefore, the initial task facing producers of scientific research is to decide which goal or set of goals is most important to pursue. This is a difficult task that is far from being accomplished in education.

The implication of attribution bias is that, as individuals, we tend to attribute to ourselves greater nobility in purpose than we do our fellow citizens, and, as a nation, we are less than clear and unified about our educational goals. Thus, the call for scientifically based practices in education will probably do little to lessen the conflict surrounding any instructional method or decision.

Confirmation Bias

Confirmation bias, as it is commonly used in psychological literature, refers to the seeking or interpreting of evidence in ways that conform to existing beliefs, expectations, or a hypothesis in hand. According to Shermer, people often believe weird things because they have a "tendency to seek or interpret evidence favorable to already existing beliefs, and to ignore or reinterpret evidence unfavorable to already existing beliefs." As a result, people tend to find what they are looking for even if it is not there.

Confirmation bias is often the result of determining the truth by checking only positive and not negative instances. Although it is certainly more pleasant to examine the reasons for our successes, a full understanding can be reached only if we consider the reasons for our failures as well. Many of the controversial treatments for disabilities appear to be supported by confirmation bias. Rather than providing clear data obtained under replicable conditions, proponents of less-accepted treatments (and some popular but refuted treatments, e.g., modality-based instruction) use anecdotal evidence about how the treatment worked for them or a given child to assure decisionmakers that it will, therefore, work for others as well.

The evidence regarding the practice of coteaching appears to be one such product of confirmation bias. Weiss and Brigham pointed out that the studies that purportedly support coteaching were highly flawed in that they often failed to define coteaching, employed only teachers who were satisfied with their instructional arrangements, employed such vague outcome indicators as "improved" or "more accepted," and failed to describe what the teachers involved in coteaching did. Weiss concluded that coteaching was often used to meet the needs of students with disabilities despite the absence of supportive evidence. In addition, she pointed out that many examples of coteaching were actually outside of the recommendations found in the literature. Nevertheless, when we discuss this evidence with teachers and parents of students with disabilities, we are often informed that the evidence may say one thing but their experience or the experience of their friends is different.

One unfortunate outcome of confirmation bias is that by focusing on information that supports a given belief, an individual's views are rarely challenged. For example, the World Wide Web, although holding the potential to open unlimited stores of information to vast numbers of people, can also have the opposite effect. Rather than focusing on a variety of viewpoints, some users simply look for statements in agreement with a given predisposition and, through repetition, reinforce the predisposition. Still another form of confirmation bias results when individuals amass large stores of information that are unified around a given proposition. Such individuals can become so entrenched in a point of view or a way of doing things that it becomes hard to see things differently.

The Impact of Attribution Bias and Confirmation Bias on Educational Research

No Child Left Behind's step in the direction of clarifying educational goals by forcing attention on academic outcomes focuses on only one of the possible goals of a school—academic achievement. Whether or not the strength of the current emphasis on academics is desirable can only be answered by science with the response "It depends." It depends on the balance that is held between academics and other ostensible goals for any given community, school, or student. The exact nature of this balance is probably better ana- lyzed politically or economically than scientifically. Once the goals are estab- lished, science can provide substantial assistance in reaching them. However, even if a unified set of goals could be established for all children in all U.S. schools, controversies would continue to erupt.

We have described two forms of bias, attribution bias and confirmation bias, that affect individual judgment regarding any source of data. Knowing that these forms of bias (and there are more that we have not discussed here) exist can help individuals guard against them. However, knowledge of the threat alone is a necessary but insufficient cure to the problems arising from bias. The self-correcting methods of scientific inquiry can, over time, mediate these forms of bias if decisionmakers and their constituents will trust data col- lected with due rigor and appropriate methods and expose their own beliefs to doubt and questioning. However, "issues of belief and doubt get into some very partisan ruts," Thus, NCLB may ask more of educational leaders, educa- tors, and parents than it does of schoolchildren.

Suggestions for Research in the Wake of No Child Left Behind

Special education practice is highly dependent on the conditions present in general education. Moreover, influences such as statewide testing and budget constraints that affect general education personnel and program managers also affect special educators. Students with mild disabilities are most often called to the attention of school officials because they have been unsuccessful in meeting the demands of general education in some way. Many of the cur- rent special education regulations and initiatives have their roots in the past 3 or 4 decades in which general education programs were expanding the num- ber of options available to students in U.S. schools. No Child Left Behind focuses attention squarely on academic achievement as the measure of educa- tional accountability. It is a bottom-line, outcome-driven approach to educa- tional decisionmaking. As such, it differs in many ways from earlier approaches to educational accountability. Furthermore, the unit of analysis applied by NCLB is actually the school and its disaggregated populations, rather than the individual, as was the case historically in special education.

The trend toward academic monitoring has already affected special education programs for many students. For example, educational programs for students with severe disabilities have moved from a developmental model to a functional model and subsequently to a model that attempts to link instructional activities to academic skills taught in the general education curriculum. Although such a trend can be viewed as opening up academic avenues that previously were closed to many students, it also closes off the opportunities for developmental and functional curricula by reallocating resources and attention to other issues. Whether or not this proves to be a positive step remains to be seen. However, the focus on academic outcomes is clearly related to enabling children to fit in to the general education environment in a more satisfactory manner. Similar trends can be seen relative to the educational programs of students with E/BD. With the emphasis on general education goals, it is difficult to imagine that programs (or remediation and community-based or vocational education will receive the support necessary to serve the populations for which they were created. Rather than isolated developments in the special education community, such trends are better understood as responses to changes in the general education program.

The NCLB focus of accountability on the academic achievement of groups of students within schools will, in our opinion, call into question earlier research findings and policy decisions made relative to IDEA. This is because the nature and focus of the general education program under NCLB is different from the nature and focus under IDEA. How these differences will manifest themselves has yet to be settled. Nevertheless, changes in the general education program will, of necessity, prompt special educators to reevaluate the findings and recommendations made earlier if they wish their research findings to remain consonant with improving student performance relative to the general education curriculum. In the following sections, we suggest some specific areas of educational research that will benefit from additional scrutiny given the requirements of NCLB.

Planning and Service Delivery

Impact of Students with Disabilities on General Education

Inclusion of students with disabilities developed in an era of mostly expanding curriculum offerings and emphasis on tolerance of individual differences. The pressures to align resources with curricular areas that are measured in state- and district-wide tests appear to be narrowing the curriculum offerings of many schools in the United States. This reduction in the number of classes, coupled with the IDEA requirement of access to the general education curriculum and pressures for inclusion, suggest that more students with disabilities will be present in classes in which teachers are already experiencing increased pressure to raise their students' achievement. Students with E/BD will likely be seen as adding unnecessary impediments to the education of other students in the general education classroom. Rather than speaking of a special education student's right to receive an individualized program of special education and related services, researchers and advocates need to be able to respond with data examining the performance of students with E/BD in classes under these new pressures and curricular demands and to provide clear evidence that the education programs of other students are unaffected. Some evidence of this currently exists; however, the extent to which the conditions under which this evidence was collected reflect conditions in schools facing the bottom-line academic accountability of NCLB is unclear.

Individualized Education Programs

The backbone of a student's special education program is the individualized education program (IEP). In an era in which developmental and functional approaches prevailed, it made a great deal of sense to single out things that a given student would be learning that were different from the curriculum presented to most students. The result of the coupling of NCLB with IDEA's access to the general education curriculum clause appears to be that more students with disabilities are taking core academic classes and are to be measured by the same standards and at the same frequency as are students who have no disabilities. Under such conditions, the traditional IEP, with its detailed mapping of goals and objectives that form the curriculum for a particular student, seems redundant because the academic program delivered for students in a given classroom or course of study is dictated by the state curriculum standards. However, there may be specific benefits to this redundancy that would be better defended through data than through insistence that IEPs are clearly needed and beneficial. For example, rather than focusing on *what* a student with E/BD will do in a particular class, the IEP may still serve a useful function in describing *how* (e.g., the conditions and timelines) a student will fulfill the requirements. While it is certainly possible to craft an IEP focusing on such aspects of a student's educational program, there is little empirical evidence that educators currently know how to do so.

Another research issue related to IEPs is the extent to which they are actually individualized. Research conducted in the past several years has not been particularly supportive of the extent to which IEPs actually reflect students' educational needs or vary according to their characteristics. Indeed, our own experience with several school districts that pride themselves on the quality of their IEPs suggests that the "I" in IEP could more accurately stand for "interchangeable." Perhaps the interchangeability of IEPs is a necessary reflection of the movement to include students in the general education curriculum; perhaps it is the result of limited time, imagination, or training. Under the NCLB opportunities, it seems prudent to examine the functionality and uniqueness of the benefits of these documents relative to their costs.

Intervention

Appropriateness of a Standard Intervention Protocol for Students with Emotional or Behavioral Disorders

By *standard intervention protocol,* we mean a set of clearly defined and well-documented treatments that should be employed as a matter of course for students with behavior problems as well as for students whose problems are serious enough to warrant identifying them as having E/BD. Multiple gating procedures in E/BD, as well as "failure to respond to treatment" models for students with learning disabilities, are predicated on the proposition that children who fail to respond to interventions that would support most students are the students who are most likely in need of special education services. In that regard, it seems imperative to have a clear idea of what the word *treatment* means.

In regard to behavioral issues, treatment could mean anything from poorly executed and inconsistent reprimands to well-designed reinforcement or cognitive behavior management programs. For newly identified students, the efforts to manage problematic student behaviors are recorded in documents such as prereferral intervention plans, reports from teacher assistance teams, and other, similar reports. With proper assistance and support, teachers have been able to create useful and effective interventions for some students who otherwise would have been referred needlessly for special education evaluation. Most classroom teachers, however, are on their own in developing and maintaining behavior management programs for their classes and treatments for individual students. It is not at all clear that most school-based practitioners possess the expertise or the time and support to develop and implement unique behavior intervention programs for individual students. Furthermore, given the relatively consistent advice about general behavior management techniques provided by different tests in the field, it is not clear that unique treatments need to be developed as a first or even second step in dealing with problematic behavior.

Efforts at creating school-wide discipline programs have established baseline conditions that could be considered essential before individual treatments are implemented. Research data could be used to establish a "what to do next" category of treatment that would be recommended for students once general school-wide and class-wide efforts had failed. Such practices are commonly found in medical treatment models but have not yet taken hold in educational settings. The enormous advantage of such a system is that students would receive effective treatments more quickly and teachers would have additional guidance and assurance that they were, indeed, providing appropriate educational services to their students.

Preferred Target Domains

The obvious focus of intervention for students with E/BD is their behavior. However, behavior can serve a variety of functions, and the relationship of behavior to academic instruction is often underplayed in discussions of students with E/BD. One of the major functions of unacceptable behavior in classrooms is escape. We know that well-designed instruction is a mediator of students' behavior, yet we see little attention paid to the academic structure of the classrooms in which the misbehavior occurs.

Research on academic instruction as an antecedent is available to scholars and policy-makers. It is clear that providing students with well-designed instruction that is within their ability to master reduces the incidence of behavior problems in the classroom. However, after NCLB's changes in academic emphasis, the extent to which teachers are able or believe that they are able to deviate substantially from state curriculum guides and time-lines related to covering material before a certain test date is unknown. It is possible that little has changed since NCLB. It is also possible that the current emphasis on performance relative to test-linked standards makes general education teachers unwilling to make substantial curriculum adaptations.

The current popularity of coteaching as a service delivery model may also mediate the ability of special education teachers to provide instruction that is supportive of students with E/BD. Through coteaching arrangements, students with E/BD are considered to have their special education programs delivered to them in the general education classroom. However, as previously discussed, the model of coteaching is poorly supported for students with special education needs. In addition, the general education classroom may be a less hospitable place to deliver special education services after NCLB than it was prior to this legislation. One reason for this is the pressure exerted on teachers to cover specific content objectives regardless of student readiness or mastery of the material covered. Many special education teachers that we work with report that they and their general education colleagues experience great pressure from their district administrators to cover the content regardless of student mastery. While it is unlikely that many students will demonstrate mastery of content that has not been taught, content-coverage approaches are likely to result in incomplete teaching and partial mastery of material, particularly for nonperforming or disengaged students. As such, the NCLB standards may actually increase rather than decrease the range of achievement outcomes for students in diverse classrooms. We suggest that it is better to find out than to wonder whether this is the case.

Possible Research Outcomes

We have suggested that a number of the traditional elements of special education programming for students with E/BD should be reexamined in light of the requirements of NCLB and the changes in general education programs that are likely to evolve from implementation of that legislation. With regard to the relationship of general and special education, it is possible that the NCLB requirements place pressures on teachers that make the general education environment a less welcoming place than it was previously. It is also likely that such changes will make the general education environment a less desirable goal for students with E/BD. Another possible outcome is that NCLB actually will result in no detectable change in general education classrooms that will be relevant to the education of students with E/BD.

We also suggest that IEPs should be reexamined to determine their necessity, function, and actual ability to promote individualized treatment for students with E/BD. Related to this question, it is possible that researchers will document the necessity of the IEP for ensuring educational treatments for students with E/BD. Conversely, it is possible, given the pressure toward a standards-based curriculum and the previous evidence that IEPs are rarely *individualized*—that they no longer serve their intended function. Another possible outcome might be documentation that the important functions of IEPs could be served by a much shorter document than is typically found in the folders of students with E/BD. If that were the case, researchers could turn their attention to the essential elements of IEPs that need to be maintained or new elements that need to be created, as well as those that are superfluous to effective intervention for students with E/BD.

Finally, we suggest that the traditional target domains of E/BD intervention may be affected by NCLB-prompted changes in the general education classroom. The flexibility of general education teachers or special education teachers working in inclusive settings or under coteaching models may be far more limited in NCLB-compliant classrooms than it was previously. It may be that teachers perceive their flexibility to be curtailed but that they would be able to offer flexible instruction with appropriate guidance. Researchers could provide a great service to the field by documenting what supports are most helpful to teachers under the pressures of test-linked standards.

We suggest that NCLB has the potential to make substantial changes in the educational landscape. The direct changes are clearly established in the legislation. Other changes may emerge as indirect effects of the legislation and will benefit from the attention of educational researchers to identify and describe them as well as to validate effective methods for dealing with these changes on behalf of students with E/BD.

Conclusion

No Child Left Behind offers a number of opportunities to the educational profession in return for a strong focus on academic accountability. One of the more commonly celebrated themes of NCLB is the call for educators to use practices that have been scientifically validated by research in their efforts to serve students with disabilities.

Although the call to use scientifically validated practices appears straightforward and within our grasp given the extant body of research, several factors suggest that it will be a more difficult and demanding task than many educators and policymakers believe. One of the difficulties affecting this enterprise is the impact of attribution and confirmation biases on the judgment of decisionmakers. Such biases work to maintain the status quo by allowing individuals to believe that their motives are somehow different from and more noble than the motives of those who disagree with them and by insulating them from evidence that contradicts or undermines personal beliefs. Furthermore, scientifically validated practices for students with disabilities are effective or ineffective in inclusive schools only relative to their interaction with the programs and expectations present in the general education curriculum. By altering the emphasis of educational programs to a predominant emphasis on performance on test-linked standards, NCLB will probably result in substantial changes in the actions, climate, and expectations of general education classrooms. How these changes will affect the service delivery, instructional, and behavioral options recommended for special education teachers has yet to be seen.

Whereas many of the findings of educational research may hold true after NCLB, others may not, and the way that they are used in the classroom may need adjustment. Components of effective special education practice interact with general education programs in much the same way that notes and scales interact with key changes in musical performance. When the rest of the orchestra changes key, it is in best interests of all the players to change at the same time. Those who do not wish to do so are better advised to be soloists or to write their own music. Special educators must respond to the key changes in general education. Transposing from one key to another can take a line of music from the comfortable range of an instrument or singing voice to a range that is impossible for the performer or vice versa. If the data suggest that the NCLB changes make general education a more productive and supportive place for students with E/BD, special educators should certainly play in the orchestra. If not, it may be time to reconsider "solo projects" and resurrect the dedicated service delivery models that have faded in recent years. In either case, we should let the data, rather than our biases, guide our actions.

POSTSCRIPT

Can Scientifically Based Research Guide Instructional Practice?

Odom and his colleagues identify "devilish details" complicating research efforts in special education: the heterogeneity of disability (consider the range within the autism spectrum alone) and the complexity of the contexts of special education (preschool to young adult; home, school. and work). To conquer these challenges, and continue the necessary pursuit of scientifically gathered data, they introduce articles that present quality indicators to establish rigor within a variety of research methods.

This range of acceptable methodology is actually encouraged by the Institute for Education Sciences, which agrees that "research designs and methods (must be) appropriate to the research question posed" (WWC, *What Is Scientifically Based Research?*). Still, to fully satisfy the gold standard, findings from other methodologies must be verified through RCT.

Originally skeptical about RCT, Forness (*Behavioral Disorders,* 2005) was convinced by its successful application in mental health. Agreeing with WWC standards, Forness believes that, despite their challenges, RCT studies are the only way to control variables and discover whether an intervention makes a critical difference.

Brigham and his co-authors maintain that controversies over instruction cannot be guided by scientific research until stakeholders agree on the purpose of education. Today's policymakers see academic achievement as the goal; special educators seek improved functioning and participation in society.

Consider inclusion, an educational practice supported by IDEA and a focus of many school interventions. Under NCLB, the efficacy of inclusion must be established through RCT studies. Could control groups be identified?

Every good study must begin with an agreement of the target phenomenon. A modest survey of preservice and practicing teachers revealed no universally agreed upon definition or model of inclusion (Snyder, Garriott, and Aylor, *Teacher Education and Special Education,* 2001). Variable definitions make conducting and analyzing research challenging indeed (Simpson, *Behavioral Disorders,* 2004).

In two districts involved in a project to increase inclusionary practices, models changed as teams developed and responded to student experience (Burstein, Sears, Wilcoxen, Cabello, and Spagna, *Remedial and Special Education,* 2004). Perhaps this change itself should be studied.

In *Improving Outcomes for Students with Disabilities* (National Council on Disability, 2004), a researcher asks, "Which is more valid, the work of an evidence-based research center or the experiences of families of children with disabilities? What is the basis for the criteria? Someone's [research] numbers or someone's real life experience?" (p. 4). For advocates, inclusion is a belief system, not a program or a research-based strategy (Villa and Thousand, 2005).

And yet, at least one researcher has devised a study of inclusionary practices within an RCT model. Russell Gersten (*Learning Disabilities Theory & Practice*, 2005), takes readers "behind the scenes," describing the complex, but rewarding, process of developing and conducting a gold-standard research project on inclusion. Other articles in this issue extend the discussion of this collaboration.

Intense partnerships with funded researchers are unavailable to most teachers. Networking through professional organizations, and the journals they publish, enables educators to become informed consumers in this evidence-driven era (Simpson, LaCava, and Graner, *Intervention in School and Clinic*, 2004). What is a teacher to do, though, when a resource such as WWC has not studied any special education methodologies?

Scientists seek evidence. Parents seek change and growth. Teachers want to use the best possible techniques to help students learn. Sometimes parents may want the school team to implement a promising treatment. Is the school compelled to reject the request if it has not been validated against a control group? Or might the successes of one child stimulate a line of research inquiry that could identify a method that would help many?

If medicine and mental health use RCT, can education become more credible by doing the same? In this high-stakes time, can we afford not to do so? Can special education research be conducted in shifting school environments and be published fast enough to help teachers?

ISSUE 11

Can One Model of Special Education Serve All Students?

YES: Wayne Sailor and Blair Roger, from "Rethinking Inclusion: Schoolwide Applications," *Phi Delta Kappan* (March 2005)

NO: Naomi Zigmond, from "Where Should Students with Disabilities Receive Special Education Services? Is One Place Better than Another?" *The Journal of Special Education* (vol. 37, no. 3, 2003)

ISSUE SUMMARY

YES: Wayne Sailor, professor of education and associate director of the Beach Center on Disability at the University of Kansas–Lawrence, and Blair Roger, an educational consultant based in Oakland, California, believe that a school-based model of support services for all students would successfully increase inclusionary practices.

NO: Naomi Zigmond, professor of education at the University of Pittsburgh, maintains that promoting one model of services over another is the wrong approach and advocates that educators and researchers need to focus attentions on individual students.

When special education laws began, people focused on getting students with disabilities into school. Initially, many children with mild disabilities received their specially designed instruction in small self-contained rooms, with little connection to their age mates. Over time, some children were enrolled in typical classes, but "pulled out" to receive help from a specialist. School focused on intensive instruction and remediation. The goal was to help students conquer the basic skills so they could return to their "regular" classes. When this remediation occurred, students often missed the curriculum and activities of the general classroom. Two separate educational systems existed. Many thought the standards and expectations of small classes were far too low.

In 1986, Madeline Will, then-Assistant Secretary of Education, launched the Regular Education Initiative (*Exceptional Children*, 1986). Acknowledging that the first 10 years of mandated special education had provided opportunities for many children, she decried the separate nature of special education. She challenged general education administrators to take responsibility for the education of students with mild to moderate disabilities and accept "the general applicability of special education techniques beyond the confines of the special education class." In words that could have been spoken yesterday, Secretary Will predicted that less segregated programming would "prepare *all* children to identify, analyze and resolve problems as they arise; to increase their ability to cope in a flexible manner with change . . . and to enter the community as informed and educated citizens who are capable of living and working as independent and productive adults."

Note that Secretary Will's emphasis was on students with mild to moderate disabilities. The *Annual Reports to Congress* indicate that the percentage of children with disabilities increased consistently from 1988 to 2000, especially students identified as having learning disabilities. In general, these students are considered to have mild disabilities. The services and supports they need are not viewed as intense. These children were the focus of Secretary Will's words.

The impact of a learning disability is deceptive. Although children might look, think, and behave much like their typical peers, they encounter significant challenges mastering the basic building blocks of reading, writing, and/or math. Educators and researchers labor mightily to identify specialized teaching methods that overcome the hurdles posed by nimble minds stymied by tasks others master so easily. Teachers identify these children as needing special education because they have not responded to traditional classroom methods.

Echoing Will's words, Wayne Sailor and Blaire Roger criticize the separation that still exists. They claim that special education continues to be disengaged from general education—too focused on individuals. Sailor and Roger present a whole-school support model, in which previously specialized services improve the learning of all students.

Naomi Zigmond notes that inclusion conversations, which once focused on access to peers, now emphasize access to the general curriculum. She has discovered no compelling reason to focus on *where* education takes place. Instead, she urges that we strive to do what is best for individual learners—and that may take place in specialized educational settings.

Sailor and Roger think special educators focus on the trees and miss the forest of the whole school. Zigmond thinks we need to focus on the trees to ensure they grow strong. As you read these articles, ask yourself which approach will provide the best education for students with disabilities.

YES

Wayne Sailor and
Blair Roger

Rethinking Inclusion:
Schoolwide Applications

As a field, special education presents an excellent case study of the paradox of differentiation and integration, wherein we seek solutions through increased specialization but, in so doing, we redefine a problem in terms of discrete parts at the expense of the whole. As Thomas Skrtic pointed out more than a decade ago, a large and ever-widening gap exists between the purpose of special education—to provide needed supports, services, adaptations, and accommodations to students with disabilities in order to preserve and enhance their educational participation in the least restrictive environment—and its practice. And that practice has evolved over three decades into a parallel and highly differentiated educational structure, often with only loosely organized connections to the general education system.

Having disengaged from general education early on, special education began to undergo a process that, at times, has seemed to mimic cell division. At one point in its ontogeny, the field could list some 30 distinct eligibility categories for special education services (e.g., learning disabilities, behavioral disorders, severe disabilities, autism, and so on). Many of these early categories further subdivided, with autism, for example, splitting into a host of subcategories lumped under "autism spectrum disorders."

How has all of this come about? The paradox of differentiation and integration—with its tensions in practice and contradictions in policy—offers a reasonable hypothesis. In our efforts to better meet the educational needs of specific identifiable groups, we have promoted differentiation at the expense of integration. If such a policy produced exemplary outcomes, the only remaining questions would concern how to direct scarce resources to meet the needs of a few individuals, and the values underlying special education would no doubt resolve the tension in favor of customization and differentiation. But the positive outcomes don't seem to be there.

In its early days, special education embraced the diagnostic/prescriptive model characteristic of modern medicine, and disability was viewed as pathology. Psychology, with its partner the test industry, became the "gatekeeper" for special education. Students referred by teachers and parents were diagnosed in one of the categories of disability and tagged for separate (highly differentiated) treatment. Indeed, special education policy handbooks at the

From *Phi Delta Kappan,* March 2005, pp. 503–509. Copyright © 2005 by Phi Delta Kappa International. Reprinted by permission of the publisher and author. References omitted.

district level came to resemble the *Diagnostic and Statistical Manual* of the American Psychiatric Association.

Then in the 1980s, the U.S. Department of Education began to advance policy reforms designed to slow the growth in the number of special education categorical placements and practices. These initiatives occurred against a backdrop of publications citing positive outcomes from integrated practices and a corresponding barrage of studies associating separate classrooms and pullout practices with negative outcomes.

The first of these reforms was called the Regular Education Initiative and was designed to stimulate the provision of special education supports and services in general education classrooms. It generated enormous controversy within special education. Indeed, a special issue of the *Journal of Learning Disabilities* was devoted entirely to an attempt to refute the research underlying the policy. Framing the reform of special education policy as general education policy ("regular" education initiative) failed completely within the community of special education.

More recently, federal policy has advanced "inclusion" as recommended practice and has expended significant funds for training, research, and demonstration purposes. This initiative, too, has failed to significantly change special education placement and service configurations, over about a 15-year period. Again, the policy has drawn fire from within special education and has failed to attract interest and enthusiasm from general education.

The No Child Left Behind (NCLB) legislation, for all its problems, does offer special education an opportunity to pursue once again the pathway to integration. First, NCLB makes clear that *all children* in public education are general education students. Second, the law is firmly anchored in accountability, even going so far as to define "evidence" and to restrict scientific inquiry to approved methodologies. If students identified for special education are placed in general education settings and provided with specialized services and supports, and if evidence for academic and social outcomes is to be evaluated according to approved methodologies, then there is an opportunity to achieve a measure of integrated education policy. And the sum of available evidence overwhelmingly supports integrated instructional approaches over those that are categorically segregated, regardless of the categorical label or severity of the disability.

A Schoolwide Approach

That inclusion policy has failed to garner much support from general education can be partially attributed to the way "inclusion" has been defined. Virtually all definitions begin with a general education classroom as the unit of interest and analysis for the provision of supports and services. The problem with a general-classroom-based model is that it doesn't seem credible to the general education teacher, whose job is usually seen as moving students as uniformly as possible through the curriculum. Students whose disabilities impede them from progressing at the expected rate and who, as a result, fall whole grade levels behind their classmates on various components of the curriculum seem to belong elsewhere. Special education has usually been there to oblige with separate categorical placements, particularly when "inclusion" has been tried and has "failed."

Alternatively, when inclusion is a core value of the school program, students with IEPs (individualized education programs) who cannot function in various components of the classroom curriculum often find themselves at tables, usually in the back of the classroom, with paraprofessionals who, in a one-on-one approach, work with them on "something else." This practice not only segregates special education students within the general education classroom but also creates a distraction that has a detrimental effect on general and special education students alike.

But does inclusion need to be tied to a classroom-based model? If the objective is to avoid separate, categorical placements as the chief alternative to general education placements, then can we shift the unit of analysis from the classroom to the school? So if Joey is a student who, because of his disabilities, cannot progress at grade level in the third grade, then we can ask, For those portions of the third-grade curriculum that Joey cannot successfully engage, even with support, where should he be? With whom? And doing what? The problem then becomes one of scheduling, personnel deployment, and the use of space, not one of alternative placement.

A schoolwide approach is not a variation on the older "pull-out" model. Under emerging schoolwide models, students with IEPs are not removed from general education classrooms to receive one-on-one therapies and tutorials or to go to "resource rooms." Following the logic of integration, all services and supports are provided in such a way as to benefit the maximum number of students, including those not identified for special education. Indeed, in recent years, special education has developed evidence-based practices that have been shown to work for general education students as well. Learning strategies, positive behavior support, and transition planning are three excellent examples. Here's a good summary of this new kind of thinking:

> In a transformed urban school, then, learning and other educational supports are organized to meet the needs of all students rather than historical conventions or the way the rooms are arranged in the building. Creative reallocation of even limited resources and innovative reorganization of teachers into partnerships and teams offer ways to break old molds and create the flexibilities needed to focus on student learning and achievement. Previously separate "programs," like special education, Title I, or bilingual education, come together to form a new educational system that delivers necessary additional supports and instruction in the same spaces to diverse groups of students. The new system anchors both organizational and professional effort in student content, performance, and skill standards that are owned by local communities and families while informed by national and state standards, curriculum frameworks, and effective assessment strategies.

The Individuals with Disabilities Education Act (IDEA) contains language in its "incidental benefits" section that encourages applications of special education that hold promise for general education students. This approach enables special educators to support students with special needs by means of integrated arrangements.

Three decades of comprehensive special education have produced an extraordinary wealth of pedagogical adaptations and strategies to enhance learning. This unique set of conditions came about through the provision of set-aside funds for research under IDEA, and much of that research has focused on problem-solving strategies that can benefit any hard-to-teach students. Today, NCLB exhorts us to teach all students to the highest attainable standards. Special education has designed instructional enhancements that can facilitate this outcome, but for these research-based enhancements to benefit all students, special education needs to be integrated with general education. Emerging schoolwide approaches and the call for a "universal design for learning" represent early efforts in this direction.

When a schoolwide approach is applied to "lowperforming" schools, such as those sometimes found in isolated rural settings or in inner-city areas affected by conditions of extreme poverty, mounting evidence suggests that integrated applications of special education practices can yield positive outcomes for all students. For example, when fully integrated applications of learning strategies designed originally for students with specific learning disabilities have been implemented, scores on NCLB-sanctioned accountability measures for all students have increased. Where social development is at issue, the use of schoolwide positive behavior support has led to higher standardized test scores for general education students in low-performing schools.

SAM

To illustrate how an integrated model works in practice, we describe below our own version of such an approach, called SAM for Schoolwide Applications Model, which is being implemented and evaluated in eight California elementary and middle schools and in one elementary school in Kansas City, Kansas. We describe this model in terms of six "guiding principles," which can be broken down into 15 "critical features." Each feature can be evaluated over time using SAMAN (Schoolwide Applications Model Analysis System), an assessment instrument designed to enable schools themselves to link specific interventions to academic and social outcomes for all students. While this approach can appear to mimic comprehensive school reform in some ways, it is specifically designed to be integrated into the existing values and culture of each individual school. In other words, under SAM, a school that wishes to unify its programs and resources is presented with the 15 critical features and instructed to use team processes to implement them according to its own culture and time lines. Across our nine research sites, we are seeing great diversity and creativity on the part of school teams.

Guiding Principles and Critical Features

Guiding Principle 1. General education guides all student learning. As a fully integrated and unified model, SAM proceeds on the key assumption that all student learning is guided by a district's framework for curriculum, instruction, and assessment and is thus aligned with state standards. Four critical features support this principle: 1) all students attend their regularly assigned school; 2) all students are considered general education students; 3) general education teachers are responsible for all students; and 4) all students are instructed in accordance with the general education curriculum.

Most teacher training programs today continue to encourage general education teachers to expect special education teachers to assume primary responsibility for students with IEPs. Special education departments at colleges and universities reinforce this notion by training special education teachers in self-contained classrooms and by having little overlap with general education departments, such as departments of curriculum and instruction. An integrated schoolwide model, on the other hand, essentially requires teachers to see their role differently. At SAM schools, the general education teacher is the chief agent of each child's educational program, with support from a variety of others. Using SAM, general education teachers have primary responsibility for all students, consider themselves responsible for implementing IEPs, and collaborate with special education professionals to educate students with disabilities.

Furthermore, this guiding principle encourages schools to avoid such alternative placements as special schools for students who need extensive services and supports. Through SAM, schools welcome these students and configure any funding that comes with them to benefit a variety of students through integrated applications.

At our research sites, it is school policy to encourage parent participation and involvement, and parents are given extensive information about the schoolwide model. In those rare cases when parents feel strongly that their child requires a separate, self-contained placement—and the district concurs—the student may be referred to a comparable non-SAM school that offers self-contained classes for students with disabilities.

SAM does not allow for separate classes for students with disabilities at the school site, so the challenge is to focus on how such students can be supported in the general education classroom, how they can be supported in other environments, and how specialized therapies and services can be provided. The use of space, the deployment of support personnel, and scheduling issues become significant. At SAM schools, very little attention is focused on the existence of disabilities among some students. Every effort is made to foster friendships and positive relationships among students with and without disabilities.

SAM differs from traditional inclusion models by ensuring that students with IEPs are pursuing goals and objectives matched to and integrated with the curriculum being implemented in the general education classroom. Under SAM, no student with disabilities would be found at the rear of a classroom, engaged with a paraprofessional on some task that is unrelated to what the rest of the class is doing. If the class is engaged in a higher-level curricular activity, say, algebra, and a student with disabilities cannot engage that material with measurable benefit, then that student might be assigned to an integrated grouping outside of the classroom for that period. In that case, instruction in remedial math would take place with general education students who are also operating at the same curricular level.

There are times, of course, when one-on-one instruction is appropriate in the general education classroom, but this option would be available to any student who could benefit rather than restricted solely to students identified for special education. For example, any child who needs intensive instruction in reading might receive a 30-minute tutorial session in the school's learning center while the rest of the class is engaged in a reading exercise.

Guiding Principle 2. **All school resources are configured to benefit all students.** Three critical features support this principle: 1) all students are included in all activities; 2) all resources benefit all students; and 3) the school effectively incorporates general education students in the instructional process.

In traditional schools, students in special education often do not accompany general education students on field trips; attend sporting events, assemblies, performances, and after-school programs; or take part in specialized reading, math, and science programs or enrichment programs in the arts. SAM schools seek to overcome such barriers to inclusion in all regular school events. All students with IEPs are members of age-appropriate, grade-level classrooms, and they attend all non-classroom functions with their classmates.

Large SAM schools, particularly secondary schools, also make use of small-group arrangements at the classroom level and small learning communities at the school level. Cooperative learning groups, student-directed learning, peer tutorials, peer-mediated instructional arrangements, and so on can greatly enhance outcomes for all students in integrated instructional settings. In addition, particularly in large middle schools and high schools, teams of general and support teachers skilled in math or literacy can use learning centers to support any student's needs. The learning center becomes flexible space for tutorial services offered by teachers or volunteer members of the National Honor Society, as well as a place to make up tests, complete homework with assistance, see a missed film, find resources for a paper or project, and so forth.

Guiding Principle 3. **Schools address social development and citizenship forthrightly.** A single critical feature undergirds this principle: the school incorporates positive behavior support (PBS) at the individual, group, and schoolwide levels. PBS was originally developed as specialized instruction in social development for students with behavioral disabilities. But it has demonstrated its efficacy for all students, particularly those in schools challenged by urban blight and poverty. SAM schools incorporate schoolwide PBS as a comprehensive intervention package to help meet the social development needs of all students.

Guiding Principle 4. **Schools are democratically organized, data-driven, problem-solving systems.** Four critical features support this principle: 1) the school is data-driven and uses team processes; 2) all personnel take part in the teaching/learning process; 3) the school employs a noncategorical lexicon; and 4) the school is governed by a site leadership team.

SAM schools are encouraged to upgrade district software to enable the leadership team to make use of all available databases that affect the social and academic performance of students. Through a process called school-centered planning, SAM schools use a variety of performance data fields, disaggregated at the district level, to make decisions regarding priorities related to school improvement.

SAM schools recognize that all salaried personnel at a school can contribute to the teaching/learning process. A custodian may have hidden talents for vocational training, or a speech therapist may be skilled in musical composition. The trick is to enable all school personnel to contribute to the primary mission of the school and not to be completely constrained by bureaucratic specifications of roles. SAM schools also seek to move away from such categorical descriptors as "learning disabilities," "inclusion," "specials," and so on. There are just two kinds of teachers in a SAM school: classroom teachers and support teachers.

A site leadership team is established at each SAM school. It represents all school personnel and may include parents and members of the local community. This team undertakes the process of school-centered planning to evaluate data related to student academic and social performance, to prioritize specific interventions to improve outcomes, and to advance the mission of the school through full implementation of SAM.

Guiding Principle 5. Schools have open boundaries in relation to their families and communities. Two critical features support this guiding principle: 1) schools have working partnerships with their students' families; and 2) schools have working partnerships with local businesses and service providers.

SAM schools go beyond the traditional structure of parent/teacher organizations and solicit the active participation of family members in the teaching/learning process. Some SAM sites have made the establishment of a family resource center at the school a top priority. Some have even created a "parent liaison" position.

SAM schools also reach beyond the "business partnership" relationship that has characterized some school reform efforts. Schools undertake a "community mapping" process to understand their respective communities. Under many circumstances, the school community may not be geographically defined. But the point is to engage the school's constituents in the life of the school.

Furthermore, effective community partnerships set the stage for meaningful service-learning opportunities and open up possibilities for community-based instruction for any student. Students with IEPs, for example, who cannot engage a secondary-level, classroom-based math curriculum, might take part in "community math" in real-life applied settings such as banks and stores. Other students who are chronically unmotivated by school may reconnect with the learning process through community-based learning opportunities.

Guiding Principle 6. Schools enjoy district support for undertaking an extensive systems-change effort. Just one critical feature is necessary here: schoolwide models such as SAM that offer a significant departure from traditional bureaucratic management and communication processes must have district support. One way to garner such support is to set up pilot projects with the understanding that expansion to additional sites is contingent on documented gains in measured student academic and social outcomes. District-level support may be expected to increase following successful demonstrations and sharing results across schools over time.

Measurement Strategies

Each SAM school employs a package of psychometrically established instruments with which to assess progress related to the priorities that were established through the school-centered planning process. These instruments include a schoolwide evaluation tool to assess support for positive behavior, SAMAN to assess the 15 critical features of SAM, and EVOLVE to assess the training of paraprofessionals and the ways they are deployed.

Districts are encouraged to use the COMPASS Data Analyzer as an adjunct to the districtwide data system to enable each SAM school to receive feedback about its own priorities and specific data of interest. The program also facilitates reporting to the other teams and committees at the school.

Structural Elements of SAM

SAM is a fully integrated and unified approach to the education of all students. As a process, it is intended to enable schools to engage in collaborative, team-driven decision making that is focused on interventions designed to enhance academic and social outcomes for students. The process of educating all students together presents both challenges and opportunities. The SAM approach requires certain structural elements to be in place. As touched upon earlier, two elements, a site leadership team and school-centered planning, must be present at the school level. And two more elements, a district leadership team and a district resource team, must be present at the district level.

Site leadership team. The SLT, usually with between eight and 12 members, evaluates schoolwide data on student progress; sets priorities, goals, and objectives for each school term; and networks with and reports to the other teams and committees that function at the school. The principal is usually a member of the SLT but does not need to be its chair. Membership on SLTs is usually determined by a combination of internal teacher nominations, with elections for one-year renewable terms; principal appointments; and invitations to specific parents and community members. Expenses incurred by parent and community participants, the cost of substitutes for participating teachers who attend out-of-class meetings, the cost of supplies, and so on, can become budget items for SLTs. SLTs follow strict team procedures with regard to agenda, floor time, minutes, and so on, so that precious time is not wasted. SLTs meet at least biweekly and undergo full-day "retreats" at least twice a year, prior to the beginning of each new term. The school-centered-planning process takes place during these retreats.

School-centered planning. The SCP process is patterned after empowerment evaluation. Using this process, a facilitator, supplied by the district or arranged through a university partnership, assists the SLT to begin with a vision for why the school decided to become a SAM school. A set of goals is derived to make the vision real, and a set of specific objectives for the coming term is spelled out for the various school/community personnel. Measurement strategies are identified for each objective so that subsequent planning and objective setting can take account of data on pupil performance that are linked to specific measurable processes. The SLT holds interim meetings to review progress in the implementation of each SCP action plan for the term.

District leadership team. The DLT consists of district personnel with an interest in implementing SAM. The superintendent may well be a member but usually will not be the chair. DLTs are frequently chaired by the head of curriculum and instruction, since SAM processes are driven primarily by general education. Other members of the DLT typically include the head of pupil support services, the special education director, the Title I director, and the director of programs for second-language learners. The superintendent may appoint other members as needed. The DLT usually meets three or four times a year to review SAM school-site plans and to consider requests for approval of policy and budget items arising from these plans.

District resource team. The final structural component is the DRT. This team is usually made up of district-level staff members who work closely with the schools, such as regional special education personnel, grade-level specialists, the parent support coordinator, and transportation officials. The function of the DRT is to help the DLT consider requests for resources from each school site for the coming term. If, for example, a SAM site requests two additional paraprofessionals to implement one or more objectives on its plan for the coming term, the DRT will consider the request, balance the needs of that site against the collective needs of all district schools, and make recommendations to the DLT. Typically, DRTs with several SAM sites in the district will meet on a fairly frequent basis to help the district stay ahead of the curve of systems change.

The Schoolwide Applications Model is a work in progress. It represents an effort to integrate all aspects of comprehensive school reform with a new and innovative approach to the delivery of special education supports and services. Research must continue if we are to determine whether the premise of SAM holds: namely, that de-differentiated educational practices can support personalized learning—in and outside of classrooms—while creating a sense of unity and a culture of belonging in the school.

Naomi Zigmond

Where Should Students with Disabilities Receive Special Education Services? Is One Place Better than Another?

The question of where special education students should be educated is not new. Lloyd Dunn raised the question in 1968, and response to his article spurred the adoption of resource room services in place of special day classes in the 1970s. The question was raised again in 1975 with the passage of the Education for All Handicapped Children Act, later known as the Individuals with Disabilities Education Act (IDEA), and its balanced support for both a continuum of services and placement in the least restrictive environment. The Act required that procedures be established

> to assure that, to the maximum extent appropriate, handicapped children . . .
> are educated with children who are not handicapped and that . . . removal
> of handicapped children from the regular educational environment occurs
> only when the nature or severity of that handicap is such that education in
> regular classes with the use of supplemental aids and services cannot be
> achieved satisfactorily.

The very first annual report to Congress by the U.S. Department of Health, Education and Welfare provided a succinct summary of this balanced position. The argument went as follows. In 1819, in *McColloch v. Maryland*, the courts maintained that the government's purpose should be served with as little imposition on the individual as possible—if less dramatic means for achieving the same basic purpose could be found, they should be taken. Years later, this court decision was interpreted to mean that children with disabilities should be educated in as mainstream a setting as possible. That interpretation was supported by the wave of civil rights litigation in the late 1960s and early 1970s, most notably *Brown v. Board of Education* (1954) and *Pennsylvania Association for Retarded Children (PARC) v. Commonwealth of Pennsylvania* (1972). *PARC*, and the subsequent *Mills v. Board of Education of the District of Columbia* (1972) case, established the proposition that children with disabilities should be placed in the least drastic, or most normal, setting appropriate, with as little interference and as normal an educational process as possible.

From *Journal of Special Education*, vol. 37, no. 3, October 2003, pp. 193–199. Copyright © 2003 by Pro-Ed, Inc. Reprinted by permission. References omitted.

Court cases established the principle of least restrictiveness, but they were only part of the story. State and federal legislation reiterated the principle. Well before the federal legislation became effective, the principle of least restrictiveness embodied in the *PARC* agreement was clearly established in the laws, statutes, or regulations of at least 20 states. In fact, in its first annual report to Congress, the U.S. Department of Health, Education and Welfare proudly proclaimed that even in 1976–1977, the school year preceding full implementation of the new federal law, "many handicapped children are already receiving their education in a regular classroom setting and appropriate alternative placements are in most cases available to accommodate children with special needs." During the following decades, efforts would be made to move services for students with disabilities out of separate schools and into regular schools, with these students being integrated (mainstreamed) into general education classes for part of the school day and provided with pull-out itinerant, resource, or part-time special education services for the rest of the day.

The question of where students with disabilities should be educated was hotly debated again in the mid-1980s, as essays on the failure of pull-out special education began to proliferate. The theme was consistent: Fundamental changes in the delivery model for special education were needed to increase the accomplishments of students with disabilities. Even Madeline Will, then Assistant Secretary of Education and head of the Office of Special Education Programs, joined the fray: "Although well intentioned, the so-called 'pull out' approach to the educational difficulties of students with learning problems has failed in many instances to meet the educational needs of these students." Will and other advocates of the regular education initiative called for children with learning problems to have completely integrated educational experiences in order to achieve improved educational outcomes.

The 1997 IDEA amendments raised the question of where students with disabilities should be educated with a new urgency. Whereas earlier definitions of *restrictiveness* had focused on access of students with disabilities to nondisabled peers, the new focus defined this in terms of their access to the general education curriculum. With the additional requirement that students with disabilities participate in (and perform respectably on) statewide assessments and accountability procedures, pressures to favor one kind of placement (e.g., inclusion in the general education classroom) over any other (e.g., providing pull-out services in some other place) mounted.

A decade earlier, McKinney and Hocott had explained that "part of the rationale for totally integrated [as compared to pull-out] programs for mildly handicapped students is based on research that questions the efficacy of special education." How solid is the research evidence indicating that any one particular place, or service-delivery model, can achieve better outcomes for students with disabilities, though? In this article I review research studies and research reviews that address the question of place. I argue, as many others have before me, that research evidence on the relative efficacy of one special education service delivery model over another is scarce, methodologically flawed, and inconclusive. But I will also argue that, in practical terms, the question of where students with disabilities should be educated is misguided.

That question is antithetical to the kind of individualized planning that is the hallmark of special education for students with disabilities. I will argue for new ways of thinking about the issue of place and the conduit of research on special education placements before progress can be made on improving results for students with disabilities.

Although I limit myself to the research literature in which students with mild and moderate disabilities are studied, I strongly believe that the arguments I make have merit across the entire range of students with disabilities promoted and protected by IDEA and that these arguments have important implications for the rhetoric of the next IDEA reauthorization.

Efficacy Studies on Place

For more than 3 decades, special education researchers and scholars have conducted research, and synthesized research, on the relative usefulness of one place or another for serving students with disabilities. Dunn concluded, on the basis of several studies conducted in the 1960s and a review of research published by Kirk, that there was no empirical support for educating students with high-incidence disabilities in special classes: "Retarded pupils make as much or more progress in the regular grades as they do in special education [and] efficacy studies on special day classes for other mildly handicapped children, including the emotionally handicapped, reveal the same results." Although Dunn called for the abandonment of special day classes for students with high-incidence disabilities, he also argued persuasively for part-time pull-out special education services to meet their special educational needs.

Ten years later, in a narrative review of 17 studies, Sindelar and Deno concluded that resource rooms were more effective than general education classrooms in improving academic achievement of students with learning disabilities (LD). At about the same time, a meta-analysis of efficacy studies completed by Carlberg and Kavale reported more complex results. Carlberg and Kavale's calculations of effect sizes showed that students with mental retardation in special class placements performed academically as well as those placed in general education classrooms. However, they also concluded that students with learning or behavior disorders in special classes (both self-contained and resource programs) had a modest academic advantage over those remaining in the general education classrooms. Leinhardt and Pallay also concluded from their research review that resource rooms were better than general education classrooms for students with LD. In addition, 1 year later, Madden and Slavin reviewed seven studies on the efficacy of part-time resource placements compared to full-time special education classes and full-time placement in the mainstream and concluded that if increased academic achievement is the desired outcome, "the research favors placement in regular classes . . . *supplemented by well designed resource programs*" (p. 530, italics added).

Research support for supplemental resource room services was, however, overlooked in the national frenzy to reshape special education that swept the country in the mid-1980s. With the introduction of newer, more inclusive service-delivery models, the early research comparing special pull-out placements with general education placements seemed dated and irrelevant. In those earlier studies, it was easy to draw stark contrasts between general education placements, in which no special services were available to students with disabilities, and pull-out services staffed by trained teachers who provided special instruction. In the newer service-delivery models, particularly the full inclusion models for students with mild/moderate disabilities that employed special education teachers in consulting or co-teaching roles, students with disabilities were supposed to be receiving specially designed instruction or supplemental aids and services right in the general education classroom. Research documenting student progress in these new inclusive settings was needed, and it proliferated.

Some studies showed positive trends when students were integrated into general education classrooms, including that full-time placement in a general education classroom resulted in student academic progress that was just as good as that achieved by students in separate settings in elementary schools. Others, however, reported disappointing or unsatisfactory academic and social achievement results from inclusion models. It should come as no surprise, then, that in a review of research on these newer special education service-delivery models, Hocutt reported equivocal findings. She concluded that "various program models, implemented in both general and special education, can have moderately positive academic and social impacts for student with disabilities." However, no intervention in the research literature eliminated the impact of having a disability. That is, regardless of the place of the intervention, students with disabilities did not achieve even at the level of low-achieving nondisabled peers, and no model was effective for *all* students with disabilities.

Manset and Semmel compared eight inclusion models for elementary students with high-incidence disabilities, primarily LD, reported in the research literature between 1984 and 1994. They reiterated Hocutt's conclusions: Inclusive programs can be effective for some, although not all, students with high-incidence disabilities. Waldron and McLeskey agreed with this conclusion. In their research, students with severe LD made comparable progress in reading and math in pull-out and inclusion settings, although students with mild LD were more likely to make gains commensurate with nondisabled peers when educated in inclusive environments than when receiving special education services in a resource room.

Holloway reviewed five studies conducted between 1986 and 1996 that compared traditional pull-out services to fully inclusive service-delivery models and models that combined in-class services with pull-out instruction. His conclusions did not offer strong support for the practice of full inclusion. Reading progress in the combined model was significantly better than in either the inclusion-only model or the resource room–only model.

In very recent research, Rea, McLaughlin, and Walther-Thomas used qualitative and quantitative methods to describe two schools and their special education models, one fully inclusive and one with more traditional supplemental pull-out services. Results showed that compared to students in the more traditional schools with pull-out programs, students served in inclusive schools earned higher grades, achieved higher or comparable scores on standardized tests, committed no more behavioral infractions, and attended more school days.

In a specific review of co-teaching as the inclusive service-delivery model, Zigmond and Magiera found only four studies that focused on academic achievement gains. In the three elementary studies, co-teaching was just as effective in producing academic gains as was resource room instruction or consultation with the general education teacher; in the high school study, students' quiz and exam grades actually worsened following the co-teaching experiment. Murawski and Swanson, in their meta-analysis of the co-teaching research literature, found six studies from which effect sizes could be calculated; dependent measures were grades, achievement scores, and social and attitudinal outcomes. Murawski and Swanson reported effect sizes for individual studies ranging from low to high, with an average total effect size in the moderate range. Both literature reviews on co-teaching concluded that despite the current and growing popularity of co-teaching as a service-delivery model, further research is needed to determine whether it is an effective service-delivery option for students with disabilities, let alone a preferred one.

Conclusions Derived From the Empirical Research Base

There is no simple and straightforward answer to the question of where students with disabilities should receive their special education instruction. The efficacy research reviewed here, which spans more than 3 decades, provides no compelling research evidence that place is the critical factor in the academic or social progress of students with mild/moderate disabilities. There are probably many reasons for reaching this conclusion, but I suggest only two. The first has to do with the body of research evidence itself. The second has to do with the appropriateness of the question.

Explanation 1: Research Base Is Insufficient

Despite the fact that the efficacy research literature on the places where special education services are provided spans more than 3 decades and that dozens of studies have been reported in refereed special education journals, Murawski and Swanson are right to ask where the data are. Studies worthy of consideration in a meta-analysis or narrative literature review, with appropriate controls and appropriate dependent measures, are few and far between. Of course, research on the efficacy of special education placements is very hard to conduct at all, let alone to conduct well. For example, definitions of service-delivery models or settings vary from researcher to researcher, and descriptions of the treatments being implemented in those models or settings are woefully inadequate. Random assignment of students to treatments is seldom an option, and appropriately matched (sufficiently alike) samples of experimental and control students and teachers are rare. As a result, *where* special education occurs is not a phenomenon that lends itself to precise investigation, and funding for research studies and publication of results in refereed journals are difficult to achieve.

Methodologically Flawed Research. Research designs used to explore the effectiveness of different service-delivery models often employ pre-post treatment group designs. The limitations of these research designs for studying the efficacy of special education have been reported in numerous previous research reviews, most notably in Kirk and Semmel, Gottlieb, and Robinson. Some studies use control groups, often samples of students experiencing "traditional" programs (sometimes referred to as "business as usual" programs) in nonexperimental schools. In some studies, the researchers manage to achieve random assignment of students to treatments, but most use intact groups of students assigned to the teacher or the school building who volunteered to participate in the experimental treatment program. Often the experimental treatment is well described, although degree of implementation is not. Descriptions of the control treatment and its degree of implementation (if indeed a control group is used) are rarely provided. Most often, replication is hindered by inadequate descriptions of the treatments and insufficient monitoring of treatment implementation. Thus, even if reliable achievement changes are demonstrated in one research study, difficulty in identifying critical treatment variables makes replicability impossible in virtually all cases. Achievement gains, or lack thereof, cannot be related to replicable interventions, and the fundamental question of whether Place A is better than Place B cannot actually be answered.

Inconclusive Research. The accumulated evidence to date has produced only one unequivocal finding: Languishing in a general education class where nothing changes and no one pays you any attention is not as useful to students with mild/moderate learning and behavior disorders as is getting some help, although it does not seem to matter for students with mild mental retardation. All other evidence on whether students with disabilities learn more, academically or socially, and are happier in one school setting or another is at best inconclusive. Resource programs are more effective for some students with disabilities than are self-contained special education classes or self-contained general education classes, but they are less effective for other students with similar disabilities. Fully inclusive programs are superior for some students with disabilities on some measures of academic or social skills development and inferior for other students or on other measures. The empirical research not only does not identify one best place but also often finds equivalent progress being made by students with disabilities across settings; that is, the research reports nonsignificant differences in outcomes. Interpreting nonsignificant findings can be tricky. Do we conclude that the proverbial cup is half full or half empty? Do we acknowledge that it does not matter where students receive their special education services and allow parents or school personnel wide berth in making choices? Or do we proclaim that one setting is preferred over another for philosophical or moral reasons with empirical evidence that it "doesn't hurt"?

Explanation 2: Efficacy Studies
Have Been Asking the Wrong Question

Failure to Specify "Best for Whom?" Special education has evolved as a means of providing specialized inter-ventions to students with disabilities based on individual student progress on individualized objectives. The bedrock of special education is instruction focused on *individual* needs. The very concept of "one best place" contradicts this commitment to individualization. Furthermore, results of research on how groups of students respond to treatment settings does not help the researcher or practitioner make an individualized decision for an individual student's plan. A better question to ask, if we dare, is "best for whom?" or best for which individual students with which individual profiles of characteristics and needs? Answering this question requires that we abandon the rhetoric in which we call for *all* students to do this, or *all* students to learn that, or *all* students be educated in a certain place.

Special educators understand about individual differences. Special educators understand that no matter how hard they try or how well they are taught, there are some students who will never be able to learn on the same schedule as most others, who will take so long to learn some things that they will have to forego learning other things, or who will need to be taught curricular content that is not ordinarily taught. Special educators understood this when they fought hard for the legal requirement of the Individualized Educational Program for children with disabilities, to permit formulation of unique programs of instruction to meet unique individual needs. By continuing to ask, "What is the best place?" we are ignoring what we know.

Restating the question as "best for whom?" would also require new research designs and data analysis. A first step in that direction might be to reanalyze group design data at the individual student level. For example, Zigmond et al. collected achievement test data for 145 students with LD in three full inclusion programs and for many of these students' nondisabled classmates. Rather than reporting average growth of the students with LD, the researchers reported the number and percentage of students with LD who made reliably significant gains (i.e., gains exceeded the standard error of measurement of the reading test) during the experimental year. They also reported on the number and percentage of students with LD whose reading gains matched or exceeded the average gain of their grade-level peers. Finally, they reported on the number and percentage of students with LD whose achievement status (i.e., their relative standing in the grade-level peer group) had improved during the school year. These analytic techniques allowed for exploration of setting effects at an individual level. Waldron and McLeskey followed this same tactic. Unfortunately, neither group of researchers took the final step of describing individual participants in enough detail to permit generalization of the findings or extrapolation of the findings to the individual case. Nevertheless, this approach seems more promising than the traditional approaches that have been used to date in terms of answering the question "best for whom?"

Failure to Specify "Best for What?"   Different settings offer different opportunities for teaching and learning. The general education classroom provides students with disabilities with access to students who do not have disabilities; access to the curricula and textbooks to which most other students are exposed; access to instruction from a general education teacher whose training and expertise are quite different from those of a special education teacher; access to subject matter content taught by a subject matter specialist; and access to all of the stresses and strains associated with the preparation for, taking of, and passing or tailing of the statewide assessments. If the goal is to have students learn content subject information or how to interact with nondisabled peers, the general education setting is the best place.

Pull-out settings allow for smaller teacher–student ratios and flexibility in the selection of texts, choice of curricular objectives, pacing of instruction, scheduling of examinations, and assignment of grades. Special education pull-out settings allow students to learn different content in different ways and on a different schedule. A pull-out special education setting may be most appropriate if students need (a) intensive instruction in basic academic skills well beyond the grade level at which nondisabled peers are learning how to read or do basic mathematics, (b) explicit instruction in controlling behavior or interacting with peers and adults, or (c) to learn anything that is not customarily taught to everyone else.

If educators value education that is different and special and want to preserve that feature of special education, it is legitimate to ask whether the general education classroom can be transformed to support this desire. Or, as Fuchs and Fuchs asked, "Can general education become special education?" Their experience (and mine) strongly suggests that the answer to this question is "no." Attempts to transport teaching methods that were developed and validated in special education to general education settings have not been successful. Instructional practices that focus on individual decision making for individual students and improve outcomes of students with severe learning problems are not easily transposed into practices that can survive in a general education classroom. General educators will make instructional adaptations in response to students' persistent failure to learn, but the accommodations are typically oriented to the group, not to the individual, and are relatively minor in substance, with little chance for helping students with chronically poor learning histories.

Over and over again, researchers and staff development personnel have come to recognize that general education teachers have a different set of assumptions about the form and function of education than do special educators. General educators cannot imagine focusing intensively on individual students to the extent that different instructional activities for different students are being implemented at the same time. This is simply impractical in a classroom of 25 to 35 students. Moreover, special education's most basic article of faith, that instruction must be individualized to be truly effective, is rarely contemplated, let alone observed, in most general education classrooms. Mainstream teachers must consider the good of the group and the extent to which the learning activities they present maintain classroom flow, orderliness, and cooperation. In addition, they generally formulate teaching plans that result in a productive learning environment for 90% or more of their students. General education settings are best for learning what most students need to learn.

For many of the remaining 10% of students, however, a different orientation will probably be needed. These students need to learn something different because they are clearly not learning what everyone else is learning. Interventions that might be effective for this group of students require a considerable investment of time and effort, as well as extensive support. Special education in a pull-out setting, with its emphasis on empirically validated practices and its use of data-based decision making to tailor instruction to the individual students' needs, might be better for teaching these students.

Conclusion

As early as 1979, federal monitoring of state programs was put into place to guard against not only too much segregation of students with disabilities but also "inappropriate mainstreaming." Although most would agree that students with mild and moderate disabilities should spend a large proportion of the school day with peers without disabilities, research does not support the superiority of any one service-delivery model over another. Furthermore, effectiveness depends not only on the characteristics and needs of a particular student but also on the quality of the program's implementation. A poorly run model with limited resources will seldom be superior to a model in which there is a heavy investment of time, energy, and money. Good programs can be developed in any setting, as can bad ones. The setting itself is less important than what is going on in the setting.

Reflecting on the 35 years of efficacy research on the settings in which special education is delivered that I have reviewed in this article, what do we know? We know that what goes on in a place, not the location itself, is what makes a difference. We know that you learn what you spend time on and that most students with disabilities will not learn to read or to write or to calculate if they are not explicitly taught these skills. We know that some instructional practices are easier to implement and more likely to occur in some settings than in others. We know that we need more research that asks better and more focused questions about who learns what best where. In addition, we know that we need to explore new research designs and new data analysis techniques that will help us bridge the gap between efficacy findings and decision making on placements for individual students.

In response to the query of what is special about special education, I can say with some certainty that place is not what makes special education "special" or effective. Effective teaching strategies and an individualized approach are the more critical ingredients in special education, and neither of these is associated solely with one particular environment. Educators must also remember that research has shown that typical general education environments are not supportive places in which to implement what we know to be effective teaching strategies for students with disabilities. Considering the research evidence to date, it is clear that placement decisions must continue to be made by determining whether a particular placement option will support the effective instructional practices that are required for a particular child to achieve his or her individual objectives and goals.

The search for the best place in which to receive special education services has tended to be fueled by passion and principle, rather than by reason and rationality. Until educators are ready to say that receiving special education services in a particular setting is good for some students with disabilities but not for others, that different educational environments are more conducive to different forms of teaching and learning, that different students need to learn different things in different ways, and that traditional group research designs may not capture these individual differences in useful ways, we may never get beyond the equivocal findings reported here. We may even fail to realize that, in terms of the best place to receive special education and related services, we have probably been asking the wrong questions.

POSTSCRIPT

Can One Model of Special Education Serve All Students?

Research findings supply grist for this controversy. According to Wehmeyer, Lattin, Lapp-Rincker, and Agran (*Remedial and Special Education,* 2003), inclusive settings provided students with mental retardation greater access to the general curriculum. However, the authors question whether access translates into greater progress, wondering whether the curriculum itself presents insurmountable barriers. Like Sailor and Roger, they advocate using universal design to increase meaningful learning.

Comparing two schools in the same district, outcomes for students with learning disabilities were significantly more favorable in an inclusive setting (Rea, Laughlin, and Walther-Thomas, *Exceptional Children,* 2002). Could the disability make a difference?

Sailor and Roger feel strongly that initiatives to increase inclusive programming have not garnered support from either special education or general education professionals. Using NCLB as a lever, their schoolwide service model extends special education supports to reach all children, instead of concentrating on a few in separate environments.

Supporting Sailor and Roger, and contrary to popular opinion, McLeskey, Hoppy, Williamson, and Rentz (*Learning Disabilities Research & Practice, 2004*) found that the drive toward inclusion is an illusion, virtually nonexistent for students with learning disabilities. Increases were slight and attributable to a few states. The most successful ventures accompanied long-term school change.

Zigmond would have educators concentrate on learners and outcomes rather than schools. Finding no one model effective for all students, and "no compelling research evidence" that *place* is the critical variable, she doubts that general education classrooms can be sufficiently restructured to make a difference. She urges educators to ask what works best for each learner. And each learner's goals.

Placement debates often occur in hearing rooms, with schools and parents supporting their preferred program. The direction of preference is unpredictable. Schools frequently advocate for services delivered in the general education environment. At other times, the same school favors a more restrictive, separate program. Some parents feel the "regular" classroom is key to learning and growth. Others believe a separate, intensive program will ensure success for their child.

Curtis (2005) was surprised by the anger of parents seeking assistance through a special education law clinic. Usually, the issue at stake was the delivery of effective services. He found general education teachers "effectively rebelling" against inclusion. Feeling they lacked the knowledge, skills, or time to take on inclusion responsibilities, some teachers did not always implement IEPs as written. Would a whole-school approach eliminate this problem? Or would it dilute specialized services for the most needy learners?

IDEA never mentions *inclusion*, although it clearly prefers the most typical setting. Yell and Katsiyannis review legal requirements for placement decisions (*Preventing School Failure,* 2004). Supporting Zigmond's recommendations, they note that IDEA requires IEP teams to consider each learner's needs first; next, appropriate goals. Only then should the team determine the appropriate setting. Decisions based on disability category, service availability, or administrative preference are not permissible.

Inclusion is an imposing endeavor. Done well, it requires hard work. Despite some opinions, it does not save money or reduce staff. Does it increase educational access or limit opportunities for targeted instruction?

Could initiatives like SAM (Schoolwide Application Model) make a difference? Would whole-school options create the best climate for all students: a well-staffed, coordinated, child-centered school? With more attention to all students, perhaps fewer needs would develop. But what about those students who need more? SAM does not "allow" separate classes in its schools.

How do the schools you know address inclusion? What is considered when making placement decisions? How are inclusion efforts supported? Have opinions and practices changed with the advent of high-stakes testing?

ISSUE 12

Is Full Inclusion the Least Restrictive Environment?

YES: Rosalind Vargo and Joe Vargo, from "Voice of Inclusion: From My Friend Ro Vargo," in Richard A. Villa and Jacqueline S. Thousand, eds., *Creating an Inclusive School*, 2d ed. (Association for Supervision and Curriculum Development, 2005)

NO: Amy Dockser Marcus, from "Eli's Choice," *The Wall Street Journal* (December 31, 2005)

ISSUE SUMMARY

YES: Rosalind and Joe Vargo, parents of Ro, use their voices to tell a powerful story of their daughter's success in fully inclusive educational programs, from kindergarten through college.

NO: Amy Dockser Marcus, staff reporter at *The Wall Street Journal,* records the voices of Eli's parents and teachers as they react to his message to leave a fully inclusive program in favor of a separate special education class.

Ask a group of people about the definition of "inclusion," and they will usually come up with a statement like, "all children being educated in the same school." Ask again, "Do you mean *all* children?" The reply is likely to be a bit less certain, "Well, maybe not *all*." Probe a bit further and someone is likely to admit (with a bit of trepidation) that inclusion should mean all students except. . . . The words that follow might vary, but usually there are exceptions for students with severe cognitive challenges—those who have mental retardation or those who have disabilities in multiple areas and require complex and broad levels of support in order to communicate, move, and learn. So inclusion, for many people, really does not include *all* children.

Proponents of full inclusion have a very different answer. They say—and mean—*all* children being educated in the same school. Full inclusion advocates proclaim that all children, regardless of level of need, have a moral and legal right to attend their home school, be enrolled in general education classes, and receive all necessary supports within those classes. In a full inclusion environment, students don't need to fit into the school; the school needs to adapt to all students. Services are brought to the child; children are not sent out (or away) because what they need is not available or difficult to deliver.

Those who oppose full inclusion cite the difficulties of adapting instruction, meeting student needs, and acquiring material, training, and professional supports. Accustomed to traditional academic curriculum for some students and vocational, life-skills–based curriculum for others, they ask how the demands of both can be met.

The challenge of full inclusion is perhaps greatest at high schools, with their focus on distinct academic disciplines and college hopes. Communication between teachers is complicated by the increased number of people who interact with each student and the large numbers of students taught by each educator. The conversation has become even more intense with the advent of high-stakes testing, causing some to wonder if the needs of every child can be met within a typical classroom.

This issue presents the compelling voices and experiences of two sets of parents who have had much in common. They each had a child—now grown—with a significant disability. Both chose fully inclusive educational programs for their children. By their accounts, both children flourished. Then their experiences diverge.

Rosalind and Joe Vargo, parents of a young woman who communicates through sign language and uses a wheelchair, describe Ro's inclusive schooling experiences, from kindergarten through university. They share vivid illustrations of how Ro was recognized for her capabilities rather than judged by her appearance.

Amy Dockser Marcus communicates the reactions of Eli's parents, who were also strongly committed to inclusion. The selection relates their surprise when their son, who has Down syndrome, reaches high school and actively rejects inclusion to be with his friends with disabilities. Although Eli's parents abide by his choice, they have different questions about the outcome of the decision.

As you read these articles, consider the experiences of both these families. What successes and challenges did they experience? Why did their paths diverge? What would you think if you were in their shoes?

YES

**Rosalind Vargo and
Joe Vargo**

From My Friend, Ro Vargo

It was Tuesday, a beautiful autumn morning at Syracuse University. Ro had just finished her class "Topics in American Music—20th Century" in Bowne Hall and was walking back to the car (with my assistance) to go home. Joe, Ro's dad, was waiting in the car. He and I looked at each other and at Ro and wondered how we had gotten here. After all, it seemed like only yesterday. . . .

Kindergarten

Among our vivid memories is kindergarten and Ro's first invitation to a birthday party. Kristen's mother phoned to ask if she should make any special arrangements for Ro to attend. Fighting back tears, we responded, "No, but thanks for asking." Kristen's mom said her daughter was so looking forward to Ro coming. Then we said it: "We love Ro because she's our daughter. But do you know why other kids like her?"

The mom replied, "Well, I can speak only for my daughter, Kristen. She says she likes Ro's smile and that Ro is someone you can really talk to . . . and that she wears really neat clothes." Kristen's mom continued, "I think kids like Ro because she isn't a threat to them; they can just be themselves around her."

2nd Grade

In 2nd grade, we invited several kids to Ro's birthday party. Because we would be picking them up at school, we needed to know who would be coming. The night before the party, we called Eric's mom and politely asked, "Is Eric coming to Ro's party tomorrow?"

She said, "I'm sorry I didn't call you, but Eric said he just told Ro in school yesterday that he was coming. Was that all right?" It was more than all right! To Eric, the fact that Ro couldn't talk didn't mean that she couldn't understand him. . . .

4th Grade

In 4th grade, a time when pressure to have the "right" clothes and hairstyles had already begun, Ro was voted "Best Friend" by her 25 "typical" 4th-grade classmates.

Somehow, Ro's inclusion in the school life was making a tremendous difference in many kids as well. Her "giftedness" was recognized and celebrated.

We recall another night when a puzzling phone call came for Ro. Sharing the same nickname as my daughter, I thought the call was for me and I replied, "Speaking."

The young girl at the other end of the line clarified, "No, I'd like the Ro who goes to Ed Smith School."

I said, "Hold on," and exclaimed to Joe, "Someone wants to talk with Ro on the phone!" We got Ro from the dinner table and put the phone to her ear. Immediately recognizing the voice of her friend Ghadeer, Ro started laughing. She then nodded her head to indicate "yes" and followed with a head shake indicating "no." Curiosity got the best of me and I took the phone, reporting to Ghadeer, "Ro's listening and nodding her head."

Ghadeer said, "Great, I'm asking her advice about a birthday present for a friend. Now, did she nod 'yes' for the jewelry or 'yes' for the board game?"

Ro's 11th Birthday

We remember with pleasure Ro's 11th birthday party. Before the party, the mother of one of Ro's friends called to ask if the present she had picked out for Ro was OK. Apparently, her daughter hadn't been with her when she went shopping. She had just wrapped it and given it to her daughter to take to school that morning. She wasn't sure if the gift was the "in" thing and feared that her daughter would die of embarrassment if it weren't.

She had bought a jump rope for Ro—a deluxe model. Without hesitation, I said that it was a wonderful idea and a gift that Ro would love using with her sisters.

With a sigh of relief, the mom responded, "Well, I am glad. I was hoping that Ro was not handicapped or anything. Is she?"

For the life of me, I wanted to say "No" and save this mom obvious embarrassment. So I said, "Well, a little bit." After many of her apologies and my reassurances, we got off the phone as friends. She had made my day, my week, my life! The thought that an 11-year-old girl had received a birthday party invitation, wanted to go, and asked her mom to buy a present, *never thinking it important to mention that her friend had a disability*, still makes me cry with wonder and happiness. . . .

When Ro unwrapped the jump rope, all the girls were elated, shrieking, "I hope I get one of those for my birthday," and "Oh, cool." The girls immediately dragged Ro down the stairs and outside to the driveway, where they tied one end of the jump rope to her wrist. With the strength of her twirling partner, Ro was able to rotate the rope for her friends. It was Ro's best adaptive occupational therapy activity in months.

A Gift for Ghadeer

Probably the most profound testimony to inclusive education occurred in January 1993. Ghadeer, Ro's friend who had called to ask for advice on gift selection, suffered a cerebral hemorrhage, or severe stroke. At the age of 12, she was comatose for almost four weeks. . . . [After] weeks of having family, teachers, and friends read at her bedside, Ghadeer miraculously, although not completely, recovered. Her voice and articulation were so severely impaired that she could not communicate orally. To the amazement of the child's doctors and nurses, her disability did not stop her from communicating; she began to use sign language. An interpreter was quickly found who asked Ghadeer, "Where did you learn sign language?"

Ghadeer replied in sign, "From my friend, Ro Vargo!"

After four months of intensive rehabilitative therapy, Ghadeer returned to school, but now as a "special education" student requiring speech and language services plus physical and occupational therapy. Her family proudly reports that Ghadeer turned away the "special" bus and rode the regular school bus on her first day back to school. Furthermore, she advocated for herself to get a laptop computer to assist her with her schoolwork. Inclusive education enabled Ghadeer to get to know someone like Ro and to learn about augmentative communication systems and her rights, particularly her right to be part of her school, class, and friendship circle. She had learned that a person can still belong even if something unexpected—like a disability—happens.

What's Hard About Being Ro's Friend?

Ghadeer was one of many of Ro's friends who became quite capable of articulating for themselves what Ro meant to them and the kinds of things that they learned at school with her. That relationship became clear when Ro and a group of her friends responded to questions from parents and teachers in a session titled "Building Friendships in an Inclusive Classroom" at a national education conference that they attended.

Tiffany said, "I think Ro should be in class with all of us because how else is Ro going to learn the really important stuff? Besides, we can learn a lot from her."

Teachers asked Ro's friends some unusual questions, such as, " 'Have you ever discussed her disability with her?' "

Stacey replied, "No, I know she is different, but I never thought it important to ask. Like, for instance, I never thought to go up to a black kid in my class and say, 'You're black. How come you're different?' "

A "popular" question among teachers and parents—judging by their nods—was "What is the hardest thing about being Ro's friend?" As Ro's parents, we held our breath, waiting for responses such as "She drools," "She walks funny," or "She's a messy eater."

But again Stacey spoke up, saying, "The hardest thing about being Ro's friend is that she always has a parent or an adult with her." Ouch! That hurt. But Stacey's observation taught us, Ro's parents, an important lesson that will surely have a positive effect on our daughter's future.

Transition to Middle School

The transition from elementary to middle school was tough socially for Ro, as it can be for any adolescent. For Ro, the first months were spent in isolation, but her isolation was not one of physical proximity. Ro attended a regular 6th grade program and had to gain acceptance from her new middle school peers. Initially, she was ignored or stared at; a few classmates even teased her. When Ro was assigned to a work group, no group members complained out loud, but Ro noticed non-verbal signs of rejection. In those first months, we began to doubt our decision to include Ro in middle school. We recalled the comment a teacher from the previous year had made: "Middle school kids don't like themselves. How can you expect them to like your kid?"

Mauricha, a classmate, became Ro's closest new friend. It was Mauricha who broke the social barrier. Asked how the two became friends, Mauricha said, "I saw her. She saw me. We've just been friends ever since." One night when I was taking Mauricha home, she looked at me and touched my arm. "You know, Mrs. Vargo," Mauricha said, "lots of teachers think I'm friends with Ro cuz it gets me more attention. That isn't true. The truth is, I need her more than she needs me."

Ro's father and I would have to summarize Ro's middle school experience as fairly typical. When reflecting on our other daughters' experiences in middle school, we realize that there were many of the same issues: isolation at times, hot and cold friendships, recognition of and a growing interest in boys, physical changes, teasing, challenging class work, and parents who didn't know anything! Oh, yes. Ro went to her first dance and danced with Jermaine. . . .

Arrival at High School

. . . Ro and six other students with disabilities entered Henninger High School. Early on, Ro communicated, "I like . . . zoology . . . , and the kids and I have learned a lot. I have had some classes I didn't like. It is hard for me when classes have no small groups and no homework for me. Sometimes there is too much information. The worst is when neither the kids nor the teachers talk to me." . . .

Inclusive education in high school was offering Ro a whole new world of opportunities and choices. She joined the Key Club. . . . She accrued service hours through her volunteer job at a . . . fully inclusive day care. Ro was acting as a role model for many young students with disabilities, as well as for the whole class and her fellow workers.

During her early high school years, Ro communicated many things to us in various ways. . . . Her "voice" gave us a clearer vision of where and what Ro wanted to do with her life. . . .

On the afternoon of her first volunteer job, Ro had to fill out an application. Her teaching assistant completed it with Ro's input. However, 10 minutes later, Ro totally dissolved into a full-blown temper tantrum.

The panicked teaching assistant questioned Ro, "Does it have anything to do with the application?"

Ro nodded, "Yes."

"Was it #1, #2, #3 . . . ." until the question, "What has been your biggest challenge?"

Without consulting Ro, the teaching assistant had written "Rett syndrome." That was the one! Ro wanted it removed. Yes, the line about Rett syndrome.

Another time that Ro clearly expressed her thoughts was when she was nominated by her teachers for Student of the Month. She had to complete an information sheet for the committee who would select the winner. After much deliberation, Ro opted not to include any of her work with local university students and their numerous papers on her life experiences or any of her work with other girls with Rett syndrome. Basically, her nomination went in with just her name, age, and favorite teacher. Ro was making it clear that she didn't think that Rett syndrome was something important to share about herself. It wasn't really who she was, or what she did, or even what she wanted to have. . . .

The voice of Ro's peers was also becoming clearer and louder. While on the zoology trip to New York City, Ro and her dad struggled for three days to keep up with the fast pace of a very busy itinerary. Ro's classmates seemed oblivious to her tiring easily and to the locomotion problems that caused her to lag behind. It appeared that they hardly noticed her at all that weekend—at least that was Joe's observation. Ro still enjoyed the trip, and it was a wonderful bonding experience for her and dad.

Months later, we came to understand the ramifications and the benefits of Ro's participation in that trip. Students in the class began to vocalize, without our knowledge, concerns about Ro's support person in school. They complained to their teacher at first about how they thought the teaching assistant was disrespectful to Ro. When the teacher heard their complaints, she notified the principal. When there was no action, kids went to their parents and parents came to us. When the school administration failed to act, Ro's peers did!

The vision for inclusive education was a reality. We had hoped that the kids who sat in class with Ro would not seek to harm her now or in the days to come. We had hoped that they would protect her and take care of her, seek the social and legislative reforms to support the inclusive lifestyle that she had grown accustomed to, and gladly be her neighbors and her friends because they had shared the same space, the same hopes, and the same dreams. Ro and her peers in an inclusive high school setting were already living out the dream, and there was no going back for any of us.

After Ro's third year in high school, . . . Ro was clearly envious of the planning and choices that her sister Josie was engaging in. College visits, college applications, and senior pictures were taking place. We were unclear about what Ro's choices could be, and she communicated that the situation was not fair.

One night I read about an inclusive college setting in Kentucky. The ONCAMPUS program had been initiated as a collaborative effort between the Inclusive Elementary and Special Education Program of Syracuse University (SU) and the Syracuse City School District. . . . ONCAMPUS brought six high school students . . . with moderate to severe disabilities to the SU campus where they would participate with other SU students in . . . learning experiences.

Ro. . . . actively communicated her absolute delight with her peers that she was going to attend SU next year. She decided which courses to take, what clubs to belong to, and where she would eat lunch.

However, getting a handicapped parking permit proved to be no easy task. After much discussion and hassle, Ro was secured her permit. When I picked it up, the receptionist asked, "Oh, is this for Ro Vargo who went to Henninger High School?"

"Yes," I replied.

"Tell her I said 'Hi.'"

"You know Ro?" I asked.

"Yeah, I graduated with her from Henninger last year."

Inclusive education . . . another voice heard and in all the right places . . . another confirmation.

Syracuse University Students

Jacqueline [,] . . . a sophomore at SU in the School of Social Work. She began to spend time with Ro on campus through her job as a residential habilitation counselor. She shared with Ro the names of all the good professors and the courses she should pass up! . . . Jackie was a member of SU's jazz and pep band, as well as the dance band. She would clue Ro in on any musical performances on campus. . . .

Justine had seen Ro on campus. . . . She was a senior in the Maxwell School of Communication at the time. As part of her final grade, Justine had to produce a short documentary. She approached Ro and asked if she would be willing to be part of a presentation highlighting the ONCAMPUS program. Ro agreed. A relationship developed that spanned a whole year. Justine introduced Ro to Gregg, another senior, who would be the codirector. They met frequently to talk and shoot videotape.

The final project culminated in a video titled *Ro*. Justine and Gregg's perspective was clearly evident in their work. It was respectful, serious, and funny, and Ro's hopes and dreams of being on a university campus were unfolded in the video. The images were searing and thought-provoking as Ro traversed the campus. Justine and Gregg's voice on this tape will last forever, and so will Ro's voice.

Ro's inclusion in high school and college settings has certainly caused my daughter some pain as she acknowledged her limitations and struggled to belong. Yet inclusion also prompted Ro's self-actualization, self-determination, and self-acceptance and her growing belief that there is nothing that she cannot do. Placing herself in a "regular" environment was a risk that Ro was willing to take.

Inclusive education has always been an emotional and physical risk for all of us, especially Ro. But it has clearly been worth it! . . . Today, Ro uses adult services, and we're starting all over again: justifying, rationalizing, sharing vision, relaying data and information.

When parents of children with disabilities become lonely and fatigued, their voices can become silent. There are limited routes of appeal and no federal mandates to support Ro's inclusive lifestyle. Frankly, we are exhausted and frustrated. Nothing prepared us for this new fight to belong in a community outside of school. This adult, segregated mentality has taken its toll. We have been diligent advocates, articulate spokespersons. We've awakened—not only in Ro but also in many other students—the idea that inclusive education can mean college.

The impact of Ro's inclusive education is made clear by the relationships she forged along the way. Ghadeer called Ro to attend Ghadeer's high school graduation party. . . . Ro received a Christmas card from Mauricha, the middle school friend who broke the social barrier for Ro. The note began, "Hi, Ro. I know you probably don't remember me, but I have never forgotten you." Mauricha explained that she was working as a home health aide and taking a sign language course at night.

Kristen, Ro's teaching assistant, married Gavin. Ro was invited to the wedding, and she reminisced with the bridal party about the last time that they had all been in a limo together! . . . In a newspaper article highlighting the . . . high school graduations in the area, Kristen told a reporter that . . . "Ro was the sister I never had."

The Future?

Our "severely impaired" child has already accomplished more than we had ever thought possible, and she continues to grow. . . . We believe in those young adults who sat in class with Ro. They will not seek to harm her but will be her community—the ones who will protect and care for her. They will advocate social and legislative reform to support the inclusive lifestyle to which Ro and they have grown accustomed. They will gladly be her neighbors, caretakers, job coaches, and friends because they shared the same classes, space, hopes, and dreams.

Eli's Choice

For years, Eli Lewis was the only student in his class with Down syndrome. The genetic condition, which causes a range of cognitive and physical impairments, made it harder for him to do his school work. But his parents felt strongly that he could succeed. They hired a reading tutor. An aide worked with his teachers to modify tests and lessons so that he could be in the same classroom as everyone else. He participated in his middle school's award-winning chorus and was treated as a valued member.

But when all the other kids in his class were making plans to go to the local high school this fall, Eli, 14 years old, said he didn't want to go. He wanted to be in a small class with other students like him. "I don't want to get lost in a big crowd," Eli says.

Eli's declaration surprised his parents. Then his mother recalled the many times she stopped by the school to check on her son, only to find him eating by himself. Once, when she came to pick him up from a dinner that chorus members attended, she says she found Eli sitting with his aide, while the other students sat at a different table.

"The kids liked him, they knew him, they spoke to him," says his mother, Mary Ann Dawedeit. "They just didn't think of him as a peer." Eli, she says, was tired of "being the only kid who was different."

Federal law mandated in the 1970s that children with disabilities be offered a "free and appropriate public education" in the "least restrictive environment," rather than being separated only in special schools or institutions. Over the years, advocacy and additional laws resulted in efforts to get children with disabilities placed in regular classrooms, with proper support, whenever possible. The process, called "inclusion" or "mainstreaming," has largely been an academic success.

Studies have shown benefits for all children, not only those with disabilities, who study together. Many researchers argue this is one reason why people with Down syndrome have made such remarkable progress in recent decades. People with Down syndrome who learn in regular classrooms do much better academically, research has found. They also have significantly higher rates of employment after they graduate and earn more money than peers who studied mainly in self-contained classes.

And yet, Eli Lewis's experience poses a difficult dilemma, one that is only now starting to be recognized and addressed. With help, he had succeeded academically in a regular classroom. But he felt isolated. In a book to be published next year, researchers at the Center for Social Development and Education at the University of Massachusetts in Boston say that although people with intellectual disabilities made enormous gains academically due to inclusion, their social integration at school "remains stagnant."

In a survey of 5,600 seventh- and eighth-grade students from 70 schools across the country, more than half of the youths said they were willing to interact with students with intellectual disabilities at school. But only one-third said they would be willing to invite such students to their house or go to the movies with them, according to the survey done by the University of Massachusetts center and the Washington-based opinion firm, ORC Macro. "Student attitudes continue to remain the most formidable barrier to inclusion," the researchers concluded.

At first, Ms. Dawedeit and her husband, Howard Lewis, thought Eli might change his mind. The couple—who have two other sons who don't have Down syndrome—felt there were many advantages to Eli staying in a regular classroom, including greater independence and more interaction with the general student body. But eventually, Mr. Lewis says he began to recognize that having Eli in a regular classroom might not be "as important to Eli as it is to me."

Ms. Dawedeit remained reluctant. She talked with a friend who had a son with Down syndrome, who was also learning in a regular classroom. "I felt like I had let her down,' Ms. Dawedeit says. "I had preached a mantra for so long to so many."

In May, at the science exposition at Eli's middle school, her feelings changed. The eighth-graders took over the school hallway and parents were invited to visit. Some students demonstrated elaborate experiments they had been working on. Eli worked with his aide to do research online about the chemical properties of silver. He learned where to find it on the periodic table. For the exposition, he printed out some of the documents he had found.

When his mother came to see his project, Eli again raised the subject of where he was going to high school. For Ms. Dawedeit, the contrast was sharp. Here was Eli, successfully participating in a science exposition with peers who didn't have disabilities—but still talking about wanting to be with other people with Down syndrome.

She says she realized she needed to try to accommodate her son's desire for a social group. "I really had to step back from my personal beliefs," she says.

In the fall, Eli enrolled in the ninth grade at Bethesda's Walter Johnson High School, a sprawling building of over 2,000 students. He is in a special program with 20 other students who have disabilities, including one who gets around in a wheelchair and has difficulty talking. Six of the students in the class have Down syndrome. Eli already knew some of the kids from various extracurricular activities, such as drama class and Special Olympics, where he participated in soccer, basketball, swimming and bowling.

Getting out of the mainstream has meant trade-offs. His school is about 10 miles from Eli's house, farther than the local high school that his older brother attends. (The local high school doesn't have a separate special-education program.) A special-education bus now comes each day to pick up Eli, along with other students with disabilities.

"This was one of our big compromises," says his mother. In middle school, Eli walked to a bus stop and rode a regular school bus. "Other kids knew him," says Ms. Dawedeit. "Now he's a special-ed kid on a bus."

One evening in November, after a dinner of chicken burritos and salad, Eli helped his brothers, ages 12 and 17, clear the dishes. Then his parents watched him, as he started making his way through his homework—a worksheet to practice using nouns and verbs. Since Eli was born, they had fought to have him included in regular classrooms. Now it sometimes felt as if Eli might end up outside the world they had tried so hard to keep him in.

All along, they shared a similar goal: for their son to be able to live independently. But Mr. Lewis, a lawyer, began to worry that the academic gap between Eli and other classmates was getting wider in the regular classroom as he grew older, and might be too difficult to bridge in high school. "I'm not married to inclusion at the expense of Eli's getting the skills he needs," he says.

Ms. Dawedeit, a manager at a retail store, was less certain. She knew how much Eli, like all kids his age, wanted to belong. But without spending significant amounts of time in regular classrooms, how would he ever learn the skills he needed to reach the goal of living on his own? "The truth is he has to go out and get a job," she says. "If he's educated with his regular peers, then maybe a regular peer will hire him."

Eli finished his English worksheet, and got up to take a break. He came over and gave his father a hug. "Are you meeting any new kids at school, Eli?" his dad asked. "Not just yet, Dad," Eli answered. "Why are you hanging out only with the kids in your class?" his father queried. "Because I know them," Eli answered, and went into the kitchen to get some cookies.

At his new school, the Parent Teacher Student Association has put the issue of how to promote the inclusion of students with disabilities in extra-curricular activities on the agenda for its January meeting. A student group that pairs students with disabilities with a buddy without disabilities has already scheduled several activities for the coming months, including ice skating and bowling.

Still, for most of his school day, Eli is now in a separate classroom from the general school population. Last month, ninth-graders in the general-education classes were reading the novel, "To Kill a Mockingbird." In the special-education classroom, the teacher was going over worksheets that had been adapted from the book, with some related questions.

Eli was signed up for a regular physical-education class, but asked his parents if he could switch to one with only special-education students. His mother was reluctant to change, because it was one of his only chances to meet kids in the general-student population. She offered a compromise: He could switch to the special-education gym class with his friends, if next semester he took weight-training as part of the regular class. Eli agreed.

Janan Slough, the assistant principal who oversees the special-education department at Eli's school, says the school has difficulty finding certified special-education teachers because of a national shortage.

The school tries to foster as many opportunities as possible for those with disabilities to be in general classrooms, she says. Still, she adds, "I feel caught" between juggling the need for socializing with the need to teach basic, crucial tasks, such as handling money. On one field trip, the special-education kids went to a grocery store; they were supposed buy something their family might use at home, pay for it, and make sure they got correct change.

Most of the kids with disabilities need to focus on independent-living and job skills, rather than college preparation. "I'm charged with thinking about where they are going to be at 21," she says. "I don't want parents to come back and say, 'It's nice they were socially included and had parallel instruction, but you didn't prepare them for the world of work.'"

For now, Eli has only one class—ceramics—that he attends with the general school population. On a recent morning, Eli sat next to a boy assigned to help him. The students were designing tiles, and from time to time his peer assistant would look at what he was doing, or go with him to get more clay. For much of the class, the boy bantered with one of his friends, who had pulled up a chair next to him and was regaling him with a story. From time to time, Eli made a joke and the boys all laughed together.

But when they walked Eli back to the special-education classroom, there was no suggestion that they meet up again that day. When Eli was asked if he enjoyed spending time with his assigned partner, he shrugged and said, "It's OK."

Eli has a lot of ideas about what he wants to do after high school. In middle school, he took a media class and worked in the school's TV studio. Along with the other kids in the class, he was given a homework assignment to make a public-service announcement. Eli made one about the Special Olympics. "I want to be a director," he said, when asked about his plans after high school.

"Eli has serious career aspirations for himself that may not have anything to do with what the rest of the world sees for him after high school," said his mother, one afternoon last month, while waiting for him at a drama class he takes outside of school. The class, made up of students with and without disabilities, was planning a variety show, and Eli was excited about performing. Every night, he went to his room to work on a dance routine he had created to accompany a song from the soundtrack of the movie, "Holes."

His girlfriend, whom he met in elementary school and also has Down syndrome, had invited him to be her date to the upcoming Winter Ball at her private school. Next month, Eli will turn 15 and is planning a big party. The only kids he plans to invite also have disabilities, his mother says.

While she's glad he has found a social circle, she still wonders about what he's missing by going to special-education classes instead of staying in regular classes. "I go back and forth on it all the time," she says. For instance, his school has a state-of-the-art TV studio with editing facilities and a control room, where a class is given. Eli's parents wanted him to be in that class, but it's not possible right now, because he needs to attend the special-education math class, which is held during the same period.

On a recent morning at school, Eli weaved around the teenagers lining the hallway. Some sprawled on the floor, catching up on homework. Others joked with each other by their lockers, or rushed to get to their next class. Eli didn't talk to any of the students. He walked with purpose, heading to the special-education room.

When he got there, his face brightened when he saw one of his friends. "This is my best friend," he said, throwing his arm around the other boy, who also has Down syndrome. He pressed his face close to his friend's until their cheeks almost touched. Eli smiled. "What table are you sitting at lunch today?" he said as they walked together down the hall. "Come on, make sure you sit with me."

POSTSCRIPT

Is Full Inclusion the Least Restrictive Environment?

How can we not respond to the compelling narratives of these parents? Eli and Ro come alive in their words. The road was not always easy and branches into two different paths.

The inclusion literature abounds with stories that melt hearts and open eyes. Horowitz and Klein (*Educational Leadership,* 2003) describe their efforts to include a child with Down syndrome into their religious school kindergarten. They discovered that, through working to include Michael, they learned to see the potential in every child and the interconnectedness of us all.

Proponents of the wisdom of full inclusion, Villa and Thousand (2005) maintain that inclusionary programs acknowledge the right of each of us to belong. No one should have to "fit in" or prove their worthiness to be part of everyday life experiences.

Taking one step further, Sapon-Shevin (*Educational Leadership,* 2003) portrays inclusion as an opportunity to teach social justice. In her eyes, building successful inclusive schools challenges people to actively create the inclusive, democratic society we envision for our children.

Most writers acknowledge that successful full inclusion is far from easy to achieve. In two instructive articles, Villa and Thousand (*Educational Leadership,* 2003) and McLeskey and Waldron (*Phi Delta Kappan,* 2002), provide numerous examples of lessons learned through schools' efforts to become inclusive. Their practical suggestions emphasize that successful inclusive programs require collaborative, sustained partnerships between administrators, teachers, and parents.

Drawing on student voices, Chadsey and Han (*TEACHING Exceptional Children*, 2005) address the peer connections essential to successful inclusion. The students think "segregation is unfair" and urge educators to provide opportunities where friendships can flourish naturally, as they would between any students.

Another group of students (Moore and Keefe, *Issues in Teacher Education,* 2004) found friendships—and inclusion—less important than their educational environment. These high school students, asked about their educational experiences, favored separate programs. Although disliking the accompanying stigma, they felt special education classes offered a more responsive environment that attended to their learning requirements.

Teachers, too, are concerned about the full inclusion learning environment. Kavale and Mostert (*Exceptionality,* 2003) reviewed several studies that explored the "empirical evidence" of full inclusion. Teachers embraced the democratic, just goals of full inclusion, but were concerned about its responsibilities. Their enthusiasm often moderated as they struggled to meet daily challenges.

How are such divergent experiences possible? Zigmond (*The Journal of Special Education,* 2003) suggests the answer may lie in our questions. Instead of asking whether full inclusion is desirable for all, perhaps we should return to the individual focus that has been the hallmark of special education to ask: For whom is full inclusion the best course? What instructional goals are best served by full inclusion?

Ro's and Eli's parents regain common ground when they speak of the future. The Vargos believe Ro's typical peers "will be her community—the ones who will protect and care for her. They will advocate social and legislative reform to support the inclusive lifestyle." Eli's mother hopes "The truth is he has to go out and get a job. If he's educated with his regular peers, then maybe a regular peer will hire him."

All teachers seek to prepare students to be successful adults. In partnership with parents, we endeavor to support and guide the young people we share along this journey. Is there one road to this ultimate destination? If not, how can any of us know which is the path best taken?

ISSUE 13

Should Students with Disabilities Be Exempt from Standards-Based Curriculum?

YES: Rex Knowles and Trudy Knowles, from "Accountability for What?" *Phi Delta Kappan* (January 2001)

NO: Jerry Jesness, from "You Have Your Teacher's Permission to Be Ignorant," *Education Week* (November 8, 2000)

ISSUE SUMMARY

YES: Rex Knowles, a retired college professor, and his daughter Trudy Knowles, an education faculty member at Westfield (MA) State College, feel that federal mandates for all students to master the same curriculum fail to consider students' individual differences and needs.

NO: Jerry Jesness, a special education teacher, stresses that students who complete school without learning the basics will be ill-equipped to succeed as adults and that any program that avoids teaching these essentials fails to address the long-term needs of students.

In 49 of the 50 states, standards-based education is the watchword. Curriculum expectations are changing. The range and dimension of these expectations differ widely across the country. Some states designed high-level academic programs to meet world-class standards. Others have embraced literacy standards, measuring the basic skills students will need to be successful in the world of work. Some states have designed their standards to apply to all students, including those with disabilities. Others have formulated separate sets of standards for students with severe disabilities. Regardless of curriculum focus, every district must now account for the performance of all students on this curriculum.

IEP expectations changed in response. While eligibility for special education has always hinged on the disability's adverse impact on classroom academic performance, once a student has entered special education, the IEP had frequently become the curriculum, seldom referencing classroom content. IDEA97 altered this pattern with its stipulation that students with disabilities must have access to the general curriculum and that IEPs must focus on ways in which this access can be facilitated.

As might be expected, these changes required some major alterations. Historically, special education programs focused on goals that include academics, sometimes going beyond them to the types of skills students would need to succeed independently in the workplace. For some students, with significant disabilities, this meant a heavy focus on communication and community-based application of a more limited range of academic skills. IDEA97 mandated a closer connection with the learning that happens in more typically academic programs.

Rex and Trudy Knowles, both college professors, believe that individual differences warrant differences in instruction and, sometimes, different curricula. They feel society bestows too much reverence on the mastery of reading, which is a supreme struggle for some children with disabilities and not terribly relevant to many rewarding jobs. Forcing the same curriculum on everyone means that some children learn to hate school, feel like failures, and do not gain the competence that they could bring to adult life.

Jerry Jesness, who teaches bilingual children with disabilities, feels holding all students to high-level curriculum may help children overcome some struggles to reach greater heights. Warning that lowered expectations can lead students into a false sense of competence, Jesness cautions that we should not confuse learning difficulty with an inability to learn or to need the same skills for lifelong success.

As you read these articles, consider these questions. How much struggling is detrimental to a child's self-confidence, and when does hard work lead to success and personal accomplishment? How would you decide whether to stop driving for mastery of the skill of reading (or math, or any other academic subject) and shift to teaching skills more related to the expected workplace? When would you make this decision? What would the student say about this change now? In 20 years? What options would this open? Close?

Have your state standards included students with disabilities, or are there separate, less academic standards for students covered by special education? How was your state's decision made, and how does it impact the education of all students? How does your own state's curriculum affect your reaction to this issue?

Accountability for What?

America instituted public education and compulsory attendance partly to save its children from exploitation. We wanted all children to be freed from the demands of sweatshops and farm labor that filled the days of 10-year-olds.

What started as a noble attempt to save children from forced labor has ended up as a daily sentence to a six- to seven-hour prison from which they have no escape. We refuse to let them leave if they feel bad; we regiment their hearing, speaking, seeing, walking, eating, arrival, departure, and bowel movements. We even tell them when they have to wear a coat.

Child abuse is a very strong term, and it rightly makes us angry. That much is clear. But our schools practice child abuse every day. That is also clear.

Every day we ask children to do what they can't do, at least at the moment we ask them. And then we grade them, as if they were eggs. "You're grade A." "You're grade B." "You're rotten." We shame them, and we embarrass them.

We could tell many stories. One lovely, considerate, and gentle 11-year-old girl studied for four hours for a spelling test. The next day she took the test and failed. According to the girl, when her teacher handed back the papers, she said to her, within earshot of the rest of the class, "You're lazy. If you'd put in any time at all on your work, you would get an A. You're just lazy! We're not going to let you hold this class back."

That young girl spells quite well orally. She is helpful and responsible around the home. She is well liked by her peers and adored by her younger brother and sister. She is bright beyond her years. And she is absolutely terrorized by school. She has a perceptual-motor problem. Writing is just not her thing. The internal details regarding the figures she draws and the words she writes get mixed up. While these facts were carefully explained to the teacher, she continued—either from ignorance or cruelty—to insult the girl. That's child abuse. And it's not an isolated incident.

A bright young man with attention deficit disorder and a severe organizational deficit consistently posted failing grades on major assignments because he couldn't seem to keep all the materials together that he needed to hand in. When it was suggested that the teacher help the student set up a system for keeping track of materials, the response was, "He's going to have to figure out how to get by in the real world sometime. Might as well do it now."

The young man continued to fail until his severe depression resulted in his being taken out of school and put in a homebound tutoring program.

We think it's time to start yelling. We have been treating our children badly for a long time now. With the new emphasis on "accountability," the abuse will only multiply. "The word in education is accountability," according to one state commissioner of education—a view no doubt shared by many of his peers. That is a worrisome sentiment. The easy acceptance of the statement by parents and teachers is even more worrisome.

If the word meant that teachers are to be accountable for the respect they show to children, we would rejoice. If it meant that teachers are to be accountable for helping students to find joy in learning and to become lifelong contributors to their society, we would rejoice. If it meant that teachers are to be accountable for ensuring that all children are successful and that those teachers will be required to find the means to guide students and to assess students in multiple ways, we would rejoice.

But "accountability" in today's discussions of education means that teachers will be held accountable for how well their students read and for what they score on achievement tests. Everyone in the class will be performing above average—or else. Teachers' salaries and promotions will depend on their ability to bring children up to grade-level norms.

Even the most naive statistician knows that half of all people who take a norm-referenced test will be below average. That's what average means. Statistical accountability automatically makes some children "leftovers." It is not true that any good teacher can teach any child to read at grade level, any more than any good physical education teacher can teach any child to be an above-average baseball player.

Reading and throwing a baseball are skills. If you're not a Greg Maddux or a Pedro Martinez, reading is probably a more important skill, but a skill it remains. Why do we make this particular skill the sine qua non of education?

Through training, almost anyone can improve his or her skills, but individual differences will remain. Some children will always be terrible baseball players (often to their shame), and some children will always be terrible readers (always to their shame). To base the notion of the "good teacher" on such "objective measurements" as test scores is to create teachers who teach not for creativity, fun, imagination, freedom, exuberance, and the love of learning, but rather for test results. And teaching merely to get test results not only deprives students of the opportunity to think, question, reason, or disagree, it also informs 50% of the group that they are below average and tells 10% that they are just no good at all!

If teachers are to be held accountable, will those students who are below average in reading be pushed, mauled, and remediated? Shouldn't we instead tinker with the regular education regimen and get on with the process of educating the child? But that's not what we do. Instead, we say, "If a child doesn't learn to read, we can't teach him anything." So we make him spend extra time working on this particular skill. If another child can't get the assigned reading in one hour, should we make her spend two? We take children with eyes that won't focus, fingers that won't cooperate, sensory pathways that won't coordinate, association areas that won't associate, neurons, that don't fire appropriately, connections that aren't connected, brains that won't attend, and we say, "Sorry, but you must read anyway. And if you don't read, you're educationally and vocationally shot. (And I don't get my raise.)" The combination of school and homework is for some students far more arduous than the 19th-century sweatshops.

Parents sometimes get angry at brutish physical education teachers who shame children who can't throw a ball because they aren't physically coordinated to do so. In enlightened schools, we even excuse some children from physical education. But we do nothing about teachers who shame children who can't read because they aren't physically coordinated to do so. And we never excuse them from reading. Instead, we pile on more. It's about accountability, after all.

Our emphasis on accountability fails to take into consideration the single clear fact of life: *children are different.* It is the only psychological truth accepted by all psychologists. Children are different. Certainly educators know this to be true. Howard Gardner has been espousing the idea of multiple intelligences for years. Teacher educators have been teaching it for years. Why, then, do federal and state mandates for accountability result in what teachers know will never work: a foolish emphasis on sameness—same classes, same books, same chronological age in the classroom, same program, same assignments, same tests, same curriculum, same instruction?

The tremendous variation in children is not abnormal, but squeezing them into a common learning mold is. In our emphasis on accountability, we operate as though individual differences *don't* exist. That's just plain stupid. But we also operate as though differences *shouldn't* exist, and that's just plain cruel.

The child with low reading ability is not diseased. That child is different in a very normal way, and if you shove a book into his or her hand, you are limiting that child's education.

There has been no essential change in schooling in more than a hundred years—except in the number of inmates being schooled. We still think students can learn only through the sacred tool of reading. We still act as if a child learns more under conditions of stress and seem to believe that the more stress, the more learning. We still think that children ought to be punished if they aren't the same as the rest and that differences—in responses, attitudes, movements—are deviant, disabling, and disturbing. We still teach children that, unless they are successful in school, they are losers. And we still hold teachers accountable for the failure of children to read.

Many school systems are guilty of child abuse, dehumanizing children, and teaching them that they are an educational waste. When children are having trouble with reading, they learn that they are not okay and that school is not where they belong.

≈◉≈

Check the dropouts. Many of them were diagnosed with learning disabilities. A great many have attention deficits. They became problem children—hyperactive, demanding attention, disruptive, aggressive, truant. They didn't really drop out by choice. They were forced out of school. In fact, they are not learning disabled; the schools are teaching disabled.

Why is it that we insist on calling a child "learning disabled" if he has difficulty reading, but we don't label a child "disabled" if she can't compose a song? Educators have set up altars to reading. They worship at its shrine and intone the doctrine "Outside of reading, there is no salvation." And if the child can't read, there are the stocks, the pillories, solitary confinement—all the torture devices.

A graduate student who teaches in a high school for students with language learning disabilities recently asked for help with some strategies for teaching *Huckleberry Finn*. She said she was having a hard time getting students to appreciate or understand the story. While thinking about strategies she could use, it suddenly became clear that perhaps there was really no point in trying to get these students to appreciate classic literature. They are a group of students who will rarely, if ever, pick up a novel to read for pleasure.

A student who recently graduated from college with a 3.7 grade-point average told us that she had to read 32 novels in high school. For her it was a painful, tearful, agonizing experience. She has never picked up a book to read for pleasure, because for her there is no pleasure in reading.

Let's be honest. Is the skill of reading classic literature that important? For students to become successful citizens, it is certainly helpful to have a command of the written word. But do we need to expose all students to courses in fiction and literature as ninth-graders, in poetry and drama as 10th-graders, in American literature and folklore as 11th-graders, and in British literature as 12th-graders? Can you pick out the slow readers and the nonreaders as you walk down the street? Does a person who hears well, remembers adequately, and works in a nonwriting or nonreading vocation (which includes most) suffer greatly from a reading disability? Only until commencement day, if there is one. The disability disappears as soon as such a student leaves school. Why should school be such an agony? Who declared that reading was so important?

Art can be viewed and created without reading. Concerts can be heard and instruments played. History can come in the form of videos, movies, photographs, and plays. Social studies and current events flow from the television sets. Films, videos, cassette tapes, records, pictures, demonstrations, and the spoken word are all available as ways of learning. And yet where do we force education to abide? In the textbook. In the written word. Imagine a book designed to show students how to assemble an engine. Then imagine a written test to see if the students have learned how to assemble an engine. Then imagine having your car fixed by a student who had passed the test but had never worked on an engine.

We "do" physical education. Why can't we "do" art and music and history and science and math? If there are good readers around, let them review the literature as their contribution. Why must everyone do so? The library is not necessarily the center of the educational process. And if learning by reading is torturous, arduous, even impossible, let's forget the reading. Give every child every opportunity to learn to read, but let's not make failure to acquire this skill mean failure in virtually all school learning. If the skill of reading makes each day a torment, makes the child feel devalued, and interferes with the acquisition of knowledge, then away with it! Let's put reading in its rightful place and get on with the learning process.

The "three R's" of reading, 'riting, and 'rithmetic are the marks of an educational elite, excellent hallmarks for what schools were meant to do a hundred years ago. We are appealing for a new way of looking at schooling, for more recognition of individual differences, for more concern for true democracy, and for fewer objective tests.

Accountability? Sure. But accountability for what? Let's make teachers accountable only for their humane treatment of children. Let's make them accountable not for how well their children test in the three R's, but for how well they function in the three "L's": living without fear or shame, loving themselves and others, and learning about this wonderful world at their own speed and in their own way.

Jerry Jesness

 **NO**

You Have Your Teacher's Permission to Be Ignorant

I once read a cheery story about a caring teacher who helped her failing students by shortening their assignments. "Don't worry," the teacher assured a crying child as she handed him a shortened list of spelling words, "I will give you an assignment at which you can succeed." The implication was that the teacher, by crossing some words off of a list, "gave" the student success. We teachers are familiar with this line of thought. It is almost a rite of passage for first-year teachers to be called into their principals' offices to be chastised after releasing their first round of grades. "If you want to fail these children," the principal begins, as if the teacher is issuing failing grades for her own pleasure. "We want these children to succeed," the teacher is told. "We don't want them to experience failure."

We teachers remember with pain, laughter, or both, the in-service sessions in which we learned to empathize with our students, to feel their pain. At one such session, a presenter gave several commands in rapid succession. "Fold your paper in nine equal parts," he commanded, and rapidly added: "Draw a tetrahedron in the upper left corner. Write the name of the capital of Outer Mongolia in the square directly above the lower left-hand corner. Write the square root of 386 rounded to the nearest whole number in the square closest to the center. Put down your pencils! Why aren't you finished?" he shouted in feigned anger.

At another workshop, participants were asked to write while viewing their hands and writing in a mirror. At another, participants were asked to assemble jigsaw puzzles which, in reality, contained mismatched pieces. The moral of these sessions was always that it hurts to fail; therefore, give the kids tasks that they can perform with relative ease. Success is good and failure is bad, so let us give our students the former.

It is truly absurd to suggest that teachers are so powerful that we can somehow grant and withhold success with mere strokes of our pens. Sixty-nine percent represents failure, 70 percent represents success, and 90 percent represents honor. So, according to this way of thinking, a teacher can bring students success or honor by simply simplifying the assignments or by devising an excuse to tack on a few extra points.

It is a linguistic fluke that the word "fail" means both to lack success and to score below a set standard. Real success is based on what the student knows,

From Jerry Jesness, "You Have Your Teacher's Permission to Be Ignorant," *Education Week*, vol. 20, no. 10 (November 8, 2000). Copyright © 2000 by Editorial Projects in Education. Reprinted by permission of *Education Week* and the author.

not on what a teacher ordains. If a 1st grade student learns to read, he has succeeded. A classmate who did not learn to read has failed, even if the teacher declares him a success by giving him a passing grade. A well-read, knowledgeable recent high school graduate has the tools for success. In fact, so does a well-read, knowledgeable dropout. A barely literate graduate armed only with an undeserved diploma and a transcript filled with inflated grades is, however, going to have problems. Only knowledge is power.

Some of the greatest frustrations that we teachers feel result from conflicting expectations placed on us. On the one hand, we are expected to honestly evaluate our students' knowledge, skills, and progress. On the other, we are expected to assure that all, or at least most, "succeed," even if we have to fabricate that success by watering down the material or inflating the grades. Teachers are expected to both follow a curriculum and to manipulate that curriculum so that all students at least enjoy the illusion of success.

Low standards, particularly for students who have known little else, can actually make a teacher look good. Feel-good activities and mind-numbing busywork can be very effective classroom-management techniques. While challenging assignments may motivate students who have come to expect them, students who have never been pushed are likely to react to such assignments by misbehaving. Veteran teachers will tell you that some of their best teaching may have appeared to be their worst. The student who refuses to open his literature textbook in August, yet somehow develops a love for reading by the following May, or one who quivers with anger or frustration while attempting new algorithms, yet becomes enthusiastic about math after mastering them, should warm our hearts.

Many competent readers had to be dragged, screaming and kicking, through their first novels, and many top math students once had to have the multiplication tables drilled into them. Helen Keller first reacted to Anne Sullivan's finger-spelling lessons by screaming, kicking, and biting. Unpleasant confrontations, however, may result in poor evaluations from administrators or complaints from parents. Smiling faces and busy fingers make for the best public relations.

✿❦✿

[Recently] a journalist for a Houston newspaper visited an inner-city high school and observed some classes. He wrote disparagingly of an English teacher whose 11th grade students were performing dismally on a test covering a Shakespeare play, but praised an algebra teacher who captured his students' attention by using games of chance to teach them about probability. What's wrong with this picture? Probability is not a part of algebra. While I do not know the teachers in question and therefore cannot judge their abilities, it is clear that the English teacher was, however unsuccessfully, covering high-school-level literature, while the algebra teacher had abandoned his assigned subject and replaced it with basic math.

I recently had a conversation with a probationary teacher who had just been told that her contract would not be renewed. I was quite impressed by both her general knowledge and her knowledge of the subject she taught. She explained to me that, despite the fact that most of her 11th graders came to her reading at only a 4th or 5th grade level, she had managed to lead them through Rudolfo Anaya's *Bless Me Ultima*, a novel appropriate for students who can at least read at a high school level. She had also managed to coax research papers from most of them. Earlier this year, she had been called into her principal's office and asked to "adjust" some of her student's grades. She was also asked to apologize to the parents of some discontented students. She refused to do either, and she is now looking for another job. She refused to give her students permission to be ignorant, so now she will pay the price.

While most teachers who give their students permission to know less than their peers do so by turning a blind eye to their failures, we special education teachers put that permission in writing. Each year, we meet with an administrator, a student's parents, and others responsible for the student's education to discuss his or her individual educational program, or IEP. At these meetings, we set the student's educational goals for the year.

I never cease to be awed by this responsibility. It is not that it is wrong to hold those of lesser skills and abilities to a lower standard. We certainly should not, for example, demand that Down's syndrome children perform differential calculus. Nor should we require illiterate children to analyze great works of literature. Still, the responsibility of determining the standard to which a child should be held is an awesome one.

≈◎≈

It is easy to succumb to the temptation to teach special-needs children at their comfort levels. The system allows and often encourages us to do so. This, however, is rarely in the child's best interest.

My school once had a 4th grade child come from a neighboring district unable to subtract or to write in cursive handwriting. Although her IEP included only the most rudimentary literacy and math skills, the girl seemed to be fairly bright, so we wrote her new IEP near her grade level. After some pushing and prodding, she mastered her basics and is now comfortably working with regular 4th grade material. Another 4th grader was reduced to tears several times in the process of learning long division, a procedure he eventually mastered. It is fortunate that I was not observed during some of those students' more difficult moments in my class.

There is nothing more heart-wrenching than a special-needs child in tears, but there is nothing more heartwarming than the smile of a child for whom schoolwork has ceased to be a mystery.

We teachers should imagine ourselves as swimming instructors whose charges will someday be thrown out of a boat half a mile from shore. If we certify that a nonswimming student is a competent swimmer, he will still sink like a stone when thrown from the boat.

In like manner, a graduate who lacks real academic skills, who has only the trappings of scholarly success, will have a difficult time swimming in the real world. Failure is failure, with or without our permission.

POSTSCRIPT

Should Students with Disabilities Be Exempt from Standards-Based Curriculum?

More exacting standards—for teachers, students, and schools—are here. There is no changing this reality. How should the reality impact students with disabilities?

Vohs, Landau, and Romano, authors of PEER (2000), an extensive parent information document on standards-based curriculum and assessment, acknowledge that while state standards range from broad to specific, all share the common goal of raising expectations—from which all students can benefit. The report concedes it is certainly easier to include all students in broad, literacy-based frameworks, but that all students can participate at some level of the new standards, with appropriate support. Addressing the specific needs of some students with more significant disabilities, the authors advocate for individualized performance standards within the common content, even for vocational goals.

Although Knowles and Knowles might be more at ease with standards stressing basic literacy, they are still concerned that some students will be unnecessarily hurt by the rigor of today's new expectations—finding that the short-term misery and struggle of learning specific skills deprives a child of the ability to feel empowered to develop life skills in which they really are competent.

In a study of legal and practical considerations for graduation of students with disabilities, Lanford and Carey (*Remedial and Special Education,* 2000) maintain that, since most students with disabilities spend most of their time in general education classes, they should work within the same curriculum. However, they also indicate that a total academic curriculum may not appropriate for all students with disabilities, whose programs should be clearly stated in their IEPs.

Jerry Jesness would counsel teachers and parents not to stray from the standard curriculum too easily, lest opportunities for success be lost. And yet, Jesness acknowledges that high expectations do not mean the same expectations for everyone. The challenge is in knowing how to balance the curriculum and individual needs.

In *Educating One and All,* exploring the involvement of students with disabilities in standards-based reform, McDonnell and McLouglin (National Research Council, 1997) wrestle with the complex balance between individualized programs and statewide standards. Referencing research concluding that post-school employment possibilities are broadened with supported community-based training best begun while students are in school, they wonder how these activities will mesh with a standard curriculum that does not include vocational or career goals.

Related to all these puzzles is new language in IDEA 2004, guiding teams to focus on academics, but also to include functional goals and those that emphasize post-secondary plans, including employment and independent living skills. Transition to post-secondary life is given a renewed emphasis.

Since educational standards are decided on a state-by-state basis, the involvement of students with disabilities are also determined locally, guided by the mandates of IDEA and NCLB. And yet, that very strategy raises a number of questions. Does what you learn depend on where you live? And if that's the case, will parents of children with disabilities move to locations where the specific needs of their children are best met? Does everyone need to learn the same curriculum, or are different life paths best served by different programs? Is there a core curriculum that everyone needs to learn? If so, who decides what that is? For students with complex needs, does a vocationally related course of study limit horizons, provide time on task for relevant skills, or offer opportunities for creative connection with academic frameworks? And who makes these decisions?

ISSUE 14

Have Schools Gone Too Far in Using Accommodations?

YES: James M. Kauffman, Kathleen McGee, and Michele Brigham, from "Enabling or Disabling? Observations on Changes in Special Education," *Phi Delta Kappan* (April 2004)

NO: MaryAnn Byrnes, from "Accommodations for Students with Disabilities: Removing Barriers to Learning," *National Association of Secondary School Principals Bulletin* (February 2000)

ISSUE SUMMARY

YES: James M. Kauffman, a faculty member at the University of Virginia, along with Kathleen McGee and Michele Brigham, both special education teachers, maintain that special education has pursued its goal of normalization to an extreme. The emphasis has shifted from increasing competence to perpetuating disabilities through the unwise use of accommodations.

NO: MaryAnn Byrnes, a University of Massachusetts–Boston faculty member, former special education administrator, and editor of this *Taking Sides*, argues that relevant accommodations are necessary to ensure that people with disabilities have a fair chance to demonstrate what they know and can do.

Have you ever used a curb-cut to ease the passage of your bike or a stroller? Have you pushed the automatic door opener button when your arms were full? Did you know that the now-ubiquitous food processor was designed to meet the cooking needs of a one-handed cook?

All of the above are accommodations. Originally designed to make the world more accessible for people with disabilities, they often make life easier for the rest of society. Federal laws require that reasonable accommodations like these be provided so that people with disabilities have fair and equal access to normal life activities.

Think about Braille texts and ramps in school. Amplification systems that expand the range of hearing aides in classrooms. Are they reasonable and acceptable accommodations to make school more accessible for children who have sensory or motoric disabilities? Most people would say they are.

Now think about scribes to transfer the words of a student into print. Or extended time for assignments and exams. Or permitting some students to submit a video or taped project instead of a written report. These are accommodations as well—for people who have difficulty writing or processing material quickly or sustaining attention. Do you accept them as easily? Many people pause here, wondering if these cross the line into making school a little too easy. Are these unreasonable accommodations?

Accommodations in school are adjustments to setting, timing, presentation mode, and/or response mode that allow students with disabilities to demonstrate what they know and can do. Their purpose is to make the task accessible. They are not intended to change the nature of a task, make it easier, or ensure that a student passes.

The issue of accommodations achieved controversial status with the advent of high-stakes testing and school accountability that includes students with disabilities. Federal laws require that schools provide appropriate accommodations to students with disabilities so they can participate fully in educational and assessment activities.

The argument is whether these accommodations are fair, just, and reasonable, or whether they go beyond leveling the playing field to create a whole new game that is just not fair to everyone else, including the students with disabilities.

Kauffman, McGee, and Brigham feel that accommodations have gone too far. Citing a number of powerful examples, they make the case that accommodations are being used indiscriminately. Bowing to threats from parents and their lawyers, educators extend accommodations that attempt to disguise a disability. In doing so, they abandon the commitment to hold students to high standards and responsibility.

Byrnes asks educators and parents to be thoughtful about the use of accommodations, choosing them to remove a barrier to learning. In her view, accommodations are to be selected carefully and matched with learning challenges so that students' disabilities don't stand in the way of acquiring, and demonstrating, knowledge and competence.

As you read these articles, ask yourself what you have seen, read, or heard about accommodations in schools. Do you think they help or hinder? Do educators and parents want to create opportunities or give excuses? In this era of high stakes, are people tempted to give the benefit of the doubt, extending accommodations in hopes of raising scores and granting diplomas? If so, does this create a climate of learned helplessness? Will students feel entitled rather than responsible?

YES

James M. Kauffman, Kathleen McGee, and Michele Brigham

Enabling or Disabling?
Observations on Changes
in Special Education

Schools need demanding and distinctive special education that is clearly focused on instruction and habilitation. Abandoning such a conception of special education is a prescription for disaster. But special education has increasingly been losing its way in the single-minded pursuit of full inclusion.

Once, special education's purpose was to bring the performance of students with disabilities closer to that of their nondisabled peers in regular classrooms, to move as many students as possible into the mainstream with appropriate support. For students not in regular education, the goal was to move them toward a more typical setting in a cascade of placement options. But as any good thing can be overdone and ruined by the pursuit of extremes, we see special education suffering from the extremes of inclusion and accommodation.

Aiming for as much normalization as possible gave special education a clear purpose. Some disabilities were seen as easier to remediate than others. Most speech and language disorders, for example, were considered eminently remediable. Other disabilities, such as mental retardation and many physical disabilities, were assumed to be permanent or long-term and so less remediable, but movement *toward* the mainstream and increasing independence from special educators were clear goals.

The emphasis in special education has shifted away from normalization, independence, and competence. The result has been students' dependence on whatever special programs, modifications, and accommodations are possible, particularly in general education settings. The goal seems to have become the *appearance* of normalization without the *expectation* of competence.

Many parents and students seem to want more services as they learn what is available. Some have lost sight of the goal of limiting accommodations in order to challenge students to achieve more independence. At the same time, many special education advocates want all services to be available in mainstream settings, with little or no acknowledgment that the services are atypical. Although teachers, administrators, and guidance counselors are often willing and able to make accommodations, doing so is not always in students' best long-term interests. It gives students with disabilities what

From *Phi Delta Kappan*, April 2004, pp. 613–620. Copyright © 2004 by Phi Delta Kappa.

anthropologist Robert Edgerton called a cloak—a pretense, a cover, which actually fools no one—rather than actual competence.

In this article, we discuss how changes in attitudes toward disability and special education, placement, and accommodations can perpetuate disability. We also explore the problems of ignoring or perpetuating disability rather than helping students lead fuller, more independent lives. Two examples illustrate how we believe good intentions can go awry—how attempts to accommodate students with disabilities can undermine achievement.

"But he needs resource. . . ." Thomas, a high school sophomore identified as emotionally disturbed, was assigned to a resource class created to help students who had problems with organization or needed extra help with academic skills. One of the requirements in the class was for students to keep a daily planner in which they entered all assignments; they shared their planner with the resource teacher at the beginning of class and discussed what academic subjects would be worked on during that period.

Thomas consistently refused to keep a planner or do any work in resource (he slept instead). So a meeting was set up with the assistant principal, the guidance counselor, Thomas, and the resource teacher. As the meeting was about to begin, the principal announced that he would not stay because Thomas felt intimidated by so many adults. After listening to Thomas' complaints, the guidance counselor decided that Thomas would not have to keep a planner or show it to the resource teacher and that the resource teacher should not talk to him unless Thomas addressed her first. In short, Thomas would not be required to do any work in the class! When the resource teacher suggested that, under those circumstances, Thomas should perhaps be placed in a study hall, because telling the parents that he was in a resource class would be a misrepresentation, the counselor replied, "But he *needs* the resource class."

"He's too bright. . . ." Bob, a high school freshman with Asperger's Syndrome, was scheduled for three honors classes and two Advanced Placement classes. Bob's IEP included a two-page list of accommodations. In spite of his having achieved A's and B's, with just a single C in math, his mother did not feel that his teachers were accommodating him appropriately. Almost every evening, she emailed his teachers and his case manager to request more information or more help for Bob, and she angrily phoned his guidance counselor if she didn't receive a reply by the end of the first hour of the next school day.

A meeting was scheduled with the IEP team. When the accommodations were reviewed, Bob's mother agreed that all of them were being made. However, she explained that Bob had been removed from all outside social activities because he spent all night, every night, working on homework. The accommodation she demanded was that Bob have *no* homework assignments. The autism specialist agreed that this was a reasonable accommodation for a child with Asperger's Syndrome.

The teachers of the honors classes explained that the homework in their classes, which involved elaboration and extension of concepts, was even more essential than the homework assigned in AP classes. In AP classes, by contrast, homework consisted primarily of practice of concepts learned in class. The

honors teachers explained that they had carefully broken their long assignments into segments, each having a separate due date before the final project,
and they gave illustrations of their expectations. The director of special education explained the legal definition of accommodations (the mother said she'd
never before heard that accommodations could not change the nature of the
curriculum). The director also suggested that, instead of Bob's sacrificing his
social life, perhaps it would be more appropriate for him to take standard
classes. What Bob's mother was asking, he concluded, was not legal. She grew
angry, but she did agree to give the team a "little more time" to serve Bob
appropriately. She said she would "be back with her claws and broomstick" if
anyone ever suggested that he be moved from honors classes without being
given the no homework accommodation. "He's too bright to take anything
less than honors classes, and if you people would provide this simple accommodation, he would do just fine," she argued. In the end, she got her way.

Attitudes Toward Disability and Special Education

Not that many decades ago, a disability was considered a misfortune—not
something to be ashamed of but a generally undesirable, unwelcome condition to be overcome to the greatest extent possible. Ability was considered
more desirable than disability, and anything—whether a device or a service—
that helped people with disabilities to do what those without disabilities could
do was considered generally valuable, desirable, and worth the effort, cost,
and possible stigma associated with using it.

The disability rights movement arose in response to the widespread negative attitudes toward disabilities, and it had a number of desirable outcomes.
It helped overcome some of the discrimination against people with disabilities. And overcoming such bias and unfairness in everyday life is a great
accomplishment. But the movement has also had some unintended negative
consequences. One of these is the outright denial of disability in some cases,
illustrated by the contention that disability exists only in attitudes or as a
function of the social power to coerce.

The argument that disability is merely a "social construction" is particularly vicious in its effects on social justice. Even if we assume that disabilities
are socially constructed, what should that mean? Should we assume that
socially constructed phenomena are not "real," are not important, or should
be discredited? If so, then consider that dignity, civil rights, childhood, social
justice, and nearly every other phenomenon that we hold dear are social constructions. Many social constructions are not merely near and dear to us, they
are real and useful in benevolent societies. The important question is whether
the idea of disability is useful in helping people attain dignity or whether it is
more useful to assume that disabilities are not real (i.e., that, like social justice, civil rights, and other social constructions, they are fabrications that can
be ignored when convenient). The denial of disability is sometimes expressed as
an aversion to labels, so that we are cautioned not to communicate openly
and clearly about disabilities but to rely on euphemisms. But this approach is
counterproductive. When we are able only to whisper or mime the undesirable

difference called disability, then we inadvertently increase its stigma and thwart prevention efforts.

The specious argument that "normal" does not exist—because abilities of every kind are varied and because the point at which normal becomes abnormal is arbitrary—leads to the conclusion that no one actually has a disability or, alternatively, that everyone has a disability. Then, some argue, either no one or everyone is due an accommodation so that no one or everyone is identified as disabled. This unwillingness to draw a line defining something (such as disability, poverty, or childhood) is based either on ignorance regarding the nature of continuous distributions or on a rejection of the unavoidably arbitrary decisions necessary to provide special services to those who need them and, in so doing, to foster social justice.

Another unintended negative consequence of the disability rights movement is that, for some people, disability has become either something that does not matter or something to love, to take pride in, to flaunt, to adopt as a positive aspect of one's identity, or to cherish as something desirable or as a badge of honor. When disability makes no difference to us one way or the other, then we are not going to work to attenuate it, much less prevent it. At best, we will try to accommodate it. When we view disability as a desirable difference, then we are very likely to try to make it more pronounced, not to ameliorate it.

Several decades ago, special education was seen as a good thing—a helpful way of responding to disability, not something everyone needed or should have, but a useful and necessary response to the atypical needs of students with disabilities. This is why the Education for All Handicapped Children Act (now the Individuals with Disabilities Education Act) was written. But in the minds of many people, special education has been transformed from something helpful to something awful.

The full-inclusion movement did have some desirable outcomes. It helped overcome some of the unnecessary removal of students with disabilities from general education. However, the movement also has had some unintended negative consequences. One of these is that special education has come to be viewed in very negative terms, to be seen as a second-class and discriminatory system that does more harm than good. Rather than being seen as helpful, as a way of creating opportunity, special education is often portrayed as a means of shunting students into dead-end programs and killing opportunity.

Another unintended negative consequence of full inclusion is that general education is now seen by many as the *only* place where fair and equitable treatment is possible and where the opportunity to learn is extended to all equally. The argument has become that special education is good only as long as it is invisible (or nearly so), an indistinguishable part of a general education system that accommodates all students, regardless of their abilities or disabilities. Usually, this is described as a "unified" (as opposed to "separate") system of education. Special education is thus something to be avoided altogether or attenuated to the greatest extent possible, regardless of a student's inability to perform in a general setting. When special education is seen as discriminatory, unfair, an opportunity-killing system, or, as one writer put it, "the gold-plated garbage can of American schooling," then it is understandable that people will loathe it. But this way of looking at special education is like seeing the recognition and treatment of cancer as the cause of the problem.

The reversal in attitudes toward disability and special education—disability from undesirable to inconsequential, special education from desirable to awful—has clouded the picture of what special education is and what it should do for students with disabilities. Little wonder that special education stands accused of failure, that calls for its demise have become vociferous, and that contemporary practices are often more disabling than enabling. An unfortunate outcome of the changing attitudes toward disability and special education is that the benefit of special education is now sometimes seen as freedom from expectations of performance. It is as if we believed that, if a student has to endure the stigma of special education, then the compensation should include an exemption from work.

Placement Issues

Placing all students, regardless of their abilities, in regular classes has exacerbated the tendency to see disability as something existing only in people's minds. It fosters the impression that students are fitting in when they are not able to perform at anywhere near the normal level. It perpetuates disabilities; it does not compensate for them.

Administrators and guidance counselors sometimes place students in programs for which they do not qualify, even as graduation requirements are increasing and tests are mandated. Often, these students' *testing* is modified although their *curriculum* is not. The students may then feel that they have beaten the system. They are taught that the system is unfair and that the only way to win is by gaming it. Hard work and individual responsibility for one's education are often overlooked—or at least undervalued.

Students who consistently fail in a particular curriculum must be given the opportunity to deal with the natural consequences of that fact as a means of learning individual responsibility. For example, social promotion in elementary and middle school teaches students that they really don't have to be able to do the work to pass. Students who have been conditioned to rely on social promotion do not believe that the cycle will end until it does so—usually very abruptly in high school. Suddenly, no one passes them on, and no one gives them undeserved credit. Many of these students do not graduate in four years. Some never recover, while others find themselves forced to deal with a very distasteful situation.

No one wants to see a student fail, but to alter any standard without good reason is to set that same student up for failure later in life. Passing along a student with disabilities in regular classes, pretending that he or she is performing at the same level as most of the class or that it doesn't really matter (arguing that the student has a legal "right" to be in the class) is another prescription for disappointment and failure in later life. Indeed, this failure often comes in college or on the job.

Some people with disabilities do need assistance. Others do not. Consider Deborah Groeber, who struggled through degenerative deafness and blindness. The Office of Affirmative Action at the University of Pennsylvania offered to intercede at the Wharton School, but Groeber knew that she had more influence if she spoke for herself. Today, she is a lawyer with three Ivy League degrees. But not every student with disabilities can do or should be expected to do what Groeber did. Our concern is that too many students with disabilities are given encouragement based on pretense when they could do much more with appropriate special education.

Types of Accommodations

Two popular modifications in IEPs are allowing for the use of calculators and granting extended time on tests and assignments. Calculators can be a great asset, but they should be used when calculating complex problems or when doing word problems. Indiscriminate use of a calculator renders many math tests invalid, as they become a contest to see if buttons can be pushed successfully and in the correct order, rather than an evaluation of ability to do arithmetic or use mathematical knowledge.

Extended time on assignments and tests can also be a useful modification, but it can easily be misused or abused. Extended time on tests should mean *continuous* time so that a test is not studied for first and taken later. Sometimes a test must be broken into smaller segments that can be completed independently. However, this could put students with disabilities at a disadvantage, as one part of a test might help with remembering another part. Extensions on assignments need to be evaluated each time they are given, not simply handed out automatically because they are written into an IEP. If a student is clearly working hard, then extensions may be appropriate. If a student has not even been attempting assignments, then more time might be an avoidance tactic. Sometimes extended time means that assignments pile up and the student gets further and further behind. The result can then be overwhelming stress and the inability to comprehend discussions because many concepts must be acquired in sequence (e.g., in math, science, history, and foreign languages).

Reading tests and quizzes aloud to students can be beneficial for many, but great caution is required. Some students and teachers want to do more than simply read a test. Reading a test aloud means simply reading the printed words on the page *without* inflections that can reveal correct answers and without explaining vocabulary. Changing a test to open-notes or open-book, without the knowledge and consent of the classroom teacher, breaches good-faith test proctoring. It also teaches students dependence rather than independence and accomplishment. Similarly, scribing for a student can be beneficial for those who truly need it, but the teacher must be careful not to add details and to write only what the student dictates, including any run-on sentences or fragments. After scribing, if the assignment is not a test, the teacher should edit and correct the paper with the student, as she might do with any written work. But this must take place *after* the scribing.

How Misguided Accommodations Can Be Disabling

"Saving" a child from his or her own negative behavior reinforces that behavior and makes it a self-fulfilling prophecy. Well-intentioned guidance counselors often feel more responsibility for their students' success or failure than the students themselves feel. Sometimes students are not held accountable for their effort or work. They seem not to understand that true independence comes from *what* you know, not *whom* you know. Students who are consistently enabled and not challenged are never given the opportunity to become independent. Ann Bancroft, the polar explorer and dyslexic, claims that, although school was a torment, it was disability that forged her iron will. Stephen Cannell's fear for other dyslexics is that they will quit trying rather than struggle and learn to compensate for their disability.

Most parents want to help their children. However, some parents confuse making life *easier* with making life *better* for their children. Too often, parents feel that protecting their child from the rigors of academic demands is in his or her best interest. They may protect their child by insisting on curricular modifications and accommodations in assignments, time, and testing. But children learn by doing, and not allowing them to do something because they might fail is denying them the opportunity to succeed. These students eventually believe that they are not capable of doing what typical students can do, even if they are. Sometimes it is difficult for teachers to discern what a student actually can do and what a parent has done until an in-class assignment is given or a test is taken. At that point, it is often too late for the teacher to do much remediation. The teacher may erroneously conclude that the student is simply a poor test-taker.

In reality, the student may have been "protected" from learning, which will eventually catch up with him or her. Unfortunately, students may not face reality until they take a college entrance exam, go away to college, or apply for a job. Students who "get through" high school in programs of this type often go on to flunk out of college. Unfortunately, the parents of these students frequently blame the college for the student's failure, criticizing the postsecondary institution for not doing enough to help. Instead, they should be upset both with the secondary institution for not preparing the child adequately for the tasks to come and with themselves for their own overprotection.

The Benefits of Demands

Many successful adults with disabilities sound common themes when asked about their ability to succeed in the face of a disability. Tom Gray, a Rhodes Scholar who has a severe learning disability, claims that having to deal with the hardest experiences gave him the greatest strength. Stephen Cannell believes that, if he had known there was a reason beyond his control to explain his low achievement, he might not have worked as hard as he did. Today, he knows he has a learning disability, but he is also an Emmy Award-winning television writer and producer. Paul Orlalea, the dyslexic founder of Kinko's, believes God gave him an advantage in the challenge presented by his disability and that others should work with their strengths. Charles Schwab, the learning-disabled founder of Charles Schwab, Inc., cites his ability to think differently and to make creative leaps that more sequential thinkers don't make as chief reasons for his success. Fannie Flagg, the learning-disabled author, concurs and insists that learning disabilities become a blessing *only if you can overcome them.* Not every student with a disability can be a star performer, of course, but all should be expected to achieve all that they can.

Two decades ago, special educators thought it was their job to assess a student's achievement, to understand what the student wanted to do and what an average peer could do, and then to develop plans to bridge the gap, if possible. Most special educators wanted to see that each student had the tools and knowledge to succeed as independently as possible. Helping students enter the typical world was the mark of success for special educators.

The full-inclusion movement now insists that *every* student will benefit from placement in the mainstream. However, some of the modifications and accommodations now being demanded are so radical that we are doing an injustice to the entire education system. Special education must not be associated in any way with "dumbing down" the curriculum for students presumed to be at a given grade level, whether disabled or not.

Counselors and administrators who want to enable students must focus the discussion on realistic goals and plans for each student. An objective, in-depth discussion and evaluation must take place to determine how far along the continuum of successfully completing these goals the student has moved. If the student is making adequate progress independently, or with minimal help, special education services might not be necessary. If assistance is required to make adequate progress on realistic goals, then special education may be needed. Every modification and every accommodation should be held to the same standard: whether it will help the student attain these goals—*not* whether it will make life easier for the student. Knowing where a student is aiming can help a team guide that student toward success.

And the student must be part of this planning. A student who claims to want to be a brain surgeon but refuses to take science courses needs a reality check. If a student is unwilling to attempt to reach intermediate goals or does not succeed in meeting them, then special education cannot "save" that student. At that point, the team must help the student revisit his or her goals. Goals should be explained in terms of the amount of work required to complete them, not whether or not the teacher or parent feels they are attainable. When goals are presented in this way, students can often make informed decisions regarding their attainability and desirability. Troy Brown, a university dean and politician who has both a doctorate and a learning disability, studied at home with his mother. He estimates that it took him more than twice as long as the average person to complete assignments. Every night, he would go to bed with stacks of books and read until he fell asleep, because he had a dream of attending college.

General educators and special educators need to encourage all students to be responsible and independent and to set realistic expectations for themselves. Then teachers must help students to meet these expectations in a more and more independent manner. Special educators do not serve students well when they enable students with disabilities to become increasingly dependent on their parents, counselors, administrators, or teachers—or even when they fail to increase students' independence and competence.

Where We Stand

We want to make it clear that we think disabilities are real and that they make doing certain things either impossible or very difficult for the people who have them. We cannot expect people with disabilities to be "just like everyone else" in what they can do. . . .

In our view, students with disabilities *do* have specific shortcomings and *do* need the services of specially trained professionals to achieve their potential. They *do* sometimes need altered curricula or adaptations to make their learning possible. If students with disabilities were just like "regular" students, then there would be no need whatever for special education. But the school experiences of students with disabilities obviously will not be—*cannot* be—just like those of students without disabilities. We sell students with disabilities short when we pretend that they are no different from typical students. We make the same error when we pretend that they must *not* be expected to put forth extra effort if they are to learn to do some things—or learn to do something in a different way. We sell them short when we pretend that they have competencies that they do not have or pretend that the competencies we expect of most students are not important for them.

Like general education, special education must push students to become all they can be. Special education must countenance neither the pretense of learning nor the avoidance of reasonable demands.

MaryAnn Byrnes

 **NO**

Accommodations for Students with Disabilities: Removing Barriers to Learning

Think about taking a driver's test without wearing glasses (if you do, that is). Not fair, you say; you need the glasses to see. You have just identified an accommodation that you need. Wearing glasses does not make a bad driver better or make driving easier; rather, wearing glasses makes driving possible. Glasses are so much a part of our lives that we do not even consider that they remove a barrier caused by a disability.

Secondary school teachers encounter students every day on an Individualized Education Plan (IEP) or 504 Plan, both of which address programs for students with disabilities. Most likely, the person charged with monitoring this plan has indicated that particular students need changes in teaching style, assignments, or testing strategies.

It is usually easy to understand the need for glasses or wheelchairs or hearing aids. These sound like changes the student must make. Other adjustments, modifications, or accommodations on these plans, such as extended time, may not be as clear.

What Is an Accommodation?

An accommodation is an adjustment, to an activity or setting, that removes a barrier presented by a disability so a person can have access equal to that of a person without a disability. An accommodation does not guarantee success or a specific level of performance. It should, however, provide the opportunity for a person with a disability to participate in a situation or activity.

Think of that pair of glasses, or the time you broke your leg and could not drive. Think of how your life was affected by these conditions. Your competence did not change. Your ability to think and work did not change. Your ability to interact with (have access to) the reading material may be very limited without your glasses. Your ability to get to (have access to) work or the grocery store may be very limited without someone to transport you. The support provided by the glasses—or the driver—made it possible for you to use your abilities without the barrier presented by less than perfect vision or limited mobility.

The accommodations in IEPs or 504 Plans serve the same purpose. They identify ways to remove the barrier presented by a person's disability.

Why Do We Need to Provide Accommodations?

Accommodations are required under Section 504 of the Federal Rehabilitation Act of 1974 as well as the Americans with Disabilities Act. Both these federal laws prohibit discrimination against individuals who have a disability. Situations that limit access have been determined to be discriminatory.

Accommodations must be provided not just by teachers to students, but by employees for workers and governments for citizens. Curbs have been cut to provide access. Doors have been widened and door handles altered to provide access to people for whom the old designs posed a barrier. Employers provide computer adaptations or other adjustments in work schedules and circumstances.

For employers and schools, individuals with disabilities may have a document called a 504 Plan, which details the types of accommodations that are required. Students who have a 504 Plan will not require special education services, just changes to the environment or instructional situation.

Students who have a disability and require special education services in addition to accommodations will have this information contained in an IEP, which also details the types of direct services that need to be provided and the goals of these services. Accommodations will be listed within this IEP.

With the recent changes in IDEA '97, the federal law governing special education, you will be addressing accommodations that must be made so a student with a disability can participate in large-scale districtwide or statewide assessment systems as well as classwork and school life.

Who Needs Accommodations?

According to Section 504, an individual with a disability is any person who has "a physical or mental impairment that limits one or more major life activities." IDEA '97, the federal special education law, lists the following disabilities: autism, deaf-blindness, deafness, hearing impairment, mental retardation, multiple disabilities, orthopedic impairment, other health impairment, serious emotional disturbance, specific learning disability, speech or language impairment, traumatic brain injury, and visual impairment.

Some conditions are covered by Section 504, but not special education. These can include attention deficit disorder—ADD, (also attention deficit hyperactivity disorder—ADHD); chronic medical conditions (such as cancer, Tourette Syndrome, asthma, or epilepsy); communicable diseases; some temporary medical conditions; physical impairments; and disorders of emotion or behavior. To qualify, there must be a demonstrated and substantial limitation of a major life activity.

Students (or adults) who have disabilities may require accommodations to have equal access to education. Not every student with a disability will require accommodations, and not every student with a disability requires the same accommodation all the time.

Think of Jim, a student who has limited mobility in his hands, affecting his ability to write. This disability will present a barrier in a class that requires the student to take notes quickly or write long essays in class. In a class that does not require either of these activities, no barrier may be present. Equal access is possible without accommodation. The student can learn and demonstrate what he knows and can do unaffected by his disability.

What Kind of Accommodations Are There?

Just as there is no limit to the range of disabilities, there is no limit to the range of accommodations. The point is to understand disability and determine if it presents a barrier to equal access. If so, decide whether an accommodation can be identified to remove the barrier—and make sure the accommodation is implemented.

Think of the student described above. The limited mobility in Jim's hands presents a barrier in a class that requires rapid note taking or the writing of long essays in class. There are several accommodations that can result in equal access. Jim might tape the lesson and take notes later. These notes could be written or dictated into a computer. Essays could be composed verbally at a computer workstation or dictated into a tape recorder or to a scribe. A computer might be adapted so typing becomes an effective way to record information on paper. In yet another type of accommodation, essays could be replaced by oral reports.

Are There Some Accommodations That Should Not Be Used?

Like many difficult questions, the answer depends on the context. An accommodation should not alter the essential purpose of the assignment. If the skill you want to measure is the ability to make multiple rapid hand movements, then there is probably no accommodation that is appropriate. Jim will not do well because of his disability. Alternately, if the purpose of a task is to see if someone has perfect vision without glasses, using those glasses is not an appropriate accommodation. If the purpose is to see if you can read, the glasses become a reasonable accommodation.

Who Decides about Accommodations?

The team that writes IEPs and 504 Plans reviews the disability and determines what accommodations, if any, are necessary. These are then written into the IEP or 504 Plan.

Once more, return to Jim. As you consider the requirements of your class, think of the most appropriate way to remove the barrier that is presented by the limited mobility Jim has in his hands.

If We Use Accommodations, How Will the Student Ever Be Prepared for Independent Life in College or the World of Work?

Some people are concerned that the supports provided in school will result in the student being unable to work productively when he or she leaves school.

As a matter of fact, Section 504 applies to colleges and employers as well. Colleges offer support centers and provide accommodations upon documentation that a disability exists. Employers are required to provide reasonable accommodations to any person who is otherwise qualified to fulfill the elements of the job.

If companies remove barriers at the workplace, educators should be willing and able to take barriers out of the school activities that prepare a student for the workplace. Teachers can help a student identify the type of accommodation that will be the least cumbersome for everyone, and those that will permit the student to be most independent.

Don't Accommodations Just Make School Easier?

That depends on how you view the world. Does wearing glasses make driving easier? Not really—for a person with limited vision, wearing glasses makes driving *possible*. With or without glasses, you need to be able to drive to pass the test. The same is true of an academic accommodation; whether or not the accommodation is provided, the students still must demonstrate that they know required material.

Think about the important elements of your class: Is it more important that Jim take notes in class or understand the material? Is it more important that Jim demonstrate good handwriting or the ability to communicate thoughts in print? Often, when you identify the main purpose of your assignments and consider the skills and abilities of a student, you will see that an accommodation lets you determine more clearly what a student knows, understands, and can do.

Does a Student Need to Follow the IEP Accommodations in All Classes?

The IEP or 504 Plan needs to address any area in which the student's disability affects life in school. Sometimes this means in all classes, but not always. For example, a student who was blind would need to use Braille in all classes dealing with written material. Jim, our student with limited mobility in his hands, might not require accommodations in world languages or physical education.

Can We Make Accommodations without Having Students on an IEP?

Many accommodations are just different ways of teaching or testing. You should be able to have this freedom in your classes. In some cases, the way in which a class is taught makes accommodations unnecessary. Accommodations change the situation, not the content of the instruction. However, accommodations on standardized tests must be connected to IEP's or 504 Plans.

May Teachers Give Different Assignments on the Same Content as a Way to Meet the Needs of Different Learning Styles without Lowering Standards?

Absolutely. The point is to remove the barrier of the disability; this is one way to accomplish that. Some teachers find they tap student knowledge best in active projects; others find that written work is best. Many secondary schools are using portfolios or performance activities to document student learning.

These assessment activities can be very compelling and they do tap different methods of expression. A student like Jim, for example, might communicate depth of understanding and analysis to a social studies debate that might be difficult to capture in an on-demand written test. A student with a disability in the area of speech or language might find barriers in the performance activities that do not exist on a paper-and-pencil task.

What if Accommodations Are Not Implemented?

Since accommodations allow equal access, refusing to provide them can be viewed as discrimination. Individuals who knowingly refuse to implement accommodations make themselves personally liable for legal suit.

This sounds serious, and it is serious. Once the accommodations are found to be necessary, everyone must implement them in situations where the student's disability poses a barrier that prevents equal access.

If no barrier exists in your class, the accommodation is not necessary. No one has the option, however, of deciding not to implement a necessary accommodation. Telling students they could not wear glasses or use a hearing aid is unthinkable. Just as inappropriate is a decision not to allow Jim to use accommodations to remove the barrier posed by his disability, even though it means making some changes to your own work.

Questions About Specific Accommodations

Now that the issues underlying accommodations have been addressed, it is time to talk about frequently-encountered accommodations that raise questions and concern. All these questions have come from secondary school faculty members in a variety of school systems.

Why Is It Fair to Read Material Aloud to Some Students?

Some students have a learning disability that makes it difficult for them to decode print. They can understand the concepts; they can comprehend the material when they hear it; they can reason through the material. They just can't turn print into meaning. If the task is to determine if the student can read, you already know they will have difficulty. If the task is to determine if the student has content knowledge, reading material aloud removes the barrier of the learning disability. Reading material aloud to a student who does not understand the material will not result in a higher grade.

Why Is It Fair to Give Some Students Extra Time on Tests?

Some students have motor difficulties that make writing an enormous challenge. They may not be able to form the letters correctly. They may not be able to monitor their thoughts while they work on the physical act of writing. They understand the material, and they know what they want to respond; it just takes longer to write the answer. If the task is to determine how quickly the student can respond, you already know they will have difficulty. If the task is to determine if the student has the knowledge, providing extra time removes the barrier of the motor disability. Providing extra time to a student who does not understand the material will not result in a higher grade.

Why Is It Fair to Permit Some Students to Respond Orally to Tests?

Think about the example above. For some students, responding orally would be a comparable accommodation. In this case, allowing an oral response will not result in a higher grade if the student does not know the material.

The Bottom Line

It all comes down to deciding what is important. Think about your assignment and expectations. Think about the disability. If the disability provides a barrier, the accommodation removes it. The accommodation does not release a student from participating or demonstrating knowledge—it allows the student to be able to participate and demonstrate knowledge. And isn't that what school is all about?

POSTSCRIPT

Have Schools Gone Too Far in Using Accommodations?

The authors agree that accommodations are necessary and can be an important educational tool. Kauffman and colleagues feel special education randomly tosses about accommodations to make life "easy" for students and, thereby, limiting opportunities to learn and excel. Byrnes says that wisely chosen accommodations provide the opportunity for students to demonstrate their capacity to achieve high standards.

Two questions are at the heart of the debate. When should accommodations be provided? Which accommodations should be provided?

Horn and Tynan (Fordham Foundation, 2001) agree with Kauffman and colleagues that accommodations are used too widely. They believe accommodations made sense early on when the intention was to ensure that students with significant sensory or motor disabilities had access to a free and appropriate public education. Now, they say, their use has been broadened to create a "lifetime of dependence," often at taxpayers' expense.

Writing in *Education Week's* 2004 Quality Counts edition focusing on the state of special education in a standards-based environment, Olson observes that states differ widely in their definition of acceptable accommodations. She references the continuing challenge of deciding whether a particular accommodation helps or gives an unfair advantage. The difficulty of selecting appropriate accommodations makes it easy to identify too many, too few, or incorrect options.

Extending the significant work of the National Center on Educational Outcomes, Bolt and Thurlow (*Remedial & Special Education, 2004)*, emphasize the need to provide appropriate accommodations to ensure students with disabilities are included in the curriculum and assessment changes of education reform. Educators must determine which accommodations enhance access without changing demands.

Some say that anyone would do better if they had more time, a reader, or a computer. The evidence seems to say that is not so. To be appropriate, an accommodation must confer a "differential boost." It must result in a gain for students with disabilities, without enhancing the scores of typical learners. This would show that students could demonstrate knowledge, once the impact of a disability was removed. Reviewing research on the differential impact of the most commonly allowed accommodations, including extended time, Bolt and Thurlow (2004) uncovered mixed results. Some had very little impact. Elliott and Marquart (*Exceptional Children*, 2004) found that extended time on math tests did not provide an advantage to students with disabilities. It did, however, help everyone feel more relaxed and provided them more time to check the accuracy of their responses.

The point, say Fuchs and Fuchs (*The School Administrator*, 1999), is to choose accommodations that result in valid, rather than optimal, performance. It is not always easy to make this determination. Students and disabilities are different. Task demands differ. The Fuchs have developed the Dynamic Assessment of Testing Accommodations (DATA) to help educators determine which accommodations are most appropriate to choose. While this evidence-based method holds much promise, it requires a substantial investment of time.

Because this field is so new, research evidence is not comprehensive. Because students differ dramatically, research is difficult to conduct. Would you want your child in the control group? Because stakes can be so high for students and schools, correct decisions are critical. How can we all be sure we make the right choices as we continue to provide meaningful education? And can we ensure that we provide appropriate accommodations when they are needed; teach required skills; and remove the accommodations when the student no longer needs them?

ISSUE 15

Should Students with Cognitive Disabilities Be Expected to Demonstrate Academic Proficiency?

YES: Kevin S. McGrew and Jeffrey Evans, from *Expectations for Students with Cognitive Disabilities: Is the Cup Half Empty or Half Full? Can the Cup Flow Over?* (National Center on Educational Outcomes, December 2004)

NO: James M. Kauffman, from *Education Deform: Bright People Sometimes Say Stupid Things About Education* (The Scarecrow Press, 2002)

ISSUE SUMMARY

YES: Kevin S. McGrew, educational researcher and director of the Institute for Applied Psychometrics (IAP), and Jeffrey Evans, consultant and educational researcher for IAP, are wary that stereotypes of individuals with cognitive disabilities are used to form limited (and limiting) expectations and self-fulfilling prophecies.

NO: James M. Kauffman, professor emeritus of education at the University of Virginia, Charlottesville, and special education philosopher-researcher, believes that educators and parents must acknowledge that some students with cognitive disabilities cannot reach high academic standards and are best served by programs that develop other skills.

Beginning with IDEA 97, districts were required to include students with disabilities in all large-scale testing programs. NCLB increased the stakes. Districts must report, and be held accountable for, the academic performance of students with disabilities.

Previously, the very fact that a student had a disability often meant they—and their performance—were excluded from testing programs. This was the case whether the student had a mild learning disability, moderate mental retardation, or a complex combination of sensory, physical, and cognitive issues. The existence of the disability was sufficient to preclude participation. Some thought this was the right thing to do; it spared students the frustration of testing on the general curriculum, which everyone knew they could not master.

To comply with IDEA and NCLB, IEP teams now decide not whether a student with a disability participates in district testing, but the way in which they can best demonstrate what they know and can do. Although parents may contest the manner of testing, they cannot ask for students to be exempt from the process. The following participation options are open:

- Regular assessment (that is administered to all students in that grade)
- Regular assessment with accommodations
- Alternate assessment based on grade-level achievement standards
- Alternate assessment based on alternate achievement standards
- Assessment based on modified achievement standards

States determine academic standards and assessment programs as well as their own method of alternate testing. In contrast to the familiar multiple choice test, some use portfolios; others select out-of-level testing, a method in which a test from a lower grade is used. All alternate assessments must be based on state academic standards.

Every school is held accountable for the adequate yearly progress of all students toward the goal of proficiency by 2013–2014. All children are expected to reach that target. States are permitted to count as "proficient" a limited number of students who take an alternate assessment based on modified or alternate achievement standards.

Should demanding standards really apply to all students? Educators generally agree that blanket exclusion of all students with disabilities was not wise and did not provide an accurate view of the accomplishments of all students. Now, some ask whether it is wise to expect all students to reach the same targets. Should students with cognitive or complex disabilities (e.g., mental retardation, traumatic brain injury, deaf-blindness) even participate if they are not expected to achieve these goals?

This issue's selections are somewhat longer than is typical for *Taking Sides*. Their length reflects the complexity of this critical controversy.

Kevin McGrew and Jeffrey Evans caution there are dangers in relying on disability labels or IQ scores to anticipate what a student might achieve. They discuss the powerful impact expectations can have on accomplishments and worry that stereotypes will limit possibilities for students with cognitive disabilities.

James Kauffman maintains that some students, particularly those with cognitive disabilities, simply will not be able to reach high academic standards. He sees this as a reality that should be accepted and urges people to focus on what these individuals can do, offering programs to develop their strengths.

As you read these articles, ask yourself if you believe all students can reach academic proficiency. Will students with cognitive disabilities surprise us all if only we raise our expectations? Or should we focus on functional, work-related areas for these students? Are lower academic expectations ever reasonable? Who decides?

YES

Kevin S. McGrew and
Jeffrey Evans

Expectations for Students with Cognitive Disabilities: Is the Cup Half Empty or Half Full? Can the Cup Flow Over?

Introduction

Over the past 30 years the United States has slowly and steadily clarified the meaning of access to a free and appropriate public education for students with disabilities. . . . Unfortunately, there is still limited consensus among educators regarding appropriate achievement expectations for students with disabilities, particularly those with cognitive disabilities.

A concern about low expectations and the need for high expectations was reflected in the IDEA's 1977 Preamble: "Over 20 years of research has demonstrated that the education of children with disabilities can be made more effective by . . . having high expectations for such children and ensuring their access to the general education curriculum to the maximum extent possible. . . ." IDEA 1997 clarified that all students with disabilities are to have access to instruction focused on the same skills and knowledge as all other students, and that their achievement is to be measured with the same district and statewide assessment programs as used for all students (and, adding an alternate assessment for those students unable to participate in the general assessment).

The *No Child Left Behind (NCLB) Act of 2001* further clarified that schools are to be held accountable for the adequate yearly progress (AYP) of all groups of students. NCLB specifically requires the disaggregation of assessment data for specified subgroups, including students with disabilities. The intended purpose of NCLB is "to ensure that all children have a fair, equal, and significant opportunity to obtain a high quality education and reach, at a minimum, proficiency on challenging State academic achievement standards and state academic assessments." In other words, the expected educational outcomes for students with disabilities . . . are the same high expectations held for all students.

McGrew, K.S., Evans, J. (2004). *Expectations for students with cognitive disabilities: Is the cup half empty or half full? Can the cup flow over?* (Synthesis Report 55). Minneapolis, MN: University of Minnesota, National Center for Educational Outcomes. References omitted.

Although data show that some students with disabilities are reaching the state-determined level of proficiency, many students with disabilities are still far from performing at this level. . . .

Many educators have grown increasingly concerned about the performance of students with cognitive disabilities who are appropriately working toward grade-level achievement standards, but whose current performance is far from a proficient level on grade-level achievement standards as measured by current statewide assessments. Considerable controversy surrounds the issue of what can and should be expected for these students. Some people argue that the vast majority of students with disabilities, when given appropriate access to high quality curriculum and instruction, can meet or exceed the levels of proficiency currently specified. Many special education advocates believe that subscribing to the same high expectations and accountability for student progress will ultimately lead to improved instruction and learning for all students. Others argue that a student's disability will ultimately prevent the student from attaining gradelevel achievement standards, even when provided appropriate instruction and accommodations. This latter group believes that it is unjust to punish schools when these students fail to perform at the proficient level.

The discrepant "expectations" arguments reflect very different perspectives regarding the nature of cognitive disabilities. These two perspectives have existed for many years. To make informed decisions about the best instruction and assessments for students with cognitive disabilities, several questions need to be answered. For instance, how many students with cognitive disabilities can be expected to achieve the same level of proficiency as other students? To what extent can we predict who these students are? Can we discern whether a student's failure to meet proficiency is due to the student's disabling condition or lack of appropriate instruction? Finally, what effects do teacher expectations have on student achievement?

This report was prepared to begin to address these issues. It includes an analysis of nationally representative cognitive and achievement data to illustrate the dangers in making blanket assumptions about appropriate achievement expectations for individuals based on their cognitive ability or diagnostic label. . . .

Overview

Few would argue that the concept of intelligence (IQ), and tests that measure the construct, have played a long and significant role in education, and special education in particular. The use of practical IQ tests is typically traced to the beginning of the century when Alfred Binet developed a battery of tasks to help identify children with learning difficulties. Binet's goal was to develop a means by which to identify struggling students who would then receive remediation via "mental orthopedics." Clearly, Binet did not believe that his measure of intelligence quantified an innate or "fixed" ability. Binet was an optimist who believed that the ability "glasses" of children with lower ability were half full, and that their vessels could be filled further.

In stark contrast to Binet's optimistic position was that of English psychologist Sir Cyril Burt, [whose] . . . work was based on the then popular view that intelligence was a genetically based fixed entity. Burt's ideas influenced the design of educational systems that segregated children in different educational tracks based on ability. According to Burt, "capacity must obviously limit content. It is impossible for a pint jug to hold more than a pint of milk; and it is equally impossible for a child's educational attainments to rise higher than his educable capacity permits." Clearly Binet and Burt viewed the proverbial half-filled glass differently.

A final view, based on the 1994 feel-good movie *Forrest Gump*, can be considered the "cup overflowing" perspective. Briefly, this movie portrayed the fictitious life history of Forrest Gump, an individual who was classified in the mental retardation range early in school. The exchange between the school principal and Forrest's mother clearly illustrated an educational approach grounded in the Burt philosophy:

School principal: "Your boy's . . . different, Miz Gump. His IQ's 75."

Ms. Gump: "Well, we're all different, Mr. Hancock. He might be a bit on the slow side. He's not going to a special school to retread tires!"

Ms. Gump's response, and the subsequent string of life achievements of her son Forrest (e.g., star football player in college, world class ping pong player, Vietnam war hero, CEO of successful shrimp company) reflects the "cup flowing over" perspective on IQ test scores. That is, Forrest's achievements were beyond his measured IQ (which was below the average sized "jug" according to Burt).

When faced with students whose classroom performances or achievement test scores surpass their measured . . . IQ scores by significant amounts, laypersons and professionals (e.g., educators and psychologists) frequently demonstrate an implicit subscription to a Burt philosophy that a person can achieve only up to his or her level of intelligence when they characterize Gump-like students as "overachievers." Ms. Gump's implicit intelligence conception, which was subsequently manifested in Forrest's accomplishments, would suggest that there is more to school learning than the size of a child's "IQ cup or jug"—other variables contribute to achievement.

Half-full or half-empty? Filled to-the-brim or the cup flowing over? Which intelligence-learning metaphor is correct? Burt versus Binet/Gump? Who should be believed during the current standards-driven educational reform fueled by the mantra that "no child shall be left behind" (NCLB), and that all children should reach grade level standards. More importantly, which philosophy should guide educational expectations for students whose primary special education classification is tied closely to IQ scores below the normal range (i.e., students with mental retardation or cognitive disabilities)? Should educational expectations for students with cognitive disabilities be grounded in a Burt philosophy (i.e., expect academic performance and achievement no higher than the student's estimated cognitive ability), or should expectations be based on the more optimistic Gump philosophy (i.e., it is possible for students with cognitive disabilities to achieve higher than their IQ test score and at grade level)? . . .

Diversity within Disability Distributions

Probably no environment elicits individual differences sooner in life than formal education. In classrooms teachers strive to arrange conditions to elicit optimal performance among a diverse class of unique learners. However, due to the only true "law" in psychology (the law of individual differences), optimal learning conditions and techniques are not universal across learners.

This holds true for all learners—those with and without disabilities. It is important that students with disabilities not be saddled with group-based stereotyped low academic expectations. Just as the diversity of learning rates for students without disabilities is acknowledged, so it should be for students with disabilities. . . .

The federally funded *Special Education Elementary Longitudinal* (SEELS) study, the first ever nationally representative longitudinal investigation of elementary students with disabilities (ages 6 to 12), recently provided empirical support for the diversity of achievement levels of students with disabilities. According to the SEELS project director . . . the data indicate that "you can find kids with disabilities who are scoring right near the top—above the 80th percentile—and you you'll find some in the middle . . . and then a lot more kids in the lowest quartile. So it's heavily weighted toward the low end but there's quite a bit of diversity." Although students with disabilities, as a group, tend to achieve in the lower half of the distribution of achievement, "individuals with disabilities can be found across the full range of academic performance." . . .

IQ and Disability: The Misunderstood Common Denominator

Despite their diversity of characteristics, the majority (58%) of students receiving special education services under IDEA share a common experience—most have been classified as having a learning disability or cognitive impairment (mental retardation) with the aid of an intelligence test. Despite many disputes over competing theoretical conceptualizations of intelligence and the utility of intelligence test scores, even the most ardent critics recognize that IQ tests "predict certain forms of achievement—especially school achievement—rather effectively."

Despite a defensible rationale for their early development and continued deployment in the schools, many people have developed . . . the inaccurate belief, often reinforced by court decisions, that measured intelligence is a genetically determined, largely fixed, global, and enduring trait that explains most of a student's success (or failure) in school learning. Such a Sir Cyril Burt conceptualization of intelligence can doom a student to low expectations if his or her IQ score is significantly below the norm. This fixed entity view of intelligence, summarized in the belief in the predictive power of the single global IQ score, represents the mental jug or cup being "half-empty" or "filled to the brim" philosophy. According to this view, to expect more academic achievement than a person's estimated or measured IQ score is simply not possible.

A recent *Education Week* (2004) national survey (*Count me in: Special Education in an Era of Standards*) of 800 special and general education teachers suggests that most educators implicitly subscribe to the Burt IQ-potential philosophy. Eighty-four percent of surveyed teachers did not believe that students in special education should be expected to meet the same set of academic standards as students without disabilities. In addition, approximately 80% of the teachers felt that students with disabilities should not be included in the same state tests as students in general education, especially if the results are used for accountability purposes.

The surprising extent to which educators appear to hold alternative (and typically lower) standards and expectations for students with disabilities, although appropriate for many of these students, is troubling given the empirical reality of the predictive power of IQ test scores—scores that are often at the root of lowered expectations. Sir Cyril Burt's IQ-fixed potential legacy appears to be alive and well in America's schools (albeit not typically adopted maliciously or explicitly articulated).

Fortunately, decades of research on intelligence tests have repeatedly converged on a near unanimous consensus on the predictive accuracy of IQ test scores[;] it is time to "leave the Burt IQ-potential philosophy behind."

Reality of the IQ-Achievement Relationship: Statistics Made Simple

In an era of standards-driven educational reform, educators and policymakers must recognize the truth about IQ test scores and the resulting disability categories that are based on a continuum of IQ test scores. . . . The reality is simple. Given the best available theoretically and psychometrically sound, nationally standardized, individually administered intelligence test batteries, three statements hold true. Each of these can be explained in depth. . . . For greater conciseness here, the statements that hold true are:

- IQ test scores, under optimal test conditions, account for 40% to 50% of current expected achievement.
- Thus, 50% to 60% of student achievement is related to variables "beyond intelligence."
- For any given IQ test score, half of the students will obtain achievement scores at or below their IQ score. Conversely, and frequently not recognized, is that for any given IQ test score, half of the students will obtain achievement scores at or *above* their IQ score.

. . . Using the general IQ and Total Achievement (average across reading, math, and written language) scores for "real" norm subjects from the standardization of the *Woodcock-Johnson Battery Third Edition* (WJ III, . . . there is a strong linear relation between IQ and achievement, as evidenced by a strong correlation of .75. . . .

[However,] . . . even IQ tests that demonstrate some of the strongest correlations with achievement . . . cannot be used to provide perfect estimates of predicted achievement for *individual* students. . . . [For] subjects with IQs from 70–80, expected achievement scores range from a low of approximately 40 to a high of approximately 110. . . . [Half] of the individuals with IQs between 70–80 achieve at or below IQ-predicted achievement, and the other half . . . score at or *above* IQ-predicted achievement.

[These] data . . . suggest that the proper metaphor for the IQ-achievement prediction relationship is that the "cup can flow over." The carte blanch assumption that all students with disabilities should have an alternative set of educational standards and an assessment system is inconsistent with empirical data. . . .

The current reality is that despite being one of the flagship developments in all of psychology, intelligence tests are fallible predictors of academic achievement. IQ test scores (and associated IQ-based disability category labels) are adequate, but not nearly sufficient metrics, by which to make reasonably precise predictions about any particular *individual* student's future expected achievement progress. It simply cannot be done beyond a reasonable doubt.

The fallibility of IQ tests, coupled with the enduring presence of the ghost of Sir Cyril Burt's deterministic IQ-achievement educational philosophy, in the context of today's high-stakes educational accountability environment, raises the specter of many children with disabilities being denied the right to appropriate and demanding expectations. Stereotyping students with disabilities (often on the basis of disability label or test scores) as a group that should be excluded from general education standards and assessments is not supported by the best evidence from current science in the field of psychological and educational measurement. The potential soft bigotry of setting a priori IQ or disability label-based low academic expectations (for students with disabilities) needs to be recognized, understood, and minimized, if all children are not to be left behind.

Expectancy Effects: A Brief History and Literature Review

Since the 1970s, the notions of the "self-fulfilling prophecy" (SFP), the "Pygmalion Effect," . . . and more recently, "expectancy effects" (EE), have become commonplace in the educational psychology literature. In general, these terms refer to similar phenomena. . . .

Merton is recognized as the first to coin the term "self-fulfilling prophecy" (which has now evolved into the more general phenomena of "expectancy effects." According to Merton, SFP occurs when an inaccurate definition of a situation elicits new behaviors which, in turn, make the originally inaccurate conception a reality. SFP is a compelling theory, largely because of its potential implications and elegant simplicity.

> The concept is simple enough: If we prophesy (expect) that something will happen, we behave (usually unconsciously) in a manner that will make it happen. We will, in other words, do what we can to realize our prophecy.

In most EE research, it is usually a person in a position of authority (e.g., an employer, medical professional, parent, teacher, . . .) who holds expectations about an individual (or group) under their supervision. According to the EE research, expectations expressed by an authority figure via verbal and nonverbal communication often influence the self-image and the behavior of the supervised person in such a way that the expectations held come to pass.

Origins of Expectancy Effects

. . . SFP is also often referred to as the "Pygmalion Effect" which was drawn from the title of the original book (Rosenthal & Jacobson, *Pygmalion in the Classroom*) that reported the phenomenon. SFP first appeared in early psychological research studies where it was demonstrated that experimenters could unwittingly influence the behavior of animal and human subjects during an experiment. In 1968, Rosenthal and Jacobson substituted teachers for experimenters in order to investigate the effects of teachers' expectancies on the intelligence test scores of their pupils. The Rosenthal and Jacobson study was designed to measure "whether those children for whom the teachers held especially favorable expectations would show greater intellectual growth than the remaining or controlgroup children" when evaluated . . . months later. Cotton provided a succinct summary of the original Pygmalion study:

> The Rosenthal/Jacobson study concluded that students' intellectual development is largely a response to what teachers expect and how those expectations are communicated. The original Pygmalion study involved giving teachers false information about the learning potential of certain students in grades one through six in a San Francisco elementary school. Teachers were told that these students had been tested and found to be on the brink of a period of rapid intellectual growth; in reality, the students had been selected at random. At the end of the experimental period, some of the targeted students—and particularly those in grades one and two—exhibited performance on IQ tests which was superior to the scores of other students of similar ability and superior to what would have been expected of the target students with no intervention.

The Rosenthal and Jacobson report suggested that teacher expectations could increase or decrease . . . IQ . . . test scores. Understandably, this report created a media sensation. The possibility that teachers could effect change (either positive or negative) in a student's IQ scores held considerable popular interest and appeal. . . .

Expectancy Effects and Intelligence

It would be an understatement to describe the EE research focused on the relations between teacher's expectations and intelligence as contentious. Post hoc re-analysis of the . . . Rosenthal and Jacobson investigation raised many questions about the study's methodology. Numerous attempts to replicate the Pygmalion effect . . . have proven unsuccessful. . . . In many of the subsequent follow-up studies the control groups often gained more IQ points than the experimental groups. . . .

Many . . . researchers have continued to examine the teacher-student expectancy effect. A clear connection between [EE] and IQ has not been established. However; *expectancy effects and academic achievement do appear to correlate positively.*

Expectancy Effects: How Large?

A frequently quoted estimate of the magnitude of Expectancy Effects (EE) in education is that 5% to 10% of student achievement performance might be ascribed to the influence of differential teacher expectations. More recently, average expectancy effect sizes from 0.1 to 0.3 have been reported. On first inspection, effect sizes of 0.1 to 0.3 appear to be of little practical import. This is wrong. According to Jussim et al., when discussing students who are the "targets" of EE, "a naturally occurring effect of 'only' .2 means, that on average, of all targets of high expectations, 10% show substantial improvement; and of all targets of low expectations, 10% show substantial decreases in performance." . . .

To reassure the reader of the importance of what appear to be significant, yet small correlations or effect sizes, one only needs to be reminded that many significant public and social policy decisions have been made on the strength of relations between variables that are of the same magnitude or lower than those reported for EE. . . . [A] special American Psychological Association . . . *Psychological Assessment Work Group* . . . provided the following examples:

- The reduction of the risk of dying from a heart attack by taking aspirin is based on $r = 0.02$
- The impact of chemotherapy on breast cancer survival; $r = .03$
- The value of antihistamines for reducing sneezes and a runny nose; $r = .11$
- The impact of Viagra on improved sexual functioning; $r = .38$

Furthermore, much like the long-term insidious effect of long-term exposure to subclinical levels of lead, asbestos, second-hand smoke, and other toxins, some research studies have suggested that even small EE can result in larger cumulative effects over time. Small EE could exert a substantial influence on student achievement, particularly for more vulnerable and "at risk" students.

Expectancy Effects and Student Characteristics

In the field of special education, EE was first investigated . . . with regard to the potential negative consequences of being labeled "mentally retarded." In general, this "stigma" research suggested that being labeled mentally retarded often led to changes in the behavior of adults who encouraged "learned helplessness." These studies reported that the attribution for success or failure for a mentally retarded person was more frequently assigned to the person's inherent low ability, while failure attribution for others was more frequently assigned to the person's effort.

Researchers have found that, in general, EE in classrooms are often related to a number of different student characteristics. "Teachers overestimate the achievement of high achievers, underestimate that of low achievers, and predict least accurately the responses of low achievers." Although low-achieving students have been found to receive more learning support, they also are communicated lower expectations via less pressure to achieve than high achieving students. Additional student characteristics associated with teacher expectations include race, ethnicity, SES, physical appearance or attractiveness, . . . use of standard English . . . , prior negative comments or evaluations about a student by other teachers, readiness/maturity, and grouping/tracking effects. Similar to the early MR-stigma research, some teachers have been found to associate success to inherent ability in the case of high achieving students and luck or chance for perceived low achievers. . . .

Expectancy Effects: Educator Behaviors

Although the claim that teacher expectancies can raise student intelligence has been effectively rebuked, most . . . critics have expressed the belief, supported by research, that expectancy effects do influence teacher-to-student performance and behavior. . . .

Expectancies can be expressed both verbally and non-verbally. Although most teachers report that they can fully control their behavioral affect and deceive students whenever necessary, at times the two primary modes of communication can send mixed signals. . . .

Even brief exposure to a teacher's face or body movements (e.g., differences in voice inflection) can provide a student with enough information to communicate expectancies. Teacher behaviors associated with the communication of low achievement expectancies to low achievement students have included:

- The provision of fewer opportunities to learn new material.
- Less "wait" time provided to answer questions.
- Providing answers or calling on someone else.
- Inappropriate feedback (more frequent and severe criticism for failure; insincere praise), limited reinforcement (e.g., giving reinforcement that is not contingent on performance), or rewarding more incorrect answers or inappropriate behavior.
- Providing less attention and more interaction in private settings.
- Providing differential treatment in grading (less frequently giving "the benefit of the doubt") and personal interactions (e.g., teachers less friendly or responsive; making less eye contact; giving fewer smiles).
- Providing briefer and less informative feedback.
- Providing less stimulating, and lower-level cognitive questions.
- Providing less effective (but time consuming) instructional methods.

Expectancy Effects: Why Do They Occur?

Although the original research on [EE] was based primarily on studies where educators were provided false information regarding student potential, "most researchers have concluded that teacher expectations are not generally formed on the basis of 'false conceptions.'" Rather, they are based on the best information available about the students. Furthermore, even if the initial expectations a teacher forms for a student are realistic and appropriate, student learning and self-concept development can be limited as a result of *sustained expectation effects*. The adverse impact of sustained expectations can occur when teachers continue to engage in behaviors that result in the maintenance of previously formed low expectations (e.g., by giving low-expectation students only drill work). . . .

Attribution Theory

Certain beliefs about intelligence and learning may lead to lowered expectations for low achieving students and students with cognitive disabilities . . . [Contemporary] social cognitive psychology research has suggested that *attribution theory* is a "useful framework for exploring teachers' response to children's academic outcomes, such as success or failure, in the general education classroom."

Briefly, attribution theory research has demonstrated that individuals (e.g., teachers) tend to attribute success or failure for an individual (e.g., students) to one of two different human characteristics—*ability* or *effort*. Graham and Weiner's studies found that the initial response of many classroom teachers to a negative student outcome is either anger or pity. Furthermore, the elicitation of anger or pity was differentially linked to the degree to which teachers perceived the student as responsible for his or her failure. Typically, when faced with student failure, a teacher pity response was elicited for students of low abilities while anger was the more frequent response to high ability students (due to a perceived lack of effort or motivation). Furthermore, these researchers found that the anticipation of future failure for students was directly related to the perceived stability of the cause of the student failure. "Failure due to causes that are viewed as stable, such as low ability, will result in a high expectation that failure will recur, whereas failure due to unstable causes, such as effort or task difficulty, will result in a lower expectation of repeated failure. . . ."

Clark found . . . [that when] students use attribution information to make inferences about their own ability and effort, these inferences are manifest in the students' self-esteem, expectations for their own future successes and failures, and their classroom performance." . . .

Group Stereotyping

Expectancy effects may also reflect the differential treatment of an individual based on group membership stereotypes. Group-based self-fulfilling prophecies differ from individual-based self-fulfilling prophecies and are relevant to the educational practices of grouping, tracking, and institutionalized segregated instruction (e.g., separate special education classrooms). . . .

Researchers have reported the communication of differential expectations as a function of placement in different ability or tracked groups in classrooms.

According to Cotton's research synthesis, "students in low groups and tracks have been found to get less exciting instruction, less emphasis upon meaning and conceptualization, and more rote drill and practice activities than those in high reading groups and tracks." . . . In general, . . . tracking or ability grouping "may lead to the type of rigid teacher expectations that are most likely to evoke self-fulfilling prophecies and perceptual biases. Teachers often prepare more for and are more supportive toward students in high ability groups."

Stereotype-based low expectations for "different" students . . . can beset anyone who belongs to a group with a specific reputation. When the stereotype or reputation is pejorative, . . . the effects can be significantly disruptive to individual development. Stereotypes have two salient characteristics: (1) they polarize perceptions and sharpen differences, and (2) they are rigidly held, readily fixated and resistant to change. Thus, the development of stereotypically-based differential student academic expectations (based on group membership or label) can serve to fixate and exaggerate existing differences. . . .

Probably one of the more potentially insidious forms of stereotype-based expectation formation is that which results from the attachment of diagnostic labels (e.g., learning disabled, mentally retarded, emotionally disturbed, . . .) to students. Although all forms of social stereotypes (e.g., gender, social class, race, ethnicity, . . .) can produce harmful effects, diagnostic educational or medical disability labels almost always have the authoritative stamp of approval by a credible expert (e.g., psychologist, doctor). This major source of lowered teacher expectations has been repeatedly demonstrated in the special education research literature. Based on the previously summarized *Education Week* national survey of teachers, lowered expectations for all students with disabilities continues to be a latent force in many of America's classrooms, and may be exacerbated by the current wave of high stakes educational accountability.

Beware of Silent, Shifting Standards

Research during the past decade has revealed that group-based stereotypes can be conceptualized as functioning as "standards against which individual members of stereotype groups are judged." Briefly, *stereotyping effects* occur when individual group members are evaluated in a direction consistent with group-based expectations or stereotypes. "For example, a man is judged a better leader than a woman; a physician is judged more intelligent than a hairdresser . . . these types of effects certainly indicate that stereotypes have been used to judge individuals and that the outcome is *assimilation*." The self-fulfilling prophesies previously described are examples of the commonly recognized assimilative stereotype effect.

Research on the "shifting standards model" suggests that assimilative effects alone fail to capture the complexity and extent to which stereotyped-based expectations operate in group settings: "Less well recognized is the fact that stereotyping can also be manifested in other ways, most notably in counter-stereotypical or contrast effects."

Within-category standards are typically used when a person evaluates or judges an individual . . . of a stereotyped group . . . on stereotyped dimensions. For example, given the stereotype that students with mental retardation are "slower learners" than students of normal intelligence, one is likely to judge the learning capability of a particular student with mental retardation relative to (lower) standards for students with mental retardation and, the learning ability of a particular non-retarded student relative to (higher) standards of competence for non-retarded students. . . . "Good" does not mean the same thing for the student with mental retardation and the student of normal intelligence. . . .

Probably the most pernicious masked effect of the shifting standards model is that "evidentiary standards are lower for members of the group stereotyped as deficient on an attribute." When an individual . . . is a member of a group that is stereotyped as deficient on a trait or attribute (i.e., intelligence), evidentiary standards or expectations are often shifted in the direction of leniency, less challenge, and minimal competencies. [This] shift, . . . in turn, often produces behavior in the evaluator in the opposite direction of the stereotype. This shifting of standards "activates low (patronizing) minimizing standards that are more readily surpassed, producing a subjective sense of positivity—a 'wow' effect. That this positivity is not borne out in outcomes that matter for the target (getting a job or the key fielding position) suggests that the favorable treatment is more apparent and ephemeral than real." The essence of this phenomena is captured in the words of Alexa Pochowski, the assistant commissioner for learning services in the Kansas education department, . . . quoted in *Education Week* as saying:

> For too long, we held these students to lower standards . . . I hate to say it: I think we almost felt sorry for them."

. . . In summary, for students with cognitive disabilities, expectancy effects can be viewed as a form of **standards-based stereotyping.** This stereotyping can either produce direct . . . or indirect "hidden" stereotyping effects, both of which can exert negative influences on academic performance. The silent, subjective shifting (towards lower) evidentiary academic standards (for students with disabilities) represents a subtle, yet potentially potent force operating against the goal of "leaving no child behind."

Education Expectations: Caveats and Concerns

Teachers, like all humans, develop personal beliefs, opinions, and stereotypes. During most teacher preparation programs, educators are taught to become aware of potential expectancy effects and how to control their overt day-to-day teaching behavior to be more equitable, and to refrain from dispensing differential praise and criticism.

Given the popularity of the expectancy effects and self-fulfilling prophesies in the educational and psychological research and popular press, one could be led to believe that these negative influences are pandemic in school classrooms. This is not the case. Although some researchers have concluded that differential treatment of students is widespread, most researchers have concluded that the majority of educators (particularly experienced teachers and teachers who are very familiar with their students) form expectations based on the initial available information and "tweak" or adjust their expectations and instruction based on changes in student performance.

It is inappropriate to infer that the majority of educators are biased simply because they may hold differential expectations for some students. Often, differential treatment of students represents the appropriate implementation of individualized adaptive instruction responsive to the individual differences in a classroom. . . .

It is important to note that educators who may hold inappropriately low expectations for some students "are rarely acting out of malice; indeed, they are often not even aware that their low expectations have developed based on specious reasoning."

Nevertheless, the literature raises numerous issues that are directly relevant to today's educational context for students with disabilities in which both IDEA and NCLB are requiring improved performance. Particularly for those students with cognitive disabilities, the information on expectancy effects should cause us much concern. Is it possible that expectancy effects have been holding students back in the past? Are we under the influence of silently shifting standards—especially for students with cognitive disabilities? These and other questions are ones that states, districts, schools, administrators, and teachers need to ask themselves and others—as our nation strives to improve the performance of all of its students, including . . . those with cognitive disabilities.

James M. Kauffman  **NO**

Education Deform: Bright People Sometimes Say Stupid Things about Education

Test Bashing is Part of the "Progressive" Rhetoric that Thwarts Progress

Standardized testing has become the Great Satan of education in the minds of some, a "monster" that must be put out of schools. For example, Alfie Kohn condemns standardized testing—not just certain tests or the misuse of tests, but standardized tests as tools. . . . His suggestions for fighting standardized tests include not only civil disobedience by educators but printing bumper stickers with slogans such as "Standardized Testing Is Dumbing Down Our Schools." Like most slogans in education, this one, too, in my opinion, is vapid. Standardized testing can, indeed, be stupid or be used stupidly, but I doubt very seriously that it is the ogre responsible for dumbing down our schools. And rejecting standardized tests can only deprive parents, teachers, school officials, and governing bodies of an important tool in monitoring students' performance. . . .

Now it is undoubtedly true that some standardized tests are poorly made or misused, as are many teacher-made tests and other forms of "alternative assessment" such as portfolios. In fact, *any* form of assessment of which I'm aware can be (and has been) crudely made and badly used. So, why the seething hostility toward "standardized" testing? The answer is not simple, but I think much of the outrage over standardized tests is prompted by fears of comparisons of various individuals and groups who take the tests. Furthermore, educational theory has become, to some, a matter of religious conviction in which evidence doesn't matter. Too many educators—and, as well, too many people who are not educators—embrace "progressive" theory that relies on pet phrases and terminology for its defense of educational "quality" that tests are said not to be able to measure. These "reformers," who actually hold educational theories originated nearly a century ago, call for "real learning" that standardized tests are assumed not to be able to assess. . . .

Kohn and others who take a position against standardized tests also often raise the specter of uniformity across schools and states, which they see

From EDUCATION DEFORM: BRIGHT PEOPLE SOMETIMES SAY STUPID THINGS ABOUT EDUCA-TION, 2002, pp. 184–192, 247–252, 254–260. Copyright © 2002 by Rowman & Littlefield. Reprinted by permission. References omitted.

as being overly rigid. Even such politically conservative opinion writers as George F. Will suggest that America probably should not have a standard examination for high school graduation or a national curriculum. Perhaps it is inevitable that people of nearly all political persuasions will figure out some day that math and reading and much of what we need to know about science and geography and the United States government is not really different in different places. People might figure out that uniformity of expectations and curricula and testing might actually be beneficial in a society in which children move often to different localities or states. But it may take decades for people to arrive at these conclusions.

All the more reason, in my opinion, that standardized testing has a valuable role to play in measuring students' progress. . . . [One] argument against standardized testing is that comparisons of schools and states—perhaps of individuals as well—are insidious. No one is to be "left behind." . . . [Any] measure of progress—but most obviously a standardized measure—produces a distribution that by nature finds some to have performed better than others; for any measure that is not simply "yes/no" or "pass/fail" or in some other way a truncated range, there is a bottom fourth (first quartile) as well as a top fourth (or any other percentage of the sample one wishes to examine). So alternative assessment procedures that obscure if not obviate comparisons seem, to some, a godsend. Such alternative measures can help maintain the fiction that all students are excellent or give the misimpression that nobody is actually behind. The "progressive" idea seems to be that an "authentic" assessment will show that everyone and everything is cool—nobody can fail.

For some purposes there is no good substitute for the test that is standardized and can be failed—normed on a large sample of test takers by which we want to judge the achievement of individuals and groups. It is easier to shoot the messenger that brings unwelcome tidings than to confront the differences among individuals and groups that tests may reveal. . . . And it is easy to overlook the advantages of standardized tests while describing the tests themselves as monsters to be driven from our schools.

Some scholars have pointed out that the current popularity of standardized testing is really based on public concern about standards or accountability. The standards of performance that a state or school adopts are nearly always linked to a standardized test, and for this reason some writers refer to "test-linked standards." We do, I think, want to know how a student's performance compares to others' and to be able to compare average student performances across schools and states. It is only through such comparisons that we can address some problems, including the problem of how well we're doing and the problem of equity. Nevertheless, some people seem to be in favor of accountability—but without knowing how students are doing on any standardized test. To them, standardized tests seem to be a way of holding people responsible for teaching a standard curriculum, which they find anathema.

Mary Anne Raywid has voiced a familiar complaint: "One problem with the vast majority of tests, of course, is that they are curriculum-based." Well, it seems to me that we do want curriculum and testing to be aligned. That is, we want to teach what students are going to be tested on and to test what we teach. In fact, curriculum-based assessment is what some of us are after. It makes no sense to test students on things they haven't been taught, and it makes good sense to base assessment on the curriculum. The curriculum could determine what is tested; the tests could determine what is taught. But, either way, it only makes sense for the two to be in sync. In fact, one is not likely to be developed without the other: Testing and curriculum *should* influence each other. To me, it makes little difference which comes first, as long as what is taught is really important stuff for students to learn. I suppose the question actually becomes what we think is important for students to know. Another way of putting it is to ask whether we think there is a common core of knowledge that most students should learn. I think there is this common content that most students should be expected to master, and I see no reason not to check up on how well we're doing it—to test it with a standardized instrument.

Others, particularly E. D.Hirsch, Jr., have described eloquently how having a core body of knowledge or core curriculum increases equity among groups of students differing in ethnicity or social privilege—or, at least, opportunities for achieving such equity. Standardized tests were invented, at least in part, to be fairer to students without social privileges—to focus on a student's performance rather than his or her genetic or social heritage that brought privilege in spite of what a student could do. Standardized tests *can* be used to increase equity if they measure important knowledge and if all schools and individuals are provided the resources needed to allow them to attain a reasonable standard. Standardized tests *can* be used to improve the clarity of schools' objectives and focus on instruction. Standardized tests *can* be used to allocate resources more efficiently, and they *can* be used as a common metric—a common, readily understood language of measurement—for communicating educational outcomes.

Please notice that I have *not* suggested that *all* students should learn exactly the same thing or be taught exactly the same way. I suggested that *most* students would benefit from a standard, core curriculum. . . . Some students are not going to be successful in the regular, general curriculum that may be right for the majority of students. I think it's essential that we provide alternatives for those students who cannot reasonably be expected to learn the core curriculum and be tested on it. . . . But, of course, here's the problem: Who should decide, and on what basis, that an alternative to the core curriculum is a better choice for a given student? Here are some givens, in my opinion: First, the decision should not be based on the student's ethnicity, gender, or social privilege. Second, the decision should be based on the student's estimated ability to learn the core curriculum. Third, there are no perfect decision makers. Any decision making scheme we can devise will produce some false positives (students thought to be able to learn the core curriculum but who cannot) and false negatives (students who are thought to be unable to learn the core curriculum but who can). The goals should be to make as few errors of judgment as possible in either direction and to correct errors as soon as they can be detected by changing the student's curriculum. But don't miss this given: Assuming that any core curriculum should be studied and mastered by *all* students simply guarantees a very large number of false positives. For a substantial number of kids and a significant percentage of the student population, it's not in the cards. The majority of the students I'm referring to have disabilities of one kind or another, although some of those with disabilities can and should learn the standard—general, core—curriculum.

Standardized tests, like every other human invention and some natural phenomena, will be abused. That is a given. We are well advised to recognize abuses without proscribing the use of the instruments that are abused, to use instruments responsibly. Obscuring or hiding differences on good standardized measures merely locks in place the social inequities that anti-testing forces say they oppose. We cannot address inequities that we will not admit are real and important. . . . [I] think we have yet to invent a better or more reliable way than standardized testing of finding out fairly what someone knows. The fact that some test questions are bad and that some people use scores unwisely should not be used as an excuse for bashing the very notion of standardized testing.

Every educational policy has a downside as far as I know, standardized testing and test-linked standards included. It is possible to narrow a curriculum unreasonably in efforts to prepare students for tests, and this is true for standardized tests or any other kind of assessment. It is possible to define good teaching simply as that which maximizes test performance—standardized tests or any other type of assessment. It is possible to use standardized test performance to devalue those who do not score well on them, but the same is true for any type of assessment—kids can be devalued because their performance is judged to be inferior, not up to expectations, not acceptable. And standardized tests or any other type of assessment can preclude certain opportunities for students who fail to meet expectations. Any kind of assessment of performance—standardized test or any alternative—can create anxiety in the person being assessed. Alternatives to standardized tests, such as "portfolio assessment" in which a student's work is judged in some way, have their downsides, too. They are cumbersome, extremely time-consuming, and present problems of reliability, validity, and comparisons across individuals and groups.

If our schools are being "dumbed down," I doubt that it's because of standardized tests. Much more likely, I think, is that the dumbing down is a result of fumbled thinking about issues in education, including mindless rhetoric that misleads people's thinking about the tools we use to assess educational progress. And make no mistake about this, either: *Standardized testing cannot take the place of the type of frequent teacher monitoring or assessment that is an essential part of good teaching.* Imagining that standardized testing provides sufficient early warning for failing students is similar to imagining that reporting tornado damage provides sufficient early warning of severe weather. Standardized tests can assess instructional success or failure long after the fact, and for that they're important, but they can't be relied upon to guide the instruction of individuals. . . .

Some who write about education policy see the advantages of good standardized testing but suggest "criterion-referenced" tests that set "benchmarks" of performance. Sometimes, these individuals even suggest that an advantage of such criterion-referencing is that the test does not rely on norms, that students' performance is simply compared to the criterion, not to other students' performance. This is quite a misleading interpretation of "criterion" or "benchmark." A reasonable person would, I think, have to ask something like this: How'd we come up with this criterion or benchmark?

A criterion or benchmark can be pulled out of the air or be based simply on someone's opinion of what a student should know at a particular age. But "pull-them-out-of-the-air" criteria are ultimately seen as arrogant and unworkable. Eventually, people come to their senses and inquire about what most students know at a given age. The criterion is then set based on a comparison to what most students can do. Otherwise, it is unreasonably high or unreasonably low.

People I think should know better than to refer to criterion-referenced tests as not comparative or non-normative. They're right in only a very restricted way—a student is judged to perform acceptably or not based only on comparison to the criterion or benchmark of performance. However, a reasonable person has to ask where the criterion comes from, and this inevitably takes us back to a normative sample or normative comparison. Witness the difficulties various states or school districts have in deciding on a "cut point" or benchmark on a standards of learning test. If the criterion is something that too few students can reach, then it's abandoned as unreasonable (and for good reason). If the criterion is something just about every student reaches without difficulty, then it's abandoned as too low (and with good reason). A criterion-referenced test does force the issue of manufacturing failure (just how much is enough, desirable, or too much?). But here's something I think you can go to the bank on: If a criterion is set that results in what is deemed a reasonable rate of failure and a few years down the road we find that nearly every child is passing it, we will see efforts to raise the bar because the benchmark is now judged too low.

Criterion-referencing might be a good idea. That is, it might be a good idea to set a standard that we think merits promotion to the next grade or graduation or the need for remediation. But nobody should be fooled into thinking that the criterion isn't based on some comparison to a normative group. And nobody should be fooled into thinking that every last student will reach whatever criterion is set. Some students will fail to reach the benchmark unless it is set at zero, and some will find reaching the benchmark ridiculously easy. That's one of the reasons we need special education. . . .

✤

Failure of Some Students with Disabilities to Reach a Standard is Predictable

Why is the failure of some exceptional students to profit from standard educational programs utterly predictable? The answer seems obvious to me. It is because they differ significantly from the modal or typical student in instructionally relevant ways. Standard programs are designed for modal (most frequently occurring) students, not those at the extremes of a distribution. These standard educational programs simply cannot, and can't be expected to, accommodate extreme differences in instructionally relevant characteristics, like abilities to read, perceive, organize, store, retrieve, and apply information to the solution of particular problems. Some students with disabilities are going to fail to meet standard educational goals regardless of the instructional strategies a teacher uses.

Some students with disabilities can meet state testing standards, but not with the standard instructional program or in the standard amount of time or by the typical chronological age. And some students who are gifted will be bored out of their minds by having to repeat and by being expected to *appear* to learn things they learned long ago.

Pixie Holbrook described the futility and cruelty of requiring all students with disabilities to take state-mandated examinations that are appropriate for the majority of students. She describes the agony for herself and one of her pupils, Sarah, a fourth-grader with a learning disability. Sarah is a good and diligent student, but because of her learning disability she hasn't the skills required for the test.

> She knows she doesn't know. And she knows that I know she doesn't know. This is so very humiliating.
>
> Her eyes are wet now, but she's silent and stoic. I check in, and she reassures me she's fine. She appears to be on the verge of weeping, but she will not be deterred. I cannot help her in any way; I can only sit nearby and return a false smile. I can offer a break, nothing more. Later, I calculated the reading level of this selection. Sarah reads like a second-grader, and the poem is at the high end of the fifth-grade scale. Her eyes are not just scanning the paragraphs. I know she has stopped reading and is just glancing and gazing. It's meaningless, and it hurts. Yet she attempts to answer every question.
>
> It is now 2 ½ hours, and my anger is growing. This is immoral and has become intolerable. And it's only the first day.

. . . Teachers and school administrators have, it seems to me, a moral obligation to recognize the fact that many special education students should not be required to take state competency exams.

Moreover, teachers have to be allowed, even encouraged, to recognize the limits of their instructional competence. Teachers should decline to teach students for whom their training is inadequate and decline to teach a curriculum that isn't right for their students. . . .

. . . [For] the life of me I can't figure out how someone . . . can . . . argue that teachers in elementary and secondary schools should just try to teach all students, regardless of students' characteristics. And, so some argue, if a teacher has a student that he or she can't seem to teach and manage or one who seriously interferes with teaching the rest of the class, then that teacher should just suck it up and learn to deal with it, never work to get the student taught in a special class or school. Maybe that teacher could ask for help, so the full-inclusion or merge-general-and-special-education argument goes, but not give up responsibility for the student and turn education of that student over to someone else.

I try to make this add up with any other profession's attitudes toward its clients, and I can't. What would we think of a dentist who said, "Well, no, I don't know what to do here, but I'm not going to refer you to someone else, because I am responsible for treating *all* of my patients? So I'll ask another dentist what to do and then do my best to follow the advice I get." Would we not want to wring the neck, if not sue, a mechanic or plumber or builder or lawyer who was in over his or her head—didn't have the skills demanded of the case and knew it—yet wouldn't give the job over to someone with the necessary skills?

Knowing the limits of one's knowledge and skill and being given the responsibility for refusing clients whose problems don't match one's training and skills are rather basic professional and moral responsibilities, it seems to me. Those who do not want teachers to decline to teach a child for whom they are not prepared believe one of two erroneous things, I think: (a) teachers shouldn't be professionals in any true sense or (b) students don't actually differ much in what's required to teach them. Teaching is teaching, they seem to believe, and if you can teach one student you can teach any student. I find that kind of denial maddening.

Students Who Fail at Certain Things Aren't Total Failures

Some people fail at few things, others at many. We have a tendency to write people off as failures if they fail at anything we think is important, regardless of the values or abilities of the person whose performance we judge to be failing. Much as we are too quick to judge someone who makes a vapid statement a stupid person, we overgeneralize. Surely, there are people whom failure seems to dog, and I believe there are people who could be described as *being* failures or as having failed generally at life. But those cases are, I think, rare. And, although some people may act like test scores are everything, we know that they're not—and we need to act like they're not.

Some people fail at something because of a disability, and their disability is then used against them in an unfair manner. True, we can't eliminate failure, and we can't and shouldn't "protect" people from confronting their own and other people's failures. But keeping failure at a particular thing or things in perspective is also important. Dan Hallahan and I, as well as many of our colleagues in special education, have noted that although people with disabilities can't do certain things (and, thus, could be said to fail in some respect) it is essential that we focus on what they *can* do, which for most people with disabilities is most of the things we consider normal or expected.

Failure at something doesn't make a person bad, nor does success make them a good person. Sometimes I think people misunderstand this and suppose that those who are gifted are better people and those who are disabled are not as good as others. Achievement or success at something doesn't make someone a better person, but it does enhance a person's opportunities. The more you know and are able to do, the more opportunities you have to learn and succeed. We do want to give students the greatest opportunity we can, and that means teaching them things that will open up new opportunities. I tried to make this clear in a previously published essay.

> Clearly, we do not want a human's worth to be measured simply by what he or she can do. That criterion would, for example, result in very little worth being attached to infants and young children. Yet, what someone can do is not a trivial matter. A just and humane society does not value people *for* what they can do, but it does unequivocally value peoples' ability to do certain things. If we do not value what people can do, then we have no reason to teach anyone anything. We value what people can do because of what accomplishment does for them, the additional opportunities it brings them—not because it makes them better people but because it makes them people who are better off.

Certainly, assuming that the test score is all that matters is perverse. It's the kind of perversion and stupidity we would be much better off without. We want kids to be happy and go to school excited about learning. Those objectives aren't incompatible with test scores unless we act as if, and teach kids that, test scores are all that matter. Still, avoiding test scores is just a way of evading reality.

One more thing here: It's important to note that failure once doesn't mean failure always. Most people can and do learn lots of things. Sometimes they have to try again, sometimes many times, before they learn a particular thing. Sometimes things just start to "click," and away they go. Sometimes people just seem to hit a "wall" and don't progress beyond it. Anyone who's practiced a musical instrument or sport knows the phenomenon most people call a learning "plateau," a point at which progress seems to stop. But persistence usually pays off, in that progress resumes with repeated practice—sometimes people experience a "breakthrough" in their progress, but not unless they're persistent. Yes, people differ in aptitudes for particular things and in skill in picking them up, but we have to be really careful not to assume that because a person is progressing only slowly (or rapidly) they'll always continue at that rate. . . .

⚜

Exceptional Students Need Options for Curriculum, Instruction, and Placement

Because public education must serve all children's educational needs, the largest part of general education must be designed for the modal (most frequently occurring) characteristics of students and teachers. Public education is by definition a service designed for the masses. Any product or service intended for the public at large has to be designed around the typical characteristics of consumers. Economies of scale alone require this. The size, shape, and abilities of the typical citizen fall within a fairly narrow band of variability around the mean, and simple economics demand that things be designed with this in mind.

Surely, what some call "universal design" is important, and good design will accommodate a large range of individual characteristics. But, like "all," "universal" has its limits, often unspoken, sometimes not even recognized. If "universal" design can accommodate a larger segment of the population, that is all well and good. But remember that it is neither economically feasible nor necessary to eliminate all stair steps because some people can't use them or to design and equip every car so that a person with quadriplegia can drive it. Neither is it feasible or desirable to design a reading program for most children that will be appropriate for students with severe mental retardation.

Education has to be designed for what the average teacher and the average student can be expected to do, not what the exceptionally able or those with disabilities can accomplish. I'm not suggesting that the performance of the average teacher or student can't be improved, simply that expectations in the general education program can't outstrip what the average teacher can do with appropriate training or what the typical student can do with good instruction.

Because public education must address all children's educational needs, it must include explicit structures ensuring the accommodation of exceptional students. By definition, exceptional students require an extraordinary response from educators—something different from the ordinary, even if the ordinary is good. The standard educational program can serve most students very well, but it can't serve exceptional students without additional, explicit components—special structures that go beyond the normal or routine in such matters as goals, lines of authority, roles and responsibilities of personnel, budgets and purchases, allocation of time and space, modification of curriculum, evaluation of performance, and assignment of students to classes. Failure to create these explicit structures to accommodate students at the extremes of the performance distribution inevitably results in their neglect. They are forgotten. They don't just fail a little. They fail a lot, and their noses are rubbed in their failures.

The requirement of alternative educational goals and programs must be explicit for exceptional students. It's as simple as this, I think: When the interests of students with disabilities or those who are gifted are not explicitly mandated, they get lost in the shuffle. The implicit or explicit assumption that standard educational goals and programs will accommodate the needs of exceptional students is not just logically untenable. It also places the onus of proof that the program is inappropriate wholly on the student when questions arise about his or her performance. However, if there is an explicit requirement of alternative goals and programs for exceptional students, then the burden of proof is at least partly on the school to show that those alternatives are available to students for whom the typical program is unsatisfactory and in which an exceptional student cannot be expected to make satisfactory progress.

Alternative goals and programs must be expressed as alternative curricula and educational methods for exceptional students. It is not enough to have a separate place—a special class or school. Some exceptional learners need to learn something other than the standard curriculum, not just learn the standard curriculum in a different way or in a different place. And they may need instructional or behavior management procedures that are not needed by most students.

People not familiar with instruction may miss the distinctions of method that are important for exceptional students. For example, students with disabilities may require more trials, more examples, a different pace, smaller steps in a sequence, more reinforcement (praise, encouragement, or other rewarding consequences, more careful monitoring, more structure (e.g., higher predictability, more explicit instructions, more immediate consequences) than is desirable for typical students. There may be other distinctions that I have not listed here, but at least all of these are involved In more precise teaching. In short, the instruction of students with disabilities may need to be considerably more precise than the instruction that produces good results for typical students.

In many types of performance, it is the precision with which something is done that makes the difference, not the basic operation. This is true in driving, flying, playing music, shooting guns, and so on. Just consider the differences in level of performance of the same basic operations in the following comparisons: the typical drive to work versus driving in a high-speed race; flying from city *A* to city *B* versus flying with a stunt team; playing in a municipal band versus playing in one of the world's virtuoso combos; shooting targets in the backyard versus sharp-shooting for a SWAT team. Highly expert, precision performance requires extensive training. You don't give all soldiers the competence of the Special Forces by giving them a beret. You don't make every teacher a special educator by telling them good teaching of exceptional children is just good teaching because, after all, kids are more alike than they are different and good teachers use the same basic operations regardless who their students are.

POSTSCRIPT

Should Students with Cognitive Disabilities Be Expected to Demonstrate Academic Proficiency?

People sometimes live up to our expectations for them—or down to those same expectations. The power of positive thinking motivates many to unimagined levels of success. McGrew and Evans remind us not to let IQ scores limit the opportunities offered to children with cognitive disabilities.

Testifying at an NCLB hearing, Martha Thurlow (2004), a noted scholar of including students in large-scale testing, emphasized that the existence of a disability should not automatically mean students cannot reach high standards. Expectations must be raised.

Listen to the voices of teachers who have used alternate assessments to engage their students in academic standards. "My attitude [about her abilities] was denying her the opportunity to succeed." "Now I look at the possibilities instead of the limitations." "He is doing things I didn't realize he could do." These optimistic comments represent the findings of Moore-Lamminen and Olsen (Alliance for Systems Change, n.d.), who documented the positive experiences of teachers who have stretched their students to excel.

James Kauffman would likely be pleased that these teachers and their students had found success. Simultaneously, he would doubt that this increased academic focus will bring all students to proficiency.

A New Jersey high school teacher (Karp, *Rethinking Schools Online,* 2004) bemoans the fact that the proficiency hurdle masks significant student change. "On a test. . . where a passing score is 200, helping a bilingual, special education student from a low income household raise his/her test score from, say, a 50 to 199 counts for nothing. . . . Moving a student from 199 to 200 is success."

U.S. Secretary of Education Margaret Spellings appears to have acknowledged that holding all students to one standard may not be the best way to reflect a school's progress. Holding firm to the "bright-line principles" that all students must participate and reach proficiency targets, she has announced pilots for growth models of accountability.

These pilots, approved through a peer-reviewed process, will track the achievement of individual children from year to year. Schools receive credit for the progress of each child, instead of the number of students who reach targets. Such a model, first approved in Tennessee and North Carolina, would address Karp's concerns and also document the incremental growth of students with disabilities.

Growth models are receiving initial approval. Some are pleased that schools will be held accountable for steady progress of each student (Hershberg,

312

Phi Delta Kappan, 2005). The Council for Exceptional Children (CEC) (http://www.cec.sped.org), an international professional association, has long advocated a longitudinal growth model to document and validate the progress of students who may not reach grade-level standards.

Even with growth models, can all students reach proficiency? The *Education Week* study (Olson, 2004), cited by McGrew and Evans, noted discrepant opinions among the participating teachers. The majority of special education teachers surveyed were more optimistic about their students' content progress than were general education teachers. In addition, the special education teachers felt more prepared to tackle the content challenge than the general education teachers felt about teaching students with disabilities. Which group is optimistic? Which is realistic? How will these different opinions affect student performance?

Do expectations hold students back, or do they set reasonable, reachable targets that make a productive adulthood more likely? Can higher academic standards for schools raise our expectations for students with cognitive disabilities? Will growth models accurately reflect individual performance or reinforce lower expectations?

Internet References . . .

Autism Society of America

The mission of the Autism Society of America is to promote lifelong access and opportunity for all individuals within the autism spectrum, and their families, to be fully participating, included members of their community. Education, advocacy at state and federal levels, active public awareness and the promotion of research form the cornerstones of ASA's efforts. This Web site contains a wide range of information regarding autism, treatments and supports for families.

http://www.autism-society.org

Children and Adults with Attention-Deficit/Hyperactivity Disorder

Children and Adults with Attention-Deficit/Hyperactivity Disorder (CHADD), founded in 1987 by families seeking information about this disorder, is now a national organization linked to a variety of activities. The CHADD Web site contains extensive information on ADHD and ADD and is helpful to anyone who wants to learn more about these conditions.

http://www.chadd.org

Council for Exceptional Children (CEC)

The CEC is the largest international professional organization addressing issues surrounding education of students with disabilities, as well as those who are gifted and talented. CEC's site introduces you to current events in the field, recent legislative developments, and an array of specialized divisions focused on particular aspects of special education.

http://www.cec.sped.org

LD OnLine

A service of the Learning Project at WETA (FM) in Washington, D.C., LD OnLine is supported by numerous foundations. Oriented toward parents and children, this Web site provides a range of information, personal stories, homeschooling ideas, and resources for children, parents, and teachers who are interested in learning disabilities.

http://www.ldonline.org

National Reading Panel (NRP)

This NRP Web site leads readers to the full NRP reports, along with additional videos and information.

http://www.nationalreadingpanel.org

PART 3

Issues About Disabilities

*E*arlier sections of this book focused on global issues regarding the education of children with disabilities. Apart from these issues of law, policy, and practice, exist controversial issues about the reality of particular disabilities and the efficacy of unique methodologies. The fervent desire of parents and educators to help children nurtures the development of approaches that promise success. The challenge of evaluating new ways of thinking will be with us so long as there are children who need extra support in order to learn.

- Can Brain Scans Unravel the Mystery of Learning Disabilities?

- Is Attention Deficit (Hyperactivity) Disorder Overdiagnosed?

- Are There Scientifically Effective Treatments for Autism?

- Should One-on-One Nursing Care Be Part of Special Education?

ISSUE 16

Can Brain Scans Unravel the Mystery of Learning Disabilities?

YES: Sally E. Shaywitz and Bennett A. Shaywitz, from "Reading Disability and the Brain," *Educational Leadership* (March 2004)

NO: Gerald Coles, from "Danger in the Classroom: 'Brain Glitch' Research and Learning to Read," *Phi Delta Kappan* (January 2004)

ISSUE SUMMARY

YES: Sally and Bennett Shaywitz, codirectors of the National Institute of Child Health and Human Development—Yale Center for the Study of Learning and Attention, and Yale University professors, summarize their recent research findings suggesting that advances in medicine, together with reading research, can virtually eliminate reading disabilities.

NO: Gerald Coles, an educational psychologist and former member of the Robert Wood Johnson Medical School, University of Medicine and Dentistry of New Jersey, contests the claim that neurological procedures can identify reading disabilities and identify the methods to help children read.

Specific learning disability:

> A disorder in one or more of the basic psychological processes involved in understanding or in using language, spoken or written, that may manifest itself in an imperfect ability to listen, think, speak, read, write, spell, or to do mathematical calculations, including conditions such as perceptual disabilities, brain injury, minimal brain dysfunction, dyslexia, and developmental aphasia. This does not include learning problems that are primarily the result of visual, hearing or motor disabilities, of mental retardation, of emotional disturbance, or of environmental, cultural, or economic disadvantage. (IDEA 2004)

Have you ever met a student who seems to be very capable in many ways—can communicate, compute, and reason well—but who struggles to read? Or who is proficient in all academic areas except for the ability to compose a coherent narrative? The puzzle is that the student seems so competent—except in one specific area. Motivation, family support, and good teaching have all been present, but performance in this one area persistently lags behind success in others.

Curiosity and frustration about this student have been the source of discussion for the last century. In 1963, Samuel Kirk formalized thinking into a condition he termed "learning disabilities." Education has never been the same since.

Since the advent of special education law, educators, parents, and attorneys have argued over the shape and meaning of specific learning disabilities, a set of conditions that seem to be defined mostly by what they are not. The federal definition cited above describes a disability that is most apparent while learning academic subjects and occurs in a child who appears to have the background and capability to learn easily. For much of the twentieth century, researchers sought to identify specific neurological differences hypothesized to be the basis for learning disabilities.

More than half the children receiving special education services have been identified as having a specific learning disability. Most frequently, reading is identified as the primary area of difficulty.

No Child Left Behind (NCLB) sets a goal of having all children learn to read by the end of third grade, emphasizing the use of "effective, research-based reading programs." How do children with learning disabilities fit into this goal?

Sally E. Shaywitz and Bennett A. Shaywitz are prolific researchers in the area of learning. They, along with Reid Lyon, have been instrumental in shaping the reading foundation of NCLB. Shaywitz and Shaywitz believe that learning disabilities exist. In their research, results of functional magnetic resonance imaging (fMRI) identified "glitches" in the brains of struggling readers. They cite evidence that the right type of instruction can eliminate these glitches.

Gerald Coles, a pioneer researcher in the area of learning disabilities, feels that fMRI data do not provide a clear link between brain functioning and reading. He is concerned that the scientific glitz of new technology leads people to think that a glitch exists. By focusing only on brain activity, he fears that critical information about how and why children struggle to learn may be overlooked.

As you read the articles, decide whether or not you think that advances in medical technology have found the long-sought-for neurological cause of learning disabilities.

YES

Sally E. Shaywitz and
Bennett A. Shaywitz

Reading Disability and the Brain

The past decade has witnessed extraordinary progress in our understanding of the nature of reading and reading difficulties. Never before have rigorous science (including neuroscience) and classroom instruction in reading been so closely linked. For the first time, educators can turn to well-designed, scientific studies to determine the most effective ways to teach reading to beginning readers, including those with reading disability (National Reading Panel, 2000).

What does the evidence tell us? Several lines of investigation have found that reading originates in and relies on the brain systems used for spoken language. In addition, accumulating evidence sheds light on the nature of reading disability, including its definition, prevalence, longitudinal course, and probable causes. Although the work is relatively new, we have already made great progress in identifying the neural systems used for reading, identifying a disruption in these systems in struggling readers, and understanding the neural mechanisms associated with the development of fluent reading.

Reading and Spoken Language

Spoken language is instinctive—built into our genes and hardwired in our brains. Learning to read requires us to take advantage of what nature has provided: a biological module for language.

For the object of the reader's attention (print) to gain entry into the language module, a truly extraordinary transformation must occur. The reader must convert the print on the page into a linguistic code: the phonetic code, the only code recognized and accepted by the language system. Unless the reader-to-be can convert the printed characters on the page into the phonetic code, these letters remain just a bunch of lines and circles, totally devoid of meaning. The written symbols have no inherent meaning of their own but stand, rather, as surrogates for the sounds of speech.

To break the code, the first step beginning readers must take involves spoken language. Readers must develop *phonemic awareness*. They must discover that the words they hear come apart into smaller pieces of sound.

On the basis of highly reliable scientific evidence, investigators in the field have now reached a strong consensus: Reading reflects language, and reading disability reflects a deficit within the language system. Results from large and

Reading Disability and the Brain, an article based upon the book OVERCOMING DYSLEXIA, by Sally E. Shaywitz (NY: Knopf, 2003). Grateful acknowledgement is made to Sally Shaywitz c/o Writers' Representatives LLC. (to whom all rights inquires should be directed) for permission to reprint "Dyslexia and the Brain."

well-studied populations with reading disability confirm that in young school-age children and in adolescents, a weakness in accessing the sounds of spoken language represents the most robust and specific correlate of reading disability. Such findings form the foundation for the most successful, evidence-based interventions designed to improve reading (National Reading Panel, 2000).

Understanding Reading Disability

Reading disability, or *developmental dyslexia*, is characterized by an unexpected difficulty in reading in children and adults who otherwise possess the intelligence, motivation, and education necessary for developing accurate and fluent reading. Dyslexia is the most common and most carefully studied of the learning disabilities, affecting 80 percent of all individuals identified as learning disabled and an estimated 5–17 percent of all children and adults in the United States.

Incidence and Distribution of Dyslexia

Recent epidemiological data indicate that like hypertension and obesity, reading ability occurs along a continuum. Reading disability falls on the left side of the bell-shaped curve representing the normal distribution of reading ability.

Dyslexia runs in families: One-fourth to one-half of all children who have a parent with dyslexia also have the disorder, and if dyslexia affects one child in the family, it is likely to affect half of his or her siblings. Recent studies have identified a number of genes involved in dyslexia.

Good evidence, based on surveys of randomly selected populations of children, now indicates that dyslexia affects boys and girls equally. Apparently, the long-held belief that only boys suffer from dyslexia reflected bias in school-identified samples: The more disruptive behavior of boys results in their being referred for evaluation more often, whereas girls who struggle to read are more likely to sit quietly in their seats and thus be overlooked.

Longitudinal studies indicate that dyslexia is a persistent, chronic condition rather than a transient "developmental lag." Children do not outgrow reading difficulties. The evidence-based interventions now available, however, can result in improved reading in virtually all children.

Neurobiological Origins of Dyslexia

For more than a century, physicians and scientists have suspected that dyslexia has neurobiological origins. Until recently, however, they had no way to examine the brain systems that we use while reading. Within the last decade, the dream of scientists, educators, and struggling readers has come true: New advances in technology enable us to view the working brain as it attempts to read.

Perhaps the most convincing evidence for a neurobiological basis of dyslexia comes from the rapidly accumulating and converging data from functional brain imaging investigations. The process of functional brain imaging is quite simple. When we ask an individual to perform a discrete cognitive task, that task places processing demands on specific neural systems in the brain. Through such techniques as functional magnetic resonance imaging (fMRI), we can measure the changes that take place in neural activity in particular brain regions as the brain meets those demands. Because fMRI uses no ionizing radiation and requires no injections, it is noninvasive and safe. We can use it to examine children or adults on multiple occasions.

Using functional brain imaging, scientists around the world have discovered not only the brain basis of reading but also a glitch in the neural circuitry for reading in children and adults who struggle to read. Our studies and those of other investigators have identified three regions involved in reading, all located on the left side of the brain. In the front of the brain, Broca's area (technically the inferior frontal gyrus) is involved in articulation and word analysis. Two areas located in the back of the brain are involved in word analysis (the parieto-temporal region) and in fluent reading (the occipito-temporal region, also referred to as the word form area).

Studies of dyslexic readers document an underactivation of the two systems in the back of the brain together with an overactivation of Broca's area in the front of the brain. The struggling readers appear to be turning to the frontal region, which is responsible for articulating spoken words, to compensate for the fault in the systems in the back of the brain.

Researchers have observed this neurobiological signature of dyslexic readers across cultures and across different languages. The observation of this same pattern in both children and adults supports the view that reading difficulties, including the neural disruption, do not go away with maturity. To prevent failure for students with reading disability, we must identify the disability early and provide effective reading programs to address the students' needs.

The Importance of Fluency

In addition to identifying the neural systems used for reading, research has now revealed which systems the brain uses in two important phases in the acquisition of literacy.

Beginning reading—breaking the code by slowly, analytically sounding out words—calls on areas in the front of the brain (Broca's area) and in the back of the brain (the parieto-temporal region).

But an equally important phase in reading is fluency—rapid, automatic reading that does not require attention or effort. A fluent reader looks at a printed word and instantly knows all the important information about that word. Fluent reading develops as the reader builds brain connections that eventually represent an exact replica of the word—a replica that has integrated the word's pronunciation, spelling, and meaning.

Fluency occurs step-by-step. After systematically learning letters and their sounds, children go on to apply this knowledge to sound out words slowly and analytically. For example, for the word "back," a child may initially represent the word by its initial and final consonants: "b–k." As the child progresses, he begins to fill in the interior vowels, first making some errors—reading "back" as "bock" or "beak," for example—and eventually sounding out the word correctly. Part of the process of becoming a skilled reader is forming successively more detailed and complete representations of familiar words.

After the child has read the word "back" correctly over and over again, his brain has built and reinforced an exact model of the word. He now reads that word fluently—accurately, rapidly, and effortlessly. Fluency pulls us into reading. A student who reads fluently reads for pleasure and for information; a student who is not fluent will probably avoid reading.

In a study involving 144 children, we identified the brain region that makes it possible for skilled readers to read automatically. We found that the more proficiently a child read, the more he or she activated the occipito-temporal region (or word form area) in the back of the brain. Other investigators have observed that this brain region responds to words that are presented rapidly. Once a word is represented in the word form area, the reader recognizes that word instantly and effortlessly. This word form system appears to predominate when a reader has become fluent. As a result of this finding, we now know that development of the word form area in the left side of the brain is a key component in becoming a skilled, fluent reader.

Helping Struggling Readers Become More Fluent

Our study of 144 children also revealed that struggling readers compensate as they get older, developing alternate reading systems in the front of the brain and in the *right* side of the brain—a functioning system, but, alas, not an automatic one. These readers do not develop the critical left-side word form region necessary for rapid, automatic reading. Instead, they call on the alternate secondary pathways. This strategy enables them to read, but much more slowly and with greater effort than their classmates.

This research evidence of a disruption in the normal reading pathways provides a neurobiological target for reading interventions. In a new study, we hypothesized that an evidence-based, phonologically mediated reading intervention would help dyslexic readers develop the fast-paced word form systems serving skilled reading, thus improving their reading accuracy and fluency. Under the supervision of Syracuse University professor Benita Blachman, we provided 2nd and 3rd grade struggling readers daily with 50 minutes of individual tutoring that was systematic and explicit, focusing on helping the students understand the *alphabetic principle*, or how letters and combinations of letters represent the sounds of speech.

Students received eight months (105 hours) of intervention during the school year in addition to their regular classroom reading instruction. The experimental intervention replaced any additional reading help that the students might have received in school. Certified teachers who had taken part in an intensive training program provided the tutoring.

Immediately after the yearlong intervention, students in the experiment made significant gains in reading fluency and demonstrated increased activation in left hemisphere regions, including the inferior frontal gyrus and the parieto-temporal region. One year after the experimental intervention ended, these students were reading accurately and fluently and were activating all three left-side brain regions used by good readers. A control group of struggling readers receiving school-based, primarily nonphonological reading instruction had not activated these reading systems.

These data demonstrate that an intensive, evidence-based reading intervention brings about significant and durable changes in brain organization so that struggling readers' brain activation patterns come to resemble those of typical readers. If we provide intervention at an early age, then we can improve reading fluency and facilitate the development of the neural systems that underlie skilled reading.

Evidence-Based Effective Reading Instruction

In addition to new neurological research on the nature of reading, educators can draw on a body of rigorous, well-designed, scientific studies to guide reading instruction. In 1998, the U.S. Congress mandated the National Reading Panel to develop rigorous scientific criteria for evaluating reading research, apply these criteria to existing reading research, identify the most effective teaching methods, and then make findings accessible for parents and teachers. As a member of the Panel, I can attest to its diligence. After two years of work, the Panel issued its report (2000).

The major findings of the report indicate that in order to read, all children must be taught alphabetics, comprising phonemic awareness and phonics; reading fluency; vocabulary; and strategies for reading comprehension. These elements must be taught systematically, comprehensively, and explicitly; it is inadequate to present the foundational skills of phonemic awareness and phonics incidentally, casually, or fragmentally. Children do not learn how letters represent sounds by osmosis; we must teach them this skill explicitly. Once a child has mastered these foundational skills, he or she must be taught how to read words fluently.

Good evidence now indicates that we can teach reading fluency by means of repeated oral reading with feedback and guidance. Using these methods, we can teach almost every child to read. It is crucial to align all components of a program with one another—for example, to provide so-called decodable booklets that give the student practice in the specific letter-sound linkages we are teaching. The use of decodable booklets enables the repeated practice necessary to build the automatic systems in the word form region that lead to fluent reading.

Neuroscience and Reading Research Agree

We are now in an era of evidence-based education. Objective scientific evidence—provided by brain imaging studies and by the National Reading Panel's rigorous scientific review of the literature—has replaced reliance on philosophy or opinion.

In considering a reading program, educators should ask several key questions:

- Is there scientific evidence that the program is effective?
- Was the program or its methodology reviewed by the National Reading Panel?

- In reading instruction, are phonemic awareness and phonics taught systematically and explicitly?
- How are students taught to approach an unfamiliar word? Do they feel empowered to try to analyze and sound out an unknown word first rather than guess the word from the pictures or context?
- Does the program also include plenty of opportunities for students to practice reading, develop fluency, build vocabulary, develop reading comprehension strategies, write, and listen to and discuss stories?

Children are only 7 or 8 years old once in their lifetime. We cannot risk teaching students with unproven programs. We now have the scientific knowledge to ensure that almost every child can become a successful reader. Awareness of the new scientific knowledge about reading should encourage educators to insist that reading programs used in their schools reflect what we know about the science of reading and about effective reading instruction.

Gerald Coles

 **NO**

Danger in the Classroom: 'Brain Glitch' Research and Learning to Read

Did you know that recent studies of the brain and reading support the reading instruction mandated in George W. Bush's No Child Left Behind (NCLB) legislation? And did you know that this research also supports the legislation he has proposed to dismantle Head Start's comprehensive approach to preschool education? And were you aware that, thanks to this brain research, we now know how children learn to read and which areas of the brain must first be stocked to promote skilled reading? Did you realize that we now have strong brain-based evidence that the best reading instruction is heavily prescriptive, skills-emphasis, building-blocks teaching that starts with small pieces of written language and proceeds to larger ones—and teachers are fortunate because these features are contained in reading programs like Open Court?

You didn't know all that? Good, because none of it is true, although you would never know that if you just listened to the President, the educators and assorted researchers who support his educational agenda, and the media who repeat their assertions.

Over 25 years ago, when I began appraising theories about faulty brain wiring in beginning readers, my criticism of the research then being conducted was limited to ersatz explanations of so-called brain dysfunctions in children called "learning disabled," "reading disabled," or "dyslexic." Contrary to the assertions made then, the research had never shown that the overwhelming number of these children did not have normal brains. Certainly a portion of poor readers had problems that were the result of exposure to such toxins as lead and cadmium, to food additives, and to other environmental influences. But, I argued, there was no evidence that they accounted for more than a small portion of the large numbers of children given these labels and shunted into special education programs.

At some point, thanks to increased, widespread criticism of these "brain-based" explanations, I had thought a change had started toward more informed, measured interpretations. However, my naive thinking has long been gone. Not only are explanations about "brain glitches," to use the term employed by reading researcher Sally Shaywitz, now being applied more forcefully to "dyslexics," but they have also been reworked to explain how all children learn to read, what single method of instruction must be used to teach them, and why the single method mandated in Bush's Reading First, part of the NCLB legislation, is a wise, scientifically based choice. Thus never have these "brain glitch" explanations been more pervasively intrusive for all beginning readers and their teachers in classrooms across the nation. . . .

A new best seller, *Overcoming Dyslexia*, by Sally Shaywitz, who has received considerable NICHD [National Institutes of Child Health and Human Development] funding for her research, claims to present "the advances in brain science" that inform what "at last we know," which are "the specific steps a child or adult must take to build and then reinforce the neural pathways deep within the brain for skilled reading." Shaywitz served on the panel whose findings, she proudly explains to readers, "are now part of the ground-breaking No Child Left Behind Legislation," . . .

In this article I will argue that, despite all the unbridled assertions about the wonder of it all, this new "brain glitch" research is theoretically, empirically, and conceptually deficient, as was the deficit-driven work that preceded it by decades. . . . More than ever, claims about the research constitute an ideological barrier to a sounder understanding of the connections between brain activity and learning to read. More than ever, this work is a danger in the classroom both because it applies unproven labels to an ever-larger number of children and because it promotes a single kind of instruction that, based on the actual empirical evidence mustered for it, contains no promise for leaving no beginning reader behind. To all of this, add the false and cruel expectations that these claims generate in parents.

To help illustrate my critique, I will use as an example a recent, highly publicized study on reading and brain activity whose co-authors include Reid Lyon, Sally Shaywitz, and several other researchers whose work argues for building-blocks teaching and has been used as evidence for Reading First instruction. (For convenience I call it the Shaywitz/Lyon study).

Is the Brain "Reading"?

Functional magnetic resonance imagery (fMRI) is a valuable diagnostic and investigative technology that can measure blood flow in the brain and thereby provide information about certain kinds of brain activity when someone is performing a task. However, like every technology used in research, its value and the information it produces are never better than the initial theory and concepts that steer its application. Perhaps the biggest misrepresentation in the "brain glitch" research is that the color scans produced by fMRI provide information about "reading." In fact, they provide no such thing, because the "reading" tasks under study are largely a person's performance on simple sound and sound/symbol (phonics) tasks with words and parts of words, rather than performance in reading as conventionally defined, that is, reading and comprehending sentences and paragraphs. (The same misrepresentation appears in claims about "reading" contained in the report of the National Reading Panel, the chief research document cited in the Reading First legislation.)

The puny definition of reading used in this research appears not to concern the investigators, though, because they design their studies on the assumption that these simple tasks involving words and parts of words embrace the core requirements for beginning readers: that is, mastery of phonological awareness (distinguishing and manipulating sounds in words) and sound/symbol relationships. As the Shaywitz/Lyon study explains, there is now "a strong consensus" (that is, a broad unanimity of professional opinion) that phonological awareness is the first building block within the sequence and that reading disability reflects a deficit in this "lower level component" of "the language system." Only after mastering this component can beginning readers effectively continue to master other reading skills.

That's the claim. The reality is that the so-called strong consensus does not exist. I and others have published thorough research reviews that critique—and dismiss—the "lower level component" model and the supposed empirical evidence showing the superior effect of early, direct, and intensive instruction in word sounds on later reading. As I have also argued, this narrow, do-as-you're-told instruction not only pushes aside numerous issues that bear on beginning literacy—such as children's backgrounds, interests, problem-solving approaches, and definitions of "reading" —it also masquerades as a bootstrap policy solution for poor children that takes off the table all other policies required to address the many needs that influence learning success or failure. However, for the advocates of this "strong consensus," especially those linked to the political power pushing these claims, conflicting views are never allowed to ruffle their harmony.

Hence, an experiment, such as those reported in the Shaywitz/Lyon study, can be designed in which subjects do "lower level component" tasks, such as deciding if nonwords rhyme ("Do leat and bete rhyme?") or making judgments requiring both phonological and semantic knowledge ("Are corn and rice in the same category?"), and the researchers can claim that the data generated tell us a great deal about "reading," the reading process, and the best kinds of instruction. The conclusions in this work display no awareness of the self-fulfilling prophecy at play when the research focuses solely on "lower level components" decontextualized from a full appraisal of reading, uses no other model of reading and instruction, and then concludes that these components are the initial and key ones in learning to read.

A Real "Brain Glitch"?

Looking more deeply into the research design of the "brain glitch" studies, we find a problem that dyslexia researchers have long encountered but not overcome when organizing an experiment so that data on brain activity can be meaningfully interpreted: the experiment must start by grouping dyslexics separately from other kinds of poor readers. This distinction is required because even in studies using the fMRI, the data are about brain activity associated with the word-level tasks, not about micro brain damage. Therefore, fMRI differences in brain activity among a group of unsorted poor readers would not provide information about the cause and meaning of the various differences in activity.

To solve the problem, these studies and previous ones employing simpler technologies try first to separate from a group of poor readers those whose problems are assumed to have non-neurological causes, such as emotional, familial, social class, and similar "exclusionary" influences, as they have been called. If these poor readers are excluded, researchers have reasoned, the probability is high that the reading problems of those who remain are caused by a "brain glitch." While this might make sense in theory, in practice it has not worked, because researchers have not created evaluation methods and criteria for separating the two groups of poor readers.

Even worse, for decades, researchers have frequently stated that they have used a thorough process of distinguishing between the two groups, but the assertion has rarely been accompanied by evidence. In the Shaywitz/Lyon study, for example, dyslexics were supposedly identified after the researchers had determined that the subjects' reading problems were not caused by emotional problems or "social, cultural, or economic disadvantage." Yet the researchers, so dedicated to obtaining and reporting a surfeit of brain data, offered not a whit of information on this process of elimination. Presumably, readers of the published study were expected to accept without question the assertion that genuine dyslexics had been identified and that these children could then be compared to "nonimpaired" readers (an odd term, since it refers to normal or average readers but is used in the study to underline a priori the assumption that the dyslexics' brains were impaired).

The need to provide evidence of thorough appraisals of the roots of subjects' reading problems is usually obvious to anyone who has actually taught poor readers and, therefore, knows that there can be numerous contextual causes of poor reading in middle-class children that will not be readily apparent. In my extensive work with children, young adults, and adults with severe reading problems, I have found that causes can be uncovered only after spending considerable time *both* evaluating and teaching a student, with the latter especially necessary. Poor teaching—such as using a one-size-fits-all reading program, insufficient individualized instruction, too much phonics, too little phonics—is just one of the many influences that can produce reading problems in a variety of ways, but those problems will not be apparent without thorough analysis of a person's instructional history and current active reading.

Many unusual family circumstances and stresses can impair a child's early reading progress. A parent losing a job, a family moving to another city in the middle of the first grade, overworked parents, grandparents dying around the time a child began school are all examples of problems I have identified. These experiences hinder reading development by distracting and stressing a child, but they are not overt "emotional" problems. Even when a poor reader comes from a family that appears "normal," only an extensive exploration of the family dynamics can determine whether this appearance might cloak problems that have affected a child's beginning reading.

By not providing criteria and evidence that the "dyslexics" are different from other poor readers, the brain research studies use another self-serving, self-fulfilling prophecy: because the fMRI shows differences in brain activity between "dyslexic" and "nonimpaired" readers, the differences in brain activity must be visual demonstrations of impairment and nonimpairment. How do we know the fMRI data reveal impairment? Because one of the groups was initially identified as impaired. How do we know the group was impaired? Because the group was first identified as impaired and the fMRI data corroborated the impairment. No other explanations can explain the dyslexics' different brain activity. Impaired, for sure! No question about it. . . .

Fixing the "Brain Glitch"

Beyond finding "brain glitches," researchers have reported other good news: building-block skills instruction can remedy the glitch. "An effective reading program" can produce "brain repair," Shaywitz reports. "The brain can be rewired.". . .

Nearly 20 years ago, Leonide Goldstein and I published a study on differences in brain hemisphere activation in adult beginning readers as they were learning to read. We found that these adults, when they were poor readers or nonreaders, did, indeed, demonstrate brain activation that was different from that found among good readers. However, as their reading improved, through the use of a holistic, comprehensive teaching approach over many months, their brain activation changed toward that commonly found in good readers. We interpreted these data as evidence that new knowledge and competencies were linked to concomitant changes in brain structure and functioning, as one would expect for *all kinds of learning*. There was nothing in the data to suggest that these beginning readers started learning to read with anything other than normal brains that were configured as they were at the beginning of the study because the students had not learned to read; no data suggested that the educational intervention we provided somehow repaired or circumvented dysfunctional brain areas.

To restate a central point for appraising these glitch-fixing interventions: although researchers insist that the training programs they use repair or ameliorate brain hardware or glitches, there is no evidence in any of their studies that this rewiring was different from that which is concomitant with the learning that continues throughout our learning lives. Nor does this so-called repair demonstrate that phonological processing is the *initial* key component in learning to read. The subjects apparently lacked this ability and then learned this ability, and their brain processing changed accordingly. Using modern technology to identify and track brain changes related to changes in reading ability is an extraordinary achievement. Using the achievement for ideological ends is not.

Emotionless "Cognition"

Like the assumed "consensus" on building-blocks instruction, "brain glitch" research assumes that cognition—that is, the process that creates images, concepts, and mental operations—is not a construct but an independent reality that actually describes the brain processes associated with reading. Ignored in this assumption is the ever-growing evidence suggesting that thinking is an inseparable interaction of both cognition and emotion (feelings, desires, enthusiasms, antipathies, etc.) . . .

Unfortunately, none of this new perspective on the "continuous and interwoven cognitive-emotional fugue," . . . has entered the "brain glitch" research. As a result, the question of whether diminished activity in a portion of the brain of someone doing a reading task might be a consequence of an emotional response, in that emotional memories can exert a powerful influence on "thought processes," remains unaddressed. By purging emotions and focusing only on cognition, the "brain glitch" research also purges the alternative: a holistic instructional approach based on the assumption that classrooms are filled with whole children for whom learning is always grounded in the fugue of cognition and affect.

How the Brain Works: Modules?

The interrelationships and interactions missing from the narrow cognitive model of "brain glitch" research lead us to a final concern. A chief premise of this research holds that the brain has specific modules for specialized operations that work in sequence with other modules in learning written language and that foremost of these is at least one module that can process basic sound and sound/symbol skills. This kind of modular model has a certain palpable, visual appeal (not unlike "building-blocks instruction"), but the actual existence of such modules is a theory, not a fact, that has increasingly been questioned. Most likely, the modular model is not one that explains how the brain actually works.

For instance, Merlin Donald, a psychologist who has written extensively on human consciousness, rejects the explanation that modules perform "specialized operations," such as deciphering portions of language. While language areas of the brain, such as those related to aspects of reading, are important in processing particular functions, all are intertwined in extensive networks (a polyphony) of brain areas that are simultaneously and interactively communicating and constructing and reconstructing particular areas within the whole. Yes, the brain has fundamental mechanisms for beginning to learn written language, but it does not begin with a "fixed pattern of connectivity." Instead, the "connectivity pattern is set by experience" with "countless interconnection points, or synapses, which connect neurons to one another in various patterns." In other words, learning and experience create and shape the brain's circuits and how they are used in learning to read; the circuits are not predetermined.

Linguist Philip Lieberman has also criticized modular explanations, calling them "neophrenological theories," that is, theories that "map complex behaviors to localized regions of the brain, on the assumption that a particular part of the brain regulates an aspect of behavior." In these theories, he remarks, the functional organization of the brain is run by "a set of petty bureaucrats each of which controls a behavior." Like Donald, Lieberman proposes that converging behavioral and neurobiological data indicate that human language is composed not of a hierarchical system but of neural networks, including the traditional cortical "language" areas (Broca's and Wernicke's areas), formed through circuits that link populations of neurons in neuroanatomical structures that are distributed throughout the brain. Lieberman stresses, "Although specific operations may be performed in particular parts of the brain, these operations must be integrated into a *network* that regulates an observable aspect of behavior. And so, a particular aspect of behavior usually involves activity in neuroanatomical structures distributed throughout the brain" (emphasis in original). . . .

The view of a "connectivity pattern" that emerges and is activated as children learn to read contrasts with the model of step-by-step progression from module to module. If the former is an accurate model of brain organization and functioning, it suggests that the connectivity pattern should be the focus of research because only by looking at the overall pattern can researchers begin to determine the functioning and interrelationships of any part and the causal, consequential, or interactive function of that part within the entire pattern.

From the perspective of a connectivity pattern model, not only do the brain areas involved in grasping the sound/symbol correspondence *not* have to be primed first before other areas of the pattern can become effectively operable, the creation and functioning of these areas depends on connections within the entire pattern. And because the pattern is not innately fixed, if instruction were to stimulate certain areas more than others, a particular connectivity pattern would emerge. That specific pattern, however, might not necessarily be the sole one required for reading success and might not be superior to other connectivity patterns. Moreover, a more complex connectivity pattern could be created through richer written language learning. None of this is addressed in the "brain glitch" research.

Conclusion

Philip Lieberman offers a caveat worth emphasizing when appraising "brain glitch" research, learning to read, and the Bush agenda for education: "We must remember that we stand on the threshold of an understanding of how brains really work. The greatest danger perhaps rests in making claims that are not supported by data." Unfortunately, not only have "brain glitch" researchers seldom been guided by such a caveat, they have tended to misconstrue the data and have drawn conclusions that serve to justify unwarranted beliefs, instructional policy, and the politics that have driven the research in the first place. . . .

For research on the brain and reading to become productive, what is needed most is the discarding of fundamental assumptions that have not been validated. Building-blocks instruction has not been proved to be the best way to teach reading. Phonological awareness has not been proved to be the initial, essential component that determines reading success. Thinking does not involve "cognition" alone. The modular organization of the brain is, at best, a disputed theory. Brain activation differences do not necessarily reflect "brain glitches." Dyslexia remains no more a proven malady among a substantial percentage of beginning readers than when Glasgow ophthalmologist James Hinshelwood first discussed it as "congenital word-blindness" at the end of the 19th century.

To make research on the brain and reading work, it must be informed by the complexity of reading acquisition, and it must begin to address such questions as: Will alternative teaching approaches configure brain activity in alternative ways? Will children's differing assumptions about what it means to "read" correspond to differing brain activity and organization? How do different aspects of reading, such as comprehension, syntax, and word analysis, interact in certain reading tasks and what kinds of brain activity do the interactions produce? How does the knowledge children bring to literacy learning affect brain activity?

These and similar questions can begin to contribute to a better understanding of the relationship between brain function and reading acquisition, which in turn can help promote ecological approaches that are grounded in an understanding of the unified interrelationships of brain, active child, and learning environment. They can also begin to help identify genuine brain-related reading impairments. Developing this kind of understanding of integrated interrelationships will require that we eschew views that are either "brain based" or conceive of the brain as an extraneous "black box."

By adding to the current pretensions about the superiority of one brand of "scientifically based" reading instruction, "brain glitch" research remains a danger in the classroom. Unfortunately, because of the political power connected to this sham science and brainless instruction, a mighty effort is required to end that danger.

POSTSCRIPT

Can Brain Scans Unravel the Mystery of Learning Disabilities?

By Christmas of the first-grade year, parents and teachers alike begin to worry about children who don't seem to be catching on to the magic of reading—understanding the connection between the sounds we make and their written symbols. Heated disputes about the best way to help struggling readers have existed for hundreds of years.

The latest round of this debate was sounded with the release of the National Reading Panel Report (2000). Using a tool called meta-analysis, the National Reading Panel (NRP) reviewed a number of research studies. Based on this analysis, the NRP concluded that most children would learn to read with systematic and intensive instruction, emphasizing phonemics and phonics.

The NRP report generated much controversy, especially from theorists who believe in a more holistic, literature-based method of reading instruction. Researchers argued (and continue to argue) about the studies selected and the studies eliminated from consideration. They argued about types of students included in the studies and criticized the fact that many of the studies did not seem to include struggling readers. They argued about the definition of reading—is it decoding individual words or gaining meaning from the print? The fervor increased when NCLB authors used the NRP's findings to set expectations for the type of research-based instruction schools should be using.

The drive to help all children learn to read easily has generated so much disagreement that it has often been termed "The Reading Wars." A promising method is identified, only to be dashed in a few years in a headline proclaiming reading researchers failed, yet again, to solve the reading crisis. In an attempt to define common ground, Rona Flippo (2004, 1999, 1998) surveyed "The Experts." Working for over 10 years, she learned that 11 prominent researchers with varying philosophies agreed on a number of points. One was that there is no "one best method" of teaching reading. The experts agreed that it was critical for teachers to match instructional methods to individual children, in response to their specific needs, interests, and learning styles.

Shaywitz and Shaywitz use fMRI results to provide evidence that brain "glitches" exist and can be corrected with the right kind of reading instruction. They strongly believe that the type of reading instruction advocated by NCLB can help "virtually" all students learn to read, even those with disabilities. Shaywitz and Shaywitz have great confidence that "teaching matters and good teaching can change the brain."

Coles cautions that demonstrating differences in brain activity is not enough—brains change as they learn. Some students have difficulty reading, he notes, because they have not had sufficient language support or because they might be preoccupied with troubled lives. According to Coles, the reasons for reading problems are not always simple—neither are the solutions. He is wary that the results of a few studies have been used to further a political agenda that dictates specific reading methodologies for use by all schools.

In the next 10 years, what will we discover about reading and the brain? Will fMRI (or its successor) unlock the mysteries of thinking and learning? Will in-school testing be replaced by visits to the neurologist? Will research identify teaching techniques to match with brain scan patterns? Or will the next set of studies find that the puzzle of reading disability has multiple explanations and solutions?

ISSUE 17

Is Attention Deficit (Hyperactivity) Disorder Overdiagnosed?

YES: Arthur Allen, from "The Trouble With ADHD," *The Washington Post* (March 18, 2001)

NO: Russell A. Barkley, from *Taking Charge of ADHD: The Complete, Authoritative Guide for Parents*, 2d ed. (The Guilford Press, 2000)

ISSUE SUMMARY

YES: Arthur Allen, reporter for *The Washington Post,* believes that attention deficit hyperactivity disorder (ADHD) exists but thinks that too many children are given this diagnosis, masking other conditions (or simply normal behavior) and resulting in the prescribing of drugs that do more harm than good.

NO: Russell A. Barkley, director of psychology and a professor at the University of Massachusetts Medical Center, addresses several current beliefs about ADHD and maintains that ADHD is underdiagnosed and undertreated in today's children.

$\mathbf{A}$ttention deficit hyperactivity disorder, or ADHD, describes someone who cannot stop moving, has difficulty concentrating, and is distracted by what happens around him or her. Without the H (hyperactivity), ADD refers to someone who can sit relatively still, but has difficulty concentrating and is likely distracted by internal thoughts. Although ADD and ADHD refer to variations of the same condition, ADHD will be used here to refer to both. Here are the official diagnostic criteria for ADHD:

A. Either (1) or (2):

8. Six (or more) or the following symptoms of inattention have persisted for at least six months to a degree that is maladaptive and inconsistent with developmental level: often fails to give close attention to details or makes careless mistakes; often has difficulty sustaining attention in tasks or play; often does not seem to listen when spoken to directly; often does not follow through on instructions

and fails to finish chores or duties (not due to oppositional behavior or failure to understand); often has difficulty organizing tasks and activities; often avoids, dislikes, or is reluctant to engage in tasks that require sustained mental effort; often loses things necessary for tasks or activities; often forgetful.

9. Six (or more) of the following symptoms of hyperactivity-impulsivity have persisted for at least six months to a degree that is maladaptive and inconsistent with developmental level: often fidgets with hands or feet or squirms in seat; often leaves seat unacceptably; often runs about or climbs excessively when inappropriate (in adolescents or adults, may feel restless); often has difficulty playing quietly; often talks excessively; often blurts out answers before questions completed; often has difficulty awaiting turn; often interrupts or intrudes on others.

B. Some symptoms present before age 7

C. Present in two or more settings

D. Clear evidence of clinically significant impairment

E. Symptoms are not due to another disorder

—Adapted from *DSM-IV-TR*, 2000

ADHD is one of the most frequently cited medical/behavioral conditions known. Likely, it is the topic of at least one article in at least one of the magazines on the rack at your supermarket's checkout counter. Although a medical condition, ADHD is frequently considered by parents and teachers when a child seems to have difficulty in school.

About 7 percent of children have received a diagnosis of ADHD. The authors of both selections believe that ADHD exists, but they have very different opinions about whether or not this diagnosis is being used appropriately.

Arthur Allen examines the life stories of a number of children—cast in the light of educators, psychologiests, and researchers—to identify how easy it is to apply the ADHD label and prescribe medication to address the "symptoms."

Russel A. Barkley, in a selection from an extensive book that also considers the experiences of children and families, believes that educators and parents are only just beginning to recognize and appropriately treat the challenging problems of the disorder known as ADHD.

As you read the following selections, ask yourself how often you have wondered if you or someone you know has ADHD. Is it possible for us to concentrate fully all the time, or is there a real biological disorder that deserves our attention? Are we leaping too quickly to seize a label—and medical cure?

YES

Arthur Allen

The Trouble With ADHD

It's a struggle for Andrew Fraser just to be here.

He is sitting politely in the dining room of a Silver Spring church, where each Thursday morning all 36 students at the tiny Quaker middle school Andrew attends gather for silent meeting. The season is midwinter and the group, described by the school's headmaster as mostly "bright underachievers," is midway between childhood and teenagerdom. . . . In the opening moments of worship, the room is remarkably quiet.

The silence is finally broken by a teacher who mentions that in this season of short days, ancient cultures treasured light, which explains why winter celebrations center on lavish displays of it. In the Quaker tradition, you pray for someone by "holding him in the light," and the teacher suggests that the students of Thornton Friends Middle School might do that now.

A boy raises his voice to hold his mother and little sister in the light. His father, he says, is leaving the family—"he says he hates me." Soon others chime in, sharing worries about sick grandparents and aggrieved friends. . . . Andrew, a rail-thin eighth-grader, . . . announces he is holding in the light a gym teacher who twisted his knee. . . .

Andrew has been struggling to get into the light his whole life. At 6 months he fell off the growth curve; in his toddler years, rough textures and loud sounds vexed him. When he was in second grade, a psychiatrist declared Andrew to have the worst case of "attention deficit disorder" he'd seen in 27 years. Andrew ricocheted and fidgeted through grade school, unable to tolerate more than a few minutes in class. He couldn't bear to write. He left his seat constantly. He got into scuffles all the time.

Home life wasn't much better. The Fraser home, a Rockville rambler with a sunken den, frequently shook with Andrew's tantrums. One morning, when Andrew was in fourth grade, he went after his older sister with a knife. Another, he was so enraged at life that he ripped the folding doors off his closet and threw them into the back yard, where he stomped them into slivers. Most mornings Andrew was a reptile coiled in his room, so unready to face the cruel exposures of the school day that his father had to dress him.

Yet Andrew could be a nice kid—open, friendly, communicative. For that grace his teachers and therapists never entirely gave up on him. "Through it all, Andrew was liked," says his mother, Wendy.

His parents took him to a psychiatrist who diagnosed attention deficit hyperactivity disorder (ADHD) with "co-morbidities"—depression and possible conduct disorder. There were drugs to treat each malady.

. . . [W]hen he was all of 11 years old, Andrew was on an enormous dose—70 milligrams—of Ritalin for his ADHD, plus two antidepressants, Prozac and Pamelar, and the anti-hypertensive Clonidine, to counter the side effects of Ritalin. To make sure his heart could stand the stimulation of so much Ritalin, Andrew had his blood pressure checked weekly. Yet he seemed as distracted, irritable and unhappy as ever. Sometimes the drugs seemed to be making things worse. His father, Bruce, . . . and Wendy . . . were at wit's end.

"He'd cry. He'd threaten to jump out of the car. It was hard to see how he'd make it in middle school," Wendy recalls.

That summer, she got a call from counselors at a day camp that Andrew was attending. Her son had threatened to run into the street, they said, and was marauding around the place with a branch, intimidating counselors and other kids. Come get him. So they did. But this time, when they took Andrew to his psychiatrist, it was clear they had arrived at a threshold. The psychiatrist suggested putting him on a fifth drug, the antipsychotic Risperdal, whose side effects, the doctor explained, included tics, tremors and the risk of permanent brain damage.

Andrew's parents were floored. "He didn't try to hard-sell us," Bruce recalls, but it dawned on them that ever-stronger behavioral drugs were all the psychiatrist had to offer. And Risperdal was "the last club in his bag."

Children who are hyperactive and distracted, who can't focus on what's in front of them or control their behavior, have always been with us. They entered the medical lexicon in 1902, when a British physician, George Frederic Still, described a group of children with "morbid defects of moral control." Still thought he could detect a child's moral propensities by taking measurements of his skull. Since then, the medical definition of this disorder has certainly undergone many revisions. But in some ways it has come full circle.

. . . In 1972, Virginia Douglas, a Canadian researcher, characterized it as attention deficit disorder, and her terminology became the accepted way of referring to children like Andrew Fraser. It was part of a turning point in child psychiatry toward defining mental illnesses more on the basis of observable behaviors and less on a patient's life history. This approach located the problem in the child's brain—separated it, in a way, from the child's character. That opened the way for large-scale use of medication to change the behaviors. . . .

The scientists who study ADHD believe these children are predisposed to it by particular patterns of brain chemistry, with most cases having some sort of genetic basis, others possibly the result of environmental factors during pregnancy or after birth.

Because there are no blood-borne proteins that define when a kid has ADHD, no lumps on the head or in it, no physical marks of any kind that clearly distinguish a child with ADHD from anyone else, the diagnosis remains controversial in society at large, even as the number of children—and, increasingly, very young children—who are treated for it is skyrocketing. . . .

Today an estimated 3 million children in this country have been diagnosed with ADHD—including perhaps 200,000 between age 2 and 4. With numbers like these it is not surprising that the diagnosis is controversial or that it has become enmeshed in many of the cultural battles of the past two decades, America's fretful internal argument over the proper way to parent and educate the young.

While scientists struggle to provide a unifying theory of what's different about the brains of children with ADHD, critics charge that it's wrong to view these kids' behavior as pathological in the first place; the fault lies with overcrowded schools, stressed-out parents with little time for the children and a society that wants to dull its rough edges and is intolerant of anything but success. Other, less radical critics of the system still believe that ADHD is severely overdiagnosed in America.

At the heart of the controversy over hyperactive disorder is that most children diagnosed with it get the same treatment: a stimulant. . . .

It wasn't until the 1960s that doctors began regularly treating hyperactive children with methylphenidate—trade name Ritalin. Researchers had long reported that Ritalin at low doses had a paradoxical effect—it was "speed" that slowed children down. Eventually it was recognized that stimulants had the same effect on almost everyone: They improved short-term concentration. It was just that people with ADHD needed more help focusing than the rest of us.

There was a brief backlash against Ritalin in the 1970s, when some studies suggested it might stunt a child's growth, but later research indicated those worries were overblown, and by the early 1990s, when society had generally embraced the idea that many problems could—and should—be dealt with by a pill, Ritalin had taken off again.

Even the biggest proponents of drug therapy agree that drugs work best in combination with behavioral modification and talk therapy. But talk is not cheap in the era of managed health care. And the thing about Ritalin and other stimulants is, they get results. Study after study has shown that low-dose stimulants will improve short-term concentration and reduce impulsivity and fidgetiness in about three-quarters of the kids who get them, as long as they're on them. These kids will often do better in school. They won't anger and alienate friends and teachers as much. That makes their parents saner. As a result of these things, the children often feel better about themselves.

How does Ritalin work? As with much about ADHD, no one is exactly sure, but it is evident that Ritalin increases the availability of dopamine, a chemical that's key to movement and attention and other nervous functions, to certain cells in the brain. By adding to the dopamine pool, the drug seems to speed the flow of impulses through the circuits that help people control the instinct to respond to each and every stimulus. In a way, you could say that Ritalin strengthens willpower.

Or, as Ellen Kingsley, the mother of a 13-year-old who has been on ADHD drugs since age 5, puts it: "It enables him to do the things he wants and needs to do and would not be able to do." Kingsley, . . . who . . . puts out a magazine about ADD, says her son T.K. would never have made it through school without drug therapy. Like many parents of children with ADHD, Kingsley is impatient with people who don't recognize that kids like hers are deeply impaired and need help. "I could give him all the therapy in the world, but it won't sink in without medication because he can't attend to the task," Kingsley says.

Parents with a morbidly hyperactive or inattentive child, most specialists agree, should be no more reluctant to try Ritalin than to give eyeglasses to a nearsighted child, if Ritalin will calm their child and improve his or her life. But among the millions of parents who have put their children on a permanent ration of behavior-modification drugs, many have undoubtedly had to overcome an initial queasiness and feeling of guilt. Laura and Barney Gault certainly did last fall, when a pediatrician suggested that their son, Sam, might need to be medicated.

"My first thought was denial," recalls Barney, Sam's father. "He's a kid—you aren't going to do this to my son. And then I was a little sad. I was thinking, 'Are we going to alter his personality?'"

It is a dreary winter evening in the [school] cafeteria . . . , and Sam's den leader, Jeff Bush, is attempting to get Sam and eight other rambunctious 9-and-10-year-old Webelos to drill for their civics merit badge. The den leader's presentation isn't really pulling in the audience. The boys, a few in their blue uniforms with yellow kerchiefs, most in ordinary kid clothes, are popping up and down in their seats like ducks in a shooting gallery. They all seem to be talking at the same time, except for the kids who are falling off their chairs. . . .

At the far end of the table, quietly fabricating spitballs and loading them into a straw, sits Sam Gault. You wouldn't necessarily know that he's the one with ADHD. He doesn't seem hyper. And he's very focused—not on Jeff Bush, unfortunately, but he's very focused on his spitballs. He fires across the room at his mother, Laura, and narrowly misses.

Laura . . . is keeping a close eye on her son. . . . On the previous Saturday, the den took a field trip to a firehouse. During the tour Sam got bored and started making silly remarks: "Is this an atomic bomb?" he asked about a high-pressure hose. "Is this a nuclear weapon?" Finally the fire chief turned and scolded him. Laura finds such incidents painful and hopes that, eventually, Sam will be embarrassed, too, and change his behavior. "When kids are continually singled out, it just whittles away at their self-esteem," she says.

It was partly concern about self-esteem that led the Gaults to take Sam in for a psychiatric evaluation more than a year ago, when he was 8 and in third grade. Sam was bright and thoughtful and didn't do poorly in school, but he couldn't sit still. Time and again, his second-grade teacher reported that Sam had trouble following through with her instructions. He raised a ruckus in the halls and played the class clown. He literally climbed the walls at times. Sam was an inquisitive, detail-oriented child, but his mind had a way of meandering from the critical to the banal. You could hear it in his speech as he drifted from one topic to the next—teachers, Game Boys, his ADHD—without clearly completing his thoughts on any of them.

Laura Gault had had forebodings before Sam was diagnosed with ADHD. She felt that Sam's ADHD might have had a hereditary connection—Sam's paternal grandfather . . . probably had ADHD, though in his era, of course, such a thing was not recognized. Even as an adult, he was impatient and impulsive like Sam, and sometimes he blurted out off-color remarks in mixed company.

And that's partly what bothered Laura about her son—the social improprieties. "I noticed that the other kids would be acting out, but they could stop when an adult said stop," she says. "Sam really couldn't stop. He'd just continue to wiggle."

Kids who wiggle too much stand out in a big classroom, where sheer management is a real challenge. Sam's class had 28 other children.

After Sam was diagnosed with moderate ADHD, the Gaults were urged by their pediatrician to start out with a behavioral modification routine. They got his teacher to provide daily reports on Sam, and rewarded good behavior with trinkets: a sleepover for being especially on-task. But within a couple months it was clear this regimen was not enough to motivate Sam. That's when the Gaults turned to Adderall, . . .

"He didn't have the maturity or ability to control his behavior on his own," says Laura. So Sam began taking the drug . . . , and his parents waited to see how it would affect him. Tonight, as his den leader winds up the civics session and the games begin, the effects of Adderall have long since worn off, and Sam is lost in his own world. The boys . . . divide into teams for sock ball, which is dodge ball using balled-up socks. Everyone runs around, yelling and throwing sock bombs at the kids on the opposing team. Sam wads up a pair of socks to make what he calls a "megabomb."

"Throw it, Sam!" shout two of his friends.

Sam does not respond. He is carefully folding the edges of the sock to make a rounder, more compact megabomb. One quality of Sam's mental architecture, it's plain to see, is a certain perfectionism. For better or worse, Adderall hasn't done anything to change that.

"Come on, throw it, Sam!"

Finally he throws and—whack!—the sock bomb smacks a boy named Chris as he attempts to flee.

Teammates cheer. Sam betrays no emotion but lets out a belch of conquest. "He's very proud of that," Laura says, rolling her eyes.

Notwithstanding that ADHD can be a serious disease, the diagnosis of ADHD in America is an inexact science shaped in large part by the socioeconomic milieu of the kid in the middle of it. All it takes is a look at the diagnostic guide to see that.

The guide divides ADHD into three types: inattentive, hyperactive/impulsive or combined. A hyperactive diagnosis requires that the child exhibit six symptoms from a list that includes fidgeting, frequently leaving classroom seat, interrupting often, excessive climbing and running about, excessive talking, inability to quietly engage in leisure activity, acting "as though driven by a motor." An inattentive diagnosis is for children with symptoms that include failure to listen, failure to follow through, tendency to lose things, etc. It's clear that subjective judgment enters into any diagnosis—almost anyone with a child could imagine him or her meeting the diagnostic criteria, on a bad day at least.

To be sure, the diagnostic guide also requires that to be ADHD, the symptoms must exert a significant impact on the child's life at home and school. But "significant impact" requires a context and that's where the controversy about ADHD begins.

Every November, just after parent-teacher conference days in many schools, Barbara Ingersoll, a leading ADHD diagnostician, . . . begins to get calls from parents. Ingersoll, a psychologist, performs assessments of children that parents can use to procure medications, therapy or classroom accommodations—all tools employed to get ADHD children through school with a modicum of success.

"After the parent-teacher conferences, when the honeymoon's over," the parents start seeking assessments, she says. "Wouldn't it be great if we had schools that let them be themselves?" she asks a bit facetiously. "But it ain't going to happen. You can't let them run amok."

Often, it's not the parents but the schools that drive the diagnosis. The principal of an elite . . . private school several years ago gave the parents of a 5-year-old kindergartner a gentle bit of advice that was almost an ultimatum. The child, who had a photographic memory of almost anything ever read to him and who could spend hours working on art and science projects, was unable to sit still in the classroom. The school referred him to another D.C. psychologist—not Ingersoll—for an assessment that lasted three hours, cost about $2,500 and resulted in what the parents viewed as a preordained conclusion: Their son had ADHD. "He may need to be on Ritalin," the principal said, "to stay in the school."

The family decided to get a second opinion. A child psychiatrist at Washington's Children's National Medical Center rolled his eyes when he heard about the diagnosis. ADHD was a "garbage can label," he told them, the diagnosis for any kid who was out of the box. Their boy was too young to be diagnosed definitively, he said, and the diagnosis wasn't a trivial matter.

Ritalin could mask an underlying condition, or it could cause serious side effects. The kindergartner had tics, and children with tics sometimes developed full-blown Tourette's syndrome after going on Ritalin.

Deep in their guts it felt wrong to the parents and they worried it would stifle their son's nascent creativity. When he was reassessed at a clinic two years later, the ADHD label turned out to be wrong. The boy was dyslexic. He wouldn't sit still in school, it turned out, because he couldn't make sense of the words put in front of him. In the meantime, the family had switched their child to a public school. . . .

What almost happened to this family captures society's fear of Ritalin, that the drug is being used to convert spirited children into docile sheep. But for most children on medication, the real problem isn't that the "meds" turn them into robots; it's that they rarely work as one would hope. At least half of the children diagnosed with ADHD also suffer from complex mixtures of other problems—learning disabilities, anxiety, depression—that can mandate a complex mixture of other drugs.

Theoretically, you can find a drug to treat each symptom. But the relationship between a behavior and the underlying biological facts isn't cut and dried, particularly in children.

Sometimes, Ingersoll acknowledges, she sees children with mood disorders who've been misdiagnosed as ADHD and put on high doses of stimulant that leave them subdued and distant. "You get better behavior, but it's using medicine as a chemical straitjacket," she says. "You get zombies."

Others wonder if some of the "co-morbidities" described by the psychiatrists are caused by the medicines themselves. "Here's the conundrum—I put you on stimulants because you're running around the classroom too much and you're too impulsive and in people's faces," says Julie Magno Zito, a professor at the University of Maryland School of Pharmacy who tracks the growing tendency to prescribe mind drugs for preschoolers. "About three months later, it looks like the treatment works, and then you go home at night and need medication to go to sleep. Enter Clonidine to help you sleep. Now we've gone from one drug to two. I have to worry about interactions, a wider spectrum of side effects. Then after a couple months it becomes apparent that you cry more easily, you're more sensitive. Now somebody says, 'He needs an antidepressant.' Now you're on three drugs. We could call it co-morbid depression. But to me it's equally possible that it's behavioral medicine toxicity. You probably wouldn't have the insomnia and crying if the other drugs were not on board. You can't just keep treating symptom by symptom."

. . . Zito and a colleague, Daniel Safer, a child psychiatrist at Johns Hopkins University, made headlines when they published an article in the *Journal of the American Medical Association* that tracked a threefold increase in the use of stimulants, antidepressants and other psychotropic drugs among 2- to 4-year-old Medicaid patients. . . . The article set off a new round of critical news stories about overuse of psychotropic drugs. And like previous Ritalin scares, the uproar put many physicians and parents who believe the drug can save lives on the defensive.

"When you ask me why I put a child on four drugs, I say look at asthmatics," says Larry Silver, a former NIH [National Institutes of Health] official who now has a large child psychiatry practice in Rockville. "With asthma you have multiple maintenance and emergency drugs, and there's a reason for each of the psychotropic medicines, too."

"The people who tend to criticize the use of these medications," he adds, "are usually in the media, or people who've never had to live with or treat the patients."

For a long time, Andrew Fraser and his parents hewed to this logic and followed the pharmaceutical trail wherever their psychiatrist advised them it led. They spent thousands of dollars and hundreds of hours in therapy and classes and doctor's appointments for Andrew. But when the psychiatrist suggested Risperdal, with its terrible potential side effects, it was a step too far.

"We've got to try something else," Bruce Fraser told his wife.

And so they stepped out of the mainstream and into the . . . office of Peter Breggin, who provided an unexpected answer to the problem of their son.

"Andrew," Breggin said, looking at the thin, . . . boy . . . sitting in front of him, "they say you're mentally ill, my friend. But actually you're a brat."

Peter Breggin, whose office is within mortar distance of the National Institute of Mental Health, is the bete noire of psychiatrists. He has written several books attacking the misdiagnosing and overmedicating of America's children. Some view him as his profession's prickly conscience, but his point of view, that there is no such thing as ADHD, is a fringe one among psychiatrists. Many of them believe that his crusading ways have done more harm than good by driving parents away from treatments that could help sick kids. Yet at least a few parents with difficult children view him as a savior who gives voice to their doubts and worries.

Breggin . . . believes that ADHD is essentially a "bunch of behaviors that make it difficult to teach kids in a big classroom. That's all it is! You wouldn't have a parent coming in and saying, 'Joey squirms in his seat.' What parent would claim that was an illness? It's the teacher saying, 'You're out of control, take some Ritalin.'"

Most of the worst symptoms of ADHD, he believes, are caused by the drugs that are used to treat it. "Once psychiatry went in the direction of drugs, it basically lost its knowledge and skills," he says. "If you look at the leading psychiatric journals today, there's nothing about family therapy, child development, how to handle an out-of-control kid. It's all about drugs. They act as if children don't need parents, they need drugs! Quite literally! We've abandoned our kids."

Breggin is the medical consultant in . . . class action lawsuits . . . on behalf of children medicated with Ritalin. The lawsuits, filed . . . by some of the same lawyers involved in anti-tobacco litigation, accuse[d] Novartis Pharmaceutical Corp., the maker of Ritalin, the American Psychiatric Association, and CHADD [Children and Adults with Attention-Deficit/Hyperactivity Disorder], an advocacy group for people with ADHD, of conspiring to poison America's children. . . .

"Breggin's effect has been to make families wary of medical treatment," says Laurence Greenhill, a Columbia University child psychiatrist who is leading a clinical trial of Ritalin for preschoolers, which he hopes will provide a means of testing Breggin's theory that Ritalin itself causes brain changes that scientists attribute to ADHD. "He feels that the kids don't get enough tender loving care, they aren't hugged enough. But he doesn't believe in evidence-based medicine and that's the standard now."

The Frasers had had enough of evidence-based medicine when they first stepped into Breggin's office . . . , and they instantly took to him and his message. Breggin told them that "in the overload of daily issues we'd failed to pay attention to teaching basic human dignity," Bruce recalls. "Breggin saw a lack of attention had been paid to the basic nurturing of a child. I didn't take umbrage. It sounded reasonable."

. . . Breggin took Andrew off the medications, one by one. In family and individual therapy, . . . he told the Frasers that Andrew had to learn to act civilized. He could learn to check his impulses, to pay attention, to show respect. Willpower was his to grasp. Wendy and Bruce had to love him tough and tender. The Frasers were happy to toss out the biological psychiatry, with its talk of titration and syndromes and EEG patterns. Ceremoniously, in the presence of his parents, Andrew flushed the leftover pills down the toilet: Out with impersonal chemicals! Human beings rule!

But Andrew did not immediately improve. He struggled through a year at a public middle school . . . then a year in a . . . special ed program. Finally, this fall, Andrew began something new—Thornton Friends. The small Quaker school . . . was created expressly for kids with promise who had trouble sitting still or paying attention, kids who got teased or harassed in traditional schools, kids who were a little different—but reachable. Thornton Friends stressed individual growth and community feeling. "We want to help people understand themselves and find a style that works for them," says the headmaster, Michael DeHart.

Roughly one-third of the kids in Thornton's middle school are on psychotropic medications of some kind, DeHart says. He agrees with Breggin, who has written positively about Thornton, that the surge in prescription drug use in children reflects our society's anxiety to produce kids who fit expectations, and its inability to create schools that handle their needs. But he also believes—unlike Breggin—that drugs sometimes are necessary. "It's clear to us that some kids, in order to make it work here, need to be on medication. That's where we kind of part ways with Peter."

When Andrew arrived at Thornton, the administrators were up to the challenge of educating a drug-free Andrew. But it wasn't a lovefest. In his first three months Andrew showed little patience and a lot of anger. In the middle of English once, he'd gotten up and yelled that he hated poetry.

"I'm not going to say Andrew needs to be medicated, and I'm not going to say he doesn't," says Jonathan Meisel, the principal of the middle school. "There have been times when it's been very difficult for him. He's very easily distracted. Does that mean it's not worth continuing to try being off them? I'm not sure. Ultimately, is this the right place for him to be as a student, medication aside? We don't know."

Sitting on the couch in Meisel's office, . . . Andrew says he is embarrassed to tell old friends he goes to this school. "I hate it here," he says matter-of-factly. "A lot of kids here have a lot of problems. They feel like they don't fit in. They are like really big dorks."

At the same time, Andrew, now 13, knows he never wants to take medication again. He hated himself on drugs: "Nothing seemed fun; everything seemed boring." His goal is to get back to public school, which he knows will be impossible unless he shapes up. "I don't want to, but I think I'll end up here," he says. "I'm going to try to make do with what I've got."

Do Andrew and Sam do what they do because of flaws in the wiring of brain circuits that inhibit inappropriate action, or is the apparent difference in their brains more in the nature of an evolutionary mismatch with modern life, an alternate state of readiness that represents a holdover from prehistoric times when extremely alert, impulsive people presumably had advantages in the struggle to survive? These are two of the untestable hypotheses of pop psychology concerning ADHD.

This much is clear: Our brains evolved with a great deal of variation. If children's height was as variable as the size of their brains, some would be giants stooping to get in the classroom door each morning while others would barely be tall enough to reach their computer keyboards.

That fact poses one of the formidable challenges for researchers such as Xavier Castellanos, a doctor who has been studying ADHD for a decade in the child psychiatry branch of the National Institute of Mental Health. . . . "Some kids' brains are twice the volume of those of other kids, with both completely normal and healthy," he says. "There's a wide range in brain volume that we don't understand."

For the past several years, Castellanos has been studying the brains of ADHD children as they appear in magnetic resonance imagery (MRI). He's doing the measurements to see if size can tell us something about the seat of abnormality. The current theory is that ADHD may derive from abnormal neural circuits linking the frontal lobes, the deep brain structures called the basal ganglia, and the cerebellum.

But Castellanos . . . , is the first to admit how few facts have been established. "The problem with neuroscience at this point is that everything in the brain seems to be related to everything else," he says. "It's like you're attempting to make out which notes of a symphony come from the different instruments, but you are listening from the hall through the wall with a stethoscope."

Castellanos and others have found that the brains of children with carefully diagnosed ADHD are approximately 4 percent smaller, on average, than those of healthy children. Some parts of the brains of ADHD children can be particularly small—the posterior-inferior vermis, a tiny segment of the cerebellum, for instance, is 10 to 15 percent smaller, on average. Castellanos doesn't want to make too much of that—or too little. For the record, he doesn't know what that teaspoon-size region of the brain does.

But he was extremely excited when a study . . . found that in macaque monkeys the posterior-inferior vermis was packed with dopamine receptors. That's interesting to Castellanos because an inadequate supply of dopamine is believed to hamper attention and self-control. So the smallness of the posterior-inferior vermis in ADHD kids might mean a shortage of the right neural circuitry.

The smaller the brain size in these children, the worse the ADHD symptoms tend to be. But there's an awful lot of variation, Castellanos says. Two-thirds of the brains of ADHD children are indistinguishable, in size, from those of healthy kids. If you're a skeptic, you say size has nothing to do with it.

Similar caveats cover the genetic work on ADHD so far. "My favorite nightmare is there are going to turn out to be 300 or 500 genes, each of which contributes a couple percent of risk here and there," Castellanos says. The leading candidate gene for ADHD is a variant of the gene known as DRD4. This variant apparently causes a receptor on certain brain cells to have trouble sucking dopamine out of brain synapses. That presumably slows the feedback messages in the brain that inhibit impulses. But you can't call it a defective gene because it turns out fully 30 percent of the U.S. population has it, and not all of those people have been diagnosed with ADHD. And not everyone with ADHD has that particular DRD4 gene variant. . . .

At least two drug companies are said to be working on DRD4-related drugs that could be used to improve the brain circuitry of ADHD patients. But Jim Swanson, one of the UC-Irvine professors involved with the study, has an intriguing hypothesis that the ADHD patients with the suspect DRD4 variant might be the subgroup that benefits most from behavioral modification strategies—rather than medication.

Because it was treatment, rather than diagnosis, that was the most contentious element of the ADHD debate, the National Institute of Mental Health set out to settle the issue of how best to treat ADHD by funding a six-site, 14 month study comparing Ritalin with behavioral modification and combined therapy. The researchers who designed the study included Ritalin advocates . . . and behavioral modification proponents. . . .

. . . The study found that, overall, combined therapy worked best, but drugs alone were significantly more effective than behavioral modification therapy alone.

Swanson was surprised. "We thought intensive behavior modification would meet or beat the medication effects, and it didn't," he says. "We have to face the facts."

But there was another way of looking at the study. More than one-third of the . . . kids in the study who were treated with behavioral techniques alone improved their ADHD symptoms. Which means, in Swanson's words, "If there are 3 million kids medicated in the United States, maybe 1 million of them could have a good response to non-drug therapy."

And that would be a good thing. Because the drugs have side effects, and they don't work perfectly, and there will always be parents who, for a variety of reasons, refuse to give their kids mind-altering chemicals.

Before she started him out on Adderall . . . , Laura Gault wrote a letter to Sam that explained his disorder and compared the drug to the glasses a nearsighted kid would have to wear. She wanted him to have something to look at in case he started to worry about being called ADHD.

Sam tried to avoid telling friends at school that he had the condition; one reason his parents chose to give him Adderall was that it was long-acting. A single dose, it was hoped, would get him through the entire school day. Kids on Ritalin, which the body metabolizes faster, often have to see the school nurse at lunchtime to get a booster dose—and Sam felt that would be embarrassing.

In the first month on the drug, Sam lost four pounds, and he was a skinny boy to begin with. "I was very concerned about that," Laura recalls. "You can tell a child to eat, but you can't make them eat."

"But," she says with a shrug, "it did help with his behavior." Sam no longer seemed compelled to pester his neighbors in class. He could walk from room to room without climbing the walls or rattling a pen along the lockers.

But the tiny blue . . . pill he takes at breakfast wears off by 2 p.m., and from that point Sam's teachers and parents use their wits and wisdom to keep Sam on track. One evening a week, Sam attends a group therapy session with other children with ADHD who need help learning how to act appropriately in social settings. He says he doesn't like it, but he clearly tunes in—you can tell by his recall of some details.

"If you see two people having a conversation there are six things you do," he recites. "First, you stand near them. Then you move closer, and smile. Then you see if they smile back. If they do, then you smile again. Then if you know something about what they're talking about, you join in the conversation, but maybe just a small comment at first."

Laura doesn't give Sam the medication on weekends or evenings, mainly because she worries about his weight. Too, she doesn't want him to be on medication forever. "Our goal is eventually to get him off," she says. "From what I've read, a lot of boys, once they go through puberty can . . . not outgrow it exactly, but the hyperactivity can be less.

"In the meantime I want him to learn how to cope."

For now coping begins with the pills, which clearly have an effect. Sam forgot to take his medication the first day back at school after winter break this year—and the teacher noticed right away. He couldn't sit still and his attention wandered. Which got Laura thinking again about the dosage. "I've been kind of waiting to see if there's a need to increase it," she says.

Before Thornton Friends' two-week winter break, Jonathan Meisel had written up a contract for Andrew. It was a one-page list of do's and don'ts, and it essentially stipulated that if Andrew's behavior didn't improve, he was out of the school.

One thing the contract required was more frequent therapy, and so Andrew began seeing Breggin weekly, instead of every few months. But the new system also made a concession: Instead of writing by hand, which was torture for Andrew as it is for many ADHD kids, he was allowed to bring a laptop to school so he could type his notes.

All in all, it was a challenge.

The family drove to South Carolina to visit Bruce's parents for part of the school vacation. The trip went smoothly. One evening, back in town but before he returned to school, Andrew joined his father and a family friend in a sort of woodshed behind the friend's house. While the adults drank cognac and smoked cigars, they talked with Andrew about his future. "You could just tell how excited he was to be treated as an adult," Bruce says, "and at the end my friend said, 'This is a good kid. He doesn't need to be in special education.'"

Recently, Andrew has begun to feel he has a goal in life. He downloads music from the Internet and burns CDs for his friends, earning a little money that way. He's been thinking he'd like to take a mail-order computer course. "That's what I'd like to do when I'm older," he says, "become a computer programmer."

In written evaluations submitted at the end of the third week of the new trimester, all of Andrew's teachers had noted a remarkable turnaround. "Andrew has developed some qualities in the science classroom since holiday break that I have not usually seen," one teacher wrote, "—improved attentiveness to discussion and explanation, more thoughtful questioning and answering, and decreased distractions with other students. . . ."

His parents are keeping their fingers crossed.

"It took a lot of people—his teachers and friends and therapists and family and him—to get this far," Wendy says. "We feel like he's turned a corner."

Russell A. Barkley    **NO**

What Is Attention-Deficit/ Hyperactivity Disorder?

Attention-deficit/hyperactivity disorder, or ADHD, is a developmental disorder of self-control. It consists of problems with attention span, impulse control, and activity level. But, as you will discover here, it is much more. These problems are reflected in impairment in a child's will or capacity to control her own behavior relative to the passage of time—to keep future goals and consequences in mind. It is not, as other books will tell you, just a matter of being inattentive and overactive. It is not just a temporary state that will be outgrown, a trying but normal phase of childhood. It is not caused by parental failure to discipline or control the child, and it is not a sign of some sort of inherent "badness" in the child.

ADHD is real—a real disorder, a real problem, and often a real obstacle. It can be heartbreaking and nerve-wracking.

"Why Don't They Do Something About That Kid?"

It's easy to see why many people find it hard to view ADHD as a disability like blindness, deafness, cerebral palsy, or other physical disabilities. Children with ADHD look normal. There is no outward sign that something is physically wrong within their central nervous system or brain. Yet I believe it is an imperfection in the brain that causes the constant motion and other behavior that people find so intolerable in a child who has ADHD.

By now you may be familiar with the way others react to ADHD behavior: At first many adults attempt to overlook the child's interruptions, blurted remarks, and violation of rules. With repeated encounters, however, they try to exert more control over the child. When the child still fails to respond, the vast majority decide that the child is willfully and intentionally disruptive. Ultimately most will come to one conclusion, albeit a false one: The child's problems result from how the child is being raised. The child needs more discipline, more structure, more limit setting. The parents are ignorant, careless, permissive, amoral, antisocial, unloving, or, in contemporary parlance, "dysfunctional."

"So, Why Don't They Do Something About That Kid?"

Of course the parents often are doing something. But when they explain that the child has been diagnosed as having ADHD, judgmental outsiders typically react with skepticism. They see the label as simply an excuse by the parents to avoid the responsibility of child rearing and an attempt to make the child yet another type of helpless victim unaccountable for his actions. This hypocritical response—viewing the child's behavior so negatively, while at the same time labeling the child as "just normal"—leaves outsiders free to continue blaming the parents.

Even the less censorious reaction of considering ADHD behavior as a stage to be outgrown is not so benign in the long run. Many adults, including professionals, counsel the parents not to worry. "Just hang in there," they advise, "and by adolescence the child will have outgrown it." This is certainly true in some milder forms of ADHD: In perhaps half or more of these very mild cases, the behaviors are likely to be within the normal range by adulthood. If your preschool child has more serious problems with ADHD symptoms, however, such advice is small comfort. Being advised to "hang in there" for 7 to 10 years is hardly consoling. Worse, it is often grossly mistaken, harmful advice. The life of a child whose ADHD is left unrecognized and untreated is likely to be filled with failure and underachievement. Up to 30–50% of these children may be retained in a grade at least once. As many as 35% may fail to complete high school altogether. For half of such children, social relationships are seriously impaired, and for more than 60%, seriously defiant behavior leads to misunderstanding and resentment by siblings, frequent scolding and punishment, and a greater potential for delinquency and substance abuse later on. Failure by the adults in a child's life to recognize and treat ADHD can leave that child with an unremitting sense of failure in all arenas of life.

"Isn't ADHD Overdiagnosed? Aren't Most Children Inattentive, Active, and Impulsive?"

Imagine the toll on society when, conservatively estimated, 3–7%, or more than 2 million school-age children, have ADHD. This means that at least one or even two children with ADHD are in every classroom throughout the United States. It also means that ADHD is one of the most common childhood disorders of which professionals are aware. Finally, it means that all of us know someone with the disorder, whether we can identify it by name or not.

The costs of ADHD to society are staggering, not only in lost productivity and underemployment but also in reeducation. And what of the costs to society in antisocial behavior, crime, and substance abuse? More than 20% of children with ADHD have set serious fires in their communities, more than 30% have engaged in theft, more than 40% drift into early tobacco and alcohol use, and more than 25% are expelled from high school because of serious misconduct. Recently the effects of ADHD on driving have also been studied. Within their first two years of independent driving, adolescents with a diagnosis of ADHD have nearly four times as many auto accidents, are more likely to cause bodily injury in such accidents, and have three times as many citations for speeding as young drivers without ADHD.

Recognition of these consequences has spawned a huge effort to understand ADHD. Besides . . . thousands of scientific papers . . . , more than 50 textbooks have been devoted to the subject, with again as many books written for parents and teachers. Countless newspaper stories have addressed ADHD over the course of the 100 years that clinical science has recognized the disorder as a serious problem. Many local parents' support associations have sprung up, most notably Children and Adults with Attention Deficit Disorder (CHADD), which has grown into a national organization of more than 50,000 members. At least five professional organizations include a number of scientific presentations on the subject in their convention programs each year. . . . All this is hardly what you would expect if the disorder were not "real," as some critics have claimed.

Fact Versus Fiction

. . . [V]arious unsubstantiated claims about the legitimacy of the disorder we call ADHD have been making the media rounds [recently]. Trying to sort through these, in addition to facing the skepticism of friends, family, and teachers, can make it difficult for parents to accept a diagnosis of ADHD and move forward into productive treatment of their child. Here is what we know to date:

Fiction: ADHD is not real, because there is no evidence that it is associated with or is the result of a clear-cut disease or brain damage.

Fact: Many legitimate disorders exist without any evident underlying disease or pathology. ADHD is among them.

Disorders for which there is no evidence of brain damage or disease include the vast majority of cases of mental retardation (various brain-scanning methods reveal no obvious disease or damage in children with down's syndrome, for example), childhood autism, reading disabilities, language disorders, bipolar disorders, major depression, and psychosis, as well as medical disorders involving early-stage Alzheimer's disease, the initial onset of multiple sclerosis, and many of the epilepsies. Many disorders arise due to problems in the way the brain has developed or the way it is functioning at the level of nerve cells. Some of these are genetic disorders, in which the condition arises from an error in development rather than from a destructive process or an invading organism. The fact that we do not yet know the precise causes of many of these disorders at the level of the molecules in the brain does not mean they are not legitimate. A disorder . . . is defined as a "harmful dysfunction," not by the existence of pathological causes.

As for ADHD, the evidence is quickly mounting that we are dealing in most cases with a disorder in brain development or brain functioning that originates in genetics. Although most cases of ADHD appear to arise from . . . genetic effects and difficulties with brain development and functioning, ADHD can certainly arise from direct damage to or diseases of the brain as well. Fetal alcohol syndrome is known to create a high risk for ADHD in children with that syndrome, and so is prematurity of birth in which small brain hemorrhages may have occurred during delivery. And it is well known that children suffering significant trauma to the frontal part of the brain are likely to develop symptoms of ADHD as a consequence. All of this indicates to scientists that any process that disrupts the normal development or functioning of the frontal part of the brain and its connections to the striatum is likely to result in ADHD. It just so happens that most cases are not due to such damage, but seem to arise from problems in the development of critical brain regions or in their normal functioning. Someday soon we will understand the nature of those problems with greater precision. But for now, the lack of such a precise understanding does not mean that the disorder is not valid or real. If the demonstration of damage or disease were the critical test for diagnosis, then the vast majority of mental disorders, nearly all developmental disabilities, and many medical conditions would have to be considered invalid. Countless people suffering from very real problems would go untreated, and their problems would be unexplored.

Fiction: If ADHD were real, there would be a lab test to detect it.

Fact: There is no medical test for any currently known "real" mental disorder.

Just as we cannot identify any disease or brain damage for ADHD, we cannot give children a test to detect it. Neither is there a test for schizophrenia, alcoholism, Tourette's syndrome, anxiety disorders, or any of the other well-established mental disorders, or for many widespread medical disorders such as arthritis. Yet they are all very real in being harmful dysfunctions.

Fiction: ADHD must be an American fabrication, since it is diagnosed only in the United States.

Fact: Recent studies conducted in numerous foreign countries show that all cultures and ethnic groups have children with ADHD.

Japan has identified up to 7% of children as having the disorder, China up to 6–8%, and New Zealand up to 7%. Other countries may not refer to ADHD by this term, they may not know as much about its causes or treatment, and (depending on the countries' level of development) they may not even recognize is yet as a legitimate disorder. But there is no question that ADHD is a legitimate disorder and is found worldwide.

Remember, the United States is among the few leaders, if not the leader, in the amount of scientific research conducted on childhood mental disorders. It is therefore highly likely that the United States at times comes to recognize disorders and develop treatments for them long before other countries do.

Fiction: Because the rate of diagnosis of ADHD and the prescription of stimulants to treat it have risen markedly in the last decade or two, ADHD is now widely overdiagnosed.

Fact: As the National Institute of Mental Health (NIMH) Consensus Conference on ADHD concluded in late 1998, underdiagnosis and undertreatment of ADHD remain big problems in the United States today.

Several studies indicate that fewer than half of all children who have ADHD are diagnosed or properly treated for the disorder, and that only one-half of these are treated with medication. The greatest problems for our children continue to be that a large percentage of those with legitimate disorders in need of treatment are not being referred, diagnosed, or properly treated, and that services across the United States for children with ADHD are inconsistent, erratic, and often well below what is considered the standard of care for the disorder. So evidence for proclamations that we are overdiagnosing ADHD in the United States and overusing stimulants for its management lack credible scientific evidence.

One possible reason for the rise in diagnosis and stimulant treatment of ADHD is that the prevalence of the disorder has actually increased. However, we do not have a lot of research that has measured the rates of children's mental disorders across multiple generations. The little research we do have indicates that ADHD has not been on the rise over the last two generations of children, but that a few other disorders may be, such as oppositional defiant disorder . . . Mainly what I think we have been witnessing is an increase in the recognition of the disorder by the general population, and therefore an increase in the number of children being referred and diagnosed with the disorder. Tremendous strides have been made to educate the American public about ADHD in the last 20 years. Thanks to a substantial upsurge in research on the disorder, to the various parent advocacy groups raising the level of public and political awareness about ADHD (such as CHADD and ADDA [Attention Deficit Disorder Association] . . . , to increased professional education on the disorder, and to the recognition of ADHD as a legitimate disability in the Individuals with Disabilities in Education Act and the Americans with Disabilities Act, more children with this disorder are getting proper diagnosis and management. But again, we still have a long way to go. A recent study by Dr. Peter Jensen and colleagues at the NIMH found that as many as half or more of children with the disorder in five major regions of the United States that were studied had not been diagnosed or were not receiving appropriate treatment.

The same scenario seems to have been occurring more recently in other countries, such as Australia, Great Britain, and the Scandinavian countries, where greater efforts are under way to educate the public and professional communities about the disorder. The result has been a marked increase in the number of children being referred for professional help, properly diagnosed, and possibly being treated with stimulant medications, among other treatments, So I have to think that most of the increase in diagnosis in the United States is due to greater awareness about the disorder.

In conclusion, a number of facts suggest that we do not have widespread overdiagnosis or overmedication with stimulants, despite the marked rise in both in the United States over the last 10 to 20 years. That is not to say that there may not be some locales within the United States where more children than expected are being diagnosed or where more medication than would be prudent is being prescribed. But these appear to be very local problems and do not indicate a national scandal.

A Question of Perspective

Intense interest in demystifying ADHD has instigated voluminous research. . . . [The] research done by the time [my] book was first published in 1995 led me to a new view of ADHD—a view that has been reinforced by studies undertaken in the last five years. I see ADHD as a developmental disorder of the ability to regulate behavior with an eye toward the future. I believe the disorder stems from underactivity in an area of the brain that, as it matures, provides ever-greater means of behavioral inhibition, self-organization, self-regulation, and foresight. Relatively hidden from view in a child's moment-to-moment behavior, the behavioral deformity this underactivity causes is pernicious, insidious, and disastrous in its impact on a person's ability to manage the critical day-to-day affairs through which human beings prepare for the future, both near and far.

The fact that its daily impact is subtle but its consequences for the child's adaptive functioning are severe has led to many changes in the labels and concepts applied to the disorder over the last century. It explains why clinical science, in its attempts to pin down the nature of the problem, has moved from vague, unfocused notions of defective moral control 100 years ago to sharper, more specific concepts of hyperactivity, inattention, and impulsivity in recent decades. This evolution of our knowledge from the very general to the very specific has taken us leaps forward in understanding the abnormalities of children with ADHD, but it has caused us to lose our perspective on how those behaviors affect the social adaptation of these children over long periods of time.

Now, however, clinical science is stepping back from its microscope on the social moments of children with ADHD and once again peering through its telescope at longer-term social development. We are beginning to understand how these "atoms" of momentary ADHD behavior come to form "molecules" of daily life, how these daily "molecules" form the larger "compounds" of weekly and monthly social existence, and how these social "compounds" form the larger stages or structures of a life played out over many years. As a result, we see that ADHD is not just the hyperactivity or distractibility of the moment or the inability to get the day's work done, but a relative impairment in how behavior is organized and directed toward the tomorrows of life.

This larger, longer view of ADHD clarifies why those with the disorder struggle in their adaptation to the demands of social life and so often fail to reach the goals and futures that they have tried to set for themselves or that others demand of them. If we remember that the behavior of those with ADHD is focused on the moment, we won't judge their actions so harshly. No one would understand half of what we "normal" adults do if these actions were judged solely by their immediate consequences. Many of the actions we take have been planned with the future in mind. Likewise, we don't understand—and are quick to criticize—the behavior of those with ADHD because we are expecting them to act with foresight when they have always focused instead on the moment. We find it difficult to tolerate the way those with ADHD behave, the decisions they make, and their complaining about the negative consequences that befall them because we, who do not have the disorder, can see where it is all leading and use that vision to determine our current behavior while they cannot. Only now is clinical science coming to understand this very important feature of ADHD.

POSTSCRIPT

Is Attention Deficit (Hyperactivity) Disorder Overdiagnosed?

Allen considers whether or not ADHD reflects an "inexact science," affected by a busy and demanding society that has little tolerance for individual variation. While all treatments have their place, he wonders if adults are overlooking natural variations, seeking a "magic pill" to achieve conformity and compliance.

Barkley, on the other hand, feels that medical science is just beginning to develop the tools to help us understand how to assist all individuals reach their potential and function effectively in a demanding society. He holds that the dissemination of voluminous research on ADHD is leading a more informed set of parents and teachers to identify a disorder that can be effectively addressed.

An International Consensus Statement on ADHD (2002), signed by a consortium of over 80 international researchers, reports that there is much agreement about ADHD, beginning with it existence. The researchers attest that ADHD exists internationally and can lead to "devastating problems." Most significantly, the consortium asserts that "less than half of those with the disorder are receiving treatment." The consortium urges the media to resist distracting people by publishing "propaganda" questioning the reality or extent of ADHD.

Extensive information on ADHD is provided by Children and Adults with Attention-Deficit/Hyperactivity Disorder (CHADD), which maintains a very active Web site http://www.chadd.org, containing numerous fact sheets, legislative updates, instructional and behavioral management strategies, and a newsletter, in addition to links to related sites.

Examining "Interesting Kids Saddled with Alienating Labels," Thomas Armstrong (2001), a prolific writer, believes that we are ignoring the natural range of difference in the human population, seeking instead to attach pathological labels (and putative cures) to normal—and desirable—individual variation. Armstrong challenges adults to embrace the differences in children, seeing the possibilities rather than seeking the diagnostic label of a disorder.

Several other authors (among them Peter Breggin and Lawrence Diller) have written popular books questioning the reality and growth of interest in ADHD and the wisdom of using medication so freely with children.

In 2003 the National Institute of Mental Health reprinted its informational booklet *Attention Deficit Hyperactivity Disorder*, which reviews research data that supports a genetic basis for ADHD. Cautioning that ADHD-like behaviors can result from underachievement in school, attention lapses due to epileptic seizures, hearing problems due to ear infections, or disruptive or unresponsive behavior caused by anxiety or depression, the authors emphasize the critical need for accurate, careful analysis of the events in a child's life as opposed to a quick assumption that ADHD is present.

Real or not, the existence of ADHD is firmly established in our society. Information about the behavior of ADHD children and treatments is readily available. The scientific community has not identified a specific cause or universally effective treatments, and few believe that ADHD can be cured. Standard treatments include medication, behavioral supports, and counseling. A combination of these is usually found to achieve the most significant and long-lasting change.

Healthy caution is advisable. Many circumstances impact the behavior of children and adults alike. Medication is an important tool to use—when it is needed. Counseling and guidance from a caring adult help the most children (diagnosed with ADHD or not). Deciding whether or not a problem exists—and what to do about it—is the challenge for all of us.

Has society lost the ability to tolerate anything other than total compliance and predictability—especially from little boys? Or is it just now becoming known that there are powerful biomedical conditions that affect our ability to attend, learn, and work? Are people running to the diagnosis of ADHD (and medication) to make life easier or are they just beginning to understand its prevalence and implications?

ISSUE 18

Are There Scientifically Effective Treatments for Autism?

YES: James B. Adams, Stephen M. Edelson, Temple Grandin, and Bernard Rimland, from "Advice for Parents of Young Autistic Children," Autism Research Institute, http://www.autism.org (Spring 2004)

NO: Committee on Educational Interventions for Children With Autism, Division of Behavioral and Social Sciences and Education, National Research Council, from *Educating Children with Autism* (National Academy Press, 2001)

ISSUE SUMMARY

YES: James B. Adams, a professor at Arizona State University; Stephen M. Edelson, director of the Center for the Study of Autism; Temple Grandin, an associate professor at Colorado State University; and Bernard Rimland, director of the Autism Research Institute (ARI), recommend to parents of young children with autism an array of effective treatment options, many of them biomedically based.

NO: The Committee on Educational Interventions for Children with Autism, chaired by Catherine Lord, director of the University of Michigan's Autism and Communication Disorders Center, summarizes its examination of research studies of educational treatments for children with autism, finding little consistent evidence to support the efficacy claims made by proponents.

In 1943, Leo Kanner described a puzzling type of young child who seemed to prefer isolation from others and "aloneness." Such children did not respond readily to the smiles and games of adults. They did not react with anticipation when a caretaker reached out to pick them up, and they seemed to ignore other people. Kanner identified a combination of social isolation, significant delays in language development, and a tendency to engage in repetitive behavior and resist change. He called this group of behaviors *infantile autism*.

Early in the recognition of this disorder, Bruno Bettleheim and other psychoanalytically oriented psychologists, posited that this condition stemmed from cold, unloving "refrigerator mothers" who did not provide the child with warm and responsive parenting. This theory was disproven by other researchers who found no difference between parents of children with autism and those with typical children. In fact, parents of children with autism often had other children who developed with no difficulty.

Autism is referred to as a spectrum disorder, spanning a range of severity. Among the subtypes identified are pervasive developmental disorder (not otherwise specified), childhood disintegrative disorder, and Rett's Syndrome. Individuals who exhibit the characteristics to a lesser degree are identified as having Asperger's Syndrome, sometimes called high-functioning autism.

For the first 30 years, autism occurred two to five times per 10,000 births. Since the mid-1980s, however, prevalence figures have skyrocketed. Experts now say from ten to twelve children out of every 10,000 are given this diagnosis. In response to powerful lobbying, IDEA97 identified autism as a distinct disability category, separate from emotional disturbance.

Some say these exploding numbers are due to more refined diagnostic knowledge and practice. Others assert that something environmental must be behind these increases. Regardless of cause, experts agree that this is a serious disability, which can have disastrous consequences. Strong educational programming is essential to helping these children achieve a productive life.

Reaching agreement on what constitutes good educational programming is another matter entirely. An incredible abundance of Web sites address autism and its causes and cures. Testimonial books speak powerfully about children who have been "cured" of autism by a specific method, medical treatment, or diet. Some programs cost well over $60,000 per year per child.

Adams and his colleagues all have personal and professional connections with this field. A number of the coauthors are parents of children with autism. Temple Grandin is an adult diagnosed with autism. Offering advice to parents of young children with autism, the authors review a number of methodologies that they believe are helpful and supported by research.

At the request of the federal Office of Special Education Programs, the Committee on Educational Interventions for Children with Autism was charged with integrating information from existing research, theory, and policy. This group concludes that no one method has been substantiated as irrefutably effective for children with autism.

As you read the following selections, consider that almost every method speaks to the urgency of beginning services early—sometimes before two years of age. Parents, reeling from their child's diagnosis often feel compelled to make a rapid choice rather than lose crucial learning time. Educators want to respond to parents but also use research-based methods. How can each group make informed decisions? What happens when they disagree?

YES James B. Adams, Stephen M. Edelson, Temple Grandin, and Bernard Rimland

Advice for Parents of Young Autistic Children

Introduction

This paper is geared toward parents of newly diagnosed autistic children and parents of young autistic children who are not acquainted with many of the basic issues of autism. Our discussion is based on a large body of scientific research. Because of limited time and space, detailed explanations and references are not included.

Receiving a diagnosis of autism can be devastating to some parents, but for others it can be a relief to have a label for their child's symptoms. Many parents can be overwhelmed by fear and grief for the loss of the future they had hoped for their child. No one expects to have a child with a developmental disability. A diagnosis of autism can be very upsetting. Joining parent support groups may help. However, these strong emotions also motivate parents to find effective help for their children. The diagnosis is important because it can open the doors to many services, and help parents learn about treatments that have benefited similar children.

The most important point we want to make is that autistic individuals have the potential to grow and improve. Contrary to what you may hear from outmoded professionals or read in outmoded books, *autism is treatable*. It is important to find effective services, treatments and education for autistic children as soon as possible. The earlier these children receive appropriate treatment, the better their prognosis. Their progress through life will likely be slower than others, but they can still live happy and productive lives.

What Is Autism?

Autism is a developmental disability that typically involves delays and impairment in social skills, language, and behavior. Autism is a spectrum disorder, meaning that it affects people differently. Some children may have speech, whereas others may have little or no speech. Less severe cases may be diagnosed with Pervasive Developmental Disorder (PDD) or with Asperger's Syndrome (these children typically have normal speech, but they have many "autistic" social and behavioral problems).

Left untreated, many autistic children will not develop effective social skills and may not learn to talk or behave appropriately. Very few individuals recover completely from autism without any intervention. *The good news is that there are a wide variety of treatment options which can be very helpful.* Some treatments may lead to great improvement, whereas other treatments may have little or no effect. No treatment helps everyone. A variety of effective treatment options will be discussed below.

Onset of Autism: Early Onset vs. Regression

Autism develops sometime during pregnancy and the first three years of life. Some parents report that their child seemed different at birth. These children are referred to as early-onset autism. Other parents report that their child seemed to develop normally and then had a major regression resulting in autism, usually around 12–24 months. These children are referred as late-onset or regressive autism. Some researchers argue that the regression is not real or the autism was simply unnoticed by the child's parents. However, many parents report that their children were completely normal (e.g., speech, behavior, social) until sometime between 1 and 2 years of age. The possible causative role of vaccinations, many of which were added to the vaccination schedule in the 1980's, is a matter of considerable controversy at present . . .

Prior to 1990, approximately two-thirds of autistic children were autistic from birth and one-third regressed sometime after age one year. Starting in the 1980's, the trend has reversed—fewer than one-third are now autistic from birth and two-thirds become autistic in their second year. The following results are based on the responses to ARI's [Autism Research Institute's] E-2 checklist, which has been completed by thousands of autism families. These results suggest that something happened, such as increased exposure to an environmental insult, possibly vaccine damage, between ages 1 and 2 years.

Several brain autopsy studies have indicated that brain damage occurred sometime during the first trimester of pregnancy, but many of these studies involved individuals who were born prior to 1990. Thus, these findings may not apply to what appears to be the new population of regressive autism.

Speech Development

One of the most common questions parents ask is: Will my child develop speech?

An analysis of ARI's data involving 30,145 cases indicated that 9% never develop speech. Of those who develop speech, 43% begin to talk by the end of their first year, 35% begin to talk sometime between their first and second year, and 22% begin to talk in their third year and after. A smaller, more recent survey conducted by the first author found that only 12% were totally nonverbal by age 5. So, with appropriate interventions, there is reason to hope that children with autism can learn to talk, at least to some extent.

There are several ways to help autistic children learn to talk, including:

- Teaching speech with sign language; it is easy for parents to learn a few simple signs and use them when talking to their child. This is referred to as 'simultaneous communication' or 'signed speech.' Research suggests that the use of sign language increases the chance of children learning spoken language.

- Teaching with the Picture Exchange Communication System (PECS), which involves pointing to a set of pictures or symbols on a board. As with sign language, it can also be effective in teaching speech.
- Applied Behavior Analysis: described in more detail later
- Encouraging child to sing with a videotape or audiotape
- Vestibular stimulation, such as swinging on a swing, while teaching speech
- Several nutritional/biomedical approaches have been associated with dramatic improvements in speech production including dimethyigly-cine (DMG), vitamin B6 with magnesium, and the gluten-/casein-free diet. (To be discussed further below.)

Genetics of Autism

Genetics appear to play an important role in causing some cases of autism. Several studies have shown that when one identical twin has autism, the other co-twin often has autism. In contrast, when one fraternal twin has autism, the co-twin is rarely autistic. Studies trying to identify specific genes associated with autism have been inconclusive. Currently, it appears that 20 or more genes may be associated with autism. This is in contrast to other disorders, such as Fragile X or Rett's syndrome, in which single genes have been identified.

A large number of studies have found that autistic individuals often have compromised immune systems. In fact, autism is sometimes described as an autoimmune system disorder. One working hypothesis of autism is that the child's immune system is compromised genetically and/or environmentally (e.g., exposure to chemicals). This may predispose the child to autism. Then, exposure to an (additional) environmental insult may lead to autism (e.g., the MMR vaccine) or mercury-containing vaccine preservatives (i.e., thimerosal).

If parents have a child with autism, there is an increased likelihood, esti-mated at 5% to 8%, that their future children will also develop autism. Many studies have identified cognitive disabilities, which sometimes go undetected, in siblings of autistic children. Siblings should be evaluated for possible developmental delays and learning disabilities, such as dyslexia.

Possible Environmental Causes of Autism

Although genetics play an important role in autism, environmental factors are also involved. There is no general consensus on what those environmental factors are at this point in time. Since the word "autism" is only a label for people who have a certain set of symptoms, there are likely to be a number of factors that could cause those symptoms. Some of the suspected environmen-tal causes for which there is some scientific evidence include:

- Childhood vaccinations: The increasing number of vaccines given to young children might compromise their immune system. Many parents report their child was normal until vaccinations.

- MMR Vaccine: Evidence of measles virus have been detected in the gut, spinal fluid and blood. Also, the incidence of autism began rising significantly when the MMR was introduced in the US (1978) and in the United Kingdom (1988).
- Thimerosal (a mercury-based preservative) in childhood vaccines. The number of vaccines given to children has risen over the last two decades, and most of those vaccines contained thimerosal, which is 50% mercury. The symptoms of mercury poisoning in children are very similar to the symptoms of autism.
- Excessive use of oral antibiotics: can cause gut problems, such as yeast/bacterial overgrowth, and prevents mercury excretion
- Maternal exposure to mercury (e.g., consumption of seafood high in mercury, mercury dental fillings, thimerosal in RhoGam shots)
- Lack of essential minerals: zinc, magnesium, iodine, lithium, and potassium may be especially important
- Pesticides and other environmental toxins
- Other unknown environmental factors

Prevalence of Autism

There has been a rapid increase in the number of children diagnosed with autism. The most accurate statistics on the prevalence of autism come from California, which has an accurate and systematic centralized reporting system of all diagnoses of autism. The California data show that autism is rising rapidly, from 1 per 2,500 in 1970 to 1 per 285 in 1999. Similar results have been reported for other states by the US Department of Education. Whereas autism once accounted for 3% of all developmental disabilities, in California it now accounts for 45% of all new developmental disabilities. Other countries report similar increases.

We do not know why there has been a dramatic increase in autism over the past 15 years, but there are several reasonable hypotheses. Since there is more than one cause of autism, there may be more than one reason for the increase. A small portion of the increase of autism where speech is delayed may be due to improved diagnosis and awareness, but the report from California reveals that this only explains a minute part of the increase. However, the increase in the milder variant called Asperger's Syndrome may be due to increased diagnosis. In Asperger's Syndrome, there is no significant speech delay and early childhood behavior is much more normal. The major reason for the increase is certainly due to environmental factors, not genetics, since there is no such thing as a 'genetic epidemic.' Some *possible* environmental factors were discussed in the previous section, and an increased occurrence of one or several of those factors probably accounts for the rapid increase in autism. . . .

What is the Difference Between Asperger's Syndrome and Autism?

Asperger syndrome is usually considered a subtype of high-functioning autism. Most of the individuals with Asperger syndrome are described as "social but awkward." That is, they want to have friends, but they do not have the social skills to begin and/or maintain a friendship. While high-functioning autistic individuals may also be "social but awkward," they are typically less interested in having friends. In addition, high-functioning autistic individuals are often delayed in developing speech/language. Those with Asperger syndrome tend not to have speach/language delays, but their speech is usually described as peculiar, such as being stilted and perseverating on unusual topics.

Medical Testing and Treatments

A small but growing number of physicians (many of whom are themselves parents of autistic children) are involved in trying safe and innovative methods for treating the underlying biomedical basis of autism—the Defeat Autism Now! (DAN!) program. . . .

Routine medical tests are usually performed by traditional pediatricians, but they rarely reveal problems in autism that can be treated. Genetic testing for Fragile X syndrome can help identify one possible cause, and this testing is typically recommended when there is mental retardation in the family history. Many physicians do not conduct extensive medical testing for autism, because they believe, incorrectly, that the only useful medical treatments are psychiatric medications to reduce seizures and behavioral problems.

Some of the major interventions suggested by DAN! practitioners include:

- Nutritional supplements, including certain vitamins, minerals, amino acids, and essential fatty acids
- Special diets totally free of gluten (from wheat, barley, rye, and possibly oats) and free of dairy (milk, Ice-cream, yogurt, etc.)
- Testing for hidden food allergies, and avoidance of allergenic foods
- Treatment of intestinal bacterial/yeast overgrowth
- Detoxification of heavy metals

Psychiatric Medications

The various topics covered in this overview paper for parents of young autistic children represent, for the most part, a consensus of the views, based on research and personal experience, of all four authors. However, the authors differ in their opinions on the role of psychoactive drugs should play. . . .

Grandin has a relatively accepting position on the use of psychiatric medications in older autistic children and adults. She feels that it is worthwhile to consider drugs as a viable and useful treatment. Rimland and Edelson, on the other hand, are strongly opposed to the use of drugs except as a possible last resort, . . .— [t]hey feel the risks are great and consistently outweigh the benefits. Adams has an intermediate view. . . .

Educational/Behavioral Approaches

Educational/behavioral therapies are often effective in children with autism, with Applied Behavioral Analysis (ABA) usually being the most effective. These methods can and should be used together with biomedical interven- tions, as together they offer the best chance for improvement.

Parents, siblings, and friends may play an important role in assisting the development of children with autism. Typical pre-school children learn primarily by play, and the importance of play in teaching language and social skills cannot be overemphasized. Ideally, many of the techniques used in ABA, sensory integration, and other therapies can be extended throughout the day by family and friends.

Applied Behavior Analysis   Many different behavioral interventions have been developed for children with autism, and they mostly fall under the category of Applied Behavioral Analysis (ABA). This approach generally involves therapists who work intensely, one-on-one with a child for 20 to 40 hours/week. Children are taught skills in a simple step-by-step manner, such as teaching colors one at a time. The sessions usually begin with formal, structured drills, such as learning to point to a color when its name is given; and then, after some time, there is a shift towards generalizing skills to other situations and environments.

A study published by Dr. Ivar Lovaas at UCLA in 1987 involved two years of intensive, 40-hour/week behavioral intervention by trained graduate students working with 19 young autistic children ranging from 35 to 41 months of age. Almost half of the children improved so much that they were indistinguishable from typical children, and these children went on to lead fairly normal lives. Of the other half, most had significant improvements, but a few did not improve much.

ABA programs are most effective when started early, (before age 5 years), but they can also be helpful to older children. They are especially effective in teaching non-verbal children how to talk.

There is general agreement that:

- behavioral interventions involving one-on-one interactions are usually beneficial, sometimes with very positive results
- the interventions are most beneficial with the youngest children, but older children can benefit
- the interventions should involve a substantial amount of time each week, between 20–40 hours depending on whether the child is in school
- prompting as much as necessary to achieve a high level of success, with a gradual fading of prompts
- proper training of therapists and ongoing supervision
- regular team meetings to maintain consistency between therapists and check for problems
- most importantly, keeping the sessions fun for the children is necessary to maintain their interest and motivation

Parents are encouraged to obtain training in ABA, so that they provide it themselves and possibly hire other people to assist. Qualified behavior consultants are often available, and there are often workshops on how to provide ABA therapy.

Sensory Integration   Many autistic individuals have sensory problems, which can range from mild to severe. These problems involve either hypersensitivity or hyposensitivity to stimulation. Sensory integration focuses primarily on three senses—vestibular (i.e., motion, balance), tactile (i.e., touch), and proprioception (e.g., Joints, ligaments). Many techniques are used to stimulate these sense in order to normalize them.

Speech Therapy   This may be beneficial to many autistic children, but often only 1–2 hours/week is available, so it probably has only modest benefit unless integrated with other home and school programs. As mentioned earlier, sign language and PECS may also be very helpful in developing speech. Speech therapists should work on helping the child to hear hard consonant sounds such as the "c" in cup. It is often helpful if the therapist stretches out and enunciates the consonant sounds.

Occupational Therapy   Can be beneficial for the sensory needs of these children, who often have hypo- and/or hyper-sensitivities to sound, sight, smell, touch, and taste. May include sensory integration (above).

Physical Therapy   Often children with autism have limited gross and fine motor skills, so physical therapy can be helpful. May also include sensory integration (above).

Auditory Interventions   There are several types of auditory interventions. The only one with significant scientific backing is Berard Auditory Integration Training (called Berard AIT or AIT) which involves listening to processed music for a total of 10 hours (two half-hour sessions per day, over a period of 10 to 12 days). There are many studies supporting its effectiveness. Research has shown that AIT improves auditory processing, decreases or eliminates sound sensitivity, and reduces behavioral problems in some autistic children.

     Other auditory interventions include the Tomatis approach, the Listening Program, and the SAMONAS method. There is limited amount of empirical evidence to support their efficacy. Information about these programs can be obtained from the Society for Auditory Intervention Techniques' website (www.sait.org).

     Computer-based auditory interventions have also received some empirical support. They include Earobics . . . and Fast ForWord. . . . These programs have been shown to help children who have delays in language and have difficulty discriminating speech sounds. Earobics is less much expensive (less than $100) but appears to be less powerful than the Fast ForWord program (usually over $1,000). Some families use the Earobics program first and then later use Fast ForWord.

Computer Software   There are many educational programs available for typical children, and some of those may be of benefit for autistic children. There is also some computer software designed specifically for children with developmental disabilities. One major provider is Laureate. . . .

Vision Training and Irlen Lenses   Many autistic individuals have difficulty attending to their visual environment and/or perceiving themselves in relation to their surroundings. These problems have been associated with a short attention span, being easily distracted, excessive eye movements, difficulty scanning or tracking movements, inability to catch a ball, being cautious when walking up or down stairs, bumping into furniture, and even toe walking. A one- to two-year vision training program involving ambient prism lenses and performing visual-motor exercises can reduce or eliminate many of these problems. . . . More information on vision training can be found on internet Web site of the College of Optometrists in Vision Development. . . .

Another visual/perceptual program involves wearing Irlen lenses. Irlen lenses are colored (tinted) lenses. Individuals who benefit from these lenses are often hypersensitive to certain types of lighting, such as florescent lights and bright sunlight; hypersensitive to certain colors or color contrasts; and/or have difficulty reading printed text. Irlen lenses can reduce one's sensitivity to these lighting and color problems as well as improve reading skills and increase attention span. . . .

Relationship Development Intervention (RDI)   This is a new method for teaching children how to develop relationships, first with their parents and later with their peers. It directly addresses a core issue in autism, namely the development of social skills and friendships. . . .

Preparing for the Future

Temple Grandin: "As a person with autism I want to emphasize the importance of developing the child's talents. Skills are often uneven in autism, and a child may be good at one thing and poor at another. I had talents in drawing, and these talents later developed into a career in designing cattle handling systems for major beef companies. Too often there is too much emphasis on the deficits and not enough emphasis on the talents. Abilities in children with autism will vary greatly, and many individuals will function at a lower level than me. However, developing talents and improving skills will benefit all. If a child becomes fixated on trains, then use the great motivation of that fleach reading, use calculating the speed of a train to teach math, and encourage an interest in history by studying the history of the railroads."

Developing Friendships

Although young children with autism may seem to prefer to be by themselves, one of the most important issues for older children and adults is the development of friendships with peers. It can take a great deal of time and effort for them to develop the social skills needed to be able to interact successfully with other children, but it is important to start early. In addition, bullying in middle and high school can be a major problem for students with autism, and the development of friendships is one of the best ways to prevent this problem.

Friendships can be encouraged informally by inviting other children to the home to play. In school, recess can be a valuable time for teachers to encourage play with other children. Furthermore, time can be set aside in school for formal "play time" between children with autism and volunteer peers—typical children usually think that play time is much more fun than regular school, and it can help develop lasting friendships. This is probably one of the most important issues to include in a student's Individualized Education Program (IEP, or education plan for the child). Children with autism often develop friendships through shared interests, such as computers, school clubs, model airplanes, etc. Encourage activities that the autistic individual can share with others.

School Programs

For children younger than 3 years old, there are early intervention programs. For children over 3 years of age, there are pre-school and school programs available. Parents should contact their local school district for information on their local programs. In some cases a separate program for special-needs children may be best, but for higher-functioning children integration into a regular school setting may be more appropriate, provided that there is enough support (a part- or full-time aide, or other accommodations as needed). It is important that parents work with their child's teacher on an Individual Education Plan (IEP), which outlines in great detail the child's educational program. Additionally, meeting with the child's classmates and/or their parents can be helpful in encouraging other students to interact positively with the autistic child.

In some states, home therapy programs (such as ABA and speech therapy) may be funded by the school district, rather than through the state. However, it may take considerable effort to convince the school district to provide those services. Check with your local ASA chapter and other parents about how services are usually provided in your state. . . .

Long-Term Prognosis

Today, most adults with autism are either living at home with their parents or living in a group home. Some higher-functioning people live in a supported-living situation, with modest assistance, and a very few are able to live independently. Some are able to work, either in volunteer work, sheltered workshops, or private employment, but many do not. Adults with PDD/NOS (not otherwise specified) and Asperger's generally are more likely to live independently, and they are more likely to work. Unfortunately, they often have difficulty finding and then maintaining a job. The major reason for chronic unemployment is not a lack of job skills, but rather due to their limited social skills. Thus, it is important to encourage appropriate social skills early on, so they are able to live and work independently as much as possible.

Some of the most successful people on the autism spectrum who have good jobs have developed expertise in a specialized skill that often people value. If a person makes him-/herself very good at something, this can help make up for some difficulties with social skills. Good fields for higher functioning people on the spectrum are architectural drafting, computer programming, language translator, special educator, librarian and scientist. It is likely that some brilliant scientists and musicians have a mild form of Asperger's Syndrome (Ledgin, 2002). The individuals who are most successful often have mentor teachers either in high school, college or at a place of employment. Mentors can help channel interests into careers. Untreated sensory oversensitivity can severely limit a person's ability to tolerate a workplace environment. Eliminating fluorescent lights will often help, but untreated sound sensitivity has caused some individuals on the spectrum to quit good jobs because ringing telephones hurt their ears. Sensory sensitivities can be reduced by auditory integration training, diets, Irlen lenses, conventional psychiatric medications and vitamin supplementation. Magnesium often helps hypersensitive hearing.

It should also be pointed out that the educational, therapy, and biomedical options available today are much better than in past decades, and they should be much better in the future. However, it is often up to parents to find those services, determine which are the most appropriate for their child, and ensure that they are properly implemented. *Parents are a child's most powerful advocates and teachers.* With the right mix of interventions, most children with autism will be able to improve. As we learn more, children with autism will have a better chance to lead happy and fulfilling lives.

 **NO**

Educating Children with Autism

Conclusions and Recommendations

This [selection] summarizes the committee's conclusions about the state of the science in early intervention for children with autistic spectrum disorders and its recommendations for future intervention strategies, programs, policy, and research. The [selection] is organized around seven key areas pertaining to educational interventions for young children with autistic spectrum disorders: how the disorders are diagnosed and assessed and how prevalent they are; the effect on and role of families; appropriate goals for educational services; characteristics of effective interventions and educational programs; public policy approaches to ensuring access to appropriate education; the preparation of educational personnel; and needs for future research.

Diagnosis, Assessment, and Prevalence

Conclusions

Autism is a developmental disorder of neurobiologic origin that is defined on the basis of behavioral and developmental features. Autism is best characterized as a spectrum of disorders that vary in severity of symptoms, age of onset, and association with other disorders (e.g., mental retardation, specific language delay, epilepsy). The manifestations of autism vary considerably across children and within an individual child over time. There is no single behavior that is always typical of autism and no behavior that would automatically exclude an individual child from a diagnosis of autism, even though there are strong and consistent commonalities, especially relative to social deficits.

The large constellation of behaviors that define autistic spectrum disorders—generally representing deficits in social interaction, verbal and nonverbal communication, and restricted patterns of interest or behaviors— are clearly and reliably identifiable in very young children to experienced clinicians and educators. However, distinctions among classical autism and atypical autism, pervasive developmental disorder-not otherwise specified (PDD-NOS), and Asperger's disorder can be arbitrary and are often associated with the presence or severity of handicaps, such as mental retardation and severe language impairment.

Identifying narrow categories within autism is necessary for some research purposes; however, the clinical or educational benefit to subclassifying autistic spectrum disorders purely by diagnosis is debated. In contrast, individual differences in language development, verbal and nonverbal communication, sensory or motor skills, adaptive behavior, and cognitive abilities have significant effects on behavioral presentation and outcome, and, consequently, have specific implications for educational goals and strategies. Thus, the most important considerations in programming have to do with the strengths and weaknesses of the individual child, the age at diagnosis, and early intervention.

With adequate time and training, the diagnosis of autistic spectrum disorders can be made reliably in 2-year-olds by professionals experienced in the diagnostic assessment of young children with autistic spectrum disorders. Many families report becoming concerned about their children's behavior and expressing this concern, usually to health professionals, even before this time. Research is under way to develop reliable methods of identification for even younger ages. Children with autistic spectrum disorders, like children with vision or hearing problems, require early identification and diagnosis to equip them with the skills (e.g., imitation, communication) to benefit from educational services, with some evidence that earlier initiation of specific services for autistic spectrum disorders is associated with greater response to treatment. Thus, well meaning attempts not to label children with formal diagnoses can deprive children of specialized services. There are clear reasons for early identification of children, even as young as two years of age, within the autism spectrum.

Epidemiological studies and service-based reports indicate that the prevalence of autistic spectrum disorders has increased in the last 10 years, in part due to better identification and broader categorization by educators, physicians, and other professionals. There is little doubt that more children are being identified as requiring specific educational interventions for autistic spectrum disorders. This has implications for the provision of services at many levels. Analysis of data from the Office of Special Education Programs, gathered for school-age children since the autism category was recognized in 1991, would support investigation of whether the dramatic increases in the numbers of children served with autistic spectrum disorders are offset by commensurate decreases in other categories in which children with autistic spectrum disorders might have previously been misclassified or whether these dramatic increases have come about for other reasons.

Although children with autistic spectrum disorders share some characteristics with children who have other developmental disorders and may benefit from many of the same educational techniques, they offer unique challenges to families, teachers, and others who work with them. Their deficits in nonverbal and verbal communication require intense effort and skill even in the teaching of basic information. The unique difficulties in social interaction (e.g., in joint attention) may require more individual guidance than for other children in order to attract and sustain their children's attention. Moreover, ordinary social exchanges between peers do not usually occur without deliberate planning and ongoing structuring by the adults in the child's environment. The absence of typical friendships and peer relationships affects children's motivation systems and the meaning of experiences. Appropriate social interactions may be some of the most difficult and important lessons a child with autistic spectrum disorders will learn.

In addition, the frequency of behavior problems, such as tantrums and self-stimulatory and aggressive behavior, is high. The need for systematic selection of rewards for many children with autistic spectrum disorders, whose motivation or interests can be limited, requires creativity and continued effort from teachers and parents to maximize the child's potential. Although general principles of learning and behavior analysis apply to autistic spectrum disorders, familiarity with the specific nature of the disorder should contribute to analysis of the contexts (e.g., communicative and social) of behaviors for individual children and result in more effective programming. For example, conducting a functional assessment that considers contexts, and then replacing problem behaviors with more appropriate ways to communicate can be an effective method for reducing problem behaviors. . . .

Role of Families

Conclusions

Having a child with an autistic spectrum disorder is a challenge for any family. Involvement of families in the education of young children with autistic spectrum disorders can occur at multiple levels, including advocacy, parents as participating partners in and agents of education or behavior change, and family-centered consideration of the needs and strengths of the family as a unit. Nearly all empirically supported treatments reviewed by the committee included a parent component, and most research programs used a parent-training approach. More information is needed about the benefits of a family-centered orientation or combined family-centered and formalized parent training in helping parents.

It is well established that parents can learn and successfully apply skills to changing the behavior of their children with autistic spectrum disorders, though little is known about the effects of cultural differences, such as race, ethnicity, and social class, nor about the interactions among family factors, child characteristics, and features of educational intervention. For most families, having a child with an autistic spectrum disorder creates added stress. Parents' use of effective teaching methods can have a significant effect on that stress, as can support from within the family and the community. Parents need access to balanced information about autistic spectrum disorders and the range of appropriate services and technologies in order to carry out their responsibilities. They also need timely information about assessments, educational plans, and the available resources for their children. This information needs to be conveyed to them in a meaningful way that gives them time to prepare to fulfill their roles and responsibilities.

In the last ten years the widespread availability of the Internet and media attention to autistic spectrum disorders have increased parents' knowledge but often conveyed perspectives that were not balanced nor well-supported scientifically. Of crucial importance is the question of how to make information available to parents and to ensure their active role in advocacy for their children's education. . . .

Goals for Educational Services

Conclusions

At the root of questions about the most appropriate educational interventions lie differences in assumptions about what is possible and what is important to give students with autistic spectrum disorders through education. The appropriate goals for educational services are the same as those for other children: personal independence and social responsibility. These goals imply continuous progress in social and cognitive abilities, verbal and nonverbal communication skills, adaptive skills, amelioration or behavioral difficulties, and generalization of abilities across multiple environments. In some cases, reports have suggested that particular treatments can foster permanent "recovery". However, as with other developmental disabilities, the core deficits of autistic spectrum disorders have generally been found to persist, to some degree, in most individuals.

Research concerning outcomes can be characterized by whether the goal of intervention is broadly defined (e.g., "recovery" or "best outcome") or more specifically defined (e.g., increasing vocabulary or peer-directed social behavior); whether the design involves reporting results in terms of group or individual changes; and whether the goals are short term (i.e., to be achieved in a few weeks or months) or longer term (i.e., over years). A large body of single-subject research has demonstrated substantial progress in individual responses to specific intervention techniques in relatively short periods of times (e.g., several months) in many specific areas, including gains in social skills, language acquisition, nonverbal communication, and reductions in challenging behaviors. Studies over longer periods of time have documented joint attention, symbolic play, early language skills, and imitation as core deficits and hallmarks of the disorder that are predictive of longer term outcome in the domains of language, adaptive behaviors, and academic skills.

Many treatment studies report postintervention placement as an outcome measure. While successful participation in regular classrooms is an important goal for some children with autistic spectrum disorders, the usefulness of placement in regular education classes as an outcome measure is limited, because placement may be related to many variable other than the characteristics of the child (e.g., prevailing trends in inclusion, availability of other services). The most commonly reported outcome measure in group treatment studies of children with autistic spectrum disorders has been changes in IQ scores, which also have many limitations.

Studies have reported substantial changes in large numbers of children in intervention studies and longitudinal studies in which children received a variety of interventions. Even in the treatment studies that have shown the strongest gains, children's outcomes are variable, with some children making substantial progress and others showing very slow gains. The needs and strengths of young children with autistic spectrum disorders are very heterogeneous. Although there is evidence that many interventions lead to improvements and that some children shift in specific diagnosis along the autism spectrum during the preschool years, there does not appear to be a simple relationship between any particular intervention and "recovery" from autistic spectrum disorders. Thus, while substantial evidence exists that treatments can reach short-term specific goals in many areas, gaps remain in addressing larger questions of the relationships between particular techniques, child characteristics, and outcomes. . . .

Characteristics of Effective Interventions

Conclusions

In general, there is consistent agreement across comprehensive intervention programs about a number of features, though practical and, sometimes, ethical considerations have made well-controlled studies with random assignment very difficult to conduct without direct evaluation. Characteristics of the most appropriate intervention for a given child must be tied to that child's and family's needs. However, without direct evaluation, it is difficult to know which features are of greatest importance in a program. Across primarily preschool programs, there is a very strong consensus that the following features are critical:

- Entry into intervention programs as soon as an autism spectrum diagnosis is seriously considered;
- Active engagement in intensive instructional programming for a minimum of the equivalent of a full school day, 5 days (at least 25 hours) a week, with full year programming varied according to the child's choronological age and developmental level;
- Repeated, planned teaching opportunities generally organized around relatively brief periods of time for the youngest children (e.g., 15–20 minute intervals), including sufficient amounts of adult attention in one-to-one and very small group instruction to meet individualized goals;
- Inclusion of a family component, including parent training;
- Low student/teacher ratios (no more than two young children with autistic spectrum disorders per adult in the classroom); and
- Mechanisms for ongoing program evaluation and assessments of individual children's progress, with results translated into adjustments in programming.

Curricula across different programs differ in a number of ways. They include the ways in which goals are prioritized, affecting the relative time spent on verbal and nonverbal communication, social activities, behavioral, academic, motor, and other domains. Strategies from various programs represent a range of techniques, including discrete trials, incidental teaching, structured teaching, "floor time", and individualized modifications of the environment, including schedules. Some programs adopt a unilateral use of one set of procedures, and others use a combination of approaches. Programs also differ in the relative amount of time spent in homes, centers, or schools, when children are considered ready for inclusion into regular classrooms, how the role of peers as intervention agents is supported, and in the use of distraction-free or natural environments. Programs also differ in the credentials that are required of direct support and supervisory staff and the formal and informal roles of collateral staff, such as speech language pathologists and occupational therapists.

Overall, many of the programs are more similar than different in terms of levels of organization, staffing, ongoing monitoring, and the use of certain techniques, such as discrete trials, incidental learning, and structured teaching. However, there are real differences in philosophy and practice that provide a range of alternatives for parents and school systems considering various approaches. The key to any child's educational program lies in the objectives specified in the IEP and the ways they are addressed. Much more important than the name of the program attended is how the environment and educational strategies allow implementation of the goals for a child and family. Thus, effective services will and should vary considerably across individual children, depending on a child's age, cognitive and language levels, behavioral needs, and family priorities. . . .

Public Policies

Conclusions

The Individuals with Disabilities Education Act (IDEA) contains the necessary provisions for ensuring rights to appropriate education for children with autistic spectrum disorders. However, the implementation and specification of these services are variable. Early intervention for young children with autistic spectrum disorders is expensive, and most local schools need financial help from the state and federal programs to provide appropriate services.

The large number of court cases is a symptom of the tension between families and school systems. Case law has yielded an inconsistent pattern of findings that vary according to the characteristics of the individual cases. The number of challenges to decision-making for programming within school systems reflects parents' concerns about the adequacy of knowledge and the expertise of school systems in determining their children's education and implementing appropriate techniques.

The treatment of autistic spectrum disorders often involves many disciplines and agencies. This confuses lines of financial and intellectual responsibility and complicates assessment and educational planning. When communication between families and school systems goes awry, it can directly affect children's programming and the energy and financial resources that are put into education rather than litigation. Support systems are not generally adequate in undergirding local service delivery programs and maximizing the usefulness of different disciplines and agencies, and transitions between service delivery agencies are often problematic.

A number of states have successful models for providing services to children with autism, and mechanisms are becoming increasingly efficient and flexible in some states. In most cases, existing agencies at state and federal levels can develop appropriate programs without restructuring—with the possible addition of special task forces or committees designed to deal with issues particular to children with autistic spectrum disorders. . . .

Personnel Preparation

Conclusions
The nature of autistic spectrum disorders and other disabilities that frequently accompany them has significant implications for approaches to education and intervention at school, in the home, and in the community. Approaches that emphasize the use of specific "packages" of materials and methods associated with comprehensive intervention programs may understate the multiple immediate and long-term needs of children for behavior support and for instruction across areas.

Teachers are faced with a huge task. They must be familiar with theory and research concerning best practices for children with autistic spectrum disorders, including methods of applied behavior analysis, naturalistic learning, assistive technology, socialization, communication, inclusion, adaptation of the environment, language interventions, assessment, and the effective use of data collection systems. Specific problems in generalization and maintenance of behaviors also affect the need for training in methods of teaching children with autistic spectrum disorders. The wide range of IQ scores and verbal skills associated with autistic spectrum disorders, from profound mental retardation and severe language impairments to superior intelligence, intensify the need for personnel training. To enable teachers to adequately work with parents and with other professionals to set appropriate goals, teachers need familiarity with the course of autistic spectrum disorders and the range of possible outcomes.

Teachers learn according to the same principles as their students. Multiple exposures, opportunities to practice, and active involvement in learning are all important aspects of learning for teachers, as well as students. Many states and community organizations have invested substantial funds in teacher preparation through workshops and large-audience lectures by well-known speakers. While such presentations can stimulate enthusiasm, they do not substitute for ongoing consultation and hands-on opportunities to observe and practice skills working with children with autistic spectrum disorders.

Personnel preparation remains one of the weakest elements of effective programming for children with autistic spectrum disorders and their families. Ways of building on the knowledge of teachers as they acquire experience with children with autistic spectrum disorders, and ways of keeping skilled personnel within the field, are critical. This is particularly true given recent trends for dependence on relatively inexperienced assistants for in-home programs. Providing knowledge about autistic spectrum disorders to special education and regular education administrators, as well as to specialized providers with major roles in early intervention (e.g., speech language pathologists) will be critical in effecting change that is proactive. Findings concerning change in educational and other opportunities suggest that administrative attitudes and support are critical in improving schools. . . .

Needed Research

Conclusions

There are several distinct and substantial bodies of research relevant to young children with autistic spectrum disorders. One body identifies neurological, behavioral, and developmental characteristics. Another body of research addresses diagnostic practices and related issues of prevalence. Another has examined the effects of comprehensive early treatment programs on the immediate and long-term outcomes of children and their families. These treatment studies tended to use some form of group experimental design. An additional body of research has addressed individual instructional or intervention approaches, with many studies in this literature using single-subject experimental methodology. Altogether, a large research base exists, but with relatively little integration across bodies of literature. Highly knowledgeable researchers in one area of autistic spectrum disorders may have minimal information from other perspectives, even about studies with direct bearing on their findings.

Most researchers have not used randomized group comparison designs because of the practical and ethical difficulties in randomly assigning children and families to treatment groups. In addition, there have been significant controversies over the type of control or contrast group to use and the conditions necessary for demonstrating effectiveness. Although a number of comprehensive programs have provided data on their effectiveness, and, in some cases, claims have been made that certain treatments are superior to others, there have been virtually no comparisons of different comprehensive interventions of equal intensity.

Across several of the bodies of literature, the children and families who have participated in studies are often inadequately described. Standardized diagnoses, descriptions of ethnicity, the social class, and associated features of the children (such as mental retardation and language level) are often not specified. Fidelity of treatment implementation has not been consistently assessed. Generalization, particularly across settings, and maintenance of treatment effects are not always measured. Though there is little evidence concerning the effectiveness of discipline-specific therapies, there is substantial research supporting the effectiveness of many specific therapeutic techniques.

POSTSCRIPT

Are There Scientifically Effective Treatments for Autism?

The authors on the two sides of this issue agree on several points: Autism is a serious disorder; left alone, its consequences could be disastrous; intensive, early intervention is critical; and there are many methods from which to choose.

There are critical areas of disagreement, however. Adams and his colleagues believe strongly in a biomedical cause for autism. Our environment is hurting children they say. While educational interventions are important, they advocate medical treatment as well.

The Committee on Educational Interventions for Children with Autism holds that the increased numbers of children diagnosed with autism are due to changes in diagnostic practices. As the field learns about autism, more children are given this diagnosis instead of another. Noting the wide range of characteristics in this group, the Committee says that much more systematic research is needed to find the best educational interventions.

Weighing both points of view about the increasing numbers, Goode (*The New York Times*, 2004) observes that if the increase is due to environmental problems, numbers are likely to continue to rise unless something changes. If diagnostic knowledge is behind the increase, she posits that "rates should level off as the number of previously overlooked children diminishes."

In the meantime, educators and parents need to decide what education is best. Attorneys may play the largest role in resolving disagreements through administrative hearings (Drasgow, Yell, and Robinson, *Remedial and Special Education*, 2001).

One of the most hotly debated treatments is Applied Behavioral Analysis (ABA). An intensive therapy based on the work of Lovaas and colleagues, ABA methods require many daily hours of 1:1 work, reinforcing children for increasingly complex behaviors. This approach begins with an emphasis on eye contact and basic attention and moves on to academic and social interactions. Supporters proclaim that ABA has "cured" their child of autism. Detractors claim that existing research studies are flawed and that learned behavior does not generalize to new settings. Could parental reports of improvement be flawed? Do research design problems override the observation of parents? Or do small changes delude everyone into overestimating progress?

Equally heated is the debate about whether or not autism stems from vaccines. U.S. Representative Dan Burton, chair of the Subcommittee of Human Rights and Wellness and grandfather of a child with autism, is convinced that the mercury used to preserve vaccines leads to autism. In a recent subcommittee hearing updating federal initiatives in this area, Burton claims to have convened over 20 hearings on this topic (Committee on Government Reform, 2004). Speakers at the May 2004 hearing included researchers reporting intravenous treatments to remove mercury from the bloodstream. Within the very same month, a report of the Immunization Safety Review Committee (National Academy of Sciences, 2004) "rejected the causal relationship between MMR [measles, mumps, rubella] vaccine and autism." Given conflicting views, should parents have their children vaccinated?

The conflict between the passionate parental search for a real "cure" and the need for scientific support is poignantly described in "A Father's Fight" (Bernstein, *Health*, 2004). The M.I.N.D. Institute is one of the largest research and treatment centers devoted to autism. This is a unique collaboration, funded by a group of fathers who want their children cured of autism and staffed by researchers committed to the scientific method. Dedicated to the same goal but driven by different forces, the article describes the institute as a place nurtured by "creative tension." Will this unique collaboration result in solid answers? Will they come soon enough for the children?

How do schools select effective programs? How do parents decide if their school's proposed program is effective? The evidence is clear but often contradictory. If each child is unique, how can research prove the worth of any method? Should schools follow the lead of parents excited by a promising method unsubstantiated by research? Or should they adhere to more established methods of treatment? Can ethics and approved research protocols coexist? How would you decide for a student? Would you decide differently if it were your own child?

ISSUE 19

Should One-on-One Nursing Care Be Part of Special Education?

YES: John Paul Stevens, from Majority Opinion, *Cedar Rapids Community School District v. Garret F.*, U.S. Supreme Court (March 3, 1999)

NO: Clarence Thomas, from Dissenting Opinion, *Cedar Rapids Community School District v. Garret F.*, U.S. Supreme Court (March 3, 1999)

ISSUE SUMMARY

YES: U.S. Supreme Court Justice John Paul Stevens, writing for the majority of the Court, affirms the "bright line test," establishing that school districts are required by IDEA to provide one-on-one nursing services and any other health-related services that can be delivered by individuals other than a licensed physician.

NO: U.S. Supreme Court Justice Clarence Thomas, representing the dissenting minority opinion, asserts that continuous one-on-one nursing services for disabled children are indeed medical and, as such, beyond the scope of congressional intent in IDEA. He concludes that such services are not the responsibility of special education programs within school districts.

Recognizing that some children need more than traditional educational services, IDEA directs schools to provide "related services" necessary to enable a child with a disability to access the special education program designed by the school team (IDEA, Section 300.24). Like the program, these must be provided at no cost. Related services include speech, occupational and physical therapy, and transportation. School health services and "medical services for diagnostic or evaluation purposes" are also mentioned in IDEA, though not medical procedures or treatment.

Court cases about related services began almost as soon as IDEA was passed. The first to reach the Supreme Court questioned whether a sign language interpreter was a required related service for a child with a hearing impairment (*Board of Education v. Rowley*, 1982). The Court determined that this service was not required because it felt that the child was making effective school progress with the operative special education program.

Concurrent with *Rowley*, the first medically related cases were moving through the courts. The landmark case was *Irving Independent School District v. Tatro* (1984), in which the Supreme Court required school personnel to perform clean intermittent catheterization, a procedure used to empty a child's bladder, so that she could remain in school and benefit from special education services. Although the school district felt that this procedure crossed the line into medical services, the Supreme Court established its own "bright line": If a procedure could be performed by a trained, supervised individual, it fell within the realm of the school's responsibilities. The Court acknowledged, however, that there are likely some medically related services that are too financially burdensome or complicated to be included.

Following *Tatro*, court decisions split into two lines of reasoning. Initially, lower courts adopted the "burden" and "complexity" elements of the decision, finding some medical services (tracheostomy care and cardiopulmonary resuscitation, for example) to be beyond the professional and financial responsibility of schools. About 10 years later, courts emphasized the "bright line" standard, finding that cost and complexity should not pose a barrier to access to education.

The issue crystallized with Garret Frey, a high school student who had been paralyzed since childhood. Academically successful in school, Garret required continuous medical support in order to attend. Having exhausted available personal funds, and believing that the services were well within the capacity of trained staff, Garret's parents turned to the school district. However, the district believed that the bright line standard should be overridden in this case by overall consideration of cost, complexity, time, and amount of services required, as well as liability for improper services.

In *Cedar Rapids Community School District v. Garret F.*, the Supreme Court voted 7–2 in favor of the bright line standard. The majority and dissenting opinions are reprinted in the following selections. Writing for the majority, Justice John Paul Stevens finds the continuous nursing services required by Garret to be well within the confines of school health services, noting that current federal law does not permit districts to consider the total cost or complexity of medically related assistance.

Justice Clarence Thomas, writing for the dissenting minority, holds that the services required by Garret—indeed, those discussed in *Tatro*—are medical and clearly outside the boundaries of school responsibility as written in IDEA. The minority opinion identifies financial and professional limits to the extent of a school's responsibility as well.

As you read these Supreme Court opinions, ask yourself these questions: What is the difference between medicine and education? Should there be a limit to a school's responsibilities to provide access? Where do you draw the line?

YES

John Paul Stevens

Majority Opinion

Cedar Rapids Community School District *v.* Garret F.

Justice Stevens delivered the opinion of the Court.

The Individuals with Disabilities Education Act (IDEA), 84 Stat. 175, as amended, was enacted, in part, "to assure that all children with disabilities have available to them . . . a free appropriate public education which emphasizes special education and related services designed to meet their unique needs." 20 U.S.C. §1400(c). Consistent with this purpose, the IDEA authorizes federal financial assistance to States that agree to provide disabled children with special education and "related services." See §§1401(a)(18), 1412(1). The question presented in this case is whether the definition of "related services" in §1401(a)(17)[1] requires a public school district in a participating State to provide a ventilator-dependent student with certain nursing services during school hours.

I

Respondent Garret F. is a friendly, creative, and intelligent young man. When Garret was four years old, his spinal column was severed in a motorcycle accident. Though paralyzed from the neck down, his mental capacities were unaffected. He is able to speak, to control his motorized wheelchair through use of a puff and suck straw, and to operate a computer with a device that responds to head movements. Garret is currently a student in the Cedar Rapids Community School District (District), he attends regular classes in a typical school program, and his academic performance has been a success. Garret is, however, ventilator dependent,[2] and therefore requires a responsible individual nearby to attend to certain physical needs while he is in school.[3]

During Garret's early years at school his family provided for his physical care during the school day. When he was in kindergarten, his 18-year-old aunt attended him; in the next four years, his family used settlement proceeds they received after the accident, their insurance, and other resources to employ a licensed practical nurse. In 1993, Garret's mother requested the District to accept financial responsibility for the health care services that Garret requires during the school day. The District denied the request, believing that it was not legally obligated to provide continuous one-on-one nursing services.

Relying on both the IDEA and Iowa law, Garret's mother requested a hearing before the Iowa Department of Education. An Administrative Law

From *Cedar Rapids Community School District v. Garret F.*, 119 S. Ct. 992 (1999).

Judge (ALJ) received extensive evidence concerning Garret's special needs, the District's treatment of other disabled students, and the assistance provided to other ventilator-dependent children in other parts of the country. In his 47 page report, the ALJ found that the District has about 17,500 students, of whom approximately 2,200 need some form of special education or special services. Although Garret is the only ventilator-dependent student in the District, most of the health care services that he needs are already provided for some other students.[4] "The primary difference between Garret's situation and that of other students is his dependency on his ventilator for life support." App. to Pet. For Cert. 28a. The ALJ noted that the parties disagreed over the training or licensure required for the care and supervision of such students, and that those providing such care in other parts of the country ranged from nonlicensed personnel to registered nurses. However, the District did not contend that only a licensed physician could provide the services in question.

The ALJ explained that federal law requires that children with a variety of health impairments be provided with "special education and related services" when their disabilities adversely affect their academic performance, and that such children should be educated to the maximum extent appropriate with children who are not disabled. In addition, the ALJ explained that applicable federal regulations distinguish between "school health services," which are provided by a "qualified school nurse or other qualified person," and "medical services," which are provided by a licensed physician. See 34 CFR §§300.16(a), (b)(4), (b)(11) (1998). The District must provide the former, but need not provide the latter (except, of course, those "medical services" that are for diagnostic or evaluation purposes, §1401(a)(17)). According to the ALJ, the distinction in the regulations does not just depend on "the title of the person providing the service"; instead, the "medical services" exclusion is limited to services that are "in the special training, knowledge, and judgment of a physician to carry out." App. to Pet. for Cert. 51a. The ALJ thus concluded that the IDEA required the District to bear financial responsibility for all of the services in dispute, including continuous nursing services.[5]

The District challenged the ALJ's decision in Federal District Court, but that Court approved the ALJ's IDEA ruling and granted summary judgment against the District. *Id.*, at 9a, 15a. The Court of Appeals affirmed. 106 F.3d 822 (CA8 1997). It noted that, as a recipient of federal funds under the IDEA, Iowa has a statutory duty to provide all disabled children a "free appropriate public education," which includes "related services." See *id.*, at 824. The Court of Appeals read our opinion in *Irving Independent School Dist.* v. *Tatro,* 468 U.S. 883 (1984), to provide a two-step analysis of the "related services" definition in §1401(a)(17)—asking first, whether the requested services are included within the phrase "supportive services"; and second, whether the services are excluded as "medical services." 106 F.3d, at 824–825. The Court of Appeals succinctly answered both questions in Garret's favor. The Court found the first step plainly satisfied, since Garret cannot attend school unless the requested services are available during the school day. *Id.*, at 825. As to the second step, the Court reasoned that *Tatro* "established a bright-line test: the services of a physician (other than for diagnostic and evaluation purposes) are subject to the medical services exclusion, but services that can be provided in the school setting by a nurse or qualified layperson are not." *Ibid.*

In its petition for certiorari, the District challenged only the second step of the Court of Appeals' analysis. The District pointed out that some federal courts have not asked whether the requested health services must be delivered by a physician, but instead have applied a multi-factor test that considers, generally speaking, the nature and extent of the services at issue. See, *e.g., Neely v. Rutherford County School,* 68 F.3d 965, 972–973 (CA6 1995), cert. denied, 517 U.S. 1134 (1996); *Detsel v. Board of Ed. of Auburn Enlarged City School Dist.,* 820 F.2d 587, 588 (CA2) (*per curiam*), cert. denied, 484 U.S. 981 (1987). We granted the District's petition to resolve this conflict. 523 U.S. (1998).

II

The District contends that §1401(a)(17) does not require it to provide Garret with "continuous one-on-one nursing services" during the school day, even though Garret cannot remain in school without such care. Brief for Petitioner 10. However, the IDEA's definition of "related services," our decision in *Irving Independent School Dist. v. Tatro,* 468 U.S. 883 (1984), and the overall statutory scheme all support the decision of the Court of Appeals.

The text of the "related services" definition see n. 1, *supra,* broadly encompasses those supportive services that "may be required to assist a child with a disability to benefit from special education." As we have already noted, the District does not challenge the Court of Appeals' conclusion that the in-school services at issue are within the covered category of "supportive services." As a general matter, services that enable a disabled child to remain in school during the day provide the student with "the meaningful access to education that Congress envisioned." *Tatro,* 468 U.S. at 891 ("'Congress sought primarily to make public education available to handicapped children' and 'to make such access meaningful'" (quoting *Board of Ed. of Hendrick Hudson Central School Dist., Westchester Cty. v. Rowley,* 458 U.S. 176, 192 (1982))).

This general definition of "related services" is illuminated by a parenthetical phrase listing examples of particular services that are included within the statute's coverage. §1401(a)(17). "Medical services" are enumerated in this list, but such services are limited to those that are "for diagnostic and evaluation purposes." *Ibid.* The statute does not contain a more specific definition of the "medical services" that are excepted from the coverage of §1401(a)(17).

The scope of the "medical services" exclusion is not a matter of first impression in this Court. In *Tatro* we concluded that the Secretary of Education had reasonably determined that the term "medical services" referred only to services that must be performed by a physician, and not to school health services. 468 U.S. at 892–894. Accordingly, we held that a specific form of health care (clean intermittent catheterization) that is often, though not always, performed by a nurse is not an excluded medical service. We referenced the likely cost of the services and the competence of school staff as justifications for drawing a line between physician and other services, *ibid.,* but our endorsement of that line was unmistakable.[6] It is thus settled that the phrase "medical services" in §1401(a)(17) does not embrace all forms of care that might loosely be described as "medical" in other contexts, such as a claim for an income tax deduction. See 26 U.S.C. §213(d)(1) (1994 ed. and Supp. II) (defining "medical care").

The District does not ask us to define the term so broadly. Indeed, the District does not argue that any of the items of care that Garret needs, considered individually, could be excluded from the scope of §1401(a)(17).[7] It could not make such an argument, considering that one of the services Garret needs (catheterization) was at issue in *Tatro,* and the others may be provided competently by a school nurse or other trained personnel. See App. to Pet. for Cert. 15a, 52a. As the ALJ concluded, most of the requested services are already provided by the District to other students, and the in-school care necessitated by Garret's ventilator dependency does not demand the training, knowledge, and judgment of a licensed physician. *Id.,* at 51a–52a. While more extensive, the in-school services Garret needs are no more "medical" than was the care sought in *Tatro.*

Instead, the District points to the combined and continuous character of the required care, and proposes a test under which the outcome in any particular case would "depend upon a series of factors, such as [1] whether the care is continuous or intermittent, [2] whether existing school health personnel can provide the service, [3] the cost of the service, and [4] the potential consequences if the service is not properly performed." Brief for Petitioner II; see also *id.,* at 34–35.

The District's multi-factor test is not supported by any recognized source of legal authority. The proposed factors can be found in neither the text of the statute nor the regulations that we upheld in *Tatro.* Moreover, the District offers no explanation why these characteristics make one service any more "medical" than another. The continuous character of certain services associated with Garret's ventilator dependency has no apparent relationship to "medical" services, much less a relationship of equivalence. Continuous services may be more costly and may require additional school personnel, but they are not thereby more "medical." Whatever its imperfections, a rule that limits the medical services exemption to physician services is unquestionably a reasonable and generally workable interpretation of the statute. Absent an elaboration of the statutory terms plainly more convincing than that which we reviewed in *Tatro,* there is no good reason to depart from settled law.[8]

Finally, the District raises broader concerns about the financial burden that it must bear to provide the services that Garret needs to stay in school. The problem for the District in providing these services is not that its staff cannot be trained to deliver them; the problem, the District contends, is that the existing school health staff cannot meet all of their responsibilities and provide for Garret at the same time.[9] Through its multi-factor test, the District seeks to establish a kind of undue-burden exemption primarily based on the cost of the requested services. The first two factors can be seen as examples of cost-based distinctions: intermittent care is often less expensive than continuous care, and the use of existing personnel is cheaper than hiring additional employees. The third factor—the cost of the service—would then encompass the first two. The relevance of the fourth factor is likewise related to cost because extra care may be necessary if potential consequences are especially serious.

The District may have legitimate financial concerns, but our role in this dispute is to interpret existing law. Defining "related services" in a manner that *accommodates* the cost concerns Congress may have had, cf. *Tatro,* 468 U.S. at 892, is altogether different from using cost *itself* as the definition. Given that §1401(a)(17) does not employ cost in its definition of "related services" or excluded "medical services," accepting the District's cost-based standard as the sole test for determining the scope of the provision would require us to engage in judicial lawmaking without any guidance from Congress. It would also create some tension with the purposes of the IDEA. The statute may not require public schools to maximize the potential of disabled students commensurate with the opportunities provided to other children, see *Rowley,* 458 U.S., at 200; and the potential financial burdens imposed on participating States may be relevant to arriving at a sensible construction of the IDEA, see *Tatro,* 468 U.S. at 892. But Congress intended "to open the door of public education" to all qualified children and "require[d] participating States to educate handicapped children with nonhandicapped children whenever possible." *Rowley,* 458 U.S., at 192, 202; see *id.,* at 179–181; see also *Honig v. Doe,* 484 U.S. 305, 310–311, 324 (1988); §§1412(1), (2)(C), (5)(B).[10]

This case is about whether meaningful access to the public schools will be assured, not the level of education that a school must finance once access is attained. It is undisputed that the services at issue must be provided if Garret is to remain in school. Under the statute, our precedent, and the purposes of the IDEA, the District must fund such "related services" in order to help guarantee that students like Garret are integrated into the public schools.

The judgment of the Court of Appeals is accordingly

Affirmed.

Notes

1. "The term 'related services' means transportation, and such developmental, corrective, and other supportive services (including speech pathology and audiology, psychological services, physical and occupational therapy, recreation, including therapeutic recreation, social work services, counseling services, including rehabilitation counseling, and medical services, except that such medical services shall be for diagnostic and evaluation purposes only) as may be required to assist a child with a disability to benefit from special education, and includes the early identification and assessment of disabling conditions in children." 20 U.S.C. §1401(a)(17). Originally, the statute was enacted without a definition of "related services." See Education of the Handicapped Act, 84 Stat. 175. In 1975, Congress added the definition at issue in this case. Education for All Handicapped Children Act of 1975, §4(a)(4), 89 Stat. 775. Aside from nonsubstantive changes and added examples of included services, see, e.g., Individuals with Disabilities Education Act Amendments of 1997, §101, 111 Stat. 45; Individuals with Disabilities Education Act Amendments of 1991, §2S(a)(1)(B), 105 Stat. 605;

Education of the Handicapped Act Amendments of 1990, §101(c), 104 Stat. 1103, the relevant language in §1401(a)(17) has not been amended since 1975. All references to the IDEA herein are to the 1994 version as codified in Title 20 of the United States Code—the version of the statute in effect when this dispute arose.

2. In his report in this case, the Administrative Law Judge explained that "[b]eing ventilator dependent means that [Garret] breathes only with external aids, usually an electric ventilator, and occasionally by someone else's manual pumping of an air bag attached to his tracheotomy tube when the ventilator is being maintained. This later procedure is called ambu bagging." App. to Pet. for Cert. 19a.

3. "He needs assistance with urinary bladder catheterization once a day, the suctioning of his tracheotomy tube as needed, but at least once every six hours, with food and drink at lunchtime, in getting into a reclining position for five minutes of each hour, and ambu bagging occasionally as needed when the ventilator is checked for proper functioning. He also needs assistance from someone familiar with his ventilator in the event there is a malfunction or electrical problem, and someone who can perform emergency procedures in the event he experiences autonomic hyperreflexia. Autonomic hyperreflexia is an uncontrolled visceral reaction to anxiety or a full bladder. Blood pressure increases, heart rate increases, and flushing and sweating may occur. Garret has not experienced autonomic hyperreflexia frequently in recent years, and it has usually been alleviated by catheterization. He has not ever experienced autonomic hyperreflexia at school. Garret is capable of communicating his needs orally or in another fashion so long as he has not been rendered unable to do so by an extended lack of oxygen." Id., at 20a.

4. "Included are such services as care for students who need urinary catheterization, food and drink, oxygen supplement positioning, and suctioning." Id., at 28a; see also id., at 53a.

5. In addition, the ALJ's opinion contains a thorough discussion of "other tests and criteria" pressed by the District, id., at 52a, including the burden on the District and the cost of providing assistance to Garret. Although the ALJ found no legal authority for establishing a cost-based test for determining what related services are required by the statute, he went on to reject the District's arguments on the merits. See id., at 42a–53a. We do not reach the issue here, but the ALJ also found that Garret's in-school needs must be met by the District under an Iowa statute as well as the IDEA. Id., at 54a–55a.

6. "The regulations define 'related services' for handicapped children to include 'school health services,' 34 CFR §300.13(a) (1983), which are defined in turn as 'services provided by a qualified school nurse or other qualified person,' §300.13(b)(10). 'Medical services' are defined as 'services provided by a licensed physician,' §300.13(b)(4). Thus, the Secretary has [reasonably] determined that the services of a school nurse otherwise qualifying as a 'related service' are not subject to exclusion as a 'medical service,' but that the services of a physician are excludable as such.

    . . . "By limiting the 'medical services,' exclusion to the services of a physician or hospital, both far more expensive, the Secretary has given a permissible construction to the provision." 468 U.S., at 892–893 (emphasis added) (footnote omitted); see also id., at 894 ("[T]he regulations state that school nursing services must be provided only if they can be performed by a nurse or other qualified person, not if they must be performed by a physician").

Based on certain policy letters issued by the Department of Education, it seems that the Secretary's post-*Tatro* view of the statute has not been entirely clear. E.g., App. to Pet. for Cert. 64a. We may assume that the Secretary has authority under the IDEA to adopt regulations that define the "medical services" exclusion by more explicitly taking into account the nature and extent of the requested services; and the Secretary surely has the authority to enumerate the services that are, and are not, fairly included within the scope of §1407(a)(17). But the Secretary has done neither; and, in this Court, she advocates affirming the judgment of the Court of Appeals. Brief for United States as *Amicus Curiae,* see also *Auer v. Robbins,* 519 U.S. 452, 462 (1997) (an agency's views as *amicus curiae* may be entitled to deference). We obviously have no authority to rewrite the regulations, and we see no sufficient reason to revise *Tatro,* either.

7. See Tr. of Oral Arg. 4–5, 12.

8. At oral argument, the District suggested that we first consider the nature of the requested service (either "medical" or not); then, if the service is "medical," apply the multi-factor test to determine whether the service is an excluded physician service or an included school nursing service under the Secretary of Education's regulations. See Tr. of Oral Arg. 7, 13–14. Not only does this approach provide no additional guidance for identifying "medical" services, it is also disconnected from both the statutory text and the regulations we upheld in *Irving Independent School Dist. V. Tatro* 468 U.S. 883 (1984). "Medical" services are generally *excluded* from the statute, and the regulations elaborate on that statutory term. No authority cited by the District requires an additional inquiry if the requested service is both "related" and non-"medical." Even if §1401(a)(17) demanded an additional step, the factors proposed by the District are hardly more useful in identifying "nursing" services than they are in identifying "medical" services; and the District cannot limit educational access simply by pointing to the limitations of existing staff. As we noted in *Tatro,* the IDEA requires schools to hire specially trained personnel to meet disabled student needs. *Id.,* at 893.

9. See Tr. of Oral Arg. 4–5, 13; Brief for Petitioner 6–7, 9. The District, however, will not necessarily need to hire an additional employee to meet Garret's needs. The District already employs a one-on-one teacher associate (TA) who assists Garret during the school day. See App. to Pet. for Cert. 26a–27a. At one time, Garret's TA was a licensed practical nurse (LPN). In light of the state Board of Nursing's recent ruling that the District's registered nurses may decide to delegate Garret's care to an LPN, see Brief for United States as *Amicus Curiae* 9–10 (filed Apr. 22, 1998), the dissent's future-cost estimate is speculative. See App. to Pet. for Cert. 28a, 58a–60a (if the District could assign Garret's care to a TA who is also an LPN, there would be "a minimum of additional expense").

10. The dissent's approach, which seems to be even broader than the District's, is unconvincing. The dissent's rejection of our unanimous decision in *Tatro* comes 15 years too late, see *Patterson v. McLean Credit Union,* 491 U.S. 164, 172–173 (1989) (*stare decisis* has "special force" in statutory interpretation), and it offers nothing constructive in its place. Aside from rejecting a "provider-specific approach," the dissent cites unrelated statutes and offers a circular definition of "medical services." *Post,* at 3–4 ("'services' that are 'medical' in 'nature'"). Moreover, the dissent's approach apparently would exclude most ordinary school nursing services of the kind routinely provided

to nondisabled children; that anomalous result is not easily attributable to congressional intent. See *Tatro,* 468 U.S., at 893. In a later discussion the dissent does offer a specific proposal: that we now interpret (or rewrite) the Secretary's regulations so that school districts need only provide disabled children with "health-related services that school nurses can perform as part of their normal duties." *Post,* at 7. The District does not dispute that its nurses "can perform" the requested services, so the dissent's objection is that District nurses would not be performing their "normal duties" if they met Garret's needs. That is, the District would need an "additional employee." *Post,* at 8. This proposal is functionally similar to a proposed regulation—ultimately withdrawn—that would have replaced the "school health services" provision. See 47 Fed. Reg. 33838, 33854 (1982) (the statute and regulations may not be read to affect legal obligations to make available to handicapped children services, including school health services, made available to non-handicapped children). The dissent's suggestion is unacceptable for several reasons. Most important, such revisions of the regulations are better left to the Secretary, and an additional staffing need is generally not a sufficient objection to the requirements of §1401(a)(17). See n. 8, *supra.*

 **NO**

Dissenting Opinion
of Clarence Thomas

Justice Thomas, with whom Justice Kennedy joins, dissenting.

The majority, relying heavily on our decision in *Irving Independent School Dist.* v. *Tatro,* 468 U.S. 883 (1984), concludes that the Individuals with Disabilities Education Act (IDEA), 20 U.S.C. § 1400 *et seq.,* requires a public school district to fund continuous, one-on-one nursing care for disabled children. Because *Tatro* cannot be squared with the text of IDEA, the Court should not adhere to it in this case. Even assuming that *Tatro* was correct in the first instance, the majority's extension of it is unwarranted and ignores the constitutionally mandated rules of construction applicable to legislation enacted pursuant to Congress' spending power.

I

As the majority recounts, *ante,* at 1, IDEA authorizes the provision of federal financial assistance to States that agree to provide, *inter alia,* "special education and related services" for disabled children. §1401(a)(18). In *Tatro, supra,* we held that this provision of IDEA required a school district to provide clean intermittent catheterization to a disabled child several times a day. In so holding, we relied on Department of Education regulations, which we concluded had reasonably interpreted IDEA's definition of "related services"[1] to require school districts in participating States to provide "school nursing services" (of which we assumed catheterization was a subcategory) but not "services of a physician." *Id.,* at 892–893. This holding is contrary to the plain text of IDEA and its reliance on the Department of Education's regulations was misplaced.

A

Before we consider whether deference to an agency regulation is appropriate, "we first ask whether Congress has 'directly spoken to the precise question at issue. If the intent of Congress is clear, that is the end of the matter; for the court, as well as the agency, must give effect to the unambiguously expressed intent of Congress.'" *National Credit Union Admin,* v. *First Nat. Bank & Trust Co.,* 522 U.S. 479, 499–500

From *Cedar Rapids Community School District v. Garret F.,* 119 S. Ct. 992 (1999).

(1998) (quoting *Chevron U.S.A. Inc. v. Natural Resources Defense Council, Inc.,* 467 U.S. 837, 842–843 (1984)).

Unfortunately, the Court in *Tatro* failed to consider this necessary antecedent question before turning to the Department of Education's regulations implementing IDEA's related services provision. The Court instead began "with the regulations of the Department of Education, which," it said, "are entitled to deference." *Tatro, supra,* at 892–892. The Court need not have looked beyond the text of IDEA, which expressly indicates that school districts are not required to provide medical services, except for diagnostic and evaluation purposes. 20 U.S.C. § 1401(a)(17). The majority asserts that *Tatro* precludes reading the term "medical services" to include "all forms of care that might loosely be described as 'medical.'" *Ante,* at 8. The majority does not explain, however, why "services" that are "medical" in nature are not "medical services." Not only is the definition that the majority rejects consistent with other uses of the term in federal law,[2] it also avoids the anomalous result of holding that the services at issue in *Tatro* (as well as in this case), while not "medical services," would nonetheless qualify as medical care for federal income tax purposes.

The primary problem with *Tatro,* and the majority's reliance on it today, is that the Court focused on the provider of the services rather than the services themselves. We do not typically think that automotive services are limited to those provided by a mechanic, for example. Rather, anything done to repair or service a car, no matter who does the work, is thought to fall into that category. Similarly, the term "food service" is not generally thought to be limited to work performed by a chef. The term "medical" similarly does not support *Tatro's* provider-specific approach, but encompasses services that are "of, *relating to, or concerned with* physicians *or* the practice of medicine." See Webster's Third New International Dictionary 1402 (1986) (emphasis added): see also *id.,* at 1551 (defining "nurse" as "a person skilled in caring for and waiting on the infirm, the injured, or the sick; *specif:* one esp. trained to carry out such duties under the supervision of a physician").

IDEA's structure and purpose reinforce this textual interpretation. Congress enacted IDEA to increase the *educational* opportunities available to disabled children, not to provide medical care for them. See 20 U.S.C. §1400(c) ("It is the purpose of this chapter to assure that all children with disabilities have . . . a free appropriate public education"); see also §1412 ("In order to qualify for assistance . . . a State shall demonstrate . . . [that it] has in effect a policy that assures all children with disabilities the right to a free appropriate public education"); *Board of Ed. of Hendrick Hudson Central School Dist., Westchester Cty. v. Rowley,* 458 U.S. 176, 179 (1982) ("The Act represents an ambitious federal effort to promote the education of handicapped children"). As such, where Congress decided to require a supportive service—including speech pathology, occupational therapy, and audiology—that appears "medical" in nature, it took care to do so explicitly. See §1401(a)(17). Congress specified these services precisely because it recognized that they would otherwise fall under the broad "medical services" exclusion. Indeed, when it crafted the definition of related services, Congress could have, but chose not to, include "nursing services" in this list.

B

Tatro was wrongly decided even if the phrase "medical services" was subject to multiple constructions, and therefore, deference to any reasonable Department of Education regulation was appropriate. The Department of Education has never promulgated regulations defining the scope of IDEA's "medical services" exclusion. One year before *Tatro* was decided, the Secretary of Education issued proposed regulations that defined excluded medical services as "services relating to the practice of medicine." 47 Fed. Reg. 33838 (1982). These regulations, which represent the Department's only attempt to define the disputed term, were never adopted. Instead, "[t]he regulations actually define only those 'medical services' that are owed to handicapped children," *Tatro*, 468 U.S., at 892, n. 10) (emphasis in original), not those that *are not*. Now, as when *Tatro* was decided, the regulations require districts to provide services performed "'by a licensed physician to determine a child's medically related handicapping condition which results in the child's need for special education and related services." *Ibid.* (quoting 34 CFR § 300.13(b)(4) (1983), recodified and amended as 34 CFR § 300.16(b)(4) (1998).

Extrapolating from this regulation, the *Tatro* Court presumed that this meant "that 'medical services' not owed under the statute are those 'services by a licensed physician' that serve other purposes." *Tatro, supra,* at 892, n. 10 (emphasis deleted). The Court, therefore, did not defer to the regulation itself, but rather relied on an inference drawn from it to speculate about how a regulation might read if the Department of Education promulgated one. Deference in those circumstances is impermissible. We cannot defer to a regulation that does not exist.[3]

II

Assuming that *Tatro* was correctly decided in the first instance, it does not control the outcome of this case. Because IDEA was enacted pursuant to Congress' spending power, *Rowley, supra,* at 190, n. 11, our analysis of the statute in this case is governed by special rules of construction. We have repeatedly emphasized that, when Congress places conditions on the receipt of federal funds, "it must do so unambiguously." *Pennhurst State School and Hospital* v. *Halderman,* 451 U.S. 1, 17 (1981). See also *Rowley, supra,* at 190, n. 11; *South Dakota* v. *Dole,* 483 U.S. 203, 207 (1987); *New York* v. *United States,* 505 U.S. 144, 158 (1992). This is because a law that "condition[s] an offer of federal funding on a promise by the recipient . . . amounts essentially to a contract between the Government and the recipient of funds." *Gebser* v. *Lago Vista Independent School Dist.,* 524 U.S. 274, 276 (1998). As such, "[t]he legitimacy of Congress' power to legislate under the spending power . . . rests on whether the State voluntarily and knowingly accepts the terms of the 'contract.' There can, of course, be no knowing acceptance if a State is unaware of the conditions or is unable to ascertain what is expected of it." *Pennhurst, supra,* at 17 (citations omitted). It follows that we must interpret Spending Clause legislation narrowly, in order to avoid saddling the States with obligations that they did not anticipate.

The majority's approach in this case turns this Spending Clause presumption on its head. We have held that, in enacting IDEA, Congress wished to require

"States to educate handicapped children with nonhandicapped children whenever possible," *Rowley,* 458 U.S., at 202. Congress, however, also took steps to limit the fiscal burdens that States must bear in attempting to achieve this laudable goal. These steps include requiring States to provide an education that is only "appropriate" rather that requiring them to maximize the potential of disabled students, see 20 U.S.C. § 1400(c); *Rowley, supra,* at 200, recognizing that integration into the public school environment is not always possible, see § 1412(5), and clarifying that, with a few exceptions, public schools need not provide "medical services" for disabled students, §§ 1401(a)(17) and (18).

For this reason, we have previously recognized that Congress did not intend to "impos[e] upon the States a burden of unspecified proportions and weight" in enacting IDEA. *Rowley, supra,* at 176, n. 11. These federalism concerns require us to interpret IDEA's related services provision, consistent with *Tatro,* as follows: Department of Education regulations require districts to provide disabled children with health-related services that school nurses can perform as part of their normal duties. This reading of *Tatro,* although less broad than the majority's, is equally plausible and certainly more consistent with our obligation to interpret Spending Clause legislation narrowly. Before concluding that the district was required to provide clean intermittent catheterization for Amber Tatro, we observed that school nurses in the district were authorized to perform services that were "difficult to distinguish from the provision of [clean intermittent catheterization] to the handicapped." *Tatro,* 468 U.S., at 893. We concluded that "[i]t would be strange indeed if Congress, in attempting to extend special services to handicapped children, were unwilling to guarantee them services of a kind that are routinely provided to the nonhandicapped." *Id.,* at 893–894.

Unlike clean intermittent catheterization, however, a school nurse cannot provide the services that respondent requires, see *ante,* at 3, n. 3, and continue to perform her normal duties. To the contrary, because respondent requires continuous, one-on-one care throughout the entire school day, all agree that the district must hire an additional employee to attend solely to respondent. This will cost a minimum of $18,000 per year. Although the majority recognizes this fact, it nonetheless concludes that the "more extensive" nature of the services that respondent needs is irrelevant to the question whether those services fall under the medical services exclusion. *Ante,* at 9. This approach disregards the constitutionally mandated principles of construction applicable to Spending Clause legislation and blindsides unwary States with fiscal obligations that they could not have anticipated.

⋅❦⋅

For the foregoing reasons, I respectfully dissent.

Notes

1. The Act currently defines "related services" as "transportation and such developmental, corrective, and other supportive services (Including speech pathology and audiology, psychological services, physical and occupational therapy,

recreation, including therapeutic recreation, social work services, counseling services, including rehabilitation counseling, and medical services, *except that such medical services shall be for diagnostic and evaluation purposes only*) as may be required to assist a child with a disability to benefit from special education. . . ." 20 U.S.C. §1401(a)(17) (emphasis added).

2. See, *e.g.,* 38 U.S.C. § 1701(6) ("The term 'medical services' includes, in addition to medical examination, treatment and rehabilitative services . . . surgical services, dental services, . . . optometric and podiatric services, . . . preventive health services, . . . [and] such consultation, professional counseling, training, and mental health services as are necessary in connection with the treatment"); §101(28) ("The term 'nursing home care' means the accommodation of convalescents . . . who require nursing care and related medical services"); 26 U.S.C. § 213(d)(1) ("The term 'medical care' means amounts paid—. . . for the diagnosis, cure, mitigation, treatment, or prevention of disease").

3. Nor do I think that it is appropriate to defer to the Department of Education's litigating position in this case. The agency has had ample opportunity to address this problem but has failed to do so in a formal regulation. Instead, it has maintained conflicting positions about whether the services at issue in this case are required by IDEA. See *ante,* at 7–8, n. 6. Under these circumstances, we should not assume that the litigating position reflects the "agency's fair and considered judgment." *Auer* v. *Robbins,* 519 U.S. 452, 462 (1997).

POSTSCRIPT

Should One-on-One Nursing Care Be Part of Special Education?

$\mathbf{A}$s with most complex legislation, the implementation of IDEA has been defined through court decisions. Garret's case—and others like it—highlight the complexity involved in designing education that includes all learners. All members of the Supreme Court agreed that Garret's services were costly and complicated. The majority found that these factors do not matter, almost requesting a renovation of IDEA to be more specific about limits in this area. In short, while it did not seem very happy about the decision, the majority felt that it was the only choice under the current law. The bright line may not be the best line, but it is clear and easy to apply. Now it is clear that schools have no choice.

The minority contends that *Garret* and *Tatro* have crossed a boundary that was very clear in IDEA. Schools cannot fulfill their educational mission when their energies are focused on medical care. If Congress had meant to include daily medical attention, it would have said so. IDEA limits medical services to diagnosis and evaluation, argues the minority. Continuous care does not fall within that limit.

Despite the clear connections to health-related conditions, parental medical insurance is not a resource for schools. Because families of children with significant disabilities can easily exceed lifetime limits on coverage or be placed in financial risk categories with costly premiums, courts have upheld exclusionary clauses that prohibit insurance coverage for services or equipment that the insured is entitled to under IDEA (Katsiyannis and Yell, *Exceptional Children*, 2000).

As more children come to school in a fragile condition—and as the procedures to support them become more complex—district personnel must be prepared to deliver emergency care, sometimes in life-threatening situations. The consequences of not reacting fast enough or with sufficient wisdom and skill raise fears of liability among educators. To date, this issue has not been tried in the courts, which have determined that concerns about consequences should not prohibit implementation of accommodations and services by individuals who have been adequately trained.

As medical science continues to advance, will schools soon be required to provide even more extensive and expensive medical services? Is this what IDEA meant? Should the federal law be rewritten to refocus human and financial resources on education and to delegate medical responsibilities to other agencies? Can the line be drawn more clearly in a different location, or will any change simply spawn more debate? Should there be any line at all?

Contributors to This Volume

EDITORS

DR. MARYANN BYRNES is associate professor in the Graduate School of Education at the University of Massachusetts–Boston. Dr. Byrnes consults with schools and districts on issues of policy and the implementation of IDEA. Additional school-based activities include long-term consultation for system change, curriculum alignment, and staff development as well as program and budget evaluation. MaryAnn served as a special education administrator for 18 years, having taught at elementary, middle, and high school levels. A past president of the Massachusetts Association of Administrators of Special Education (ASE), Dr. Byrnes is president of MCEC (Massachusetts Federation of the Council for Exceptional Children). Dr. Byrnes earned her undergraduate degree at the University of Chicago, her master's degre at Northwestern University, and her doctorate at Rutgers University. She has written numerous articles on standards-based instruction and assessment and students with disabilities.

STAFF

Larry Loeppke	Managing Editor
Jill Peter	Senior Developmental Editor
Susan Brusch	Senior Developmental Editor
Beth Kundert	Production Manager
Jane Mohr	Project Manager
Tara McDermott	Design Coordinator
Nancy Meissner	Editorial Assistant
Julie Keck	Senior Marketing Manager
Mary Klein	Marketing Communications Specialist
Alice Link	Marketing Coordinator
Tracie Kammerude	Senior Marketing Assistant
Lori Church	Pemissions Coordinator

AUTHORS

JAMES B. ADAMS is a father of a young girl with autism, diagnosed in 1994, and that is what led him to eventually shift much of his research emphasis to autism, focusing on biological causes and treatments. He is currently a Full Professor in the department of chemical and materials engineering at Arizona State University. He created and teaches a course on Heavy Metal Toxicity, focused on lead and mercury toxicity.

ARTHUR ALLEN is a Washington-area writer whose work appears in *The Washington Post* magazine, the *New Republic* and *Salon.com*.

LEWIS M. ANDREWS is executive director of the Yankee Institute for Public Policy Inc. at Trinity College, a Connecticut research and educational institute.

RICHARD A. BAKER, JR., is a middle school teacher at Hurst Middle School in the St. Charles Parish public schools.

DR. RUSSELL A. BARKLEY is the director of psychology and professor of psychiatry and neurology at the University of Massachusetts Medical Center, and has written 14 books and more than 150 scientific articles related to the nature, assessment, and treatment of AD/HD. As the leading expert on the subject, he speaks eloquently and passionately about the need to recognize the complexities of the disorder and to treat it properly.

JENNIFER BOOHER-JENNINGS is a doctoral candidate in the department of sociology at Columbia University in New York City. Her research focuses on accountability, school organization, and school choice.

ELLEN BRANTLINGER is professor emeritus, School of Education, Indiana University. She earned her B.S. at Antioch College in 1963 and her Ed.D. at Indiana University in 1977. She is an expert on how parents, educators, and caregivers view the sexuality of the mentally handicapped and on the sterilization of people with mental disabilities. She is the author of *Fighting for Darla* (1994) and *The Politics of Social Class in Secondary School*.

FREDERICK J. BRIGHAM is an assistant professor of education in the Department of Curriculum, Instruction, and Special Education at the Curry School of Education of the University of Virginia. He has also taught at Dickinson State College and served as director of special education for the West River Special Education Unit in Dickinson, North Dakota. He earned his M.Ed. from Bowling Green State University in 1983 and his Ph.D. from Purdue University in 1992.

MICHELE ST. PETER BRIGHAM is the choral music director and special education instructor at Western Albemarle High School and adjunct faculty in the School of Continuing Education and Professional Studies at the University of Virginia.

GERALD COLES is an educational psychologist, full-time researcher, writer, and lecturer on literacy, learning, and psychology. The author of numerous articles in education, psychology, and psychiatry journals, his 1978 *Harvard Educational Review* paper on learning disabilities was identified by The Institute of Scientific Information as a "Citation Classic" because of the number of times it has been cited and its influence on other authors in the field.

CHRISTOPHER T. CROSS is a senior fellow at the Center for Education Policy and a distinguished senior fellow at the Education Commission of the States. During his 32 years in Washington, D.C., he served in both the executive and legislative branches, as an assistant secretary at the U.S. Department of Education, the Republican staff director of the House Committee on Education and Labor, and a deputy assistant secretary in the old Department of Health, Education and Welfare.

M. SUZANNE DONOVAN is a senior program officer at the National Research Council's Commission on Behavioral and Social Sciences and Education and study director for the Committee on Minority Representation in Special Education. Her interests span issues of education and public policy. She has a Ph.D. from the University of California, Berkeley, School of Public Policy, and was previously on the faculty of Columbia University's School of Public and International Affairs.

JUDY DAVIS-DORSEY is director of human resources with the York County schools in Yorktown, Virginia. Her research interests include workplace disability issues and professional development and its relationship to employee retention.

STEPHEN EDELSON, M.D., has practiced medicine for more than 20 years. As an autoimmune specialist and founder of the Edelson Center for Environmental and Preventative Medicine in Atlanta, he has successfully treated thousands of patients using innovative and effective alternative therapies. Dr. Edelson lives and works in Atlanta, Georgia.

JEFFREY EVANS does research with the Institute for Applied Psychometrics (IAP) and the Woodcock-Johnson development team. He has published in the area of reading achievement. Jeff is currently working on educational test development and writing projects with IAP. He also serves on the volunteer board of directors of United Cerebral Palsy (UCP) of Central Minnesota. Jeff holds a master's in communications disorders from St. Cloud State University.

GREG FORSTER is a senior research associate at the Manhattan Institute's Education Research Office. He is the co-author of several education studies and op-ed articles. He received a Ph.D. with distinction in political science from Yale University in May 2002, and his B.A. from the University of Virginia, where he double-majored in political and social thought and rhetoric and communications studies, in 1995.

RUSSELL GERSTEN is executive director of Instructional Research Group. Currently, he directs the Mathematics component of the Center of Instruction, a comprehensive Technical Assistance Center for No Child Left Behind. He is also professor emeritus in the College for Education at the University of Oregon. He received his Ph. D in special education from the University of Oregon in 1978.

TEMPLE GRANDIN is a designer of livestock handling facilities and a professor of animal science at Colorado State University. Facilities she has designed are located in the United States, Canada, Europe, Mexico, Australia, New Zealand, and other countries. In North America, almost half of the cattle are handled in a center track restrainer system that she designed for meat plants. She obtained her B.A. at Frankin Pierce College and her M.S. in animal science at Arizona State University. Dr. Grandin received her Ph.D. in animal science from the University of Illinois in 1989.

JAY P. GREENE is a senior fellow at the Manhattan Institute for Policy Research where he conducts research and writes about education policy. He has conducted evaluations of school choice and accountability programs in Florida, Charlotte, Milwaukee, Cleveland, and San Antonio. He has also investigated the effects of school choice on civic values and integration.

WILLIAM E. GUSTASHAW III is as assistant professor in the College of Education, Special Education and Rehabilitation Counseling at the University of Virginia. His research interests include effective instructional practices for students with disabilities, teacher education, and special education policy.

KAREN R. HARRIS is the Currey-Ingram Professor of Special Education and Literacy at Vanderbilt University, Nashville, Tennessee. Dr. Harris' research focuses on the theoretical and intervention issues in the development of academic and self-regulation strategies among students who are at-risk and those with severe learning challenges such as learning disabilities and attention deficit hyperactivity disorder.

FREDERICK M. HESS is an assistant professor of education and government at the University of Virginia in Charlottesville, Virginia. He is the author of *Spinning Wheels: The Politics of Urban School Reform* (Brookings Institution Press, 1999) and *Bringing the Social Sciences Alive* (Allyn & Bacon, 1999).

JOHN HOCKENBERY is an award-winning television commentator, radio host and foreign correspondent, became a paraplegic in an auto accident when he was 19. He lives in Brooklyn, New York, with his wife, Alison, and their two sets of twins—Zoe and Olivia, and Zachary and Regan.

ROBERT H. HORNER is a professor in the department of special education at the University of Oregon, Eugene. Dr. Horner has published over 150 professional papers and six texts. He currently co-directs the OSEP Technical Assistance Center on Positive Behavior Interventions and Supports and the OSEP Research and Demonstration Center on School-wide Behavior Support. Dr. Horner also co-directs the Positive Behavior Research and Support research unit at the University of Oregon.

KAY S. HYMOWITZ is a senior fellow at the Manhattan Institute and a contributing editor of *City Journal*. She writes extensively on education and childhood in America. Ms. Hymowitz has also written for many major publications including *The New York Times, The Washington Post, The Wall Street Journal, The New Republic, New York Newsday, The Public Interest, Commentary, Dissent,* and *Tikkun*. A native of Philadelphia, Hymowitz received a B.A. magna cum laude with honors in English and American literature from

Brandeis University, an M.A. in English literature from Tufts University, and a masters of philosophy from Columbia University. Before becoming a full-time freelance writer, she taught English literature and composition at Brooklyn College and Parsons School of Design.

JERRY JESNESS is a special education teacher at Las Yescas Elementary School in Los Fresnos, Texas. His extensive writings on many aspects of education have appeared in such publications as *Principal, Reason,* and *Teacher.*

JAMES M. KAUFFMAN is the Charles S. Robb Professor of Education at the University of Virginia in Charlottesville, Virginia, where he also serves as director of the doctoral program in special education. His primary areas of interest in special education are emotional and behavioral disorders and learning disabilities. He is coeditor of *Behavioral Disorders*, the journal of the Council for Children with Behavioral Disorders, and he is coprincipal investigator of the Center of Minority Research in Special Education (COMRISE). Among his many publications are *Characteristics of Emotional and Behavioral Disorders of Children and Youth,* 7th ed. (Prentice Hall PTR, 2000) and *The Least Restrictive Environment: Its Origins and Interpretations in Special Education*, coauthored with Jean B. Crockett (Lawrence Erlbaum, 1999). He received his M.Ed. in teaching in the elementary school from Washburn University in 1966 and his Ed.D. in special education from the University of Kansas in 1969.

REX KNOWLES is a retired college professor living in Claremont, California.

TRUDY KNOWLES is an associate professor of education at Westfield State College in Westfield, Massachusetts, where she helps coordinate the middle-level education program. She is actively involved in the education of young adolescents through her work in local schools, the Commonwealth of Massachusetts Middle-Level Educators, the New England League of Middle Schools, and the National Middle School Association. She is coauthor, with David F. Brown, of *What Every Middle School Teacher Should Know* (Heinemann, 2000).

DANIEL J. LOSEN is a research associate with The Civil Rights Project at Harvard University and the principal investigator for the Conference on Minority Issues in Special Education. He is presently developing research and policy fact sheets for members of Congress on the topics of Dropouts and Title I of the Elementary and Secondary School Act. Before becoming an attorney, he taught in public schools for nearly 10 years, including work as a founder of an alternative public school.

KANYA MAHITIVANICHCHA is a research analyst at the American Institutes for Research.

AMY DOCKSER MARCUS is a Boston-based staff reporter for the New York bureau of the *Wall Street Journal*. Born in Boston, Massuchusetts, Marcus earned a bachelor's degree from Harvard University.

KEVIN S. McGREW is the director of the Institute on Applied Psychometrics (IAP) and is currently a visiting professor in the department of educational psychology at the University of Minnesota. McGrew has extensive experience in both clinical (1:1) and large-scale assessment and data management and analysis. Dr. McGrew has published over 60 different journal articles, books, or book chapters covering many areas of special education.

JAMES McLESKEY is professor and chair of the department of special education, University of Florida. His state and federal grants have addressed school reform and school improvement, preparation of teachers to meet the needs of a diverse range of students in general education classrooms, and preparation of leadership personnel in general and special education.

BARBARA MINER is former managing editor of the Milwaukee-based newspaper *Rethinking Schools* and has two children in the Milwaukee public schools. She recently co-edited the book *Failing Our Kids: Why the Testing Craze* Won't Fix Our Schools.

NATIONAL COUNCIL ON DISABILITY (NCD) is an independent federal agency that makes recommendations to the president and Congress on issues affecting 54 million Americans with disabilities. The NCD is composed of 15 members appointed by the president and confirmed by the Senate. The NCD's overall purpose is to promote policies, programs, practices, and procedures that guarantee equal opportunity for all individuals with disabilities, regardless of the nature or severity of the disability, and to empower individuals with disabilities to achieve economic self-sufficiency, independent living, and inclusion and integration into all aspects of society.

SAMUEL L. ODOM is an assistant professor of education and Otting Professor of Special Education in the School of Education, Indiana University–Bloomington.

GARY ORFIELD is a professor at the Harvard Graduate School of Education and director of its Project on School Desegregation. His report, "The Growth of Segregation in American Schools: Changing Patterns of Separation and Poverty since 1968," was recently issued to the National School Board Association.

ROD PAIGE is the seventh U.S. Secretary of Education. Paige rallied the department to create the Blueprint for Management Excellence in order to build an organization worthy of the taxpayer's trust and the president's vision–a vision grounded in the belief that good government is not only closer to the people, but also more accountable to the people. Dr. Paige earned a bachelor's degree from Jackson State University in his home state. He then earned both a master's and a doctoral degree from Indiana University.

THOMAS PARRISH is the managing director of the Education and Human Development Program at the American Institutes for Research (AIR) and is a consulting professor in the School of Education at Stanford University.

PATRICIA JORDAN REA is an assistant professor in educational leadership at The George Washington University. Her research interests include distributed leadership and the impact of leadership on organizational outcomes.

BERNARD RIMLAND is a research psychologist (Ph.D.) and a Director of the Autism Research Institute, which he founded in 1967. He is also the founder of the

Autism Society of America (1965) and the editor of the *Autism Research Review International*. His book, *Infantile Autism: The Syndrome and Its Implication for a Neural Theory of Behavior* (1964), is widely credited with changing the field of psychiatry from its claim that autism is an emotional illness, caused by destructive mothers, to its current recognition that autism is a biological disorder.

BLAIR ROGER is an educational consultant based in Oakland, California.

DORENE D. ROSS is a professor in the School of Teaching and Learning, University of Florida. She is also a consult with school districts involved in restructuring and the establishment of collaborative professional learning environments in schools serving children of poverty. Dorene helped to design and implement the Unified Elementary PROTEACH program.

WAYNE SAILOR is a clinical psychologist, a professor of special education, and an associate director of the Beach Center on Disability at the University of Kansas, Lawrence.

BENNETT A. SHAYWITZ is professor of pediatrics and neurology and chief of pediatric neurology at the Yale University School of Medicine. Dr. Shaywitz was a pioneer in recognizing the great potential of functional brain imaging and led a national effort to apply this technology, especially functional magnetic resonance imaging (fMRI), to the study of reading and dyslexia in children and adults. The author of over 300 scientific papers, Dr. Shaywitz has received many honors for his contributions to the understanding of the basic neurobiology of reading and dyslexia.

SALLY E. SHAYWITZ is professor of pediatrics at the Yale University School of Medicine. She has devoted her career to helping children and adults who are dyslexic; her research has provided the basis for understanding this disorder. Dr. Sally Shaywitz is the author of over 200 scientific articles, chapters, and books, including *Overcoming Dyslexia: A New and Complete Science-Based Program for Reading Problems at Any Level*.

TOM E.C. SMITH is professor of special education and department head of the department of curriculum and instruction at the University of Arkansas. His research interests include disability law and inclusion.

JOHN PAUL STEVENS is an associate justice of the U.S. Supreme Court. He worked in law firms in Chicago, Illinois, for 20 years before being nominated by President Richard Nixon to the U.S. Court of Appeals in 1970. He served in that capacity until he was nominated to the Supreme Court by President Gerald Ford in 1975.

JAMES A. TAYLOR, Sr., president of Edleaders.com, believes that school administrators who design and implement an effective disciplinary code that applies to all students, including those with disabilities, can create a more orderly environment for everyone.

CLARENCE THOMAS is an associate justice of the U.S. Supreme Court. A former judge on the U.S. Court of Appeals for the District of Columbia, he was nominated by President George Bush to the Supreme Court in 1991. He received his J.D. from the Yale University School of Law in 1974.

BRUCE THOMPSON is professor and distinguished research fellow in the department of educational psychology at Texas A&M University, College Station.

H. RUTHERFORD TURNBULL III is the co-founder and co-director of the Beach Center on Disability at the University of Kansas. He is a professor of special education and former courtesy professor of law there, and his research interests include special education law and policy, disability policy generally, and, most recently, the effects of federal policy on treatment issues raised by the Schiavo cases.

U.S. DEPARTMENT OF EDUCATION promotes educational excellence for all Americans. Created in 1980 by combining offices from several federal agencies, its original directive remains its mission today—to ensure equal access to education and to promote educational excellence throughout the nation.

ROSALIND AND JOE VARGO, mother and father of Ro Vargo, use their voices to tell a powerful story of their daughter's success in fully inclusive educational programs, from kindergarten through college.

ANDREW L. WILEY joined the Center for Social Development and Education (CSDE) in 2005. Mr. Wiley has completed his doctoral coursework in special education at the University of Virginia and is currently completing his dissertation. Mr. Wiley has a bachelor's degree and a master of teaching degree from the University of Virginia. He has worked as a behavior resource teacher in an intensive center program for elementary students with emotional/behavioral disorders, as an autism resource teacher, and as a behavior specialist in Fairfax County, Virginia. Mr. Wiley has taught graduate courses in behavior management and methods for teaching exceptional children.

NAOMI ZIGMOND is a professor in the School of Education, University of Pittsburgh, Instruction and Learning. He earned his Ph.D. in learning disabilities from Northwestern University in 1966, his M.A. from Northwestern University in 1963, and his B.S. from McGill University in 1962. In 1997, Dr. Zigmond received the Research Award from the Council for Exceptional Children in recognition of research that has contributed significantly to the body of knowledge about the education of exceptional children and youth.

Index